A BOOK OF DAYS

BOOK THE FIVE

A BOOK OF
DAYS

SIR WILLIAM DARLING
C.B.E., M.C., D.L., LL.D., M.P.

A Dictionary of Dates . . .
A Chronology of Circumstance . . .
The Face of Time . . .

LONDON
THE RICHARDS PRESS

First published in 1951

Reprinted 1952

Printed in Great Britain
at The Curwen Press
Plaistow, E.13

THE RICHARDS PRESS LTD
MARTIN SECKER: DIRECTOR

CONTENTS

INTRODUCTION—AND APOLOGY

For many years dates have interested me—what happened on this day a hundred years ago—twenty years ago—to what extent does history repeat itself or how different is today from yesterday.

Over a period of years, many friends and I have collaborated in compiling a record of dates and this book of days is a result.

The trivial often appears while the significant has been omitted, of that I am aware. There may well be many inaccuracies, but these I have endeavoured to avoid.

The book as it stands is now in your hands; if you like it and find it interesting my collaborators and I are happy. If you have any criticism, we shall be glad to hear it. If you have additional dates or suggestions for future editions, we shall certainly consider them. If you can do better, we shall certainly be glad to think we have inspired you to try!

WILL. Y. DARLING

JANUARY

THIRTY-ONE DAYS

January the First

. . . . Every dog has his day . . . .

Anno Domini First of January, A.D. 1, *and ever since things have tended to happen on the First of January (as they tend, incidentally, to happen on every other day).*

The Press like the day—*The Times*, still with us, was established in 1788 and
The Athenæum—now somewhat absorbed—in 1828.

Legislators like the First of January.
The Bankruptcy Act of 1870 abolished imprisonment for debt,
First of the Old Age Pensions Acts in 1909,
The appointed day for amalgamation of British railways, 1923,
The A.R.P. Act in 1938, and
British Railways nationalized, 1948.
These things happened on the first day of the first month.

As for persons,
'The Old Pretender', as the English call him, died in 1766,
The Earl of Auckland (India) died in 1849, and
Sir Edward Lutyens, 1944.

Lorenzo de Medici (Il Magnifico) was born in 1448, and
Maria Edgeworth was born at Black Burton in 1767.

And what else? Here is a list.
THE JULIAN CALENDAR BEGAN 45 B.C.,
THE FIRST AND OLDEST CHAMBER OF COMMERCE—THAT OF
GLASGOW—WAS FOUNDED IN 1783,
THE MARRIED WOMEN'S PROPERTY ACT BECAME LAW IN
1883,
THE FIRST MEETING OF THE METROPOLITAN BOARD OF
WORKS—A PRECURSOR OF THE LONDON COUNTY COUNCIL
—IN 1885,
QUEEN VICTORIA WAS PROCLAIMED EMPRESS OF INDIA AT
DELHI IN 1877,
LOFOTEN ISLANDS RAIDED, 1942,
FIELD-MARSHAL SMUTS, ORDER OF MERIT, IN NEW YEAR'S
HONOURS, 1947,
BRITISH COAL-MINES TRANSFERRED TO THE NATION, 1947.
ALL THESE ON THE FIRST OF JANUARY.

January the Second

'However early you rise, you cannot hasten the dawn.'
IT IS BETTER TO DIE THAN TO BE BORN, DECLARED A LIFE-
WEARY ONE.

These died on January the Second,
Ovid and Livy in A.D. 18,
General Thumb in 1879,
Kinglake, the historian, in 1891,
Eleanor Rathbone in 1946, and
Edna May, American actress who created *The Belle of New York*,
in London, in 1948.

In 1951 on this day, these too died . . .
Henry Baynton, Shakespearian actor,
Sir William Robert Campion, a former Governor of Western
Australia, and
Sir Lenthal Cheatle, an authority on cancer.

But there were birthdays too . . .
The Marquis of Granby (who was he?) in 1721,
General Wolfe of Culloden and, more gloriously, of the Plains of
Abraham in 1727, and
Gilbert Murray in 1866.

In 1635 Cardinal Richelieu formally established the *Académie
Française*,
It is less authentically recorded, in 1731, that a prisoner in New-
gate was reprieved on the Second of January that year for agreeing
to submit to an operation on his ears,
Clive took Calcutta in 1757, and
John Wilkes was elected Alderman for Faringdon Without in 1769.
There was a serious fire on this day at Greenwich Hospital in 1779,
The Order of the Knights of the Bath was augmented to include a
Military Division in 1815,
The Railway Clearing House began its work in 1842,
The Battle of Nashville was fought in 1863,
Colombia and Mexico were recognized by Britain in 1875,
Air fight over Heligoland, 1940.

BRITAIN AGREED TO BUY CANADIAN SURPLUSES OF BACON,
BEEF, CHEESE AND EGGS AT INCREASED PRICES IN 1948.
WHO WILL SAY THAT JANUARY THE SECOND IS NOT ONE
OF THE DAYS!

January the Third

There was a yesterday: who dare say there will not be a tomorrow?

Two minds with but a single thought . . . it may be, but none will challenge the fact, that The Right Honourable Clement Attlee, who became Prime Minister in 1945, and The Right Honourable Herbert Morrison, Lord President of the Council in 1945, were born on the same day, the first in 1883 and the second in 1888. James Bridie (Dr. Mavor) the greatest Scottish playwright, was born on this day in 1888.

Sufficient unto this day . . . that might be, but the page must be filled.

Cicero was born on January the Third, 107 B.C. and
Douglas Jerrold, who wrote *Mrs. Caudle's Curtain Lectures*, was born on the same day, but it was 1803,
Lucretia Mott, a pioneer of women's rights in U.S.A. and Great Britain, was born on this day in 1793. Her maiden name was Coffin.

These coincidences might serve, but for the curious, let it be recounted that on this day of grace in 1838 began the trial of the Cotton Spinners of Glasgow,
The Commonwealth of Australia was inaugurated in 1901,
The Cape of Good Hope was captured in 1806, and
The British Broadcasting Corporation delivered its first broadcast in Arabic in 1938.

Death claimed Harrison Ainsworth, the novelist, in 1882 on this day,
Wedgwood, the potter of Staffordshire, in 1795,
General Monk in 1670, and
Marshal Joffre, Chief of Staff, French Army 1914, in 1931.
William Joyce, known to millions as 'Lord Haw-Haw', was executed at Wandsworth prison in 1946.
James Dooley, Labour Premier of New South Wales from 1921 to 1923, died in 1950.
Who remembers John Townson? He died on January the Third, 1881, the first to devise a means of photographing on glass, and authentic forerunner of cameras and films—and the Cinema of today.

REFLECTING ON THESE PIONEERS OF PHOTOGRAPHY ONE THINKS OF DAGUERROTYPES AND KODAKS—OF PATHÉ AND GAUMONT AND AGREES THAT 'THERE WAS A YESTERDAY' AND WE MUST DARE—HOWEVER RELUCTANTLY—TO FACE TOMORROW WHATEVER IT MAY BRING.

January the Fourth

We have all seen better days

What does it matter to recall that the history books tell that the Triple Alliance between Great Britain and France and Holland was consummated on January the Fourth, 1717 . . . There have been other events on that day.

Jacob Grimm—the fairy-tale teller—was born in 1785—perhaps that is of greater moment and was more pregnant of fine human enjoyment,
Braille, blind teacher of the blind, was born in 1809,
Sir Isaac Pitman, inventor of Pitman's Shorthand, in 1813.
What else do the researchers record?
A catalogue will do.

Silk is said to have been introduced into Europe in 536 and January the Fourth is somewhat incredibly named as the actual day. Who knows! It was one day. Why not January the Fourth?

Let exactitude resume.
Bohn—the publisher—was born in 1796,
Linley Sambourne was born in 1844,
Augustus John was born in 1879,
Nigel Douglas Hamilton, Earl of Selkirk, was born in 1906,
O. M. Reid, editor of *New York Herald Tribune*, died in 1947,
Rachel died in 1858, and only thirty-eight,
Marshal Joffre was born on this day in 1852.

Charles the First attempted to arrest Members of Parliament in 1642, and
in 1666 his son, Charles the Second, renewed the Charters of the Goldsmiths' Company.
Britain declared war against Spain in 1762,
Burma became an independent republic, 1948,
Nalchik and three other Central Caucasus towns were taken by the Russians, 1943.

DAYS IT WILL BE SEEN MAY BE JUST ANYTHING—BIRTH DAY OR DEATH DAY—MAN PUTS INTO THEM WHAT HE CAN OR WILL AND JANUARY THE FOURTH IS JUST ONE OF THEM, A DAY FORGOTTEN OR A DAY FOREVER FAMOUS.

[5]

January the Fifth

Call it a day . . . pray what else shall I call it?

For some a day of joy for others a day of mourning—for some a birthday—for some a dying day—call it a day.

What does the Fifth of January signify?
For Elizabeth of Russia it meant the day she died in 1762,
For Czartan Petrarch, a Greek, it meant death too, in 1724, at the age of 185, and for
Humbert Wolfe—fine poet and civil servant—it meant both birth and death. He was born in 1885 and died in 1940, both events on January the Fifth.

Other deaths recorded on January the Fifth are:
Edward the Confessor died in 1066 leaving Hastings to Harold later in the year,
Catherine de Medici died 1589,
Joseph Gillott—the steel-pen maker—died in 1872,
Sir Ernest Shackleton, the explorer, died on board the *Quest* in 1922.

Other births recorded on January the Fifth are:
Sir Isaac Newton, that typical practical English philosopher and genius, was born in 1642,
Sir Robert Peel was born in 1788,
Dr. Conrad Adenauer was born in Cologne, in 1876.

A TURBULENT DAY IS THE FIFTH OF JANUARY.
IN 1847 THE TRIAL OF CHRISTINA COCHRANE BEGAN IN EDINBURGH. CHRISTINA COCHRANE WAS CHARGED WITH THE POISONING OF HER HUSBAND,
IN 1916 THIS DAY SAW THE NATIONAL SERVICE BILL IN THE HOUSE OF COMMONS,
SPARTACUS WEEK BEGAN ON THAT DAY IN 1919, IN BERLIN,
BARDIA SURRENDERED IN 1941,
THE JAPANESE SUSTAINED A CRUSHING DEFEAT AT RABAUL IN 1943,
INDIA AND AFGHANISTAN SIGNED A TREATY OF 'EVERLASTING PEACE AND FRIENDSHIP', 1950.
A DAY OF MANY DEEDS DARK AND FAIR HAS BEEN THE FIFTH OF JANUARY.

January the Sixth

You do not deceive me,
O day so bright
Nor do you mock me
With pre-destined night.

Christmas Day in the old style used to be held on the Sixth of January.

Dame Fanny Burney died on this day in 1840,
Hartley Coleridge died in 1849,
Louis Braille in 1852.

Richard the Second was born on January the Sixth, 1366,
Benjamin Franklin—that painstaking person and fortunate link
between Britain, France and America—was born in 1706, and
The Earl of Carlisle was born in 1895, on this day.

But, most of all, it is surely the birthday of Joan of Arc, in 1402,
whom the English burned to death but whom ever since, they—
no less than her own countrymen—have enshrined in their affec-
tions, naming her as not least of the holy martyrs. Of no English
heroine have English writers written so lovingly and, if drama can
pay the debt of death, George Bernard Shaw has done it in his
great historical play *Saint Joan*.

SIR EDWARD COKE WAS COMMITTED TO PRISON ON JANUARY
THE SIXTH, 1622,
IN 1720, THE COMMITTEE OF INQUIRY ON THE SOUTH SEA
BUBBLE BEGAN ITS DELIBERATION AND THERE HAVE BEEN
NO SOUTH SEA BUBBLES SINCE, SO WELL DID IT DO ITS
PRICKING!
IT WAS THE DAY ON WHICH, IN 1842, THERE BEGAN THE
RETREAT FROM CABUL,
AS ALL THE WORLD'S A STAGE, IT MAY BE ADDED THAT ON
JANUARY THE SIXTH, 1931, THE NEW SADLER'S WELLS
THEATRE WAS REOPENED IN LONDON,
LORD MONTGOMERY ARRIVED IN MOSCOW AS GUEST OF
MARSHAL VASSILEVSKY, 1947,
B.E.A. VIKING FROM GLASGOW TO NORTHOLT CRASHED
NEAR RUISLIP, PILOT KILLED AND SEVEN PASSENGERS
INJURED, IN 1948,
GREEK REBELS DRIVEN FROM KONITZA AREA IN 1948.

January the Seventh

You must go, my little day,
I am with you   all the way.

'*It will be found written on my heart when I die,*' *declared Queen Mary. She spoke of Calais which was lost to England in 1558 but the streets of which were to see the English often again, hectically holidaying and hotly fighting in the days that were to be. England has not forgotten Calais, nor ever will. It is a permanent possession, wherever the stout burghers may assign their allegiance.*

And for one poet and one painter this was a day.
Allan Ramsay, poet, died in 1758, and
Sir Thomas Lawrence, than whom, as has been said, 'none more lovingly limned lovely ladies', died in 1830 when
George the Fourth was King.
On this day, Fenelon died in 1715 and
Henry Arthur Jones in 1929.

Banks are in the calendars on January the Seventh.
The First Bank was established in United States in 1782 and in 1939 the Bank of England assumed the largest transfer of gold (and perhaps the last) in its history—
Three hundred and fifty millions of pounds were on that day transferred to the Exchange Equalization account.
In that same London, but in 1857, first appeared the letters L.G.O.C. They stood for London General Omnibus Company—the first of the buses—but these letters no more are read in London's streets.
They became L.P.T.B.—London Passenger Transport Board—but now those who run (for buses or stand in the queues) read only two words—LONDON TRANSPORT.
In 1917 H.M.S. *Cornwallis* was sunk, and
Mr. Dean Acheson succeeded Mr. Marshall on this day in 1949.

Two notable births are recorded—
Lord Horder was born in 1871 and
Viscount Cunningham of Hyndhope was born in 1883.

LET'S FINISH WITH SCOTLAND. IN 1450 THE UNIVERSITY OF GLASGOW WAS FOUNDED BY A PAPAL BULL AND IN 1715 THE OLD PRETENDER ARRIVED AT SCONE AND ARRANGED FOR HIS CORONATION.

January the Eighth

You are a day—mere thing of hours
But who knows my immortal powers?

They too were born on this day and millions more beside but these rise to
the eye,
Wilkie Collins, the novelist, in 1824—he wrote The Woman in White—
and
John Curtin, the late Australian Prime Minister in 1885, and
Captain Lord Herbert in 1906.

Death is not to be denied its place on January the Eighth.
Here is a random catalogue:
Edgar, King of the Scots, 1106,
Marco Polo, 1324,
Galileo, 1642, 'and yet it moves',
John Baskerville, the printer, 1775,
Paul Verlaine in 1896,
Ada Rehan, 1916, and
Richard Tauber in 1948.

In 1916, Gallipoli was evacuated by the British, without the loss
of even a mule, under the noses of the Turks—an achievement com-
parable to the Dunkirk which then was not yet unfolded in the
scrolls of time. A year later, in the same waters, the Allies delivered
their NOTE to Greece asking her whether she was with them or
against them and Venizelos was the answer.

A year later, 1918, Woodrow Wilson presented his fourteen points
to Congress and over two hundred years earlier, in 1712, the
Treaty of Utrecht was signed, sealed and delivered.

IN 1849 ON THIS DAY THE POPE OF ROME WAS DEPRIVED
OF HIS TEMPORAL POWER: IN 1800, THE FIRST PUBLIC
SOUP KITCHENS IN LONDON WERE OPENED—PIONEERS,
ALL UNAWARE, OF THAT DESPERATELY BRITISH VENTURE,
THE BRITISH RESTAURANTS OF THE 1939–45 WAR. THE
FIRST ELECTRIC TROLLEY TRAM IN 1892: AND ANOTHER
FIRST—A WOMAN SAT ON A JURY AT QUARTER SESSIONS
AT DUDLEY IN 1921, AND, TO END, ON JANUARY THE
EIGHTH, 1940, BUTTER, BACON AND SUGAR RATIONING FOR
GREAT BRITAIN BEGAN.

January the Ninth

Why then grieve—the worries of the way,
Sin and sorrow—You have had your day.

Sin and sorrow has its place on January the Ninth.
Thomson and Bywaters—a man and a woman—were hanged in 1923.
Kaiser Wilhelm announced unrestricted U-boat warfare in 1917.
The trial of Charles the First was decided upon in 1648.
The War Council in 1915 apprehended the possibility of stalemate.

Napoleon the Third died at Chislehurst in 1873, and the great
Lord Nelson,
> 'home is the sailor,
> home from sea'
was buried in St. Paul's Cathedral in London in 1806.

Sir Edward Carson, K.C.—to die as Lord Carson—was born in
1854, and Admiral Jarvis, the Earl of St. Vincent, was born in
1754, and
Lascelles Abercrombie was born in 1881. English poet and critic—
was professor of English Literature at London University, 1929–35,
and lecturer in Poetry at Queen's University, Belfast, 1931–2,
On this day, too, there died Tommy Handley in 1949, and
Mrs. Hilton Philipson, actress and M.P., in 1951.

And there were events, too, on January the Ninth, events which
affected the lives and destinies of the lieges . . .
On this day in 1683, for example, Charles the Second issued an
Order in Council to regulate Touching for the King's Evil,
Sir Humphrey Davy's safety lamp for miners made its appear-
ance in 1816,
In 1806 the Cape of Good Hope (for the second time) was cap-
tured by the British,
Coronation Durbar at Delhi, 1903,
In 1944, the Americans landed on LUZON on their way to Tokio,
In 1492, America was discovered but on January the Ninth in the
same year the See of Glasgow was created an Archbishopric,
An Arab force from Syria attacked Jewish settlements in Palestine
and was repelled by British troops in 1948.

IT WAS NOT ALL SIN AND SORROW PERHAPS, BUT, AS
LASCELLES ABERCROMBIE WROTE, 'HAZARDOUS ARE THE
STARS'.

January the Tenth

Poor day, you merely have your hours,
Man has his purposes and powers.

On this day on the Tower Hill, at the block, William Laud, Archbishop of Canterbury, was beheaded. His were humble origins. He was, not by his own desire, brought to the councils of his King, and made many bitter enemies. He was finally charged with high treason and his long life of endeavour was brought to an end in his 72nd year by one blow of the executioner's axe. He was too 'full of fire', said a biographer, but, according to his lights, was a good and just man.

Penny Postage began in 1840 on this day and none knows when it will return.
Earlier, in no less troubled times, Nicholas Culpepper died in 1654,
The Five Members of Parliament were carried in triumph, in defiance of the King, to Westminster in 1642 and, as a result of this event, in 1649 John Bradshaw, the Chief Justice of Chester, was made President of the Court to try King Charles the First,
The Royal Exchange was burned in 1838.

In 1855 on this day, the gentle Mary Russell Mitford died and the same day was the day for dying for the Admiral Boscawen in 1761 and for Linnæus, the founder of modern naturalist science, in 1788. It was, too, the day on which, in 1948, died Reginald Kirshaw Pierson, designer of Vimy and Wellington bombers.
Sinclair Lewis, the American novelist, died on this day in 1951.

Birthdays are brighter recollections—on this day in 1837, Lord Acton, whose most pregnant saying some think is 'power corrupts —but absolute power corrupts absolutely', was born.

On January the Tenth, Lord Roberts arrived in the Transvaal in 1900, Lease-Lend was introduced in 1941, the Formal Ratification of the Peace Treaty with Germany took place on this day in 1920.

AND, PRELUDE TO THESE DAYS OF MOVING MILLIONS, THE FIRST SECTION OF WHAT THEN WAS CALLED THE METRO-POLITAN RAILWAY IN LONDON WAS OPENED TO THE PUBLIC IN 1863. AS ROBERT BURNS HAS WRITTEN 'WE'VE WAN-DERED MONY A WEARY FIT SIN THE DAYS OF AULD LANG SYNE'.

January the Eleventh

Happy the man, and happy he alone,
He, who can call today his own:
He who, secure within, can say,
Tomorrow do thy worst,
For I have lived today.

There are Pools and race meetings for horses and men and cars and grey-hounds and bookmakers and tipsters. The Englishman always was attached to the skirts of happy chance, therefore let us mark January the Eleventh, 1569, because on that date the first lottery ever was drawn in England.

Lotteries are a mixed blessing and not always blessed with public approval, but it is to be counted for righteousness that a lottery was the beginning of the British Museum, and nothing can be more British than that, though it is said that its principal glory is the Elgin Marbles which some say were stolen from Greece.

On this day, too, the New Court of Bankruptcy was opened in 1832, and the Jacobins considered (for want of a better, no doubt) the offering of the Crown of France to the Grand Old Duke of York, in 1792,

In 1783 the frost was so hard that the Thames froze and an Ice Fair was held on its frozen waters,

Charing Cross railway, London, was opened in 1864,

Mussolini (now hung up in the pages of history) greeted Chamberlain and Halifax in Rome on the Eleventh of January 1939,

In 1947 a B.O.A.C. Dakota crashed in bad weather near Folkestone—six were killed.

Ibn Saud was proclaimed King of the Hedjaz in Yeddah, on this day in 1926.

In 1753 Sir Hans Sloane died, and
In 1829, Schlegel died.

TWO BIRTHDAYS COMPLETE THIS PAGE.
GEORGE CURZON, 'A MOST SUPERIOR PERSON' AND MORE TRULY A GREAT ENGLISHMAN, DESTINED TO BECOME THE MARQUIS OF CURZON AND KEDLESTON, WAS BORN ON THIS DAY IN 1859 TO SERVE THIS COUNTRY,
SIR LEIGHTON SEAGER WAS BORN ON THIS DAY IN 1896 TO SERVE MARITIME INTERESTS.

January the Twelfth

January days seem days of death . . . spring is so far away.

' *The President of the Immortals had finished his sport . . .* '
These are some of the concluding words of Thomas Hardy's Tess of the
d'Urbervilles—*they may serve to point to the day on which Hardy himself
died.*
*It was on January the Twelfth, 1928, at his beloved Dorchester. His ashes
are in Westminster Abbey but his heart was buried in the countryside he
loved.*

The record of deaths on January the Twelfth is long,
here are three—a great diversity—
The Emperor Maximilian I in 1519,
The Duke of Alva, at Lisbon, 1583, and
John G. Lavater in 1801 at Zürich.

January the Twelfth records
Act of Supremacy passed in 1563,
In 1679 on this day it became so dark at midday one could not
read a book,
End of the Interregnum, 1689,
Aeronautical Society of Great Britain established in 1866,
The Zulu War against the British in South-East Africa began on
this day in 1879,
Bulgaria ratified Treaty of Neuilly in 1920,
Mr. Chamberlain and Lord Halifax lunched with King of Italy,
in 1938,
Sollum was captured 1942, and how!

EDMUND BURKE WAS BORN IN 1729,
JOHN H. PESTALOZZI IN 1746,
GEORGE, FOURTH EARL OF CLARENDON, IN 1800,
THE MARQUIS OF CREWE IN 1858,
THE HISTORIAN, SIR CHARLES OMAN, IN 1860,
JACK LONDON IN 1876, ALL ON JANUARY THE TWELFTH,
AND, TOO,
SIR JACK CECIL DRUMMOND, THE FOOD EXPERT WHO
PLANNED OUR WAR DIET, IN 1891.

January the Thirteenth

This is a day—Let something be done.

Maurice Jarman did something, this January the Thirteenth, in 1908—he won the Grand Prix d'Aviation. Émile Zola, ten years earlier, chose January the Thirteenth to publish his famous J'Accuse. Chillianwallah was on this day in 1849—Queen Elizabeth, the Virgin Queen, in 1559, had this day for her coronation—on this day in 1935 the Saar Plebiscite was held—on this day the Battle of New Orleans was fought in 1815—and it is on record that on this day in 1928 the War Office of Britain abolished the lance.

The patron saint of Glasgow, St. Kentigern (otherwise St. Mungo), died on this day in 601,
St. Veronica of Milan, 1597, keeps him company.

Alexander Hugh Bruce was born on January the Thirteenth in 1849 and Colonel Sir Charles MacAndrew (Conservative Member of Parliament for Bute) was born in 1888.

There died on January the Thirteenth—
George Fox, Founder of the Quakers, in 1691,
Dr. James Macknight in 1800,
The Earl of Eldon (formerly Lord Chancellor of England) in 1838,
Sir Edmund B. Phipps (formerly deputy Secretary, Board of Education) in 1947, and
The Rev. Dr. John A. Hutton (formerly editor of the *British Weekly*) in 1947.

THE IMPEACHMENT OF DR. SACHEVERELL TOOK PLACE IN 1710,
A JAPANESE LOAN WAS FLOATED IN LONDON (£2,400,000) IN 1873,
GERMAN GENERAL STAFF INTRODUCED IDEA OF RUTHLESS SUBMARINE WARFARE IN 1916,
THE SUPREME WAR COUNCIL SETTLED NEW ARMISTICE TERMS AND FIXED OPENING OF PEACE CONFERENCE FOR 1919,
TARAKAN ISLAND SURRENDERED IN 1942,
M. BLUM VISITED BRITAIN FOR TALKS WITH MINISTERS, 1947,
ALL THESE EVENTS MARK THE CALENDAR FOR JANUARY THE THIRTEENTH.

January the Fourteenth

Who has eyes to discern the beginning of a new day?

At Bradford in England it was only those with prophetic eyes who discerned the beginning of a new day on January the Fourteenth, 1893. It was on this day the Independent Labour Party was founded.
It was with saddened eyes the world read of the death of Lewis Carroll on this day in 1898, but he left behind him for the discerning of all ages the immortal classic Alice in Wonderland. *On this day the Casablanca Meeting was held in 1943—it was only the brave who discerned the beginning of the New Day on that occasion.*

Here are some other occurrences on January the Fourteenth.
It is Mallard Day at Oxford,
Pitt's India Bill was rejected by the House in 1784,
Orsini attempted to assassinate Napoleon III in 1858,
The Board of Admiralty was reconstituted, 1869,
First exhibition of the telephone in Britain in 1878,
Earthquake at Kingston, Jamaica, in 1907,
The new Man-power Bill was introduced 1918 in the House of Commons,
Mr. Churchill became Secretary of State for Air in 1919 and Pahang State was cleared by Japanese in 1942.

Prince Adam Czartoryski was born on January the Fourteenth in 1770.

Edward, Lord Bruce, died in 1610,
Dr. John Boyse, translator of the Bible, in 1643,
Madame de Sévigné in 1696,
Edmund Halley, the astronomer, in 1742,
Dr. George Berkeley, Bishop of Cloyne, in 1753,
Bishop Creighton in 1901 each died in their respective years on January the Fourteenth.

THESE SAINTS CHOSE THIS DAY:
SS. ISAIAS AND SABBAS, 273,
ST. BARBASCEMINUS, 346,
AND ST. HILARY, 368—ALL WITH DISCERNING EYES AS THE FAITHFUL KNOW.

January the Fifteenth

Let us then be up and doing,
With a Heart for any fate;
Still achieving, still pursuing,
Learn to labour and to wait.

Many holy names mark January the Fifteenth, here are three—
St. Paul, the first hermit, 342,
St. Isidore, priest and hermit, 390,
St. Bonitus, Bishop of Auvergne, 710.

Dr. Samuel Parr was born at Harrow in 1747 on this day,
Dr. John Aikin, at Knibsworth in 1747,
Talma, French tragedian, at Paris in 1763,
Thomas Crofton Croker in 1798, and earlier in time, but higher
in the rolls of fame, Molière was born in 1622.

Father Paul Sarpi, 1623, and
Sir Philip Warwick, 1683, died on January the Fifteenth—and
on the same day in 1893, Fanny Kemble quit the stage, as did
Lady Hamilton, but in 1815,
Archibald Alexander, 13th Earl of Leven and Melville, K.T., died
1947.

What do the Holy Men make of these events?

HENRY VIII ASSUMED TITLE COVERED BY ACT OF SUPREMACY,
1535,
ACT OF UNIFORMITY, 1549,
SCOTS INVADED ENGLAND, 1644,
BRITISH MUSEUM OPENED, 1759,
PONDICHERRY TAKEN BY SIR EYRE COOTE, 1780,
BATTLE OF RIVOLI, 1797,
LONDON UNIVERSITY DEGREES FOR WOMEN, 1878,
U.S.S. 'PRESIDENT' CAPTURED BY H.M.S. 'ENDYMION', 1815,
TENNYSON BECAME A PEER, 1884,
FIRST MEETING OF INTER-ALLIES COMMISSION FOR TAKING
OVER NEUTRAL TONNAGE, 1917,
PARIS CONFERENCE BEGAN IN 1919,
FIRST RUNNING COMMENTARY ON A FOOTBALL MATCH,
1927,
APPALLING EARTHQUAKE IN NORTH INDIA, OVER 7,000
LIVES LOST, IN 1934.

January the Sixteenth

Sound, sound the clarion, fill the fife,
  To all the sensual world proclaim
One crowded hour of glorious life
  Is worth an age without a name.

January the Sixteenth marks many a crowded hour of glorious life. David Beatty, who became Lord Beatty and led the British fleet to victory, was born on this day in 1871.
Sir Ian Hamilton, who commanded the troops at the landing on Gallipoli, was born on January the Sixteenth in 1853, as was Sir H. Dickens, in 1849.

Sir John Moore, the hero of the Retreat from Corunna, died on this day in 1809, and January the Sixteenth marks, too, the day of the death of Edward Gibbon, the historian of *The Decline and Fall of the Roman Empire*, in 1794.

Richard Savage, the eighteenth-century poet, was born on this day in 1697 and Edmund Spenser, the Elizabethan poet, died on January the Sixteenth in 1599.

Many are the saints who look down from early times and there were other circumstances than births and deaths. A few may be set forth here, ranging from the sixteenth century:
Mary Stuart claimed the Throne of the Three Kingdoms, Paris, 1558,
Term 'Acts of Parliament' was introduced in 1649,
Certain vails (tips) to servants were abolished in Scotland in 1760,
Captain Cook discovered the Sandwich Islands in 1778,
The Battle of Cape St. Vincent was fought in 1780,
Court of Divorce and Matrimonial Causes first sat in 1858,
The position of the Magnetic Pole was discovered in 1909,
The Kaiser decided to go ahead with submarine warfare, regardless of the United States, in 1917.

A NEW ARMISTICE CONVENTION WAS SIGNED AT TRÈVES IN 1919,
THE UNITED STATES VOTED AGAINST JOINING THE LEAGUE OF NATIONS, 1920,
FIRST MEETING OF THE LEAGUE OF NATIONS IN PARIS, 1920,
M. AURIOL ELECTED PRESIDENT OF THE FRENCH REPUBLIC 1947.

January the Seventeenth

Time is only a collection of days—in history one looks for the man and the hour.

January the Seventeenth produced the man and the hour in 1863 when David Lloyd George was born. No Welshman has so influenced affairs as he, and his memory, tempered by time, is now part of history. His leadership of the British peoples in the classic years of the 1914–18 war comes close to that of William Pitt and Winston Churchill—men who were men of their day and hour.

Benjamin Franklin was born on this day in 1706 and the people of the United States of America rightly cherish his memory. This day is marked in the books of record as the birthday of others who turn time into days:

Don Pedro Calderón in 1600,
Bernard de Montfaucon, the antiquary, in 1655,
Archibald Bower, the historical writer, in 1686,
George, Lord Lyttelton, historian and poet, in 1709,
Victor Alfieri, poet, in 1749,
Charles Kean, the actor, in 1811,
Tchekov in 1860, and Compton Mackenzie in 1883.

There died on this day
John Ray, the naturalist, in 1705,
Bishop Horne in 1792.

Six saints and more, beginning with St. Anthony, who has this for his day, in the fourth century, to St. Milgithe in the seventh century, are remembered on January the Seventeenth.

ON THIS DAY, IN 1842, THE FOUNDATION STONE OF THE NEW ROYAL EXCHANGE WAS LAID, AND A CENTURY LATER, IN 1943, THE SIEGE OF LENINGRAD WAS RAISED.

On this day, too, Buckingham House, the 'ancestor' of the Palace, was purchased for Queen Charlotte in 1775,
Sheridan's *The Rivals* was first acted on this day in 1775,
The Duke of Wellington was appointed Commander in Chief, in 1827,
The Battle of Abu Klea was fought in 1885,
Home Rule Bill passed the House of Commons, majority 110, in 1913,
Prohibition came into force in the United States in 1920, and Warsaw was captured on this day in 1945.

[18]

January the Eighteenth

Life's all getting and giving,
I've only myself to give.
What shall I do for a living?
I've only one life to live.

Rudyard Kipling died on January the Eighteenth, 1936, and his fame grows greater as he recedes into the pages of history. He looked like an Anglo-Indian Jingo when he first met the public gaze, but time showed him to be a great portrayer and lover of his country in the Shakespearian sense, and a writer of matchless verse and stirring prose. Rudyard Kipling might well be the great genius who saw most clearly the greatness of the British Empire and the destiny towards which it marched.

These things happened on January the Eighteenth:
The Houses of York and Lancaster were united by the marriage of Henry VII with Elizabeth, eldest daughter of Edward IV, 1485,
The Battle of Falkirk was fought in 1746,
The Edinburgh and Glasgow Railway was opened in 1842,
In a speech at Birmingham in 1865, John Bright said 'England is the mother of Parliaments',
William of Prussia was proclaimed First German Emperor in 1871,
General Gordon left London for Khartoum in 1884,
The Food Relief Committee first met in Paris in 1919,
Captain Scott reached the South Pole in 1912,
Malta heavily raided in 1941.

These died on January the Eighteenth:
Archangelo Corelli, 1713, founder of Roman or Ancient School of Violinists,
Sir Samuel Garth, 1719,
Sir John Pringle, 1782,
Lord Lytton, the novelist, 1873,
Original Siamese Twins, 1873.

Montesquieu was born on January the Eighteenth in 1689,
Dr. John Gillies, the historian, too, was born on this day in 1747.

THERE ARE MANY SAINTS WHO MAKE THIS DAY NOTABLE, PRINCIPALLY, ST. PAUL AND HIS THIRTY-SIX COMPANIONS IN EGYPT IN VERY EARLY TIMES.

January the Nineteenth

And neither the angels in heaven above,
Nor the demons down under the sea,
Can ever dissever my soul from the soul
Of the beautiful—Annabel Lee!

Edgar Allen Poe, who wrote *The Raven* and *Annabel Lee* was born on January the Nineteenth, 1809, in the United States. He was the first of the native poets of the Republic. He paid the price of genius in health and happiness but the English-reading world reveres his memory as it reads what he wrote.

January the Nineteenth was a day of important births:
Copernicus in 1472,
Hans Sachs in 1576,
James Watt, the architect surely of the Industrial Revolution although he never knew it, at Greenock in 1736,
General R. E. Lee in 1807, and that remarkable essayist and politician, Augustine Birrell, in 1850.
Auguste Comte was born on this day in 1798 as was another great Frenchman, Paul Cézanne, the famous painter, in 1839.

On this day too, let compilers of books of reference salute the memory of Joseph Haydn, author of the *Dictionary of Dates*, who died in 1856,
Isaac d'Israeli, who could write on any subject and wrote on most, died on January the Nineteenth, 1848,
Earlier deaths on this day are
William Congreve, poet, 1729,
Thomas Ruddiman, grammarian, 1757.

BUT JANUARY THE NINETEENTH WAS NOT GIVEN OVER TO BIRTHS AND DEATHS ENTIRELY: ON THIS DATE,
THE EARL OF DERWENTWATER AND OTHER JACOBITE LORDS WERE IMPEACHED FOR HIGH TREASON, 1716,
CIUDAD RODRIGO WAS CAPTURED IN 1812,
ADEN WAS TAKEN BY EAST INDIA COMPANY, 1839,
THE ANTARCTIC WAS DISCOVERED IN 1840,
OLD GREYFRIARS CHURCH, EDINBURGH, WAS TOTALLY DESTROYED BY FIRE IN 1845,
THE FIRST AIR RAID WAS MADE ON GREAT BRITAIN, AT YARMOUTH, 1915.

January the Twentieth

We perish, we disappear, but the march of time goes on forever.

Many famous men are reported as having died on this day—emperors and cardinals, an archbishop and an architect, writers and actors—here they are for those who are curious about the dates upon which men die:

Cardinal Bembo in 1547,
Rodolph II, Emperor, in 1612,
Charles, first Duke of Manchester, in 1722,
Sir James Fergusson in 1759,
David Garrick 'who never had his equal as an actor' in 1779,
John Howard in 1790. He was a great philanthropist.
Sir John Soane, the architect and founder of the Soanean Museum at Lincoln's Inn Fields, in 1837,
Cadell, the Scots publisher, at Edinburgh in 1849,
Sothern, the actor, in 1881,
John Ruskin in 1900,
R. D. Blackmore, author of *Lorna Doone*, in 1900, and
King George V in 1936.

Two birthdays may be noted—
Frederick, Prince of Wales, at Hanover in 1707,
Jean Jacques Barthelemy at Casis in 1716.

A number of curious happenings are related on this day—
One king was deposed and another ascended a throne—
a foreign Prince was naturalized a British subject.
In all their incongruity they are at one in this that they occurred on January the Twentieth.

ENGLAND'S FIRST PARLIAMENT, 1265,
EDWARD II WAS DEPOSED, 1327,
ARCHBISHOP OF CANTERBURY KILLED HIS PARK KEEPER BY MISTAKE IN 1621,
PRINCE ALBERT WAS NATURALIZED A BRITISH SUBJECT IN 1840,
HONG KONG WAS CEDED TO GREAT BRITAIN IN 1841,
LEFT-HANDED PERSONAL SALUTE WAS ABOLISHED BY ADMIRALTY IN 1923,
EDWARD VIII ACCEDED TO THE THRONE IN 1936,
MR. CHURCHILL INVITED NEUTRALS TO JOIN IN THE WAR IN 1940.

January the Twenty-first

I read but I vail myself behind my book.

January the Twenty-first records the death of many famous men. Of many of them nothing remains but memorial tablets or notes in books except for one—Lenin. The embalmed body of Lenin, who died on this day in 1924, lies in the Red Square of Moscow and every year it is seen by hundreds of thousands of adoring Slavs.

January the Twenty-first is the day upon which there died,
Miles Coverdale, translator of the Scriptures, 1568,
Joseph Scaliger, 1609,
James Quin, actor, Bath, 1766,
Alexander Kincaid, Lord Provost of Edinburgh—publisher and bookseller in 1777,
J. H. Bernardin de St. Pierre, 1814,
Dr. Robert Macnish, miscellaneous writer, 1837,
Henry Hallam, the historian, 1859,
Louis XVI, 1793, by the guillotine, and
Lytton Strachey, 1932.

Famous men were born, too, on January the Twenty-first:
Thomas, Lord Erskine, 1750,
'Stonewall' Jackson, 1824.

On January the Twenty-first the Pilgrim Fathers held their first service in America in 1621, and on this day
Habeas Corpus was suspended in 1716,
Letters of Junius began to appear in *Public Advertiser*, 1769,
Daily News started under editorship of Dickens, 1846,
Sir Edward Carson resigned from War Cabinet, 1918,
General Gamelin was appointed supreme commander of all French defence forces in 1938,
Rommel began his last advance in North Africa in 1942,
Russians made 23-mile advance into German Silesia, 1945, after capturing Voroshilovsk in 1943, and, in 1944, Mga, too, was captured in World War II.
Regent of Iraq and political leaders refused to ratify new treaty with Britain as it did not 'realize national aims of Iraq', 1948.

January the Twenty-second

Her court was pure: her life serene:
  God gave her peace; her land reposed;
A thousand claims to reverence closed
  In her as mother, wife and queen.

To the English-speaking peoples all the world over January the Twenty-second is the date, in 1901, when Queen Victoria died. Her long reign had seen great things for her country, not least the rise in the standards of life enjoyed by those who were born and lived in her reign.

Events connected with January the Twenty-second include:
The 'Mongrel' Parliament met in 1644,
Cromwell dissolved Parliament and ruled personally, 1655,
South Sea Bubble began, 1720, and a year later the cashier (Robert Knight) bolted,
The first mail steamer crossed from Calais to Dover in 1822,
The Battles of Isandhlwana and Rorke's Drift were fought in 1879,
President Wilson deprecated peace based on victory in 1917,
Ramsay MacDonald became Prime Minister in 1924.

The day upon which Queen Victoria died saw the deaths, too, of these,
George Stevens, editor of Shakespeare, at Hampstead in 1800,
Charles Keene, 1868,
Gustave Doré, the artist, 1883.

January the Twenty-second saw the birth day of Sir Francis Bacon in 1561—father of the English Renaissance—the 'Alter Ego' of Shakespeare, so close akin to him in thought that some thought they were not two but one man. A lively man, an original man, a great writer and scientist. . . .
His birthday is shared with

SIR ROBERT COTTON, 1570,
P. GASSENDI, 1592,
GOTTHOLD LESSING, 1729,
AMPÈRE, 1775,
GEORGE, LORD BYRON, LONDON, 1788,
AUGUSTE STRINDBERG, 1849.

[23]

January the Twenty-third

A day is a miniature eternity.

Some think that the great men and women are only of the past. There are great men and women today if you could only see them with level eyes.

Yehudi Menuhin, the marvellous violinist, was born on this day in
1917 and on the same day in
1927 Pavlova left the stage for ever.
On the same day, these took their farewell from life—
James, Earl of Moray, Regent of Scotland, in 1570,
Alison Cockburn in 1795,
William Pitt, The Younger, statesman, in 1806,
Sir Francis Burdett, political character, 1844,
Archdeacon Hare, 1855,
Charles Kingsley, 1875, and
Madame Clara Butt, 1936.

January the Twenty-third was an eventful day—at random, turning the pages of the history book, these are recorded,
Opening of First Royal Exchange, 1570, by Queen Elizabeth,
First Bishop of Manchester was consecrated, 1848,
First woman in America to take an M.D. degree, Elizabeth Blackwell, 1849,
Parcel post between Great Britain and India was established, 1873,
The French officially co-operated in Channel Tunnel Scheme, 1875,
Salisbury's fourth ministry, 1901,
Laval's Ministry resigned, 1936,
Eighth Army entered Tripoli in 1943, Burma road to China opened, 1945,
Princess Elizabeth heard foreign affairs debate in House of Commons and, with Duke of Edinburgh, lunched with the Speaker, 1948.

SEVEN SAINTS HAVE JANUARY THE TWENTY-THIRD FOR THEIR DAY,
ST. EUSEBIUS, WHO ATE ONLY ONCE IN FOUR DAYS—BUT WHEN HE ATE HE ATE A LOT ... AND
ST. RAYMOND, A SPANISH SAINT WHO SPENT HIS LIFE CONVERTING THE PAGANS ON THE ISLAND OF MAJORCA, ARE TWO OF THEM.

January the Twenty-fourth

Some are bespattered with mud, some are of the earth, earthy,
But who are these who get their hands on gold?

January the Twenty-fourth is officially the day on which gold was discovered in California in 1848. It opened a new era of prosperity, it was the magic key which unlocked the wealth of the far west of the United States but its impetus and influence were not confined to the Republic; it spread in widening prosperity all over the world. January the Twenty-fourth has another significance in the U.S., it was on this day that its people received the report of the Pearl Harbour attack in 1943.

For the British people, January the Twenty-fourth recalls that the Military Service Bill inaugurated conscription for the first time. It was passed in 1916.

Other events which cluster round this day are,
Drury Lane riot, because of abolition of half price, 1763,
Dynamite explosions at Houses of Parliament and Tower in 1885,
King Edward VII took the Oath at an impressive ceremony, 1901,
Boy Scouts organized, England, in 1908,
Dogger Bank, 1915,
Supreme War Council discussed military strength to be maintained during armistice, 1919,
Non-Fascist Trade Unions dissolved in Italy, 1924,
Society for Individual Freedom founded, 1945.

On January the Twenty-fourth there died,
Justice Henry Yelverton, 1650,
Sir George Rooke, captor of Gibraltar, 1710,
James Ralph, political writer, 1762,
Adam Black, the Edinburgh publisher, 1873,
Lord Randolph Churchill, 1895,
Ouida (Mlle Marie Louise de la Ramée), the novelist, in 1908,
John Burns, in 1943.

ON JANUARY THE TWENTY-FOURTH THESE WERE BORN,
CHARLES, EARL OF DORSET, POET, 1637,
SIR JOHN VANBRUGH, 1664,
FREDERICK THE GREAT, 1712, AND
CHARLES JAMES FOX, 1749.

January the Twenty-fifth

There was a lad was born in Kyle.

Robert Burns, who wrote There was a lad was born in Kyle, Tam o' Shanter, The Cotter's Saturday Night, Mary in Heaven, Should Auld Acquaintance be Forgot *and a whole treasury of poetry, was born on January the Twenty-fifth, in 1759, at Alloway, near Ayr.*

Scotland is proud of her poets and possibly because she cannot lay claim to as many as she would desire, but on this day, the birthday of Robert Burns, it is recorded that in 1772 James Hogg, the Ettrick Shepherd, was born. He, too, wrote many lovely poems. Less famous names whose birthdays fall on this day are
Robert Boyle, 1627, at Lismore,
Thomas Tanner, antiquary, in 1674,
Paul Whitehead, 1709,
Benjamin Robert Haydon, painter, 1786, at Plymouth,
Admiral Fisher, 1841,
W. Somerset Maugham, 1874, and
The Right Reverend James Macdougall Black, D.D., 1879.

On this day there died,
Robert Burton in 1639. He wrote the *Anatomy of Melancholy*, a book but little regarded by a world which feels perhaps it has feasted too long on stories of sadness.
A famous woman, Dorothy Wordsworth, died on this day, 1855.

In 1828, on this day, the Duke of Wellington became Prime Minister, and, walking in Hyde Park, it is said he was accosted by a gentleman who, raising his hat very politely, remarked, 'Mr. Smith, I believe', to which the Duke replied, 'Sir, if you would believe that you would believe anything'.

OTHER EVENTS ARE,
CONSTITUTIONS OF CLARENDON (GRAND JURY TRIALS), 1164,
EDWARD III ACCEDED TO THRONE, 1327,
THE BANK OF ENGLAND CHARTER WAS RENEWED FOR TWENTY-FIVE YEARS FROM 1765, IT COST THE BANK £10,000,
THE SURREY RAILWAY WAS OPENED IN 1802,
THE ANGLO-AMERICAN ASSOCIATION WAS FORMED IN 1871,
LYNSKEY TRIBUNAL REPORT IN 1949.

January the Twenty-sixth

He was the mirror and measure of true knighthood.

Charles George Gordon, an officer of the Royal Engineers, died in the discharge of his duty at Khartoum. On this day in 1885 his death shocked and shook the peoples of Britain and it was followed by firm and determined action which culminated in the overthrow of the Mahdi and the opening of the Sudan.

On the day General Gordon died there also died,
Henry Briggs, 1630, at Oxford,
Dr. Edward Jenner, introducer of vaccination, 1823,
William Clowes, the printer, 1847,
Thomas L. Beddoes, 1849,
Adam Gottlob Oehlenschläger, Danish poet, 1850,
Francis Jeffrey, 1850, of *Edinburgh Review* fame,
Prince Adolf Gustaf of Sweden (killed in an air accident), 1947,
Grace Moore, 1947.

On the day that Gordon died these things happened,
Judiciary Circuits Act passed in 1176,
Artists' Society of Great Britain incorporated in 1765,
Foundation Day in Australia, 1788,
American Church opened at Constantinople in 1834,
Australia ceased to be a convict settlement on this day in 1865,
Americans landed in Northern Ireland, 1942,
British parachute troops destroyed radiolocation post over Le Havre, 1942,
British subject kidnapped in Jerusalem by Jews, 1947,
Russians 100 miles from Berlin, 1944.

ON JANUARY THE TWENTY-SIXTH THESE WERE BORN,
LORD GEORGE SACKVILLE, 1716,
J. B. BERNADOTTE, KING OF SWEDEN, 1764, PAU,
THOMAS NOON TALFOURD, 1795,
GENERAL DOUGLAS MACARTHUR, 1880, AND
SIR ROBERT YOUNG, M.P., 1872, AND, IF THEY MET, THEY
WOULD MAKE A STRANGE BIRTHDAY PARTY.

January the Twenty-seventh

All in the golden afternoon full leisurely we glide.

It is said that Queen Victoria, having read Alice in Wonderland, *asked for other books by the same author—she intimated to her bookseller that any works by Mr. Lewis Carroll would appeal to her. She learned, however, that Mr. Lewis Carroll was the* nom de plume *of Charles Lutwidge Dodgson, Mathematical Lecturer at Christ Church, Oxford, and he continued his story-telling with* Alice Through the Looking Glass. *It has been said that it is impossible to understand the English people unless one understands* Alice in Wonderland. *That may be, indeed, a just appreciation. He was born on January the Twenty-seventh, 1832.*

On this day was born Samuel Gompers, in 1850, the founder of the American Federation of Labour,
Wolfgang Amadeus Mozart in 1756,
Richard Bentley in 1662.

On this day there died
Sir William Temple, 1699,
Thomas Woolston, 1733, King's Bench Prison,
Admiral Lord Hood, 1816,
Dr. C. Hutton, mathematician, in 1823,
The Rev. Dr. Andrew Bell, originator of the Madras System of Juvenile Education, in 1832,
Giuseppe Verdi, the composer, 1901, and
Field Marshal Baron Mannerheim of Finland, in 1951.

ON THIS DAY MEN SAW THESE THINGS,
CONVICTION OF GUNPOWDER PLOT CONSPIRATORS, 1606,
SOUTH SEA COMPANY AND BANK OF ENGLAND PROPOSED A SCHEME FOR DISCHARGING NATIONAL DEBT IN 1719,
A BRITISH ARMY OF 17,709 MEN COST £633,216 IN 1732,
JOHN WILKES WAS ELECTED M.P. IN SPITE OF OPPOSITION IN 1768,
CORN AND NAVIGATION LAWS WERE SUSPENDED IN 1847,
EDISON PATENTED ELECTRIC LIGHT IN 1880,
FINLAND HAD RED REVOLUTION IN 1919,
BURNS'S ELLISLAND FARM PRESENTED TO NATION IN 1923,
FIRST U.S. RAID ON GERMANY, 1943, WHERE THE R.A.F. HAD BEEN BEFORE.

January the Twenty-eighth

Golden days, fruitful of golden deeds.

'It does not matter very much what a man does for a living, a man can rise above his business as well as sink below it.'
Professor George Saintsbury was a great authority on English Literature and a great authority on wine and food, living, and the importance of putting a brave front on life and on death.
Some of his words are here recorded and he himself died on the Twenty-eighth of January 1933.
His Notes on a Cellar Book *is a classic and perhaps he was more proud of this success than of all the other books he wrote.*

There died on the same day,
Charlemagne, 814,
King Henry VIII, 1547, Windsor,
Sir Francis Drake, 1596,
Sir Thomas Bodley, founder of the Bodleian Library, Oxford, 1612,
Peter the Great of Russia, 1725,
Sir William Beechey, painter, 1839,
W. H. Prescott, the American historian of the Incas, 1859, and
Creasey, the English historian, in 1878.

Events crowd round this day and they include,
Maid of Norway became heir presumptive to the Kingdom of the Scots, 1283,
First Bishop of Edinburgh was consecrated in 1684,
Last execution by Act of Attainder—Sir John Fenwick—1697,
Wood got his patent for coining his halfpence, 1722,
The Lords Administration began in 1770,
Pall Mall was the first street to be lit by gas in 1807,
Paris capitulated in the Franco-Prussian war, 1871,
German daylight raid by Gothas on London, 1918,
Russians captured Kastornaya, 1943.

ON JANUARY THE TWENTY-EIGHTH THERE WERE BORN,
IN 1457 KING HENRY VII,
IN 1807 CAPTAIN MCCLURE, THE ARCTIC VOYAGER,
IN 1833 GENERAL GORDON, AND
IN 1868 FREDERICK LAMONT, A GREAT PIANIST.

January the Twenty-ninth

To do good is my religion.

Thomas Paine, who wrote The Rights of Man *and was one of the great political writers of the time, was born on January the Twenty-ninth in 1737. His life was hard, adventurous and varied, and no one knows where his remains are buried. He left an indelible mark on the life and thought of his generation.*

These share January the Twenty-ninth as their birthday,
Emmanuel de Swedenborg, 1688–9,
William Sharp, line-engraver, 1749, London,
Sir James Outram, 1803,
Frederick Delius, 1863,
Sir David Murray, painter, 1849,
Sir Ebenezer Howard, 1850.

These died on this day,
Emperor Aurelian in 275 and
Earl Haig in 1928—stout-hearted, imperturbable, just, honest, distinguished Commander-in-Chief of the British Armies at the end of the 1914–18 war—who, born in Edinburgh, rested at St. Giles Cathedral on his last journey and was interred at Dryburgh Abbey,
William Butler Yeats in 1939, and
Henry Osborne Mavor (James Bridie), the great Scots playwright, in 1951.

On this day the Victoria Cross was instituted in 1856 and still endures as the supreme honour 'For Valour'.
On this day occurred other events
The Death Warrant of Charles I was issued in 1649,
Second Barrier Treaty between Great Britain and Holland, 1713,
The first appearance of *Beggar's Opera*, Lincoln's Inn Fields Theatre, 1728,
Dr. Franklin petition from the people of Boston dismissed, 1774,
First Governor of New Zealand landed, 1840,
Naples and Sicily granted constitution, 1848.

SCOTTISH TOWNS ADOPTED GREENWICH MEAN TIME, 1848,
FIRST TANK TRIAL AT HATFIELD, 1916,
LIGHTSHIP CREWS ATTACKED, 1940, SURELY A SHAMEFUL THING!

January the Thirtieth

I strove with none, for none was worth my strife,
Nature I loved, and next to nature, art;
I warmed both hands before the fire of life;
It sinks, and I am ready to depart.

Walter Savage Landor was ready to depart when his time came to do so
. . . on January the Thirtieth, in 1775, he was born. On that day, too, in
1871, Sir Seymour Hicks, the musical-comedy actor, was born, and, down
the years, significant day for the world, was born Franklin Delano
Roosevelt in 1882.
Charles Rollin was born in Paris in 1661.

On January the Thirtieth, in 1649, King Charles I was beheaded

> He nothing common did or mean
> Upon that memorable scene;
> But with his keener eye
> The axe's edge did try.

A great evangelist and a great sceptic both died on this day—
Charles Haddon Spurgeon, 1892, and Charles Bradlaugh, 1891,
William Chillingworth died on this day in 1644,
Dr. John Robison, mechanical philosopher, in 1805, and
Edward Agar Horatio Nelson, fifth Earl and great-great-nephew
of Nelson, last recipient of the Nelson Pension, in 1951.

There were great events in the twentieth century on January the
Thirtieth. Arrangements were made provisionally for the disposal
of the German colonies on this day in 1919,
Rouse sentenced for the Blazing Car Murder, 1931,
On this day in 1933 Hitler became Chancellor,
On this day in 1943 were two significant events—the first raid by
the R.A.F. on Berlin and the surrender of the Germans in front of
Stalingrad,
Mahatma Gandhi assassinated in New Delhi, 1948.
These were in the twentieth century but January the Thirtieth
also records

THE THIRTY YEARS WAR ENDED, 1648,
FIRST LIFEBOAT WAS BUILT AT SOUTH SHIELDS, 1796,
LONDON DOCKS OPENED, 1805, AND, PEACE OR WAR, HAVE
REMAINED OPEN EVER SINCE.

[31]

January the Thirty-first

The lion is, beyond dispute,
Allowed the most majestic brute.

The most famous monument in the most famous square to the people of
Britain is the monument to Nelson in Trafalgar Square. It did not come
into being, however, all at once and it was on January the Thirty-first, in
1867, that the bronze lions, long promised by Sir Edwin Henry Landseer
were placed in position. They have remained there ever since, keeping watch
and ward over one who expected and realized his expectation, that England
would do her duty.

On January the Thirty-first were born,
Ben Jonson, at Westminster, in 1574,
Franz Peter Schubert, maker of divine harmonies, in 1797,
The incomparable Anna Pavlova in 1885, and
Robert Morris, who helped to finance the U.S. Revolution, in 1734.

Grandson of a King, son of a Pretender to the throne, himself
named The Young Pretender, Charles Edward Stuart, Bonnie
Prince Charlie, died, dispirited, unhappy, on this day in 1788.
Another Charles died, too, on this day, in 1951—Sir Charles B.
Cochran, the famous man of the theatre.

This was a day for evacuations, expulsions and prohibitions:
The plotters of the Gunpowder Plot were executed in 1606,
On this day in 1790 over two hundred and fifty people were
drowned in the canals round Amsterdam, so thick was the fog,
Canada put wartime prohibition into force in 1918, and
The British evacuated Cologne in 1926,
Trotsky was expelled from Russia in 1929,
and there were other events . . . .

ALL PERSONS WITH £40 LAND VALUE A YEAR WERE
ORDERED TO RECEIVE KNIGHTHOOD IN 1626,
CUMBERLAND TOOK OVER COMMAND OF ROYALIST ARMY
AT EDINBURGH IN 1746,
THE 'GREAT EASTERN' WAS LAUNCHED IN 1859,
ALBANIA GOT A NEW CONSTITUTION AND TIRANA BECAME
ITS CAPITAL IN 1925,
FIELD-MARSHAL MONTGOMERY WAS APPOINTED CHIEF OF
THE IMPERIAL GENERAL STAFF IN 1946.

FEBRUARY

TWENTY-NINE DAYS

February the First

. . . . The dayspring from on high hath visited us . . . .

On the First of February there are famous names—daysprings from on high indeed.
Sir Edward Coke, a speaker of the House of Commons, was born in 1552,
John Kemble, the actor, was born in 1757,
The prima donna, Madame Clara Butt, was born in 1873,
Lt.-Gen. Sir Richard McCreery was born in 1898.

Aiton of Kew Garden died in 1793,
Cruikshank, the illustrator of Dickens, died in 1878,
The Rev. Dr. James Henry Rushbrooke died in 1947,
The Rev. James Owen Hannay (George Birmingham), clergyman and novelist, died in 1950,
Sir Arthur Henry Preece, pioneer of Electricity Supply, died in 1951.

Edward the Third was crowned on this day in 1327.
Politically this day has its anniversaries.
Small Debt Courts—'Courts of Conscience' they were called—were established in England in 1517,
The Bell Rock Light House was first lit in 1811,
The Aberdeen Ministry resigned in 1855,
The Royal Naval College was opened in 1873,
On the same day, but in the year 1883, the Houses of Parliament in Quebec were destroyed by fire,
Gladstone's third ministry began this day in 1886,
In 1915 was fought the bitter Battle of La Bassée, and, back to Russia again, it was in 1924 that Britain recognized the Soviet Government,
U.S.S.R. had its Treaty with Finland in 1940,
Zuare was occupied by Eighth Army in 1943,
Torun was captured in 1945,
Mr. Trygve Lie was elected Secretary General of U.N.O. in 1946,
American forces were landed on the Marshall Islands in 1946,
Dakota airliner from Paris crashed near Lisbon—fifteen occupants were killed, in 1947,
King and Queen and Princesses sailed for South Africa in 1947.

THESE WERE SOME OF THE HAPPENINGS ON THE FIRST OF FEBRUARY IN THE DAYS GONE BY WHEN THE DAY SPRING—THE FOUNTAIN OF EVENTS — VISITED THE WORLD OF MAN.

February the Second

Hullo! there is the postman's knock,
Today must follow close the clock.

For many townsfolk the day begins with the postman's knock. It summons them to the outer world with its traffickings and commerce. It is more than that—it reminds those who hear it that today is here, unique, pristine, unprecedented but the descendent, too, of innumerable other days.

February the Second is Candlemas Day in Scotland—it is the Scottish Quarter Day—the close time for partridges begins this day.

Bishop Thomas, 1613, and
Fritz Kreisler, 1875, these are only two of the millions born on this day.

And these died—names taken at random from the histories and the biographies—
Sir Owen Tudor in 1461,
Castiglione in 1529,
Giovanni Palestrina in 1594,
Archbishop John Sharp in 1714,
Francis Hayman, the painter, in 1776,
James Stuart in 1788, one of a long line,
Dr. Olinthus G. Gregory, the mathematician, 1841,
Sir Owen Seaman, of *Punch*, in 1936,
Sir Charles H. Reilly, architect, 1940,
John Davys Beresford, novelist, 1947.

IT WAS ON FEBRUARY THE SECOND, 1625, THAT CHARLES THE FIRST, DRESSED IN WHITE AND NOT THE ROYAL PURPLE, WAS CROWNED A KING,
BURKE—THE PARTNER OF HARE—WAS HANGED IN EDINBURGH IN 1829,
IN 1845, THE INDIAN POSSESSIONS OF DENMARK WERE PURCHASED,
IN 1878, CLEOPATRA'S NEEDLE, AFTER MANY VICISSITUDES, ARRIVED IN BRITAIN,
THE TURKS ATTACKED THE SUEZ CANAL IN 1915 AND FAILED,
AT GENEVA, IN 1932, A DISARMAMENT CONFERENCE BEGAN, RUSSIANS CAPTURED EIGHT GERMAN GENERALS AND ENDED THE FIGHTING AT STALINGRAD IN 1943.

February the Third

At sunset now, there dies a day,
Embalmed—I lay its soul away.

Who were they whose souls were laid away this day—this February the Third?
Sweyn of Denmark, 1014,
John of Gaunt, 1399,
Charles X of Sweden, 1660,
Sir Thomas Lombe, 1738,
Richard Nash—'Beau Nash'—of Bath, 1761,
John Beckmann, of Göttingen, 1811,
Admiral Strachan, 1828,
Christian de Wet, 1922,
Woodrow Wilson, the American President, 1924—who were they?—it is
enough to say thay all died on February the Third.

Benjamin Franklin was examined by the House of Commons in
1766—little good came of it,
Political events include the assertion, by Parliament, of its right
to tax the—then—American Colonies in 1766, and
The expulsion of John Wilkes from the House of Commons in
1769.
The Press feature themselves on this day of the year.
In 1790 *The Times* was fined for libelling the Prince of Wales and
the Duke of Clarence—and,
Russian serfs were freed and declared emancipated on this day in
1861,
Chambers's Journal of Edinburgh celebrated its Jubilee in 1882,
Hamburg was heavily bombed in 1943,
Tudor IV aircraft were grounded pending detailed investigation,
1948,
Mr. J. W. Belcher, M.P., announced his retiral from Parliament,
1949.

MENDELSSOHN WAS BORN IN 1809,
ELIZABETH BLACKWELL, FIRST WOMAN DOCTOR OF MEDI-
CINE, WAS BORN IN 1821,
LORD SALISBURY, WHO BECAME PRIME MINISTER, WAS
BORN IN 1830,
LORD TRENCHARD WAS BORN IN 1873, AND SID FIELD,
MUSIC HALL AND STAGE COMEDIAN, DIED IN 1950 ON THIS
DAY.

February the Fourth

A day is a day even to a donkey . . .

Things that happen to men and women are of endless interest but there are few records of what the beasts of the field thought or did . . . Balaam's ass and that other donkey of which Chesterton wrote . . .

Fools! for I also had my hour:
One far fierce hour and sweet:
There was a shout about my ears
And palms before my feet

And the cat that walked by itself: and Alice's white rabbit. These are remembered but there is another which should not be forgotten.

On February the Fourth, in the year 1882, Mr. P. T. Barnum bought the world-famous elephant JUMBO.

George Lillo, dramatist, was born on this day in 1693 at Moorgate,
Tadeusz Kosciusko, Polish defender of liberty, was born in 1746,
Harrison Ainsworth, who was so popular an author in the early days of Victoria, in 1805, at Manchester, and
H. Mortimer Batten, author, was born in 1888.

February the Fourth records the deaths of poets and kings and men of fame.
Lucius Septimus Severus, Roman Emperor, at York in 211,
Egbert (of England) in 836,
John Rogers, burnt at Smithfield, in 1555,
Giambattista Porta, natural philosopher, inventor of the camera obscura, in 1615, at Naples,
George Herbert in 1633,
Rev. Robert Blair in 1746, author of *The Grave*,
Thomas Carlyle, author of *Sartor Resartus*, the sage of Chelsea, in 1881,
Lord Derby (17th Earl), famous racehorse owner, in 1948, and
The first (and last) Lord Norman, Governor for twenty-four years of the Bank of England, in 1950.

ON THE SAME DAY AS JUMBO WAS SOLD
THE FIRST BISHOP OF NEW YORK WAS CONSECRATED IN LONDON, IN 1787,
THE OLD PRETENDER AND HIS OFFICERS LEFT MONTROSE FOR FRANCE IN 1716,
THE TRIAL OF BOLO BEGAN IN 1918.

February the Fifth

Yesterday returneth not,
Perchance tomorrow cometh not,
Thine is today
Misuse it not.

These did not misuse their days—there is a scholars list for February the
Fifth.
Dr. John Lingard, the historian, was born at Winchester in 1771,
Dr. Lindley, the botanist, in 1790, and
Sir Arthur Keith in 1866.

These great scholars died on this day.
Cato—46 B.C.—'a handful of grey ashes, long, long ago at rest',
James Meyer, a Flemish scholar, in 1552,
Adrian Reland, the Orientalist, at Utrecht in 1718,
Lewis Galvani at Bologna in 1799,
Sir William Norman Raeburn in 1947.

These exchanged their day for immortality . . .
St. Agatha, the virgin martyr and patroness of Malta has February
the Fifth for her saint's-day, the year being 251,
This, too, is the saint's-day for martyrs of St. Portus, 304,
St. Avitus, the Archbishop of Vienna, 525,
St. Alice, Abbess at Cologne in 1015, and for the twenty-six
martyrs of Japan in 1697—a noble army indeed commemorate
February the Fifth.

IT IS A DIVERSE DAY IN OTHER WAYS.
THE 'LONDON GAZETTE' WAS FIRST PUBLISHED IN 1635,
LORD GEORGE GORDON, WHOM DICKENS PUT INTO 'BARNABY
RUDGE', WAS ACQUITTED OF HIGH TREASON IN 1783,
THE ORDER OF THE KNIGHTS OF ST. PATRICK WAS INSTI-
TUTED IN 1783, PRESS ASSOCIATION WAS FOUNDED IN
1870,
AT ST. JOHN'S WOOD—(WHICH ST. JOHN? MANY LONDONERS
ASK)—IN LONDON THE FIRST CABMEN'S SHELTER WAS
OPENED IN 1875,
THE R.A.F. COLLEGE AT CRANWELL WAS FOUNDED IN 1920,
PRINCESS ELIZABETH INSPECTED 16/5TH LANCERS AT
LULWORTH IN 1948.
A DIVERSE DAY INDEED IS FEBRUARY THE FIFTH.

February the Sixth

Dawn is here: come out, O fair day
Man's your companion on your way.

Edinburgh, the capital of Scotland, is the scene.
On this day, in 1886, The Edinburgh Courant *made its last appearance.*
In 1831, cholera appeared in Edinburgh, but that was earlier and it was
also its last appearance.

There were born on this day:
Queen Anne, at St. James, in 1665.
There is a modern rhymelet about this occurrence.

Queen Anne is dead is often said
With tones of varying scorn
But how few carry in their head
The date that she was born.

Antoine Arnauld at Paris in 1612, and
Augustus Calmet in 1672.

And these were not all . . . .

Sir Henry Irving was born in 1838 and
Christopher Marlowe in 1564—both made of the world no small
stage before they quitted it for immortality.

There died this day the Pope Clement, in 740
Charles the Second, King of England and Scotland, in 1685,
Dr. Joseph Priestley, chemist and electrician, Pennsylvania, in
1804,
The Rt. Hon. Ellen Wilkinson in 1947.

MORE GENERALLY, ON THIS DAY, IN 1717, THE REGENT OF
FRANCE COMPELLED THE 'OLD PRETENDER' TO MOVE TO
ITALY,
NEW ZEALAND OFFICIALLY BEGAN HER ASSOCIATION WITH
GREAT BRITAIN IN 1840,
THE RUSSO-JAP WAR BEGAN IN 1904,
THE NAVAL TREATY OF WASHINGTON, 1922,
THE FIRST FALL OF BENGHAZI TOOK PLACE ON FEBRUARY
THE SIXTH, 1941, AND
EISENHOWER BECAME COMMANDER-IN-CHIEF IN NORTH
AFRICA IN THE YEAR OF GRACE OF 1943,
KING GEORGE THE SIXTH DIED THIS DAY IN 1952.

[39]

February the Seventh

Neither fear your last day nor desire it.

James, the bonny Earl of Moray of Scottish history and Scottish song, was murdered this day in 1592.
Dr. Bedell, Bishop of Kilmore, died in 1642,
Ann Redcliffe, the novelist, died at Pimlico in 1823,
Henry Neele, the poet, died in London, 1828, and
M. Bourienne, the Secretary to Napoleon Bonaparte, departed this life in a lunatic asylum at Caen in Normandy in 1834—all these died on February the Seventh.

February the Seventh is the saint's-day of
St. Theodorus, 319,
St. Angulus, fourth century,
St. Richard, King of the West Saxons, 722 and
St. Romualdo, 1027.

The years they come: the years they go;
Man travails—joy and pain
All have their share—the High and Low—
The good Saints they remain.

On February the Seventh,
Charles Dickens was born in 1812,
The Earl of Harewood in 1923.

The formalities for the marriage of Queen Victoria were sealed, and delivered, on this day in 1840.
The London, Chatham and Dover Railway was opened in 1844,
The first meeting of the Irish Nationalist League took place in 1883.

THIS FEBRUARY THE SEVENTH IN 1859 MARKED THE FINAL ABOLITION OF PRISON HULKS, THE DAY ON WHICH A LIST OF 804 CRIMINALS WAS PRESENTED IN BERLIN IN 1920, THE DAY FROM WHICH THE GOVERNMENT TOOK OVER THE BRITISH RAILWAYS IN 1940 AND THE DAY IN 1944 WHEN AT YALTA IN THE CRIMEA, CHURCHILL, ROOSEVELT AND STALIN MET AS THE BIG THREE AND, FOR A FOOTNOTE, IT WAS ON FEBRUARY THE SEVENTH, 1845, THAT MR. WILLIAM LLOYD—A VISITOR TO THE BRITISH MUSEUM— SEIZED AND WANTONLY DASHED TO PIECES THE FAMOUS PORTLAND VASE.

February the Eighth

A day appointed—what a significant phrase!

A day appointed for death was February the Eighth.
Lovely Mary, Queen of Scots, was executed by her cousin, Elizabeth of England, in 1587.

Peter the Great died in 1725,
R. M. Ballantyne, the story-writer for boys, died in 1894, and
the son of a greater story-teller, the second Sir Walter Scott, died
in 1847,
Dr. George Sewel, the historian of the Quakers, died in 1727, and
who remembers him now?
Aaron Hill, a poet, died in 1750.

St. Proclas, the patriarch of Constantinople, was born on this day
in 1412,
There were many more—millions of unrecorded births. Here are
some who had February the Eighth for their birthday.
John Ruskin, 1819, an artist philosopher,
Jules Verne, 1828, a scientific novelist,
Samuel Butler—the poet, the author of *Hudibras*, not the philo-
sopher—1612,
Mary I, Queen of England, 1516,
Jenny Lind, 1820, a sweet singer,
William, Earl of Pembroke, 1580 (who was he?),
Peter Daniel Huet, 1630, Bishop of Avranches (and who was he?),
Charles Henault, *littérateur*, 1685, born at Caen (but what else?),
A Genevese philosopher in 1727, to wit—John Andrew de Luc,
and Arthur Greenwood in 1880 and Anthony Hope, born 1863.

THESE ARE EVENTS:
ON THIS DAY, IN 1750, THE LAST EARTHQUAKE OF ANY
CONSIDERABLE VIOLENCE IN GREAT BRITAIN OCCURRED,
CONCILIATORY ACT WAS PASSED IN 1778,
SARDINIA WAS GRANTED A CONSTITUTION IN 1848,
THE RUSSIAN AMBASSADOR LEFT LONDON IN 1854,
GLADSTONE INTRODUCED HIS PRELIMINARY RESOLUTION
ON POST OFFICE SAVINGS BANK BILL IN 1861,
CARDINAL MINDSZENTY SENTENCED TO LIFE IMPRISON-
MENT AT BUDAPEST, 1948.
PROCLAMATION OF QUEEN ELIZABETH, 1952.

February the Ninth

All is even at eventide.

*Martyrdom marks February the Ninth for St. Apollonia, the virgin
martyr of Alexandria, in 249,*
St. Nicephorus at Antioch, in 260,
*And away down the years, at the stake by burning in 1555, Bishop Hooper
found it at Gloucester,*
And Doctor Rowland Taylor at Hadleigh in the same year.

In 1401, a Lollard named Sawtre—the first heretic so called—was
burned at the stake.
Lord Darnley, consort of the ill-starred Mary, Queen of Scots, was
murdered on this day in 1567.

Fortunately, there are happier things.
Mrs. Patrick Campbell, the actress, was born on February the
Ninth in 1865, to delight the world and to enchant Mr. Bernard
Shaw into the bargain.

Fame! What is it? I have all,
Time is a swallowing maw,
Careless now I take my call,
I enchanted Bernard Shaw!

In 1700, Bernoille—a Swiss mathematician of note—was born and,
in 1747, Volney, the French philosopher, chose the same day to
make his bow,
Field-Marshal Sir Evelyn Wood, v.c., in 1838 preceded
Lord Carson in 1854 in choosing this day for a birthday.

And many died on this day.
Agnes Sorel in 1450,
Dr. John Gregory, of Edinburgh, the author of *A Father's Legacy to
his Daughters*, in 1773,
Nevil Maskelyne, the Astronomer Royal, in 1811,
The philosopher, Benjamin Martin, in 1872, and
Röntgen, famous for X-rays, in 1922.

COMING NEARER STILL TO THESE DAYS OF GRACE. FEB-
RUARY THE NINTH LIVES IN THE CALENDAR AS THE DAY
WHEN THE FRENCH LINER 'NORMANDIE' WAS BURNED AND
THE DAY ON WHICH SOAP RATIONING BEGAN, BOTH IN
1942.

February the Tenth

The gates of hell are open—night and day.
Smooth the descent and easy is the way.

Robert the Bruce murdered the Red Comyn in 1305, that was a
red day in Scotland on February the Tenth.

Red is the rose and red the dawn
Is man fated still to tread
A path whereon he is a pawn
In the pocket of the red?

On February the Tenth, in 1746, the Bath Administration took
office and lasted only a few days,
Paris came virtually into the British Empire when the Peace
Treaty was signed at Paris on this day in 1763 at the end of the
Seven Years War.
There are other public events which mark this day.
Queen Victoria was married in 1840,
The first Dreadnought was launched in 1906,
Conscription, by means of the First Military Service Bill, began in
Britain in 1916, and
The King's College at Aberdeen had its charter by Papal Bull
dated February the Tenth, 1494.
This date marks the death of Lister in 1912, and the assumption of
dictatorship by Bolivar in Peru in 1824,
Heavy fighting in the Anzio beachhead in 1944,
Parliament of Dominion of Ceylon opened by Duke of Gloucester
in 1948.

Pope Leo XII died in 1829,
Pushkin left the Russian scene for ever in 1837.

Wars continued and peace was enacted, but, for some, the day is
best remembered as the birth day, in 1775, of the gentle Elia—
England's one and only Charles Lamb, essayist, critic, humanist,
Samuel Plimsoll was born in 1824,
Sir John Black was born in 1895,
William Henry Denham Rouse, former Head of Persse School,
Cambridge, died 1950.

THE GATES OF HELL ARE OPEN—NIGHT AND DAY
BUT NOT FOR CHARLES LAMB, PLEASE GOD!

February the Eleventh

The prosperous day dawns, be propitious with your tongues and thoughts.

These on this day were born:
The Princess Elizabeth (of York) in 1466,
Sir Maurice Denny, the shipbuilder, in 1886.

These died.
The Emperor Heraclius, 641,
Elizabeth Plantagenet of York, 1502,
René Descartes, the French philosopher, 1650,
William Shenstone, the poet, 1763,
Macvey Napier, of *Encyclopaedia Britannica* fame, in 1847, and
Lt.-Col. James Grant, African explorer, in 1892.

In 1765, on February the Eleventh, a petition was presented to King George III, by the Master Peruke-makers, lamenting the decline of their trade because gentlemen were beginning to wear their own hair!
In the twentieth century, the League of Nations took over Danzig but did not hold it,
The Vatican City was established by Treaty in 1929,
The *Scharnhorst* affair occurred on February the Eleventh in 1942, and
The Fifth Regiment of Guards, the Welsh Guards, came into being in 1915.

Men died, men of letters, and not least notable was
John Buchan (Lord Tweedsmuir) in 1940, but journals, too, are mortal.
The *Athenæum* produced its last number on this day and gave over its world to the *Spectator*, the *New Statesman* and the *Week End Review*.

Tuscany had its Constitution in 1848,
Nicaragua had its Treaty in 1860, and
The Charter was granted to the University of London in 1826.

Across the Atlantic, in the United States, modern electric science took its beginnings, in the birth of Thomas Alva Edison in 1847.

PROSPEROUS AND PROPITIOUS WERE THESE DAYS,
O! MAY MANKIND FIND EVER BETTER WAYS.

February the Twelfth

Anthony—it is my name
Constantinople gave it fame:
Can I bring it further fame,
In these less and later days?

February the Twelfth joins Barcelona and Anian and Constantinople in its
saints'-days. These are St. Anthony Cauleas, the patriarch of Constantinople,
896, St. Eulalia, the virgin of Barcelona, a blessed martyr, about 305,
St. Benedict of Anian, an abbot, 821.

On this day, first dawned the light of life on
Gabriel Naude, a *littérateur*, in 1600 at Paris,
Bishop (John) Pearson, 1613, at Snoring,
Elias de Crébillon, the French romanticist, 1707, also at Paris,
Abraham Lincoln, 1809, and Charles Darwin in the same year,
Edward Forbes, naturalist, 1815, at Douglas, Isle of Man. How
rarely does the Isle of Man figure in the pages of history!

On this day there died, Bishop David ap Owen in 1512,
Sir Nicholas Throckmorton, Chief Butler of England to Elizabeth,
in 1571,
George Heriot ('jingling Geordie' of *The Fortunes of Nigel*) died in
London 1623–4, interred at St. Martin's-in-the-Field.
Gabriel Brotier, editor of Tacitus, 1789,
Lazaro Spallanzani, naturalist, 1799, both at Paris,
Sir Astley Cooper, the surgeon, in 1841,
Lily Langtry, 1929.

IN 1688, JAMES II, HAVING FLED TO FRANCE, THE CON-
VENTION ADOPTED, ON FEBRUARY THE TWELFTH, THE
RESOLUTION 'THAT WILLIAM AND MARY, PRINCE AND
PRINCESS OF ORANGE, BE DECLARED KING AND QUEEN OF
ENGLAND, FRANCE AND IRELAND, AND THE DOMINIONS
THERETO BELONGING'.
THIS DAY COMPLETED THE REVOLUTION OF 1688,
ON SATURDAY, FEBRUARY THE TWELFTH, 1881, MAIL
SERVICE FROM LONDON TO BRISBANE WAS INAUGURATED
BY BRITISH INDIAN STEAMSHIP COMPANY WHEN S.S.
'MERKARA' LEFT THE VICTORIA DOCKS UNDER THE COM-
MAND OF CAPTAIN J.J. BALLANTYNE,
A REPUBLIC WAS ESTABLISHED IN CHINA IN 1912.

February the Thirteenth

'Tis a lucky day, boys, and we'll do good deeds in it.

Was it a lucky day for:
John Hunter, surgeon, born 1728,
Alexander Wedderburn, Earl Rosslyn, born 1733 at Chesterhall,
David Allan, the Scottish painter, born 1744 at Alloa,
Charles Maurice de Talleyrand-Périgord, the diplomatist, 1754,
Lord Randolph Churchill was born in 1849—born never to be Prime Minister, but to beget one,
Mr. Stephen Gwynn, author, politician and soldier, born 1864.

Was it a lucky day for:
Catherine Howard, beheaded in 1543 in the Tower,
Elizabeth of Bohemia, 1662, at Leicester House,
Dr. Cotton Mather, 1728, at Boston,
Dr. Samuel Croxall, fabulist, in 1752,
Charles, Count de Vergennes, the French diplomatist, in 1787 at Versailles,
The Duc de Berri, assassinated in 1820 at Paris,
Henry Hunt, a political character, in 1835,
Sharon Turner, historian, in 1847,
Richard Wagner in 1883—all these—in diverse ways—died on February the Thirteenth, and
Rafael Sabatini, an historical novelist, died 1950.

And was it well for mankind that the Bill of Rights was passed on this day 1689, or that the
Massacre of Glencoe befell on the morning of the Thirteenth in 1692,
Martinique was taken and Grenada surrendered in 1762,
The trial of Warren Hastings began in 1788,
The first steam locomotive moved on rails in 1804,
The Peace Treaty with the Ashantees was signed in 1874,
The Mersey Tunnel was opened in 1885,
Viscount Nuffield notified his munificent gift of £10,000,000 for research and welfare, 1943,
The Russians took Budapest in 1944.

A LUCKY DAY FOR PAINTERS, FABULISTS, HISTORIANS, BUT IS NOT EVERY DAY A LUCKY DAY FOR SOMEONE? 1,000 TONS OF BOMBS DROPPED ON LORIENT, 1943.

February the Fourteenth

It is never a bad day that hath a good night.

February the Fourteenth is St. Valentine's Day.
St. Valentine is placed in the calendar as c. 270, a priest and a martyr and
the patron of the millions who:
Come foul—come fair—come frost—come fine
Dear, will you be my Valentine?

He takes precedence over all the other saints of this day for this
alone, but none the less, they companion him this day.
Here they are:
St. Abraemes, Bishop of Carres, 422,
St. Auxentius, Hermit of Bithynia, *c.* 470,
St. Conran, Bishop of Orkney, seventh century.

And from the saints let us turn to the uncanonized. There were
born this day
Camille, Duke of Tallard, 1652,
Archdeacon Waterland, eminent theologian, 1683, and
Israel Zangwill, the Jewish novelist, was born in 1864 on this day.

On this day there died . . .
Pope Innocent I, 417,
Richard II, King of England, murdered, alas! in 1400,
Benvenuto Cellini, died 1576,
Lord Chancellor Talbot, 1737,
Captain James Cook, killed at Owhyhee, 1779, a grievous thing,
Sir William Blackstone, author of the *Commentaries on the Laws of*
England, 1780.

The events which mark the calendar on February the Fourteenth
are,
The Government by Council of State was set up in 1649,
The discovery of Prendergast's Plot against William III in 1696,
The day on which Williams, the publisher of *The North Briton,*
stood in the pillory in 1765,
The opening of the Singapore base in 1938.

'IT IS NEVER A BAD DAY THAT HATH A GOOD NIGHT' IS A
COMFORTING REFLECTION FOR THOSE WHO ARE DIS-
APPOINTED ON ST. VALENTINE'S DAY.

[47]

February the Fifteenth

A day is only a day.

February the Fifteenth is old Candlemass,
Singapore was lost on this day in 1942,
A day is only a day, alas!

There died on this day many, but included in the uncountable
and uncounted multitude are:
Oswy (of Northumbria), 670,
John Philips, poet, 1708,
Anthony, Earl of Shaftesbury, author of characteristics, 1713,
Bishop Atterbury, 1732,
John Hadley, inventor of the sextant, 1744,
Lessing, the German critic and dramatist, 1781,
Cardinal Wiseman, 1865,
General Lew Wallace, who wrote *Ben-hur*, in 1905,
The Earl of Oxford and Asquith in 1928, some think, of our
generation, the noblest Roman of them all.

Born on this February the Fifteenth were:
Galileo Galilei, the astronomer, 1564, at Pisa,
Louis XV (of France), 1710,
Jeremy Bentham, 1748,
Susan B. Anthony, worked to free Negro slaves and for women's
rights, United States, 1820,
Sir Bannister Fletcher, 1866,
Chaliapin, 1873,
H. M. Bateman in 1887, whose pictures made Guardsmen laugh,
Mr. Brendan Bracken in 1901.

AND WHAT OF OTHER EVENTS?
CEYLON WAS TAKEN BY THE BRITISH IN 1766,
PITT'S MAIDEN SPEECH ON REFORM BILL HEARD 1781,
KIMBERLEY, IN 1900, WAS RELIEVED ON THIS DAY,
THE FIRST CHIMPANZEE EVER BORN IN LONDON CHOSE
THIS AS A BIRTH DAY IN 1935,
RUSSIANS BROKE THROUGH MANNERHEIM LINE IN 1940,
KISMAYU, ITALIAN SOMALILAND, CAPTURED, 1941,
THE CASSINO MONASTERY WAS BOMBED IN 1944.
A DAY IS ONLY A DAY, ALACK! ALAS!!
FUNERAL OF KING GEORGE VI, 1952.

[48]

February the Sixteenth

A day holds more than twenty-four hours.

On this day there died:
Alphonso III of Portugal, 1279,
Archbishop Henry Deane, 1502, Canterbury,
Dr. Richard Mead, virtuoso, 1754, St. Pancras,
Lindley Murray, grammarian, 1826, and
Lionel Lukin, inventor of the lifeboat, in 1834,
Dr. Kane, American Arctic explorer in 1857, Havana,
A strange concourse indeed to share the same day of departure and, let there
be added, Baron Trenck in 1726—a different sort of man.

But these born on this day are no stranger a company.
Philip Melanchthon, the reformer, 1497, at Bretton,
Gaspard de Coligny, Admiral of France, Protestant leader, 1516,
Archbishop John Sharp, 1644, Bradford,
George Macaulay Trevelyan, the great modern historian, 1876,
Sir Oliver Franks in 1905.

And, of course, there are the saints'-days . . . from
St. Onesimus, disciple of St. Paul, martyr, 95, to
St. Gregory X in 1276.

Here are some performances:
In 1643 the first Committee of England and Scotland was appointed, a kind of 'working party' in modern parlance,
1801 saw Pitt's resignation,
1869 saw the first meeting of the Reform Parliament,
1909 saw a colliery accident in Durham when 168 lives were lost,
1915 saw British planes in action over the Belgian coast,
1923 saw Tutankhamen's tomb opened,
The *Altmark* raid and rescue took place on this day in 1940, and
three years later Kharkov was recaptured.

SUNSET AND DAYS-END
PUT THE HOURS AWAY
BUT THESE HOURS WILL LEND
MUCH FOR ANOTHER DAY,
MUCH FOR JOY AND
MUCH FOR SORROW,
IF THEY WILL LEND—
THEN, WE WILL BORROW.

February the Seventeenth

Are there no saints, these days, Samuel?

Saints'-days are mostly long ago.
Is that because we think so,
Mankind has fallen very low,
Perhaps because he drinks so!

Born on this day were
Francis, Duke of Guise, the French warrior, 1518,
Horace Benedict de Saussure, the Genevese traveller, 1740,
John Pinkerton, a historian and antiquary, 1758, Edinburgh,
Selwyn Image, artist, 1849.

There died on February the Seventeenth in their respective
centuries,
Giordano Bruno, Neapolitan philosopher, burnt at Rome, 1600,
Jean Baptiste Poquelin de Molière, 1673, Paris, the French
Shakespeare,
Antoine Galland, translator of the *Arabian Nights' Entertainments*,
1715,
John Martin, historical painter, 1854,
John Braham, singer and composer, 1856, London,
The Grand Duke Sergius of Russia—assassinated—1905.
The list is incomplete—none could number it—but there are some
to be added.
Heine, for example, died in 1856 and, the great contemporary of
Molière, Corneille, died on the same day in 1684,
Albert of Belgium died tragically on February the Seventeenth in
1934,
Sir Wilfred Laurier, the first French-Canadian Prime Minister,
died in 1919,
C. S. Calverley—who wrote so understandingly of tobacco as the
solace of man—died in 1884.

BURKE ON THIS DAY IN 1786 EXHIBITED ARTICLES OF
IMPEACHMENT AGAINST WARREN HASTINGS,
THE CORN LAWS WERE INTRODUCED IN 1815,
IN 1917 THE BATTLE OF THE ANCRE WAS FOUGHT,
THE ROYAL FAMILY ARRIVED IN CAPE TOWN IN 1947.
IT WILL DO. EVERY DOG HAS HIS DAY. EVERY DAY ITS
DOINGS, AND PERHAPS EVERY DAY ITS SAINTS.

February the Eighteenth

Each day's march takes us nearer home,
Albeit far afield we roam,
Freighted the hours with certain doom
Gordon—on this day—reached Khartoum.

In 1884, General Gordon reached Khartoum,
In 1808, Russia invaded Swedish Finland,
In 1797 the island of Trinidad was taken—all on this day.

The Birth Days include,
Mary I, Queen of England, 1517, at Greenwich,
Isaac Casaubon, the scholar, 1559, at Geneva,
James Cassini, the astronomer, 1677, at Paris,
Alexander Volta, the discoverer of Voltaism, 1745, at Como, and
Wilson Barrett, in 1846.

There died too, on this day,
Pope Gregory V, 999, doubtless in his bed,
George, Duke of Clarence, murdered, 1478,
Martin Luther, the Protestant Reformer at Wittenberg, 1546,
Michelangelo, 1564—he joined the other angels,
Sir Richard Baker, chronicler, 1645, Angoulême,
Dr. Thomas Hyde, orientalist, 1702, at Hamburg,
Sir Jeffrey Wyatville, architect (who did the Windsor Castle restoration), in 1840, at Windsor, and
Rt. Hon. Sir James Andrews, 1951.

What else in these fleeting pages of history?
Paganini was born in 1784,
Madame Roland's birthday in 1734—and this Eighteenth of February marks the Second Commune of Paris in 1871,
It is challenged by some, but it is accepted by others, that on this day, 1725, the Order of the Bath was revived.
Jefferson Davis was elected President of the Confederacy, 1861.
The World's a stage; let it be recalled that
Tom Walls, the actor, was born on February the Eighteenth, 1883.

WE LIVE AND LEARN, LET US REMIND OURSELVES, LORD ACTON ON FEBRUARY THE EIGHTEENTH, 1895, WAS APPOINTED REGIUS PROFESSOR OF MODERN ENGLISH HISTORY—THE FIRST ROMAN CATHOLIC SO APPOINTED SINCE THE DAYS OF JAMES II OF ENGLAND.

February the Nineteenth

In sooth the sorrow of these days
  Is not to be expressed,
When he that takes and he that pays,
  Are both alike distressed.

There were born on this day:
Nicolaus Copernicus, astronomer, in 1473, at Thorn in Prussia,
Henry Frederick, Prince of Wales, in 1594, at Stirling Castle in Scotland,
David Garrick, in 1717,
The Admiral Rodney, in 1718,
Richard Cumberland, dramatist, 1732, at Cambridge,
Sir Roderick Murchison, geologist, 1792, at Tarradale,
Adelina Patti, in 1843, surely one of the sweetest of sweet singers,
Sven Hedin, in 1865—the explorer.

And on this day there died:
Decimus Albinus (Emperor) killed in battle, 198, on the Rhône River,
Erasmus Reinhold, astronomer, in 1553,
Lucilio Vanini, 1619, burnt as an atheist at Toulouse,
Sir Henry Savile, mathematician, 1622, Eton College,
Francis de Sauvages, the nosologist, 1767, at Montpellier,
Elizabeth Carter, classical scholar, 1806, translator of Epictetus and still the best,
Bernard Barton, poet, 1849, and
Sir William Napier, military historian of the Peninsular War, 1860, and friend of the great Duke of Wellington.

BUT BIRTHS AND DEATHS ARE BUT BEGINNINGS AND ENDINGS—THERE ARE, TOO, THE GREAT EVENTS:
PARLIAMENT ROSE AFTER PASSING BILL TO MAKE JUDGES INDEPENDENT OF THE CROWN, 1761,
CATO STREET CONSPIRACY FORMED, 1820—AND FAILED,
NEW HOUSES OF PARLIAMENT OPENED, 1835—A HOPEFUL AUGURY,
ÉMILE ZOLA TRIED, SENTENCE QUASHED, 1898, IN THE GREAT DREYFUS CASE,
BEGINNING OF DARDANELLES BOMBARDMENT, 1915—ON FEBRUARY THE NINETEENTH—ONE OF THE PHASES OF THE GREAT WAR OF 1914–18 ON WHICH MUCH HOPE RESTED BUT WAS NOT FULFILLED.

February the Twentieth

Each day is the scholar of yesterday.

They make a strange quartette. They have little else in common.
The great Voltaire, 1694,
David Garrick, actor and dramatist, 1717, Hereford,
Rev. James Dallaway, antiquary, 1763, Bristol,
Adam Black, 1784, in Edinburgh,
Lord Macmillan, 1873,
All these were born on February the Twentieth and were doubtless a joy to their mothers on that day.

These all died on February the Twentieth:
Archbishop Arundel, 1413–14, at Canterbury,
James I, murdered at Perth, 1437,
Sir Nicholas Bacon, Lord Keeper, 1579, York House, Strand,
Dorothy Sydney, Countess of Sunderland, 1684, Brington,
Mrs. Elizabeth Rowe, philanthropic religious writer, 1737,
Charles II (of Savoy), 1773,
Dr. John Moore, novelist, 1802, Richmond,
Richard Gouch, antiquary, 1808, Wormley,
Joseph Hume, the statesman, 1855,
Scribe, French dramatist, 1861,
Isaac Croper, last survivor of *Shannon-Chesapeake* fight (1813), 1878,
Gen. Sir Charles Fergusson, New Zealand, 1951, and in the same year Sir Cyril Maude, veteran actor manager.

ON THIS DAY IT IS RECORDED . . .
EDWARD THE SIXTH WAS CROWNED IN 1546,
COVENANTERS REBELLED AND DECLARED FRENCH KING THEIR SOVEREIGN IN 1639,
THE HOUSE OF LORDS WAS VOTED 'USELESS AND DANGEROUS' IN 1648—THERE IS NOTHING NEW!
FIRST PERFORMANCE OF 'BARBER OF SEVILLE' IN 1816,
SIND WAS ANNEXED IN 1843—BUT NO ANNEXATION LASTS FOR EVER,
RUSSELL'S MINISTRY WAS DEFEATED IN 1858,
LETTERS WERE SENT BY PNEUMATIC TUBE FROM EUSTON STATION TO G.P.O. IN 1863,
LORD WAVELL, VICEROY OF INDIA, RESIGNED IN 1947,
A LIST OF HAPPENINGS NEVER BEFORE RECORDED TOGETHER ON ONE SINGLE PAGE!

February the Twenty-first

Get ye to rest—try then to sleep
Yours is a lot forlorn
It is indeed your fate to keep
For you are bound to mourn.

The words were those of Robert Burns: the sentiment belongs to all mankind.

On this day there died:
Caius Agrippa, A.D. 4,
Pope Julius II, 1513,
Henry Grey, Duke of Suffolk, beheaded, 1555,
Robert Southwell, a poet, executed at Tyburn, 1595,
Pope Benedict XIII, 1730,
Eugène de Beauharnais (shades of Empress Josephine), Duke of
Leuchtenberg, 1831, Bristol,
Charles Rossi, R.A., sculptor, 1839,
John Quincey Adams, sixth President U.S.A., 1825–9, in 1848,
Colonel Nicol Burns, last surviving son of Robert Burns, 1872 and
Spinoza, the philosopher, 1677, the gentlest of them all—died in
Holland, the world lamenting, but by the world unforgotten,
Gogol died this day in 1852.

Here are battles, cruelties and wars:
Colonel Desparit, and six associates, executed for High Treason,
1803,
Verdun, 1916, 'How deep the corn,
                where the battlefield had been'
Jericho captured 1918, and Allenby's campaign was over,
The battleship *King George V* was launched at Newcastle, 1939,
Bremen was heavily bombed, 1943.

ON THIS DAY WERE BORN:
PIERRE DU BOSE, 1623, BAYEUX (AND WHO WAS HE?)
MRS. ANN GRANT, AUTHOR OF 'LETTERS FROM THE
MOUNTAINS', 1755, GLASGOW,
CARDINAL NEWMAN, 1801—WAS HIS 'LEAD, KINDLY
LIGHT'?
GEORGE LANSBURY, 1859, A SAINT OF SOCIALISM,
SACHA GUITRY, 1885, AN ACTOR AND SURELY MORE,
CARDINAL BERNARD W. GRIFFIN, 1899, AND
THE POET, WYSTAN HUGH AUDEN, IN 1907.

February the Twenty-second

Once to every man and nation
Comes the moment to decide
In the strife of truth with falsehood
For the good or evil side.

Born on February the Twenty-second, in U.S.A., James Russell Lowell
wrote the challenge 'Once to every man and nation'. He understated
opportunity. Fortunately opportunity comes more than once to most but one
never knows whether it may not be the last opportunity.

There were also born on February the Twenty-second:
George Washington, 1732, the great Englishman who made
U.S.A.,
Charles, Duke of Richmond, 1735,
Schopenhauer, 1788, who saw the world as a will and an idea,
Sarah Flower Adams, 1805, the poetess,
Frederick Chopin, 1810, pianist and composer, exile and patriot,
who found, happily for himself and the world, an expression in
divine harmonies of the sadness which was his daily companion, and
Baden-Powell, 1857, who proved that boys will always be boys.

There died on this day:
David II (of Scotland), 1371, at Edinburgh Castle,
Amerigo Vespucci, 1512, who gave his name to America,
Frederick I (of Tuscany), 1609,
James Barry, painter, 1806, Marylebone,
Adam Ferguson, philosopher, 1816,
Rev. Sydney Smith, 1845, who was so witty and so wise,
J. F. Gravelet (Blondin), 1897, who crossed Niagara on a rope,
Dame Nellie Melba, 1931, who sang so sweetly.

SOME WERE BORN—SOME DIED, BUT THERE WERE OTHER
EVENTS:
FLORIDA WAS CEDED TO U.S. BY SPAIN, 1819, ON THIS DAY,
BRITISH CENTRAL AFRICA PROTECTORATE, 1893,
TERMINOLOGICAL INEXACTITUDE DESCRIBED BY CHUR-
CHILL, 1906,
THESE WERE THINGS THAT HAPPENED.
AND FOR A POSTSCRIPT—IT MAY BE RECALLED THAT
HINKLER FLEW FROM LONDON TO AUSTRALIA IN SIXTEEN
DAYS—1927, BEGINNING THIS DAY.

[55]

February the Twenty-third

Daisy, Daisy, this is your day
Lazy, lazy, do what you may.

It was Pinero who wrote,
> *Mind the paint—Mind the paint*
> *A girl is not a sinner because she's not a saint.*

And to be at all, one must be born.
These had their birth days on February the Twenty-third:
Samuel Pepys in 1633, all the world knows what he wrote,
G. F. Handel in 1685, brought harmony to a disharmonious world,
Cardinal York, last of the Stuarts, in 1725,
William Mason, poet, in 1725, at Hull. What did he write?
John G. Winant, the American Ambassador, 1889.

These died this day:
Pope Eugenius IV, 1447,
Sir Thomas Wyatt, beheaded in 1555 in the Tower of London,
Stanislaus I (of Poland) in 1766,
Sir Joshua Reynolds, 1792, who adorned, as few have done, this
fleeting world,
Dr. Joseph Warton, professor of poetry, Oxon, 1800, at Wickham,
John Keats, 1821, whose name is writ in water but forever,
Joanna Baillie, 1851, the poetess,
Sir Edward Elgar, 1934—'Pomp and Circumstance' was his—and
is now ours,
Stefan Zweig, the novelist, 1942.

SIR WALTER SCOTT ACKNOWLEDGED AUTHORSHIP, 1827,
AND THE GREAT UNKNOWN WAS REVEALED,
EARL OF DERBY'S FIRST MINISTRY, 1852, TOOK UP ITS
WORK,
ORANGE FREE STATE CREATED, 1854, ONLY TO DISAPPEAR
IN 1902 AND LATER TO BECOME PART OF THE DOMINION
OF SOUTH AFRICA,
CONSECRATION OF THE FIRST BISHOP OF BIRMINGHAM,
1902, THE CHURCH WIDENS ITS FOUNDATIONS,
THE RED ARMY INSTITUTED, 1918, AFTER THE REVOLU-
TION,
TURKEY DECLARED WAR ON GERMANY AND JAPAN, 1945,
BUT NO TURK KILLED EITHER GERMAN OR JAP.

February the Twenty-fourth

But the tender grace of a day that is dead
Shall never come back to me.

These saints are remembered on February the Twenty-fourth:
St. Lethard, Bishop of Senlis, 596, Canterbury,
St. Ethelbert, first Christian King of England, 616 and
Robert of Abrissel, of whom too little is known.

It is easier to be born—than to be a saint.
These were born on February the Twenty-fourth:
John Picus, Count of Mirandola, 1463, and
Charles V (of Spain) in 1500, at Ghent, historians know these.
James Quin, actor, 1693,
Clive of India, 1726,
Robert, Lord Gifford, Master of the Rolls, in 1779, and
Wilhelm Karl Grimm, in 1786, brother of Jakob Ludwig Karl—
who was a philologist as well as a fairy-tale teller,
Grant Allen, in 1848, scientist and novelist,
Viscount Templewood (formerly Sir Samuel Hoare), 1888,
Ralph Assheton, M.P., born 1901.

Death took Francis, Duke of Guise, assassinated, 1563,
Charles Bonaparte, 1785,
The Hon. Henry Cavendish, the amateur chemist, in 1810,
Coutts, the banker, 1822, a Scotsman, of course,
Thomas Bowdler, 1825, the first 'bowdlerizer',
Admiral Henry Loftus Tottenham, of Naval Brigade at Tel-el-Kebir, 1950,
Sir Arthur William Street, Deputy Chairman of National Coal
Board, 1951.
Death took these on February the Twenty-fourth.

SOME EVENTS ARE RECORDED TOO:
SCOTTISH LAND BILL TO ABROGATE FEUDAL TENURE,
INTRODUCED BY LORD ADVOCATE, 1820,
BURMESE CONCESSION TO GREAT BRITAIN, 1826 (WHERE
IS IT NOW?)
LOUIS PHILIPPE OF FRANCE ABDICATED, 1848,
THE BRITISH RETOOK KUT-EL-AMARA, 1917, AND
WILHELMSHAVEN WAS HEAVILY BOMBED IN 1943, ALL ON
FEBRUARY THE TWENTY-FOURTH.

February the Twenty-fifth

Be not therefore anxious for the morrow:
For the morrow will be anxious for itself.

What a day was February the Twenty-fifth.
The Earl of Essex was executed, 1601,
Slave trade was abolished in 1807,
The Garrick Club was instituted, 1831,
Colt patented his revolver in 1836 on this day,
The Second Derby Administration began, 1858,
The Third Derby Administration ended, 1863,
The beginning of the Wolf Pack Theory, 1941,
Nuremberg was heavily bombed, 1943,
Augsburg bombed, 1944,
U.S. armies eighteen miles from Cologne, 1945,
New Czechoslovak Government formed under Communist leadership, 1948.
These things made the Twenty-fifth a day.

These died on this day:
William Lily, master of St. Paul's School, London, 1523,
General Count Wallenstein, 1634,
Frederick I (of Prussia), 1713,
Sir Christopher Wren, 1723, architect of St. Paul's Cathedral,
Dr. William Buchan, 1805, St. Pancras,
Thomas Moore, the poet, 1852, 'Oft in the stilly night',
George Don, naturalist, 1856,
Charles Peace, the notorious criminal, was hanged in 1879,
Baron de Reuter, 1899, who founded Reuter's Agency,
Sir John Tenniel, 1914, who made much of his fame in *Punch* as
a cartoonist,
Trade agreement signed by India and Pakistan at Karachi
broke seventeen months' deadlock, 1951.

THESE WERE BORN:
GERMAIN DE SAINT FOIX IN 1703 AT RENNES,
P. A. RENOIR, IN 1841, A GREAT PAINTER,
SIR GEORGE REID IN 1845, A GREAT AUSTRALIAN STATES-
MAN,
ENRICO CARUSO IN 1873, A GREAT SINGER,
AIR CHIEF MARSHAL SIR ARTHUR BARRATT, 1891.
BUT LET US REMEMBER TO CALL NO MAN GREAT UNTIL HE
IS DEAD. FAME EMBALMS ALL GREATNESS.

February the Twenty-sixth

'What do I know?'—the dying man asked,
And no answer did obtain,
None since the day the world began
Could answer him—the great Montaigne.

Here are birth days:
Anthony Cooper, Earl of Shaftesbury, 1671, at Exeter House,
Arago, the philosopher, 1786,
Victor Hugo, 1802,
Émile Coué (optimist), 1857, and
Fred Ramo, 1866.

Here are death days:
Manfred (of Tarento) killed, 1266,
Robert Fabian, chronicler, 1513, Cornhill,
Sir Nicholas Crispe, Guinea trader, 1665, Hammersmith,
Thomas d'Urfey, wit and poet, 1723, St. James's,
Sir Christopher Wren, 1723,
Maximilian (of Bavaria), 1726, Munich,
Joseph Tartini, musical composer, 1770, Padua,
Dr. Geddes, the theologian, 1802,
John Philys Kemble, the actor, 1823,
Dr. William Kitchiner, *littérateur*, 1827, St. Pancras,
Sir William Allan, R.A., painter, 1850,
Thomas Tooke, author of the *History of Prices*, etc., 1858, London.
Sir Harry Lauder, Scottish comedian and singer, 1950.

HERE ARE EVENTS:
PUBLICATION OF FIRST BOOK OF CONSTITUTIONS OF FREE-
MASONS, 1722,
£1 AND £2 BANK-NOTES ISSUED IN 1797,
NAPOLEON ESCAPED FROM ELBA, 1815,
POLAND WAS ANNEXED BY RUSSIA, 1832,
FRENCH REPUBLIC PROCLAIMED IN 1848,
MACREADY THE ACTOR RETIRED IN 1851,
THE 'BIRKENHEAD' WRECKED IN 1852, OFF CAPE AGULHAS,
BERLIN'S HEAVIEST RAID OF THE WAR IN 1945,
MR. LEWIS WILLIAMS DOUGLAS APPOINTED U.S. AMBAS-
SADOR TO GREAT BRITAIN, 1947.

February the Twenty-seventh

When you go home, tell them of us and say,
For your tomorrow—they gave their today.

She has now passed into history. It is more than a hundred years since she
was born, on February the Twenty-seventh in 1848, but the glamour and
glow of her personality still shine. 'I once saw Ellen Terry'—those who can
say that, know they are to be envied. They have a precious possession for all
their days.

There were born on this day:
George Morley, Bishop of Winchester, 1597, Cheapside,
John David Michaelis, orientalist, 1717,
Lord William George Frederick Bentinck, 1802,
Henry William Longfellow, 1807,
Sir Hubert Parry, 1848.

There died on this day:
The Emperor Geta, murdered, 212,
Philip Nye, Nonconformist, 1673, London,
John Evelyn, the diarist, 1706,
Dr. John Arbuthnot, 1735, Cork Street, London,
Sir John B. Warren, G.C.B., 1822.

These events occurred on this day:
First Russian embassy to Great Britain, 1557–8,
Charles II withdrew Declaration of Indulgence, 1673,
Younger Pitt resigned his military commission rather than fight
the Americans, 1776,
Battle of Majuba Hill, 1881,
Convention of London, 1884,
First wireless message between Great Britain and France, 1899,
Surrender of Cronje, 1900,
British Labour Party founded, 1900,
Burning of the Reichstag, 1933,
Java Sea fight, 1942.

WHICH OF THESE WAS THE GREATER? WHO SHALL SAY?
ST. NESTOR, MARTYR IN 250, OR ELLEN TERRY—THE
BURNING OF THE REICHSTAG OR THE FOUNDATION OF THE
BRITISH LABOUR PARTY—OR THAT FIRST WIRELESS
MESSAGE BETWEEN BRITAIN AND FRANCE.

February the Twenty-eighth

Even now the eye beholds a flowery scene . . .

St. Romanus, about 460, and
St. Lupicinus, 479,
St. Proterius, patriarch of Alexandria, martyrs, 557, are some of the saints
whose names are joined with February the Twenty-eighth.

Montaigne was born in 1533,
Henry Stubb, the most noted Latinist and Grecian of his age, was
born on this day in 1631,
Dr. Daniel Solander, naturalist, in 1736,
Rachel, in 1821,
Viscount Hailsham in 1872, better remembered by some as Sir
Douglas Hogg,
Sir John Simon, now Viscount Simon, a former Lord Chancellor
and notable politician, in 1873,
These were born on this day.

Humphrey, Duke of Gloucester, murdered at St. Albans, 1447,
Christian IV (of Denmark) in 1646,
Edward Moore, dramatist, in 1757,
Dr. Richard Grey, in 1771,
Mrs. Susan Cromwell, great-great-grand-daughter of the Protector
and last of the line, 1834.
All died on February the Twenty-eighth.

THE POPE ALLOWED A TRANSLATION OF THE BIBLE IN
CATHOLIC COUNTRIES, IN 1759, NOT THE FIRST,
FOX WAS DISMISSED FROM THE TREASURY, 1774,
GLADSTONE RETIRED FROM THE OFFICE OF PRESIDENT OF
THE BOARD OF TRADE, 1845,
COLORADO WAS ORGANIZED AS A TERRITORY IN 1861,
CREPE PUT ON THE ALSACE-LORRAINE STATUE IN THE
PLACE DE LA CONCORDE, PARIS, 1871,
FIRST CONTESTED SCHOOL BOARD ELECTION TOOK PLACE
IN SCOTLAND IN THE PARISH OF EASTWOOD, 1873,
END OF TICHBORNE CASE AFTER 188 DAYS, IN 1874,
THE RELIEF OF LADYSMITH, 1900 and
MORE RECENTLY BRUNEVAL WAS RAIDED IN 1942.
THESE EVENTS MARK THE CALENDAR ON FEBRUARY THE
TWENTY-EIGHTH.

February the Twenty-ninth

O happy day—and one to be marked for me
With the whitest of chalk.

February the Twenty-ninth is Leap Year day—An extra day—a bonus in
the Calendar. The wise make much of the Leap Year days that come in
their lives. Something they would not otherwise have done—Some deed of
noble note before the end—Something should mark this day indelibly.
'I did it on Leap Year Day, I remember,' should be a recollection everyone
should possess and should cherish!

St. Oswald, Bishop of Worcester, and Archbishop of York, 992,
is a remembered saint for February the Twenty-ninth.

Ann Lee, 1736, was born:
So was, in 1792, Gioachino Rossini, and so was
Edward Cave, the printer and publisher, in 1692, whom all the
friends of Doctor Johnson will remember,
Montcalm was born on this day in 1712.

St. Barbas, Bishop of Benevento, died in 684,
Archbishop Whitgift, died on this day in 1604,
In 1852, the Victorian, Landseer, finished his work on February
the Twenty-ninth, but the world can still see his solid achievements,
E. F. Benson, celebrated as the author of *Dodo* and other novels,
departed this life in 1940.

AMONG THE EVENTS THERE ARE TO BE FOUND THESE:
REFORMS GRANTED IN BADEN IN 1848,
FIRST DISRAELI MINISTRY, 1868,
ST. GOTHARD TUNNEL PIERCED, 1880,
GREAT STRIKE OF COAL MINERS—1,000,000 MEN OUT,
1912,
IN 1932 ADOLPH HITLER STOOD AS A CANDIDATE,
BERLIN BOMBED, 1944.
FEBRUARY THE TWENTY-NINTH IS LEAP YEAR DAY. IT
CARRIES ITS RECORD.
AN EXTRA DAY FOR EXTRA DEEDS,
THAT LITTLE MORE SHOULD BE AN AIM,
THAT LITTLE MORE—THIS SAD WORLD NEEDS,
IF WE DENY IT—OURS THE SHAME.

MARCH

THIRTY-ONE DAYS

March the First

March comes in like a lion.
What is lion-like in these events? Sufficient unto the day is the evil thereof!

No one knows who fixed this day, in 1516, for the foundation of Corpus
Christi College at Oxford, and the swearing, in Edinburgh, of the first
Solemn League and Covenant in 1638.

John Murray chose this day for the publication of *Childe Harold's*
Pilgrimage and made Lord Byron forever famous in 1812,
Napoleon chose this day for landing on the Riviera in 1815,
George Russell chose this day to introduce his Reform Bill in 1831,
On March the First the Indo-European Telegraph was opened, 1865,
On March the First the Germans entered Paris in 1871,
On March the First the first battle of Adowa was fought, 1896,
On March the First the Allies declared a total blockade of Germany in 1915,
In 1936, on March the First, His Majesty the King broadcast a
message to the Empire,
In 1941, on the same day, Bulgaria joined the Axis,
In 1944 Stuttgart and Munich were raided,
In 1945 München-Gladbach was captured by the Americans,
In 1948 a Petition was presented by Peeresses for admission to the
House of Lords,
U.S.S.R. agreed to preliminary talks in 1951, Foreign Ministers,
and on the same day British Trade Mission arrived at Buenos
Aires to reopen the negotiations for supply of meat.
. . . these are only a few of the events which the records show on
the First Day of March.

ST. DAVID'S DAY.
SIR SAMUEL ROMILLY, LAWYER AND POLITICIAN, WAS
BORN IN 1757 AND AIR CHIEF MARSHAL SIR RODERICK
HILL WAS BORN ON THE SAME DAY IN 1894,
MANUEL JOHNSON, ASTRONOMER, DIED ON MARCH THE
FIRST, 1859,
GEORGE GROSSMITH, 1912, AND
GRIFFITH BREWER, PIONEER IN AVIATION, ON THE SAME
DAY IN 1948.
A LEEK I FOUND BUT FOUND NO LAY,
IS THERE NO SONG FOR DAVID'S DAY?

March the Second

So foul and fair a day I have not seen.

The events which fell on March the Second include the day when the Speaker was maintained in his Chair by force, 1628, and the Serjeant was detained by the House of Commons and Black Rod refused admittance, Parliament first moved against Charles I, 1641,
The fifth attempt on life of Queen Victoria was made in 1882, fortunately —as all others—unsuccessful.

Let the saints go unrecorded, let Births and Deaths take note and give account of themselves. Here are the events—
Thames Tunnel commenced, 1825,
Wild's electric light displayed, 1867,
Victory in Bismarck Sea, 1943,
The Rhine was reached by United States forces on March the Second, 1945.

There died on March the Second:
Robert Abbot, Bishop of Salisbury, 1618,
John Wesley, 1791,
Henry Archer, inventor of perforated stamps, 1863,
Field Marshal the Viscount Gough, 1869,
Horace Walpole, 1897.

There were born on this day
D. Junius Juvenal, Latin poet, *c.* 40, Aquinum,
William Murray, Earl of Mansfield, Lord Chief Justice, 1705,
Friedrich Smetana in 1824, the Czech composer.

LITTLE ENOUGH, YOU WILL SAY. WHERE ARE THE SEEKERS AND RESEARCHERS? WAS MARCH THE SECOND A 'DIES NON' ON WHICH NOTHING OF MOMENT OCCURRED? IT MAY BE SO —BUT DON'T YOU WISH YOU HAD BEEN THERE WHEN MELBOURNE TOOK ITS NAME FROM THE PRIME MINISTER OF THE DAY—IN THE FIRST YEAR OF VICTORIA'S REIGN— OR WOULD YOU RATHER HAVE BEEN AT THE BEGINNING OF THE THAMES TUNNEL TWELVE YEARS EARLIER? PER- HAPS NOT, PERHAPS YOU WOULD LIKE TO HAVE SEEN THE MAKING OF THAT TREATY IN 1918 WHICH BEGAN THE U.S.S.R. OR MORE HAPPILY IN EDINBURGH WHEN SIR WALTER SCOTT BECAME A FREEMASON, IN 1801. YOU MAY CHOOSE. THE PAST IS ALL OURS.

[65]

March the Third

Any day is every day.

On March the Third the Forth Bridge across the Firth of Forth was opened in 1890. It was then the wonder of the world in bridge-building. Some think it is still and some think that beside it soon will be a road bridge—a nobler prospect than ever Doctor Johnson dreamed.

On March the Third these were born:
Gisbert Voet, the Leyden theologian, 1589,
Edmund Waller, the poet, 1605,
Sir William Davenant, a Poet Laureate, 1606,
Thomas Otway, the dramatic poet, 1651,
William Godwin, the novelist, 1756, at Wisbech,
Macready, the great actor, 1793,
Sir Ernest Cassel, 1852,
Van Gogh, in 1853,
Sir Henry Wood, 1869.

There died this day . . .
Sir Nicholas Carew, beheaded, 1539, at Aldgate,
John Frederick, the Magnanimous, of Saxony, 1554,
John Sturm, Lutheran teacher, 1589,
Robert Hooke, philosopher, 1703,
Camillo, Duke de Tullard, French Marshal, 1728,
Rev. Dr. William Stukeley, antiquary, 1765, East Ham,
Dr. William Hunter, 1783, London,
Robert Adam, the Scots architect, 1792,
Copley Fielding, landscape painter, 1855.
All men of mark in their day and generation.

What more . . .

THE COCK LANE GHOST WAS DETECTED IN 1762,
RUSSIAN SERFS EMANCIPATED, 1863,
NEW SOUTH WALES CONTINGENT LEFT FOR SUDAN, FIRST TIME ON WHICH A BRITISH COLONY SENT TROOPS AT OWN COST TO AID THE MOTHER COUNTRY, IN 1885,
TREATY OF BREST-LITOVSK WAS IMPOSED ON RUSSIA IN 1918,
CARDIFF ATTACKED BY FIRE BOMBS, 1941,
LONDON AIR RAID SHELTER DISASTER IN 1943.
THESE ALL BEFELL ON MARCH THE THIRD.

March the Fourth

Who knows what a day will bring forth?

On March the Fourth in 1882 the first electric tramway opened in England in Essex. On March the Fourth Mr. Samuel Plimsoll began his demand for the Plimsoll Line in 1873. On March the Fourth in 1842 the first Income Tax was carried with only slight opposition in the House of Commons. Which of these were the most far-reaching events?

On this day Edward IV, in 1461, ascended the throne of England,
Dollars (4/9) issued by Bank of England, 1797,
Royal National Lifeboat Institution founded, 1824,
James Knox Polk elected President of the U.S.A., 1844,
General Zachary inaugurated President of the U.S.A., 1848,
Lofoten Islands were raided in 1941.

There departed this day of March the Fourth,
Saladin, 1193,
Bernard Gilpin, rector of Houghton-le-Spring, 1583,
Matthias Hoe, 1645, Dresden,
John Anstis, Garter King-at-Arms, 1744,
Thomas Rickman, architect, 1841, Birmingham,
W. Willett, of 'daylight saving' fame, in 1915.

And on this day these were born:
Don Pedro, of Portugal, 1394,
Lord Chancellor Somers, 1652, Worcester,
James, Earl of Waldegrave, 1715,
Charles Dibdin, 1745,
Sir Henry Raeburn, 1756,
Emma Cons, 1838.

IN 1493, SURELY THIS WAS THE DAY . . . COLUMBUS DIS-
COVERED AND LANDED IN THE NEW WORLD. MARCH THE
FOURTH IS AN ENCOURAGEMENT TO ALL BUT THE PLAN-
NERS. DID HE NOT, AS HAS BEEN OFTEN SAID, SAIL WITH A
FALSE MAP AND ANOTHER OBJECTIVE, YET REACHED HIS
HEART'S DESIRE AND—LET US PRAY—WITH THE HOPE OF
A BETTER WORLD,
AND ON THAT SAME DAY—IN 1789—THERE WAS INAUGU-
RATED THE FEDERATION OF THE UNITED STATES,
FRANCO-BRITISH FIFTY-YEAR PACT SIGNED, 1947.

March the Fifth

Today holds tomorrow.

On March the Fifth, 1933, Adolph Hitler entered the Reichstag as a member of that body with all its consequences to the Reichstag, to Germany, to the world and to Adolph Hitler himself. It is a significant day in history.

The saints were not consulted. They are:
St. Adrian and St. Eubulius, of Palestine, martyrs, 309,
St. Kiaran, of Ireland, bishop, fourth century,
St. Roger, a Franciscan, 1236.

The dead lie unheeding in their resting graves,
Odoacer, King of Italy, A.D. 493,
Alphonso II of Portugal, 1223, Alcobaca,
Correggio, the painter, 1534,
James, Duke of Hamilton, 1649, beheaded, Old Palace Yard,
Bishop Beveridge, 1708,
Dr. Arne, the musician, in 1778,
Flora Macdonald, in 1790,
Alexander Volta (Voltaism), 1827, Como,
Miss Ann Wallace, descendant of the Patriot, 1873.

There were born, unheeding—
John Collins, F.R.S., accountant, 1624, Woodeaton,
Dr. George Stanhope, Dean of Canterbury, 1660, Hartshorne.

THESE EVENTS WERE INSIGNIFICANT IN COMPARISON,
CATHOLIC EMANCIPATION BILL INTRODUCED, 1829,
THE THAMES TUNNEL OPENED, 1843,
LORD CAMPBELL TOOK THE OATH AS LORD CHIEF JUSTICE
OF ENGLAND, 1850,
COVENT GARDEN THEATRE DESTROYED BY FIRE, 1856,
RAILWAY FROM BOMBAY TO CALCUTTA WAS COMPLETED,
1870,
CLEOPATRA'S NEEDLE SALVAGE CASE AWARDED AT
£25,000, 1878,
MAXIM GUN FIRST DESCRIBED IN 'NATURE', 1885,
DISTRICT COUNCILS SET UP, 1894,
HOLLAND REFUSED TO HAND OVER KAISER WILLIAM II,
1920,
ESSEN HEAVILY RAIDED, 1943.
BUT THEY ALL HAPPENED ON MARCH THE FIFTH.

March the Sixth

Dear, dead women, with such hair, too—
What's become of all the gold
Used to hang and brush their bosoms?

March the Sixth, let it be a Ladies' Day.
It is the saint's-day of Colette, the virgin and abbess in 1447,
On March the Sixth, 1888, Louisa May Alcott died and left Little Women
to the world.
Nelson's daughter, Horatia, died on this day in 1881 . . . But,
Best remembered of all surely is Elizabeth Barrett, the Barrett of Wimpole
Street, who became Mrs. Robert Browning and gave us the Sonnets from
the Portuguese *and that novel in verse* Aurora Leigh, *born in 1806.*

In 1475, Michelangelo was born, and Francesco Guicciardini,
in 1482, at Florence began the days which raised him to diplomacy,
In 1662 on March the Sixth, Francis Attenbury, Bishop of
Rochester, was born and in 1786 Charles Napier of Merchiston
Hall, nr. Falkirk, who became Admiral Sir Charles Napier, a
famous sailor and author of books about the Navy, and
Lord Beveridge was born in 1879.

On this day, these departed this mortal life . . .
Roger, Lord Grey de Ruthyn, 1352,
Zachary Ursinus, German divine, 1583, Neustadt,
Beaumont, the dramatist, 1616.
Lord Chief Justice Sir John Holt, 1710, Redgrave,
G. T. F. Raynal, philosophical historian, 1796, Passey,
Dr. Samuel Parr, scholar and divine, 1825,
George M. Kemp, architect of the Scott Monument, in 1844,
Benjamin Travers, surgeon, 1858,
John Redmond, 1918,
Albert Lebrun, last President of Third Republic of France, 1950,
Ivor Novello, actor, composer, 1951.

OF THE REST THAT MAKE THIS DAY NOTABLE THESE
EVENTS OCCURRED.
NAPOLEON DRIVEN FROM ACRE BY SIR SIDNEY SMITH, 1799,
SERVIA WAS PROCLAIMED A KINGDOM, 1882,
RUSSIA WAS FORCED TO BUY IN AMERICA FOR GERMANY'S
WAR NEEDS, 1940,
CAPTURE OF COLOGNE, 1945.

March the Seventh

When wilt thou save thy people!

March the Seventh saw the birth (and much else) of Ebenezer Elliot in 1781. He was the Corn Law rhymer and his cry is still heard in the land.

When wilt thou save thy people
O God of Nations when
Thy People, Lord, thy people
Not kings and thrones—but men
Flowers of thy heart are they
Thou wilt not let them pass like weeds away
Their heritage an empty day
God save the People.

On the same day as Ebenezer Elliot, in their respective century, were born—
Sir John Fortesque Aland, 1670,
Antonio Sanchez, 1699,
Herschel, the astronomer, 1792,
Maurice Ravel, 1875,
T. G. Masaryk, 1850, first President of Czecho-Slovakia.

There died on March the Seventh
Antoninus Pius, Roman emperor in 162, at Lorium,
William Longsword, first Earl of Salisbury, in 1226,
Bishop Thomas Wilson in 1755, at Isle of Man,
John Richard Green, the historian, in 1883 (who was aware of Ebenezer Elliot beyond doubt),
Blanchard, aeronaut, in 1809,
Admiral Lord Collingwood in 1810,
Aristide Briand in 1932.

ON MARCH THE SEVENTH, THE BRITISH AND FOREIGN BIBLE SOCIETY WAS FORMED IN 1804,
A ROYAL LEVEE WAS HELD AT WHICH OFFICERS OF NEWLY FORMED RIFLE VOLUNTEERS WERE RECEIVED, 1860,
ALBERT MEDAL APPOINTED BY ROYAL WARRANT, 1866,
GERMANY REPUDIATED LOCARNO TREATY, 1936,
THE 'QUEEN ELIZABETH' REACHED NEW YORK HAVING RUN THE GERMAN BLOCKADE IN 1940.
MARCH THE SEVENTH HAS HELD MUCH OF HISTORY.

March the Eighth

What use did he make of his days . . . This is the question the great recorder will ask!

What use did these make of their days:

Born on March the Eighth at Paris in 1817
Austen H. Layard, a Member of Parliament, explored the antiquities of Nineveh.

William of Orange, who died on March the Eighth, 1702, left a record in the Book of Kings as surely too did Karl Johann Bernadotte, King of Sweden, who also died on this day, 1844. And what use of his days made Francis, Duke of Bridgewater, of canal navigation fame, who died in 1803?—or
Hector Berlioz, who died in 1869, or, more sinister perhaps, the Baron F. V. Zeppelin who went to his account in 1917—
What has the Great Recorder to say of these, to all of whom March the Eighth closed the record?

These events, too, occurred on March the Eighth.
Title 'Chief Justice of the King's Bench' first conferred in 1628,
Commercial treaty concluded between U.S.A. and Japan in 1854,
Russia and Turkey agreed on naval reductions in Black Sea in 1931,
Americans crossed the Rhine in 1945.

These were born on March the Eighth,
St. John of God, 1495,
Dr. John Campbell, historical writer, 1708, Edinburgh,
Dr. John Fothergill (Quaker), 1712, Carr-end,
William Roscoe, miscellaneous writer, 1753, Liverpool,
Kenneth Grahame, 1859, a banker and a writer.

THESE DIED ON MARCH THE EIGHTH.
BISHOP JOHN HOUGH, 1743,
THOMAS BLACKWELL, LL.D., CLASSICAL SCHOLAR, 1757,
EDINBURGH,
SIR WILLIAM CHAMBERS, R.A., ARCHITECT, 1796,
W. SAWREY GILPIN, LANDSCAPE PAINTER, 1807, BROMPTON,
JOSEPH JEKYLL, F.R.S., NOTED WIT, 1837, LONDON,
THE REV. HENRY WARD BEECHER, 1887.

March the Ninth

Let my name be remembered that my days will not be forgotten.

It might have been called Columbus's or Cabot's Land or New Britain or New England, but it was none of these. It is called America and it is called America because Amerigo Vespucci was born on March the Ninth in 1451. It is he who finds his name remembered although his days are forgotten. On this same March the Ninth was born William Cobbett at Farnham in 1762—who went in due course to Amerigo Vespucci's America as a soldier of the King and who died famous as an Englishman and as a political and economic writer.

St. Aloysius, Lewis Gonzaga, was born too on March the Ninth in 1568, and—
Strange companion for a birthday—Doctor Joseph Franz Gall, the founder of the science of phrenology, saw the light on the same day in 1775, as did
Ernest Bevin in 1881. On his seventieth birthday he left the Foreign Office, was appointed Lord Privy Seal, being succeeded by Mr. Herbert Morrison, Viscount Addison becoming Lord President. Mr. Chuter Ede followed Mr. Morrison as Leader of the House of Commons, 1951.

These died violent deaths on March the Ninth,
David Rizzio, murdered at the Palace of Holyrood House, in the presence of his Queen in 1566, and
John Calas in 1762 at Toulouse broken on the wheel.
These died more happily on March the Ninth—let their names be re-lamented—
Francis Beaumont, dramatist, 1616,
Anna Barbauld, child's writer, 1825,
Arnold Toynbee, the social reformer, in 1883.

THESE EVENTS OCCURRED ON MARCH THE NINTH:
COLONEL BLOOD FAILED IN HIS ATTEMPT TO STEAL THE CROWN JEWELS IN 1671,
ACTION BETWEEN 'MERRIMAC' AND 'MONITOR', 1861,
SIR ROWLAND HILL, THE GREAT POST-OFFICE REFORMER, RESIGNED POST AS SECRETARY OF THE POST OFFICE, 1863, IN 1893 PROFESSOR DEWAR ANNOUNCED THE SOLIDIFICATION OF AIR, AND
IN 1942 JAVA SURRENDERED.

March the Tenth

Life is short, but art is long.

The artists find in March the Tenth some names which make, for them, history.

William Etty, the painter, was born on March the Tenth, 1787, and Raven Hill, the *Punch* black-and-white artist, in 1867.

Benjamin West, the painter, died in 1820, but there are more than births and deaths on this day.

Famous witch trials took place at Bury St. Edmunds in 1665,
King Edward VII married Queen Alexandra in 1863,
Electric trams from Kew to Hammersmith were run in 1883,
And ten years earlier, 1873, the Guildhall Library was opened,
Suffragettes rioted in London in 1914,
Battle of Neuve Chapelle in 1915,
British aircraft carrier *Hermes* sunk in 1942,
Uman was taken by the Russians in 1944.

The saints too have their places on March the Tenth:
It is the date of the Forty Martyrs of St. Sebaste, 320,
It is the date of St. Mackessog, Bishop in Scotland, in 560,
And of the good abbot St. Droctovaeus, about 580.

On March the Tenth were born . . .
Bishop Duppa in 1598,
Marcellus Malpighi, the microscopic anatomist in Bologna in 1628, and later by a century and more the great Professor of Natural Philosophy, Professor Playfair, in 1748,
Sergei Diaghilev, 1872,
Lord Marchwood of Penang in 1876.

There died on this day
Heliogabalus the Emperor, beheaded in A.D. 222,
In 858 Pope Benedict III,
In 1333, Ladislaus III of Poland, and
Thomas, Lord Seymour of Sudley, was beheaded in 1549,
On this day in 1826 John VI of Portugal died, and the same day marks the death of the great Mazzini in 1872.

THINGS HAVE HAPPENED ON MARCH THE TENTH. WHO KNOWS WHAT WILL HAPPEN IN THE DAYS YET UNBORN WHICH TOO WILL BE MARCH THE TENTH?

March the Eleventh

What shall I do today? Shall I make war or just have my breakfast?

On March the Eleventh the soldiers of the Third Reich entered Austria and occupied Vienna in 1938. None knew that on this day in 1544, Tasso was born—none of these Nazi soldiers knew, and if they had known it would not have stopped them. On this day at the same time, equally indifferent agents of the Irish Republican Army arranged a series of explosions and other outrages in Birmingham . . . yes, March the Eleventh was important . . . .

There are the saints for example—here they are
St. Sophronius, Patriarch of Jerusalem, 639,
St. Aengus, the Culdee, Bishop in Ireland, 824, and less known.

On this day:
John Peter Niceron, the French biographer, was born in 1685 at Paris,
Sir George Beharrell was born in 1873, and
Huskisson, the politician who was killed in a railway accident, began his career in 1770.

John Toland, a miscellaneous writer, died in 1722 at Putney, and, too, Mrs. Cowley, a dramatist, in 1809,
General Sir James Outram, of Mutiny fame, in 1863,
Earl Beatty died in 1936,
Dr. Victor Hely-Hutchinson, composer and director of music to B.B.C., 1947,
Sir Ralph Freeman, designer of Sydney Harbour Bridge, 1950.

A MR. ELIAS ASHMORE WAS MADE A FREEMASON IN 1682, ON MARCH THE ELEVENTH THE FIRST LONDON DAILY PAPER COMMENCED IN 1702,
NAPOLEON HAS HIS SECOND WEDDING DAY WITH MARIE LOUISE IN 1810,
THE LUDDITE RIOTS BEGAN IN 1811 AND THE KING LUD STILL STANDS AT LUDGATE HILL (ALTHOUGH IT WAS NOTHING TO DO WITH IT),
BRITAIN BEGAN MEAT RATIONING 1940—1s.10d. WORTH,
LEASE LEND WAS SIGNED ON THIS DAY IN 1941,
MR. MCKELL SWORN IN AS GOVERNOR-GENERAL OF AUSTRALIA, 1947,
ALL ON MARCH THE ELEVENTH.

March the Twelfth

Begone, self-depreciation—Let us be good to ourselves today!

The English are by their critics sometimes considered a vain and conceited people. The man who began it all, some think, was Pope Saint Gregory the Great. March the Twelfth is his day and he is remembered as the discriminating one who, on seeing some fair-haired young prisoners of war, asked of what nation they were. He was told they were ANGLES. 'Not Angles surely,' he said, 'Angels.'

March the Twelfth then is of some importance to the English and it makes March the Twelfth a day of note to them.

There were other events on this day.
First baseball match to be played in this country in 1889,
The Russian Revolution in 1917—the event which shook the world,
Finland signed peace with Russia, in 1939,
Strike of 100,000 Welsh miners ended in 1944.

There died on this day:
George Wishart, burnt at the stake, in 1546,
The Rev. Dr. George Gregory, editor of the *New Annual Register*, 1808, at West Ham,
Rev. R. Polwhele, a photographer and a poet, 1838,
Caesar Borgia in 1507,
And tragic, innocent figure, Lady Jane Grey beheaded, 1554,
Sun Yat Sen, 1925,
Heinrich Mann, German novelist, 1950,
Charles Gideon Murray, 2nd Viscount Elibank, Colonial Administrator and M.P., 1951.

On this day there were born:
Godfrey Bidloo, the anatomist, in 1649 at Amsterdam,
John Frederick Daniell, chemist and meteorologist, in 1790,
'The Learned Bishop Berkeley', 1684, and a year earlier,
Desaguliers, the philosopher, in 1683, and
Sir W. H. Perkin, 1838.

ST. GREGORY SHARES MARCH THE TWELFTH AS HIS SAINT'S-DAY WITH TWO OTHER SAINTS,
ST. MAXIMILIAN OF NUMIDIA, MARTYR, 296 AND
ST. PAUL OF CORNWALL, BISHOP OF LEON, ABOUT 573.

March the Thirteenth

Who can say what is a happy day?

On March the Thirteenth was born Hugh Walpole in 1884. Some surveying the world of events with which March the Thirteenth is associated would not put his birth day as the most important. Others would. Hugh Walpole gave happiness to millions in these unhappy years between 1900 and the end of the Second World War and, although he is dead, many still find happiness in Fortitude, *in* Mr. Perrin and Mr. Traill *and in* Rogue Herries.

These share with Sir Hugh Walpole, March the Thirteenth as a birth day:
Charles, Earl Grey, the statesman, 1764,
Joseph II (of Germany) in 1741,
Dr. Priestly in 1733, and
Esther Johnson (Swift's Stella) in 1681.

These died.
Belisarius, the general, 565 at Constantinople,
Cardinal d'Ossat, 1604, Rome,
Cowley, the actor, 1618,
Richard Burbage in 1619,
John Gregory, scholar, 1646,
Pierre Mignard, French painter, 1695,
Jean de la Fontaine in 1695,
Nicholas Boileau, French poet, 1711,
Sophia Lee, novelist, 1824,
J. F. Daniell, chemist and meteorologist, 1845,
Regina Maria Roche, novelist, 1845,
Richard, Lord Braybrooke, Editor of Pepys's *Diary*, 1858,
G. E. Buckle, 1935, and
Angela Brazil, 1947.

THESE EVENTS OCCURRED ON MARCH THE THIRTEENTH.
FIRST DIAMOND, 'STAR OF SOUTH AFRICA', FOUND, 1867,
RUSSIAN AMERICA SOLD TO U.S.A., 1867—HOW STRANGE THAT READS,
DISSOLUTION OF THE REFORM LEAGUE, 1869,
SIEGE OF KHARTOUM BEGAN, 1884,
END OF LAST BIG RUSSIAN TRIALS, 1938,
OSAKA GOT 2,000 TONS OF INCENDIARY BOMBS IN 1945.

March the Fourteenth

Who can say what he has done with his days.

In 1883 on March the Fourteenth died a refugee in London, the German Jew Socialist philosopher Karl Marx. He is buried in Highgate Cemetery, but he never dreamed that his ideas would dominate—fifty years after he with his friend Frederick Engels published the Communist manifesto—more than half the world. It is so and none surely would be more surprised than he who often felt himself misunderstood, underrated and derided. Marx never dreamed he would become a myth but so his adherents have made him.

In 1757 Admiral Byng was shot on this day and, in 1663, Simon Morin was burned to death.
These had a happier fate and died, as far as is known, in bed:
John, Earl of Bedford, 1555,
William Melmoth, accomplished scholar, 1799, Bath,
Daines Barrington, antiquary, lawyer, naturalist, 1800, Temple,
Earl St. Vincent, 1823,
George Papworth, architect and engineer, 1855,
General Wade, 1751, the soldier and road builder.

Albert Einstein was born on this day in 1879 and Johann Strauss in 1804.

These saints claim March the Fourteenth:
St. Acepsimas, bishop in Assyria, Joseph and Aithilahas, martyrs, 380,
St. Boniface, bishop of Ross in Scotland, 630, and
St. Maud, Queen of Germany, 968.

THESE EVENTS MAKE MARCH THE FOURTEENTH MEMORABLE:
REFORM ACT: FIRST READING, 1831,
DISCOVERY OF ALBERT NYANZA ANNOUNCED, 1864,
TICHBORNE CLAIMANT MADE FIRST APPEARANCE, 1868,
FIRST PERFORMANCE OF 'MIKADO', 1885—A HAPPY EVENT,
THE PEERAGE BILL, 1917 (SCOTS PEERS FOR THE HOUSE OF LORDS),
'TEN-TON TESS' DROPPED ON GERMANY, 1945,
BRITISH PRESENTED NOTE TO PERSIA DECLARING OPERATIONS OF ANGLO-IRANIAN OIL COMPANY COULD NOT BE TERMINATED BY NATIONALIZATION, 1951.
MARCH THE FOURTEENTH CARRIES THESE IN THE RECORDS OF THE DAYS THAT ARE PAST.

[77]

March the Fifteenth

You may be a saint, but it will be after your days are done.

March the Fifteenth is the day chosen for Saint Abraham, the Hermit of Mesopotamia and for his niece Saint Mary—that was in the fourth century. Pope Saint Zachary in 752 and Saint Leocritia, the virgin martyr at Cordova, in 859, have the same day—the day, too, which in 44 B.C. saw Julius Caesar stabbed to death in Rome. Honour is the subject of that story.

The Royal Academy was established, 1768,
Czar Nicholas abdicated in 1917,
Independence of Egypt was recognized, 1922,
Germans entered Prague in 1939,
Over 1,000 R.A.F. bombers raided Stuttgart in 1944,
These events make this day.

These were born . . .
Theophilus Bonet, eminent Genevese physician, in 1620,
General Andrew Jackson in 1767, the American general,
Dame Madge Kendal, a great actress, in 1849,
Lord Catto in 1879,
The second Earl Haig in 1918.

All these died . . .
Thomas, Lord Chancellor Egerton, 1617, Dodleston, Cheshire,
John, Earl of Loudon, Chancellor of Scotland, 1663,
The Rev. Dr. Thomas Franklin, eminent Greek scholar, 1784,
Admiral John Jervis, Earl of St. Vincent, 1823, Stone,
Otto Kotzebue, navigator, 1846,
Cardinal Mezzofanti, an extraordinary linguist, 1849,
Captain Sir Samuel Brown, civil engineer, 1852,
Sir Richard Bessemer, 1878—and his name means steel—and
Walter Crane in 1915,
Floods in England, worst ever known, 1947.

THE IDES ON THE ROMAN CALENDAR WERE THE THIR-
TEENTH DAY OF THE MONTH, EXCEPT IN MAY, JULY,
OCTOBER AND MARCH WHEN THEY FALL ON THE FIF-
TEENTH.
MARCH THE FIFTEENTH IS THE IDES OF MARCH WHICH
WILLIAM SHAKESPEARE MADE FAMILIAR AND FAMOUS.

March the Sixteenth

The curtain rises, the curtain falls: it is a day.

*Events which mark this day—this March the Sixteenth—were dissolution
of the Rump Parliament, 1680,
Duke of Newcastle's Ministry, 1754,
Trial of George Chapman (Jack the Ripper), 1903.*

Booklets of stamps first issued, 1904,
Port of London Authority held its first meeting, 1909,
Germany repudiated the military clauses of the Versailles Treaty,
1935,
Germany annexed Bohemia and Moravia, 1939, and
Lastly in this record, on this day the Allies entered Cassino, 1944.

There are two saints with whom this day is associated. They are:
St. Julian, of Cilicia, martyr about 303, and
St. Finian, surnamed Lohbar (or the Leper) of Ireland in the
eighth century.

René de Bossue, French classical scholar, was born on March the
Sixteenth in 1631, so was
Jacques Boileau, the French theologian, 1635,
Madame Chapman, the historical writer, 1752,
Sir C. H. Firth, 1857,
That brilliant star of the London stage, Elsie Janis, in 1889, and
General Sir William Bartholomew in 1877.

THESE DIED:
ALEXANDER II OF SCOTLAND, 1286,
LORD BERNERS, TRANSLATOR OF FROISSART, 1532,
JOHANN SEVERIN VATER, GERMAN LINGUIST AND THEOLO-
GIAN, 1826, AT HALLE,
GOTTFRIED NEES VON ESENBACH, BOTANIST, 1858,
R. S. SURTEES IN 1864,
A GREAT SCOTSMAN, ROBERT CHAMBERS, AUTHOR, PUB-
LISHER AND FOUNDER OF THE FAMOUS CHAMBERS'S
'ENCYCLOPAEDIA', IN 1871,
AUBREY BEARDSLEY IN 1897,
SIR AUSTEN CHAMBERLAIN IN 1937, AND
SELMA LAGERLOF, SWEDISH AUTHORESS, NOBEL PRIZE
WINNER, IN 1940.

March the Seventeenth

The Sportsman said: 'It is a fine day: let us go out and kill something.'

March the Seventeenth is St. Patrick's Day. The Irish Guards get their Shamrock. It is for the Irish a holiday in Ulster and a holy day in Eire— and a proper day of pride, passion, patriotism and partisanship. There is no other day like it in all the calendar of days and saints.

There are other saints who share this day, however, but they do it meekly and modestly. They are Saint Joseph of Arimathea, the patron of Glastonbury, the gentle virgin Saint Gertrude of Brabant in 659 and many martyrs of Alexandria about 392, but none of these has inspired, as has St. Patrick, such lines as these:

St. Patrick was a gentleman
And came of decent people
He built a church in Dublin Town
And on it put a steeple.

The Birthday Book of March the Seventeenth reveals that on this day these were born:
Dr. Thomas Chalmers, 1780, the Scottish Divine and Reformer,
Otto Niebuhr, the great traveller, 1733,
Sir Robert Burrows in 1884.

The Register of Deaths for this day records that these died.
William, Earl of Pembroke, 1570, London,
Thomas Randolph, poet, 1634, Blatherwick,
Bishop Burnet, 1715, the historian,
George, Earl of Macclesfield, astronomer, P.R.S., 1764,
Charles Kirkpatrick Sharp who died in Edinburgh, 1851, and
Adam McKinlay, Labour M.P. for West Dunbartonshire, died 1950.

THESE WERE SOME OF THE EVENTS:
FIRST ENGLISH DUKE WAS CREATED IN 1337, HE WAS EDWARD III'S ELDEST SON,
PETITION OF RIGHTS PRESENTED TO CHARLES I, 1628,
ADDINGTON MINISTRY FORMED, 1801,
STRAITS SETTLEMENTS ACQUIRED FROM DUTCH, 1824,
BERBERA, CAPITAL OF BRITISH SOMALILAND, RECAPTURED, 1941,
COBLENZ CAPTURED, 1945.

March the Eighteenth

How many share in some way a day!

March the Eighteenth was significant to Neville Chamberlain, the Dardanelles, Laurence Sterne and Robert Walpole and the population of Berlin in 1944. All these found something of moment in the day designated March the Eighteenth.
Neville Chamberlain was born on that day in 1869: the attack on the Dardanelles began on that day in 1915; Laurence Sterne and Robert Walpole died on that day in 1768 and 1745 respectively and on that day the population of Berlin in 1944 endured the biggest daylight air raid of the Second World War.

These events seem less by comparison but they, too, occurred on March the Eighteenth:
First public omnibus in Paris, 1662,
American stamp duty repealed, 1766,
Reform conceded to Hanover, 1848,
Political opening of the Suez Canal, 1869,
French religious orders dissolved, 1903,
Hitler and Mussolini met at the Brenner Pass in 1940,
U.S. aircraft raided Tokyo, 1942,
Members of Parliament raised their salaries to £1,000 a year, 1946.

These—as they say—took the Ferry—on this day:
Edward, King and martyr, 978,
Pope Honorius II, 1227,
Bishop Forbes, 1635,
Dr. George Stanhope, eminent divine, 1728, Lewisham,
John Horne Tooke, 1812,
Sebastian Pether, painter of moonlight scenery, 1844, Battersea,
Sir Henry Pottinger, G.C.B., military commander in India, 1856,
Playfair, the architect, 1857—many lives but one day on which they died.

PHILIP DE LAHIRE, THE FRENCH GEOMETRICIAN, WAS BORN AT PARIS THIS DAY IN 1640,
JOHN CADWELL CALHOUN, AN AMERICAN STATESMAN, 1782 IN SOUTH CAROLINA,
RIMSKY-KORSAKOV IN 1844,
MAJOR-GENERAL FRANCIS PIGGOTT IN 1883, AND
ROBERT DONAT IN 1905.

[81]

March the Nineteenth

I saw the sun-rise: I saw the dawn
Twelve hours of day were mine
They're gone—am I then just a pawn
Who cannot life define.

On March the Nineteenth in 1887 the closure was devised by the House of
Commons. It indicated that enough was as good as a feast even for Members
of Parliament.
The Emperor Alexander Severus was murdered on this day in A.D. 235,
The Lord Lovat was condemned for treason on this day in 1747,
H.M.S. 'Eagle'—the largest aircraft carrier launched in 1946.

St. Alemuns of England—a blessed martyr—has March the Nine-
teenth as his day in the calendar.
Enough—call it a day for these.
John Astruc, an eminent French physician, born 1684 at Sauve,
Tobias George Smollett, in Dumbartonshire, in 1721,
The Rev. Edward Bickersteth the writer on Religious subjects
1786 at Kirby-Lonsdale, and
On this day David Livingstone, the African explorer and mis-
sionary, was born at Blantyre in Scotland in 1813, as also were
Sir Richard Burton, 1821, the great Orientalist,
Alfred von Tirpitz, Father of the German Navy, 1849, and
Wilkie Bard, the comedian, in 1874.

ON MARCH THE NINETEENTH DIED:
SPENCER COMPTON, EARL OF NORTHAMPTON, KILLED AT
HOPTON HEATH IN 1643,
BISHOP THOMAS KEN, FROME, ON THIS DAY IN 1711,
POPE CLEMENT II IN 1721,
NICHOLAS HAWKSMOOR, ARCHITECT, PUPIL OF WREN, 1736,
ADMIRAL PALLISER IN 1786,
STEPHEN STORAGE, MUSICAL COMPOSER, IN 1796, LONDON,
JOHN, DUKE OF ROXBURGHE, BIBLIOPHILE, IN 1804,
SIR JOSEPH BANKS, THE NATURALIST, IN 1820,
THOMAS WILLIAM DANIELL, R.A., PAINTER OF ORIENTAL
SCENERY IN 1840,
EARL OF BALFOUR, 1930,
EDGAR RICE BURROUGHS, AMERICAN NOVELIST AND
CREATOR OF 'TARZAN', 1950.

[82]

March the Twentieth

Little boy, this is your birth day.

March the Twentieth, 1811, was a great day for Napoleon and he had many great days, had Napoleon Bonaparte!
It was greater than Marengo, greater than that day when he wrote to Josephine, in 1796, to tell her that he had been given command of the Army of Italy in place of Scherer: greater than when he was acclaimed First Consul—it was the day on which was born to him his son, the Duke of Reichstadt and the King of Rome.

The King of Rome shared his birthday—this March the Twentieth
—with Publius Ovidius Naso, 43 B.C.,
Bishop Morton, 1564, and
The great dramatist, Ibsen, 1828.

On this day there died:
The Emperor Publius Gallienus, A.D. 268, assassinated at Milan,
Henry IV, 1413,
Ernest, Duke of Luneburg, 1611,
Bishop Parker, 1687,
Sir John Vanbrugh, 1726,
The very great Isaac Newton, 1727,
Frederick, Prince of Wales, 1751, at Leicester House,
Lord Chief Justice, Earl of Mansfield, 1793,
H. D. Inglis (Derwent Conway), traveller, 1835,
Mademoiselle Mars, the actress, 1847,
That fighter for freedom, Louis Kossuth, in 1894, and
Marshal Foch, 1929.

THESE, TOO, FIND MARCH THE TWENTIETH THEIR DAY OF DESTINY:
MARBLE ARCH UNCOVERED 1850 AND STILL BEAUTIFYING HYDE PARK,
'UNCLE TOM'S CABIN' PUBLISHED IN 1852 BY HARRIET BEECHER STOWE,
EX-EMPEROR NAPOLEON III SETTLED AT CHISLEHURST, 1871,
PONDOLAND ANNEXED, 1894,
EMPIRE WAR CABINET FIRST MET IN 1917,
BRITISH COUNCIL FORMED, 1935,
END OF BATTLE OF MANDALAY, 1945.

March the Twenty-first

The soldier saw the dawn of day
When the darkness fell—a corpse he lay.

March the Twenty-First, 1918, was the day when Germany began her
last attack against the Allies. The British Fifth Army was its objective.
The battle began on this misty morning, waged throughout the summer, but
ended in the eleventh hour of the eleventh day of the eleventh month, when on
November the Eleventh, 1918, Germany accepted the terms of the Armistice.
Many who saw the dawn of this day did not see that victory.
March the Twenty-first figures more than once in the history books. In
1899, on March the Twenty-first, the French withdrew from the Nile
Valley and the Eighth Army in 1943 attacked the Mareth Line.

On this day was the accession of Henry V, 1413,
The Militia Bill was passed in 1851,
Persia was re-named Iran in 1935,
Paul Reynaud became French Premier, 1940, and
In Korea, Chunchon was occupied without a shot being fired, 1951.

On March the Twenty-first
Edmond of Woodstock, Earl of Kent, was beheaded in 1330,
Cranmer burnt, 1556,
Peter Ernest, Count de Mansfield, 1604, at Luxembourg,
Charlotte Tremouille, Countess of Derby, heroic defender of
Latham House, and of the Isle of Man, 1663, died at Ormskirk,
Archbishop Usher died 1656,
Richard Dawes, eminent Greek scholar, 1766, died at Haworth;
Michael Bryan, biographer of painters and engravers, died 1821,
Robert Southey, the poet, died 1843, and
Rev. W. Scoresby, Arctic voyager, died 1857.

BORN ON THIS DAY WERE:
ROBERT THE BRUCE, KING OF SCOTLAND, 1274,
HUMPHREY WANLEY, ANTIQUARY, 1672, COVENTRY,
JOHN SEBASTIAN BACH, 1685,
J. B. J. FOURIER, MATHEMATICIAN, 1768,
ALBERT CHEVALIER, 1861, A TENDER SINGER OF COCKNEY
SONGS,
H. A. L. FISHER, 1865,
MR. GEORGE TOMLINSON, WHO BECAME MINISTER OF
EDUCATION, IN 1890.

[84]

March the Twenty-second

I depict today and the world hails it as belonging to all time.

March the Twenty-second was the Birth Day of two great artists who depicted their day and generation and whose work now belongs to all time —Vandyck, the great portrait painter, born in 1599 and Rosa Bonheur, the great animal painter, born in 1822. There was a writer too, who gave his days to tomorrow. Johann Wolfgang Goethe, who died on March the Twenty-second, 1832, the greatest German poet and prose writer, who found in Thomas Carlyle his disciple.
On March the Twenty-second there was sudden death. On this day in 1322, Thomas, Earl of Lancaster, was beheaded at Pontefract and on the same day in 1421 another Thomas, Thomas, Duke of Clarence, was slain in Anjou.

March the Twenty-second saw:
Templars suppressed, 1312,
Colonial Stamps Act, 1765,
Italy annexed to Sardinia, 1800,
The first Reform Bill second reading in 1831,
Constitution promised for Poland, 1848,
Proposal, afterwards accepted, to raise Income Tax to 10d. in the £1 in 1860,
Finnish seaport of Hango handed over to the Russians, 1940.

These died on March the Twenty-second:
Anne Clifford, Countess of Pembroke, 1676,
Lully, the musician, in 1687,
Jonathan Edwards, 1758,
John Canton, electrician, 1772,
Stendhal in 1842,
Rev. David Williams, Warden of New College, 1860,
Tom Hughes, 1896, and
Sir Muhammad Azizul Hugue, former High Commissioner for India in London, died 1947.

ON MARCH THE TWENTY-SECOND THESE WERE BORN,
WARWICK, 'THE KING-MAKER', IN 1428,
EDWARD MOORE, A DRAMATIC WRITER, 1712, ABINGDON,
CARL ROSA IN 1842,
RANDOLPH ALDECOTT, 1866, AND
THE MASTER OF ELPHINSTONE IN 1914.

[85]

March the Twenty-third

Who can say what makes today memorable?

Milner was born in 1854 on this day: Laplace, the savant, was born on this day in 1749: Emperor Paul of Russia was assassinated in St. Petersburg in 1801: Pope Julius died in 1556 on this day: Paris in the 1914–18 war came under long-range shelling—who can say which of these makes today most memorable?

Saints'-days:
St. Victorian, proconsul of Carthage, and others, martyrs, 484,
St. Edelwald, of England, 699,
St. Alphonsus Turibius, Archbishop of Lima, 1606.

Other birthdays were:
William Smith, 'The Father of English Geology', 1769,
Sir Muirhead Bone, 1876,
Sir Charles Wyndham, the actor, in 1837,
Viscount Esher in 1881.

These died on March the Twenty-third:
Peter the Cruel, King of Castile, 1369,
Duchess of Brunswick, sister of George III, 1813,
August Frederick Kotzebue, German dramatist, 1819, assassinated at Mannheim,
Carl von Weber, the German composer, in London in 1826,
Archdeacon Nares, philologist, 1829,
James Morier, 1849,
Sir Charles Trevelyan, the historian, 1879.

AND SOME OF THE EVENTS WERE:
ENGLAND LAID UNDER AN INTERDICT, 1208,
CAMDEN HOUSE BURNT, 1862,
JAMAICA GOVERNMENT ACT PASSED, 1866,
BOMBAY, ADEN AND SUEZ JOINED BY CABLE, 1870,
RIEL'S REBELLION BREAKS OUT IN CANADA, 1885,
LOSS OF THE 'MAINE', 1898,
ARMENIA JOINED THE U.S.S.R., 1937,
BERLIN, KIEL AND HANOVER BOMBED, 1941,
GENERAL PATTON'S THIRD ARMY CROSSED RHINE, 1945,
KING GEORGE VI CONFERRED ON BURGH OF CAMBRIDGE TITLE AND DIGNITY OF CITY, 1951.

March the Twenty-fourth

And these shall be ours—and all men's
And none shall lack their share
Of the toil—and the gain of living
In the days when the world grows fair!

The days when the world grows fair—these are the words of William
Morris, poet, craftsman and Socialist, who was born on this day—March
the Twenty-fourth—in 1834. Are these ours and all men's? Who can say? It
can be said that William Morris, believed, lived and practised his Socialism.

Mahomet II, 1430, was born on this day at Adrianople,
Cardinal York was born on this day in 1725,
Silas Kitto Hocking, novelist, 1850,
Sir Jonathan Trelawny, one of the 'Seven Bishops', 1650,

Here are eleven names—each has its place: they have each this
in common: they died on this day.
Pope Nicholas V, 1455,
Queen Elizabeth, 1603,
Dr. Daniel Whitby, celebrated divine, 1726, Salisbury,
Chesterfield, 1773,
John Harrison, inventor of 'The Time Keeper', 1776,
Haroun-al-Raschid, twenty-fifth Caliph, 809,
Miss Mary Tighe, classic poetess, 1810, Woodstock, Ireland,
A. B. Thorvaldsen, 1844,
Rev. Thomas Gisborne, miscellaneous writer, 1846,
Longfellow, 1882,
John M. Synge, 1909.

THESE OCCURRED ON THIS DAY,
ACCESSION OF JAMES I AND VI AND UNION OF TWO CROWNS,
1603,
GREAT SEAL OF ENGLAND STOLEN AND DESTROYED, 1784,
FIRST DEAD HEAT TO OCCUR IN THE BOAT RACE, 1877—
OXFORD VERSUS CAMBRIDGE, OF COURSE,
ANGLO-ITALIAN AGREEMENT OVER ABYSSINIA, 1891,
FOUR-POWER PACIFIC TREATY RATIFIED BY U.S. SENATE,
1922,
BRITISH SOMALILAND RECAPTURED, 1941,
BRITISH CROSSED THE RHINE, 1945, UNDER FIELD-
MARSHAL MONTGOMERY.

March the Twenty-fifth

Not day-dreaming—but doing the day's work,
Not designing plans—but
Achieving them—this is what days are for . . .

John Drinkwater, insurance man, dramatist and poet died on March the Twenty-fifth in 1937. His great play was *Abraham Lincoln*. He wrote fine poetry. Here are some lines . . .

Knowledge we ask not—knowledge Thou hast lent,
But Lord, the will—there lies our bitter need,
Give us to build above the deep intent,
The deed, the deed.

There were born on March the Twenty-fifth,
Archbishop John Williams, 1582, at Aberconway,
Bishop George Bull, 1634, at Wells,
Sir Richard Cox, Lord Chancellor of Ireland in 1650 at Bandon, Ireland,
Toscanini, 1867, and going back over the years
Henry II of England, in 1133.

There died:
Sir Thomas Elyot, an eminent English writer in the times of Henry VIII, in 1546,
Bishop Aldrich, 1556, at Horncastle,
Archbishop John Williams, 1650, at Llandegay,
Henry Cromwell, fourth son of the Protector, 1674, peacefully at Soham in Cambridgeshire,
Anna Seward in 1809.

AROUND THIS DAY THERE CLUSTERS THESE EVENTS:
OLD NEW YEAR'S DAY TILL 1582,
CHARITY SCHOOLS FOUNDED, 1688,
PADRE NEARLY HANGED BY DRUNKEN HANGMAN, 1738,
VEHICLES (COACHES) FIRST TAXED, 1747,
LEGAL NEW YEAR'S DAY DOWN TO 1752,
SLAVE TRADE ABOLITION BILL PASSED, 1807,
REVOLT OF GREEKS AGAINST TURKS, 1821, AND IN 1827
GREECE WON ITS INDEPENDENCE FROM TURKEY,
KING GEORGE II OF GREECE DEPOSED, REPUBLIC DECLARED
1924, AND A FORMER PRIME MINISTER WAS KILLED BY
RELIGIOUS TERRORIST, 1951.

March the Twenty-sixth

Saints and sinners go their way
Even dogs, they have their day.

St. John Ervine wrote, when Gerald du Maurier, the English actor, died,
that something indescribable went out of English life and particularly the
theatre. He called it 'Geraldry'. It was the indefinable quality which was
Sir Gerald du Maurier who was born on this day in 1873.

Cecil John Rhodes died on March the Twenty-sixth, 1902.
He is buried in the Matoppo Hills and on the covering stone is one
word—RHODES.
It tells everything. It is enough.

On this day too, there died,
John Winthrope in 1649,
Bishop Brian Duppa, 1662, at Richmond,
William Courten, traveller and virtuoso, 1702, at Kensington,
C. P. Duclos, French romance writer, 1772, Paris,
The great Beethoven, 1827,
John Mitchell Kemble, Anglo-Saxon scholar and historian, 1857,
John Seward, engineer, 1858,
Lord Lloyd George, the great Liberal statesman in 1945, and
Sir Charles Alexander Harris, in 1947.

On March the Twenty-sixth,
The Royal Agricultural Society of England was incorporated by
Royal Charter in 1840,
First cremation, at Woking in 1885,
Field-Marshal Hindenburg was elected President of Germany on
March the Twenty-sixth, 1925, and
University boat race won by Cambridge by a quarter of a length,
1949.

THESE ARE THIS DAY'S BIRTHDAYS:
GESNER, 1516,
WILLIAM WOLLASTON, AUTHOR OF 'THE RELIGION OF
NATURE DELINEATED', 1659, COTON CLANFORD, STAF-
FORDSHIRE,
GEORGE JOSEPH BELL, WRITER ON LAW AND JURIS-
PRUDENCE, 1770, FOUNTAINBRIDGE, EDINBURGH,
LORD RHONDDA, 1856, AND
ROBERT FROST, AMERICA'S POET, WAS BORN IN 1875.

March the Twenty-seventh

There's room enough and room to spare
No room! No room for dark despair.

For myself, I have never despaired and I will not despair. In the language
of one of our old poets . . . I will not despair. For I have seen a ship in
haven fall after the storm had broke, both mast and shroud.

John Bright said these words.
He never despaired and died on March the Twenty-seventh, 1889,
full of hope for humanity.
On the same day, in Antarctic wastes, died Captain Scott in 1912.
He did not despair of men; he set a new standard of devotion to
duty and courage the most sublime.

They died—these famous men—on March the Twenty-seventh.
Ptolemy XIII of Egypt, 47 B.C., drowned in the Nile,
Pope Clement III, 1191,
James the First of England and Sixth of Scotland, 1625,
Sir Gilbert Scott, R.A., famous 'restorer' of Gothic architecture,
1878,
Walt Whitman in 1892,
Enoch Arnold Bennett in 1931.

James Keill, the mathematician, 1671, at Edinburgh, and
Rt. Hon. J. R. Clynes in 1869, were born on this day.

THESE OCCURRED ON MARCH THE TWENTY-SEVENTH:
THE BRUCE BECAME KING OF SCOTS, 1306,
CEYLON CEDED TO GREAT BRITAIN BY PORTUGAL, 1802,
ROME DECLARED CAPITAL OF ITALY, 1861,
FIRST ALLIED WAR CONFERENCE MET, 1916,
BRITISH VICTORY OVER TURKS AT GAZA, 1917,
THE LAST V2 FELL ON ENGLAND IN 1945,
ARGENTINA DECLARED WAR ON GERMANY AND JAPAN,
1945,
CIVIL ESTIMATES SHOWED THAT £400,000,000 WOULD BE
REQUIRED FOR NATIONAL HEALTH SERVICE IN 1951-2,
1951, AND
UNITED STATES CHIEFS OF STAFF INSTRUCTED GENERAL
MACARTHUR TO MAKE NO MORE POLITICAL STATEMENTS
WITHOUT GOVERNMENT APPROVAL, 1951.

March the Twenty-eighth

Why! Why! must people mar
The hopeful day by making war.

France and Britain, for centuries at war with each other, became allies at last in the middle of the nineteenth century. They signalized this happy association by the discovery—so it was believed—that Russia had expansionist aims on Turkey. There were many complications and there still is much confusion and obscurity about the whole business but on March the Twenty-eighth the Crimean War began in 1854. Disaster, misfortune, disease, mismanagement were the victors.
The Treaty of Paris in 1856 brought the Crimean War to an end.

Garnet, the Jesuit, was tried in 1606,
The Royal Exchange was opened by Queen Victoria in 1844,
First German Navy Bill passed, 1898,
Massed German onslaught at Vimy Ridge, 1918,
Madrid fell and Franco triumphed in 1939,
Battle of Cape Matapan in 1941,
St. Nazaire docks were raided by the British, 1942,
Gdynia was taken in 1945,
Recorded on successive years on March the Twenty-eighth.

These died:
Pope Martin IV, 1285,
Lord Fitzwalter, and Lord John de Clifford was killed at Ferrybridge, in 1461,
George I in 1660,
Margaret Woffington, the celebrated actress, 1760,
General Sir Ralph Abercrombie, Battle of Alexandria fame, 1801,
Rev. Dr. Valpy, classical scholar at Reading, in 1836,
Archbishop Trench, 1886.

THERE WERE, FOR THESE, BIRTH DAYS ON MARCH THE
TWENTY-EIGHTH:
SIR THOMAS SMITH, AUTHOR OF 'THE ENGLISH COMMON-
WEALTH', 1514–15, AT SAFFRON WALDEN,
DR. ANDREW KIPPIS, NONCONFORMIST DIVINE, EDITOR OF
'BIOGRAPHIA BRITANNICA', 1725, NOTTINGHAM,
THOMAS CLARKSON, 1760, THE COMPANION OF WILBER-
FORCE IN THE FIGHT FOR FREEDOM FOR SLAVES, AND
ARISTIDE BRIAND, WHO STOOD FOR FRANCE, 1862.

March the Twenty-ninth

Names and places; strange; forgotten
How rich the fancy paints
These were men—of man begotten
They were not plaster saints.

Sanzio Rafaelle, the painter, was born on this day in 1483 at Urbino,
Dr. John Lightfoot, a Scripture commentator, in 1602, Stoke-on-Trent,
Joseph Ignace Guillotin, physician, originator of the guillotine—a certain cure for all ills—in France, 1783, at Xaintes,
Sir Edward Geoffrey Stanley, fourteenth Earl of Derby, the statesman, 1799, and
Sir Edwin Lutyens in 1869, the designer of the Cenotaph in Whitehall—and the architect of New Delhi.

Raymond Lully, the enlightened doctor, died on this day in 1315, at Majorca,
Henry Percy, third Earl of Northumberland, killed at the battle of Towton, 1461,
Captain Thomas Coram, originator of the Foundling Hospital in London, 1751,
Emanuel Swedenborg, 1772, Coldbath Fields, London,
Charles Wesley, 1788,
Sir William Drummond, learned historian, 1828,
Lieutenant Stratford, R.N., editor of the *Nautical Almanac*, 1853, (let almanac makers be remembered),
Mrs. Fitzherbert, 1837,
John Keble, 1866,
Sir Charles Stanford, 1924,
These—each in the appointed place and the appointed year—died on this day.

FOUR EVENTS ARE NOTED ON MARCH THE TWENTY-NINTH. IT WAS DECIDED THAT BY A STANDING ORDER, ONLY A MINISTER OF THE CROWN COULD PROPOSE A MONEY BILL IN 1707,
A SURPLUS ON THE BUDGET OF £4,165,000 WAS DISCLOSED IN 1844, AND THE ALBERT HALL WAS OPENED BY QUEEN VICTORIA IN 1871,
HEAVY RAIDS IN THE BRUNSWICK AREA IN 1944.

March the Thirtieth

How happy is he born and taught
That serveth not another's will:
Whose armour is his lowest thought
And simple truth his utmost skill.

Happy indeed was Sir Henry Wotton who has described in his poem *The Character of a Happy Life*, many proper things. He did not tell that he was indeed himself such a happy warrior. Educated at Winchester and Oxford he studied law and sciences, wrote a play, did some journalism, dabbled in diplomacy, did some secret service, it has been alleged, was entangled in plots and schemings in a dozen foreign lands, loved a Queen, fished with Izaak Walton and died Provost of Eton College. In 1568, on March the Thirtieth, he was born at Bocton Hall in Kent. He died happy—having lived in full measure—in 1639.

On March the Thirtieth there were born:
Archbishop Somner, antiquary, 1606, at Canterbury,
Francis Pilatre de Rozier, aeronaut, 1756, Metz,
Lord Radcliffe, 1899.

Under the heading, DEATHS, there are on this day recorded:
Sir Ralph Sadler, diplomatist (*Sadler Papers* are his memorial), in 1587, at Standon in Herts,
Dr. John King, Bishop of London, in 1621,
Archbishop Somner in 1669, Canterbury,
Dr. William Hunter in 1783, at Windmill Street, St. James's,
Beau Brummell in 1840, the man of fashion, *arbiter elegantiarum*,
Sir John Gilmour, Minister of Shipping, in 1940,
Leon Blum, Leader of French Socialists and former Prime Minister, 1950.

MARCH THE THIRTIETH KNEW THESE OCCURRENCES,
THE SICILIAN VESPERS, 1282,
SAMUEL JOHNSON WAS 'TOUCHED' BY QUEEN ANNE IN 1741
FOR 'KING'S EVIL',
CRIMEAN WAR TREATY OF PEACE SIGNED, 1856,
U.S. BOUGHT ALASKA FROM RUSSIA, 1867,
ANDREW JOHNSON, U.S. PRESIDENT, IMPEACHED, 1868,
FIRST AIR MAIL TO INDIA, 1929,
ALLIED NAVAL VICTORY MEDITERRANEAN, 1941,
RUSSIANS CAPTURED DANZIG, 1945.

March the Thirty-first

Stay, O Sweet, and do not rise
The light that shines comes from thine eyes,
The day breaks not: it is my heart
Because that you and I must part.

On March the Thirty-first, 1631, died Doctor John Donne.
John Donne wrote Stay, O Sweet, and do not rise *and many other poems,*
the noblest in the opinion of some, being his sonnet Death.

Why swell'st thou then?
One short sleep past, we wake eternally,
And death shall be no more: death, thou shalt die.

The son of an ironmonger, his career was run in the reigns of
James I and Charles II. He died Dean of St. Paul's: his biography
was written by Izaak Walton—and his statue is in St. Paul's
Cathedral to this day.

On this day, these deaths are recorded:
George, Earl MacCartney, Ambassador to China, in 1806,
John Constable, R.A., the landscape painter, in 1837,
Charlotte Brontë (Mrs. Nicol), novelist, in 1855,
Lady Charlotte Bury, novelist, in 1861, at Sloane Street.

Born on March the Thirty-first were:
René Descartes, the French philosopher, in 1596, at La Haye,
Francis Joseph Haydn, the musical composer, in 1732, at Rohrau,
Edward Fitzgerald was born on this day in 1809. He was born
Edward Purcell but his father changed his name to Fitzgerald.
His fame rests on his *Rubá'iyát* of Omar Khayyám. He was
acclaimed a poet but his happiness was in friendship,
Andrew Lang in 1844,
His Royal Highness the Duke of Gloucester in 1900.

EVENTS ON THIS DAY INCLUDE:
SWORD OF STATE PRESENTED TO JAMES IV BY JULIUS II
IN 1507,
NAPOLEON'S FIRST ABDICATION, 1814,
EIFFEL TOWER INAUGURATED, 1889,
REPRESENTATIVE GOVERNMENT GIVEN TO TRANSVAAL,
1905, AND—
IN 1947—WETTEST MARCH SINCE 1856 WAS ANNOUNCED.

APRIL

THIRTY DAYS

April the First

'Oh to be in England now that April's here.'
All Fools' Day, of course, but much else there is besides on April the First.

Manchester was made a city by Royal Charter in 1853,
The Royal Flying Corps and the Royal Naval Air Service were
amalgamated on April the First, 1918,
The Post Office of Ireland, which Anthony Trollope had laboured
to create, separated from the United Kingdom in 1922,
Boards of Guardians in England came to an end in 1930,
The declaration of Aden made it a separate colony in 1937,
The Spanish Civil War officially ended in 1939,
Uganda reached its Jubilee officially in 1943,
Peter Fraser appointed Prime Minister of New Zealand, 1940,
British Electricity Industry nationalized, 1948,
Newfoundland became part of Canada, 1949,
Prices of bread and flour increased in 1951.

But there were people too, as well as events:
Cicely Courtneidge confessed to choosing April the First for her
birthday in 1892 and on the selfsame day in 1815 the great
Bismarck was born.
April the First brings more than April showers for mankind.
William Harvey, discoverer of the circulation of the blood, 1578,
Folkestone,
Charles de St. Evremond, 1613, St. Denis le Gat,
Solomon Gesner, painter and poet, author of *The Death of Abel*,
1730, Zürich,
Sir Thomas F. Buxton, baronet and philanthropist, 1786, Essex.
All were born on April the First.

THESE MEN DIED ON THIS DAY,
SULTAN TIMUR (TAMERLANE) CONQUEROR OF PERSIA,
1405 (THE DATE OTHERWISE GIVEN AS 19TH FEBRUARY),
ROBERT III, KING OF SCOTS, 1406, PAISLEY,
SIGISMUND I, KING OF POLAND, 1548,
JEAN BAPTISTE THIERS, A MISCELLANEOUS WRITER, 1702,
DR. JOHN LANGHORNE, POET, TRANSLATOR OF PLUTARCH,
1779,
DR. ISAAC MILNER, DEAN OF CARLISLE, THEOLOGICAL
WRITER, 1820, AT KENSINGTON GORE.

April the Second

When heads are heavy and ardour faints
And hearts are lonely and things deride
Think how they loved us, these ancient saints,
The older saints who as martyrs died.

For April the Second there is
St. Ebba, or Abba, the abbess and martyr, in 874,
St. Francis of Paula, founder of the Order of Minims, 1508, and
St. Bronacha of Ireland, all ancient saints who glorified their generation
and to whose memory men's minds still turn.

History has strange bed-fellows. These were bed-fellows in that
they all were born on April the Second:
Charlemagne, 742, now dead in history but still glorious,
Casanova, 1725, a character and a scoundrel,
Hans Christian Andersen, 1805, who wrote fairy-tales that did
not seem to be too good to be true,
Émile Zola, 1840,
J. B. Squire, 1884.

There are listed as died on April the Second,
Arthur, Prince of Wales, 1502, Ludlow,
Jean Bart, French naval commander, 1702,
Thomas Carte, historian, 1754, Yattendon,
Dr. James Gregory, compounder of Gregory's Mixture, professor
of medicine, author of *Conspectus Medicinae*, 1821, Edinburgh,
Thomas Morier, the 'Oriental' novelist, 1849,
T. P. Cooke, the actor, 1864,
Richard Cobden, 1865, and by the hand of a madman,
Edward Terry, the actor, in 1912.

THE THINGS MEN CONSUMMATED ON APRIL THE SECOND
INCLUDE:
FIRST AMERICAN CONGRESS, 1781,
DUKE OF PORTLAND'S MINISTRY, 1783,
THE BATTLE OF COPENHAGEN, NELSON PUT HIS TELESCOPE
TO HIS BLIND EYE AND WON THE BATTLE, 1801,
ANNEXATION OF THE PUNJAB, 1849,
WORLD SAFE FOR DEMOCRACY, WOODROW WILSONS'
DECLARATION IN 1917,
RUSSIANS IN RUMANIA IN 1944.

April the Third

Hours piled on hours are all too little
The days too short for what I dream.
Lord, take it all, the jot and tittle.
And make them nobler than they seem.

George Herbert was born on this April the Third in Montgomery Castle
in Wales. He has been described by Arthur Waugh as one of those 'Beacons
of a quiet hope', whose lives have lightened not only the Church of England,
but men everywhere. His poetry still consoles and comforts those who turn
to it.

Born on this day were:
Richard II, King of England, 1366, Bordeaux,
Roger Rabutin, Count de Bussy, 1618, Epiry,
Dr. John Abernethy, surgeon and inventor of the biscuit named
after him, 1764, and
Reverend Dionysius Lardner, scientific and miscellaneous writer,
1793, at Dublin.

Died on this day,
Prince Arthur, Duke of Brittany, the English prince murdered,
1203, at Rouen,
John Napier, of Merchiston, inventor of logarithms, 1617,
Merchiston,
Edward, Marquis of Worcester, 1667, Raglan,
Jacques Ozanam, French mathematical writer, 1717, Paris,
Dr. John Berkenhout (medical and scientific writings), 1791,
Bishop Heber, 1826, who wrote 'What though the spicy breezes
blow soft o'er Ceylon's isle', and other missionary hymns,
Christopher North (John Wilson), at Edinburgh, 1854, professor
of moral philosophy,
Admiral Ross, the Arctic navigator, 1862,
D'Oyly Carte in 1901, who gave us Gilbert and Sullivan.

EVENTS ON APRIL THE THIRD INCLUDE:
BATTLE OF BEAGUE, BEGINNING OF ENGLISH LOSS OF
FRANCE, 1421,
NAPOLEON DEPOSED IN 1814,
GARIBALDI ARRIVED IN ENGLAND, 1864,
TWO AEROPLANES FLEW OVER EVEREST, 1933,
BUDAPEST RAIDED IN 1944.

April the Fourth

We've missed the bus: we've missed the bus
   But must we go on foot?
We've missed the bus! Alas! Alas!
   There is another route.

April the Fourth was a day of destiny in 1940. Neville Chamberlain, Prime Minister of Great Britain, told the world on this day that Adolph Hitler, Führer of Germany had 'missed the bus'. Omnibus was, however, not the only method of travel available to Hitler. In fact it is not on record that he ever tried to catch the bus. He got to his appointed end all the same.

On April the Fourth,
The first book was printed in Scotland, 1508,
Drake was knighted by Elizabeth, 1581,
The Self-denying Ordinance in 1645 was promulgated on this day,
The steamer *Sirius* set out for New York, 1839,
Gold was reported in the Yukon, 1896,
Formation of Royal Armoured Corps, 1938,
Britain lost Benghazi, 1941—all on April the Fourth.

St. Ambrose in 397, at Milan, died on April the Fourth; so did
Pope Nicolas IV, 1292,
Sir Robert Naunton, 1634,
Robert Ainsworth, 1743, at Poplar,
Oliver Goldsmith, the poet and miscellaneous writer, 1774, in the Temple,
Lloyd Kenyon, Lord Chief Justice of England, 1802, Bath,
André Masséna, Duke of Rivoli, Marshal of France, 1817, Ruel,
Rev. John Campbell, missionary to South Africa, 1840,
Sir Cuthbert Wilfrid Whitaker, editor of *Whitaker's Almanack*, 1950,
Sir Henry Mendelssohn Hake, Director of National Portrait Gallery, 1951.

THESE FOUR BEGAN THEIR LIVES ON THIS DAY,
GRINLING GIBBONS, THE ENGLISH WOOD-CARVER, IN 1648,
JOHN JACKSON, THE LEARNED ENGLISH DIVINE, IN 1686,
EARL OF DERBY IN 1865,
THE DUKE OF BEAUFORT IN 1900,
KIEL BOMBED, 1943,
BUCHAREST HEAVILY RAIDED, 1944,
NORTH ATLANTIC TREATY SIGNED IN WASHINGTON, 1949.

April the Fifth

What is a day—it calls for fortitude, endurance, patience, for is not all life nasty, brutish and short.

'Life is nasty, brutish and short.' These works, admittedly out of their context, come to the English speech from Thomas Hobbes, the philosopher, who wrote The Leviathan *and who was born on April the Fifth at Malmesbury in 1588. Life for Englishmen has been lengthened. It is not as short as it was.*

These share April the Fifth as a birth day with Thomas Hobbes:
Dr. Edmund Calamy, 1671, Aldermanbury,
Catherine the First of Russia, 1689, Ringen,
Hardy, 1769, Nelson's captain,
Sir Henry Havelock, 1795,
Lord Lister, 1827, whose name is ever associated with antiseptics,
Swinburne, 1837, who wrote *Songs before Sunrise*, and was Poet Laureate.

They died on April the Fifth,
William, Lord Brounker, mathematician, P.R.S., 1684, St. Catherines,
The Rev. William Derham, Speaker of the House of Commons, in the reign of Queen Anne, editor of Shakespeare, 1746,
Danton, guillotined, 1794, a creator and victim of the Revolution,
Robert Raikes, first institutor of Sunday-schools, 1811, Gloucester, who suffered little children and gave them the means of grace and hope of glory,
Lord Carnarvon, 1923.

THESE OCCURRED ON THIS DAY,
PARLIAMENTARY GRANT FOR FORMATION OF BRITISH MUSEUM, 1753,
END OF DEVONSHIRE AND PITT MINISTRY, 1757,
KHYBER PASS, 1842,
WINDOW TAX ABOLISHED, 1851,
KING EDWARD VII VISITED PRESIDENT LOUBET IN PARIS, 1905,
ADDIS ABABA, 1941,
PAY AS YOU EARN, 1944, AND
THE BRITISH GOT BACK AGAIN TO MINDEN, 1945, AND MARLBOROUGH WAS THERE.

April the Sixth

Just for a handful of silver he left us
Just for a riband to put in his coat.

Robert Browning wrote much that pleases, delights and inspires. He wrote one bitter poem. He wrote it about another poet. He wrote it because he felt that poet had apostasized his principles—he had renounced them, 'just for a handful of silver'.

William Wordsworth on April the Sixth, 1843, accepted the office of Poet Laureate at the hands of Sir Robert Peel and attended an official function wearing another coat and a borrowed sword. Perhaps it was not so bad after all. Tennyson when he became Poet Laureate had to get himself into the selfsame coat.

These are among the death of the great, recorded on this day,
Albrecht Dürer, 1528,
John Stow, the antiquary, 1605,
Sir William Hamilton, 1803.

This was the day of Badajos in 1812 in the Peninsular War,
In 1917 on this day United States of America declared war on Germany,
The Registration for Military Service of the twenty and twenty-five-year-olds began on this day in 1940,
In 1941 on this day Germany invaded Yugoslavia and Eastern Macedonia,
On April the Sixth, 1945, the Russians were fighting in Vienna.

AND WHAT OF THESE EVENTS?
COVENT GARDEN OPENED FOR ITALIAN OPERA, 1847,
EAST INDIA COMPANY SENT QUEEN VICTORIA THE KOH-I-NOOR DIAMOND—THE LARGEST IN THE WORLD, 1850,
FIRST NEWS OF THE KU-KLUX-KLAN, 1868,
ON APRIL THE SIXTH, 1942, THREE BRITISH INDIAN STEAMSHIPS OF THE COMPANY WERE LOST, THE 'GANDARA' WENT DOWN OFF MASULIPATAM, THE 'MALDA' AND THE 'INDORA' IN THE BAY OF BENGAL,
DRAFT OF RUSSO-FINNISH PACT SIGNED IN MOSCOW, 1948.

MARTIN SECKER WAS BORN AT 24 HOLLAND ROAD IN KENSINGTON, 1882,
SIR EDWARD SALISBURY WAS BORN IN 1886.

April the Seventh

There was no arsenic and lace,
Ladies were gracious—knew their place:
On April the Seventh they went their way,
For that was then old Lady Day.

April the Seventh was Lady Day in days gone by. Let its memory be
preserved and recorded in less gracious times.
On April the Seventh, 1939, Italy invaded Albania, in 1739 Dick
Turpin the highwayman was hanged at York, in 1571 the Scots hanged an
archbishop, and King Stephen on this day was deposed in 1141.
These were not very gracious things but they may well have been foreseen, for
it is on record that black was first used for public mourning on this day
away back in 1488.

On this day were born:
François de Xavier, 1506,
William Wordsworth, 1770,
Sir Francis Chantrey in 1781, and
Archbishop Lord Davidson, 1848.

On April the Seventh in 1199, Richard the First, King of
England, died, and
On April the Seventh, 1891, Barnum, the American showman, died.
When we are on the American Continent with Mr. Barnum, it
may be added that on this day, in 1865, the *Alabama* Dispute
opened and, more usefully, the Canadian Pacific Railway was
completed in 1914.

THE RANELAGH GARDENS WERE OPENED IN 1742,
THE ROYAL TITLES BIBLE WAS APPROVED ON APRIL THE
SEVENTH IN 1876,
THE GREAT ASQUITH LIBERAL MINISTRY BEGAN IN 1908,
CUBA DECLARED WAR ON GERMANY IN 1917,
THE PRESIDENT OF SPAIN WAS DEPOSED IN 1936,
MALTA—THE GEORGE CROSS ISLAND—RECEIVED ITS
HEAVIEST RAID IN 1942,
EIGHTH ARMY CAPTURED EL AKARIT IN 1943,
GREAT BRITAIN ANNOUNCES MINING NORWEGIAN TERRI-
TORIAL WATERS AT THREE POINTS, 1940, AND
GERMANY ADMITTED TO FULL MEMBERSHIP OF COUNCIL OF
EUROPE BY STANDING COMMITTEE AT STRASBOURG, 1951.

April the Eighth

The skies seem strange: the Dutchman sees
Inverted tulips overhead
Scores and scores—O! what are these
That make the heavens a flower bed:
It is the British airborne troops
Landing that Holland may be freed
The Netherland no longer stoops
And liberty has come indeed.

On April the Eighth the airborne armies of Great Britain landed in Holland in 1945 and the Netherlands was freed. On the same day in 1939 King Zog of Albania abdicated and Italy completed the rape of Easter Day—taking yet one other irrevocable step to inevitable disaster and defeat under Mussolini.

Let us go back in time to 1141. On this day Matilda assumed the title of Queen but was never crowned,
On April the Eighth in 1663, the mummers were merry for it was on this day that Drury Lane issued its first Play Bill,
On this day in the High Court of Parliament in 1763, the Bute Administration came to an end, and
On the same day in 1886 William Ewart Gladstone introduced the first Home Rule for Ireland Bill,
On April the Eighth a General Order was issued from the War Office reorganizing Regular Enlistments and Militia Enlistments on a territorial basis in 1881,
Beam service to Australia began in 1927,
The League of Nations held its Final Assembly in 1946.
On this day were born Sir Adrian Boult, 1889 and Mary Pickford, 1893.

THESE DIED,
JOHN THE GOOD, KING OF FRANCE, 1364, SAVOY PALACE,
LORENZO DE MEDICI ('THE MAGNIFICENT') 1492, FLORENCE,
DR. THOMAS GALE, LEARNED DIVINE AND EDITOR, 1702,
HENRY FORD, 1947, AND
VACLAV NIJINSKY (THE GREATEST DANCER OF HIS DAY) 1950.

JOHN C. LOUDOUN, WRITER ON BOTANY, WAS BORN IN 1783, AT CAMBUSLANG, LANARKSHIRE, AND
SIR MALCOLM TRUSTRAM EVE WAS BORN IN 1894.

April the Ninth

The caravan moves on—the dingo barks
Lenin is born and now there dawns for Marx
A prospect large: a hope: no let nor bar,
The chief architect of U.S.S.R.

Nikolai Lenin was born on April the Ninth in 1870 and with his birth the Soviet Union of today was heralded. His embalmed body lies in the Red Square of Moscow, symbolical of the triumph of an idea—the idea of Karl Marx, first embodied in Das Kapital, *and announced over his name and that of Frederick Engels in the Communist Manifesto of 1848.*

James Matthew Barrie was born on April the Ninth at Kirriemuir, in Scotland, in 1860, and Peter Pan is the surviving fruit of that fortunate day. Léon Blum, too, was born on this day in 1872. Blum, Barrie and Lenin made a strange birthday party.

Died on this day are recorded,
Constantine II, Roman Emperor, assassinated, 340,
Edward IV of England, 1483,
Gabrielle d'Estrées (La Belle Gabrielle) 1599,
Francis Bacon in 1626, the philosopher and writer,
'Simon Frazer, Lord Lovat', last victim publicly beheaded on Tower Hill, 1747,
Christian Wolf, philosophical writer, 1754, Halle,
Jacques Necker, French financial minister, 1804, Geneva,
Dr. William Prout, scientific writer, 1850, London,
Chevreul, 'Father of fatty acids', 1889.
On April the Ninth, 1932, Gunner Arthur P. Sullivan, an Australian V.C., was killed by accident in London. A bronze tablet on the railings of Wellington Barracks, St. James's Park, London, commemorates him.

EVENTS ON THIS DAY INCLUDE,
NATIONAL GALLERY WAS OPENED, 1838,
HUDSON'S BAY COMPANY CEDED ALL ITS TERRITORIAL RIGHTS, 1869,
BRITISH DEFEATED ON THE TIGRIS, 1916,
BATTLE OF VIMY RIDGE, 1917,
BOLIVIA AND BRAZIL DECLARED WAR ON GERMANY, 1917,
GERMANY INVADED DENMARK AND NORWAY, 1940,
'ADMIRAL SCHEER' SUNK IN KIEL HARBOUR, 1945.

April the Tenth

In days of wrath and days of woe
Tired men about their business go
A weary road—a long, long mile
The saints above look down—and smile.

Born on this day were,
James V, 1512,
Sir John Pringle, P.R.S., medical writer, 1707, Stitchel,
General Booth, 1829—he founded the Salvation Army,
Pulitzer, the newspaper king of U.S.A., in 1847,
George Arliss, the film star, 1868.

On this April the Tenth there died,
William, Earl of Pembroke, 1630,
William Cheselden, anatomist, 1752,
Admiral John Byron, 1786,
Erasmus Darwin, poet, 1802,
Cardinal Weld, 1837, Rome,
Alexander Nasmyth, painter, 1840, Edinburgh.

Of Algernon Charles Swinburne, the Poet Laureate who died on
this day at the Pines, Putney, London, in 1909, there were written
these lines on his death . . .

'From the unheeding world without, none cries.
The Pilgrims only mourn thee gone.
Mourn the singer of the songs of sunrise,
Asleep and silenced ere the dawn.'

His principal collection of poems is *Songs Before Sunrise*, in which
appears the poem 'The Pilgrims'.

EVENTS OF THE DAY—HERE A FEW . . .
COPYRIGHT ACT, 1710,
CONTRACTS FOR NELSON'S MONUMENT IN TRAFALGAR
SQUARE PLACED, 1840,
TREATY OF ALLIANCE BETWEEN GREAT BRITAIN AND
FRANCE, 1854,
BATTLE OF NARVIK AND FIRST V.C. IN SECOND WORLD
WAR, 1940,
BRITISH IN ACTION IN GREECE, 1941,
RUSSIANS CAPTURED ODESSA, 1944,
HANOVER CAPTURED, 1945.

April the Eleventh

The day is short—the work is much.

On April the Eleventh, 1918, it was a short day for many, but they did their work. It was on that day that Haig issued his immortal message to the armies of Britain, bidding them stand with their backs to the wall. It was obeyed and the free world breathed again.
It was on this day that Napoleon abdicated in 1814 and went to Elba.

On April the Eleventh there passed out of the sight of men,
Cardinal Beaufort, 1447, Winchester,
Sir Thomas Wyatt, 1554,
Pope Gregory XIII, 1585,
Stanislaus Poniatowski, last king of Poland, 1798,
John Galt, novelist and miscellaneous writer, 1839,
Charles Reade, the novelist, 1884.

History reports these.
Henry VI deposed for second time, restored 1471,
Gibraltar became British, 1713,
A man sold his wife—had a rope round her neck—at Dartmoor, to her first lover, for two guineas, 1817,
American Civil War began, 1861,
Alfonso XIII of Spain abdicated, 1931,
British landed in Norway, 1940,
Belgrade occupied by German forces, 1941,
Soviet forces advanced into the Crimea, 1944,
Essen captured, 1945,
The Coronation Stone was placed inside Arbroath Abbey with letters to the King and General Assembly expressing hope that it should remain in Scotland, 1950.

BORN ON THIS DAY WERE:
CHRISTOPHER SMART, POET, 1722, AT SHEPBURNE, KENT,
DAVID HAMILTON, ARCHITECT, 1768, AT GLASGOW,
MARSHAL LANNES, DUKE OF MONTEBELLO, 1769,
GEORGE CANNING, A STATESMAN, 1770, LONDON,
SIR CHARLES HALLE, 1819,
LORD HARLECH, 1885,
SIR ALAN LASCELLES, PRIVATE SECRETARY TO H.M. THE KING, 1887, AND
FREDERICK HENRY GRISEWOOD, 1888.

April the Twelfth

Once all men proclaimed the glory,
The glory of the skies.
Alas, now in mankind's story
The heavens are fraught with sighs.

On April the Twelfth, 1941, the first full-scale daylight raid was made by
the Royal Air Force. The airplane as a hopeful harbinger of the exploration
of the beauties and blessings of the heavens above had failed men.
It was destined as a bird of ill omen bringing sorrow and sighing.
On the same day in 1918 the last of the Zeppelin raids was made on Britain.

On April the Twelfth these came into the world of men to do their
work:
Dr. Burney, born on April the Twelfth, in 1726,
Edward Bird, eminent *genre* painter, 1772, born at Wolverhampton,
John George, Earl of Durham, statesman, 1792, born at Durham,
Admiral Sir Rhoderick McGrigor, Commander-in-Chief of the
Home Fleet, hero of midnight convoy battle in 1944, commander
of the *Renown* at the sinking of the *Bismarck*, was born on April
the Twelfth, 1893.

These finished their course on this day,
Seneca, Roman philosopher, ordered to death by Nero, 65, at
Rome,
Dr. George Cheyne, eminent physician, 1742, Bath,
William Kent, painter, sculptor, and architect, 1748, at Burling-
ton House, Chiswick,
Dr. Edward Young, poet, 1765, at Welwyn,
Dr. Burney, 1814, dying on his birthday,
Flora Annie Steel, 1929, the Anglo-Indian novelist,
Chaliapin, 1938,
President Roosevelt in 1945, the friend of Britain and of Winston
Churchill, and
H. de Vere Stacpoole, Novelist, 1951.

THERE WERE OTHER HAPPENINGS BESIDES BIRTHS AND
DEATHS.
CROMWELL UNITED SCOTLAND AND ENGLAND, 1654,
CAGLIOSTRO INITIATED AS A MASON, 1777,
TRANSVAAL ANNEXED BY PROCLAMATION, 1877,
CHINA PROCLAIMED A REPUBLIC, 1912.

April the Thirteenth

The night passes: man's days are brief,
But not too short for all his grief.

April the Thirteenth is the saint's-day for St. Hermengild, a martyr in 586,
for St. Guinoch of Scotland in the ninth century, and for St. Caradoc, a
priest and martyr in 1124, but it is also a Handel day.
George Frederick Handel, the musical composer, died on this day in 1759,
but it was also on April the Thirteenth that there took place the first per-
formances in Dublin, in 1742, of Handel's Messiah.

Vienna was captured on this day in 1945, the second Battle of
Narvik took place in 1940, U.S.S.R. captured the capital of the
Crimea in 1944, and away back in 1598 the Edict of Nantes was
promulgated.

The Globe Theatre, Bankside, was demolished, 1644,
The Catholic Emancipation Act, 1829,
Magdala was stormed on April the Thirteenth in 1867,
Major H. R. Armstrong was convicted for murder at Hereford
assizes on April the Thirteenth in 1922,
Croydon to Australia by air, first regular service, 1935,
The Stone was returned to Westminster Abbey, 1950.

These died on April the Thirteenth,
Henry, Duke of Rohan, French military commander, 1638,
Switzerland,
Charles Leslie, controversialist, 1722, Glaslough,
Christopher Pitt, translator of Virgil, 1748, Blandford,
Captain Hugh Clapperton, traveller, 1827,
Sir Henry de la Beche, geologist, 1855,
Sydney, Lady Morgan, miscellaneous writer, 1859, London.

THESE ON APRIL THE THIRTEENTH WERE BORN:
THOMAS WENTWORTH, EARL OF STRAFFORD, STATESMAN,
1593, LONDON,
JEAN PIERRE CROUSAZ, SWISS DIVINE, PHILOSOPHER,
AND MATHEMATICIAN, 1663, LAUSANNE,
FREDERICK NORTH, EARL OF GUILFORD, STATESMAN, 1732,
THOMAS JEFFERSON IN 1743, VIRGINIA, U.S.A.,
PHILIP LOUIS, DUKE OF ORLEANS, 1747, ST. CLOUD,
AIR MARSHAL SIR JOHN BALDWIN IN 1892.

April the Fourteenth

At Easter time the lilies fair,
And lovely flowers bloom everywhere.
At Easter time: at Easter time:
How glad the world at Eastertime.

At Easter time, the angels said
That Christ had risen from the dead.
At Easter time; at Easter time,
How glad the world at Easter time.

Easter time is April the month of spring . . .
There is always Easter . . . There is always hope . . .
It is the redeemer of the world.

On April the Fourteenth were born
William Henry, Duke of Portland, the statesman, in 1738, and
Dr. George Gregory, a miscellaneous writer, in 1754, at Dublin,
The Earl of Athlone, youngest brother of Queen Mary, in 1874,
and John Gielgud, actor, in 1904.

Ethelred—called the unready—was buried in St. Paul's in 1066,
on April the Fourteenth.
These died on this day:
Richard Neville, Earl of Warwick, killed, 1471, Barnet,
Earl of Bothwell, husband of Mary Queen of Scots, 1577,
Thomas Otway, poet, 1685, London,
Madame de Sévigné, 1696, Grignan,
John Gilbert Cooper, poet, 1769,
Rev. James Granger (*Biographical History of England*), 1776,
William Whitehead, 1785, London,
Thomas Wright, the prison philanthropist, 1875,
Sir Thomas Baxter, 1951,
Rt. Hon. Ernest Bevin, 1951,
Lt.-Col. Sir Charles H. Bressay, 1951.

EDINBURGH UNIVERSITY FOUNDED ON THIS DAY, 1582.
THESE EVENTS COMPANION IT ON THIS DAY:
WASHINGTON ACCEPTED PRESIDENCY, 1789,
THE U.S. CIVIL WAR BEGAN IN 1861,
FIRST JAPANESE WARSHIP TO BE BUILT LAUNCHED, 1877,
MARSHAL FOCH MADE GENERALISSIMO, 1918,
THE BRITISH CAPTURED ARNHEM, 1945.

April the Fifteenth

He hath out-soared the night,
Above is endless light
He hath outlived these days
But not an endless praise.

On April the Fifteenth, President Abraham Lincoln died in 1865. He hath out-soared the night and his memory shines forever in the firmament to which men's eyes return to find hope and inspiration.

These died on April the Fifteenth—ladies and gentlemen—peers and poets and men of science and men of skill.
George Calvert, Lord Baltimore, 1632,
Madame de Maintenon, 1719, St. Cyr,
Dr. Alexander Murray, philologist, 1813,
John Bell, eminent surgeon, 1820, Rome,
Thomas Drummond, eminent in physical science, 1840, Dublin,
Last survivor of Trafalgar, Lieut.-Col. Fynemore, R.M., 1887,
Matthew Arnold, the critic and poet, 1888,
Sir Charles Hallé, 1895.

On April the Fifteenth were many odd events. Here are a few:
Published—the great dictionary of Dr. Johnson, 1755,
Duchess of Kingston tried at West Hall for bigamy, 1776,
Completion of Pacific Railway uniting New York and San Francisco, 1869,
Naturalization Treaty with Great Britain ratified by U.S. Senate, 1869,
Moody and Sankey's revivalist meeting attended by the Princess of Wales, 1875.
Titanic sunk, 1912,
Von Papen captured, 1945,
Budget introduced by Mr. Dalton, 1947,
Sir Walter Hankinson, appointed U.K. Ambassador to Irish Republic, 1951.

WILLIAM AUGUSTUS, DUKE OF CUMBERLAND, 1721,
SIR JAMES CLARK ROSS, NAVIGATOR, 1800,
BENJAMIN JOWETT, 1817,
HENRY JAMES, 1843,
VISCOUNT BRUCE OF MELBOURNE, 1883—
THESE CLAIM APRIL THE FIFTEENTH AS BIRTH DAY.

April the Sixteenth

I toil, I plan, I strive, I plod:
Of work I make my very god,
Why not? How can I fill these days
And who can show me better ways?

Samuel Smiles died on April the Sixteenth in 1904. His was the doctrine of self-help—work—and independence. He is less esteemed today than in his life-time. The world is not better for the scorning of his counsel.

There were other significant figures who mark April the Sixteenth. These died:
Aphra Behn, poetess, 1689,
Georges Louis, Comte de Buffon, naturalist, 1788, Montbard,
Henry Fuseli, artist, 1825, Putney Hill,
Muzio Clementi, celebrated pianist, 1832,
Pietro Dragonetti, eminent musician, 1846, London,
Madame Tussaud, artist and exhibitor of wax figures, 1850,
Sampson Low, the publisher and founder of the firm, died 1886.

These were born,
William the Silent, founder of Dutch Republic, 1533,
Charles Montagu, Earl of Halifax, 1661, Horton,
John Law, a speculative and original financier, 1671, Edinburgh,
Sir John Franklin, the explorer, 1786,
William Chambers, Lord Provost of Edinburgh and writer, 1808,
Anatole France, the wisest of the critics, 1844, in Paris,
The Earl of Halifax, wartime Ambassador of the United States,
a former Viceroy of India, in 1881,
Charlie Chaplin, 1889.

ON APRIL THE SIXTEENTH THESE OCCURRED,
EVENING PRAYER, FIRST READ IN ENGLISH (IN KING'S CHAPEL), 1547,
DRUMMOND'S BANK FOUNDED, 1717, AND STILL POWERFUL IN FINANCE,
BATTLE OF CULLODEN, 1746,
RIGHT HON. W. E. GLADSTONE, INSTALLED RECTOR OF EDINBURGH UNIVERSITY, 1860,
RUSSO-GERMAN TREATY OF RAPALLO, 1922,
LAST ORGANIZED GERMAN RESISTANCE COLLAPSED 1945,
O.E.E.C. ESTABLISHED 1948.

April the Seventeenth

What is a day?
Define it. A day consists in time between sunrise and sunset.

Whose day is April the Seventeenth? Ian Hay was born on it in 1876, and so was Pierpont Morgan in 1837. Benjamin Franklin found it his day whereon to die in 1790 at Philadelphia. It was a day on which some important things happened.

For example, on April the Seventeenth
Quebec made seat of Canadian Government, 1856,
Revised edition of the New Testament issued, 1881,
First shots fired at submarine by British armed merchantmen, 1915,
Portsmouth raided, 1941,
Russians closed in on Sebastopol, 1944,
Britain restricted liberty of Diplomatic missions, 1944,
Leipzig invested, 1945.

On this day too, died
Marino Falieri, doge of Venice, executed, 1355,
Joachim Camerarius, German Protestant scholar, 1574, Leipzig,
George Villiers, second Duke of Buckingham, 1688,
Bishop Benjamin Hoadley, 1761, Winchester,
James Thom, 'The Ayrshire sculptor', 1850, New York,
James Abercrombie, the politician, at Edinburgh, 1858.

And these were born,
John Ford, dramatist, 1586, Islington,
Bishop Edward Stillingfleet, 1635, Cranborne, Dorset,
Henry Vaughan, 1622.

THE REPORT OF ROYAL COMMISSION ON BETTING PROPOSED CONTROL OF POOL BETTING AND PROVISION OF FACILITIES FOR OFF COURSE BETTING, 1951,
SUBMARINE 'AFFRAY' SUNK, ALL ON BOARD LOST, 1951,
GENERAL MACARTHUR, RELIEVED OF HIS COMMANDS IN JAPAN AND KOREA, ARRIVED BY AIR AT SAN FRANCISCO, 1951,
FOREIGN MINISTERS OF SIX EUROPEAN NATIONS REACHED FINAL AGREEMENT ON SCHUMAN PLAN TREATY AT CONFERENCE IN PARIS, 1951.

April the Eighteenth

So every day is holy day,
For you and me, the saints do pray.

It was the day of the earthquake at San Francisco in 1906.
In 1857 it was spent more quietly in London. The British Museum
Reading Room was opened and one day Karl Marx was going to
use it, but that was not foreseen.

Born on April the Eighteenth were:
Sir Francis Baring, baronet, eminent merchant and banker, 1740,
George H. Lewes, miscellaneous writer, essayist and husband of
George Eliot, 1817, London,
Mr. Justice Barnard, born 1891, and
Queen Frederika of Greece in 1917.

On April the Eighteenth, there died,
John Leland, eminent English antiquary, 1552, London,
John Fox, author of *The Acts and Monuments of the Church*, 1587,
Judge Jeffreys, 1689,
Alexandre Lainez, French poet, 1710,
Charles Pratt, Earl of Camden, Chancellor of England, 1766–70,
statesman, 1794.
Dr. Erasmus Darwin, poet, 1802, Breadsall,
Sir Robert Smirke, the architect, 1867,
John Addington Symonds, 1893,
H. A. L. Fisher, 1940,
Senator Arthur Hendrik Vandenberg, Republican supporter of
United Nations, 1951.

IT WAS NOT ALL BEING BORN OR DYING. THESE HAPPENED.
FOUR INDIAN CHIEFS ARRIVED IN LONDON, 1710,
BATTLE OF CULLODEN, 1746,
MELBOURNE'S SECOND MINISTRY, 1835,
GENERAL MAUDE ANNIHILATED 18TH TURKISH ARMY
CORPS, 1917,
GERMANY SENT PLENIPOTENTIARY TO VERSAILLES, 1919,
TOKYO WAS ATTACKED BY U.S. AIRCRAFT IN 1942,
BRITISH TANKS WERE SEVENTEEN MILES FROM HAMBURG
IN 1945,
EIRE LEFT BRITISH COMMONWEALTH AND BECAME A
REPUBLIC IN 1949.
ALL ON APRIL THE EIGHTEENTH.

April the Nineteenth

Made every day he had to live
To his last minute—a preparative.

The nineteenth-century men filled the unforgiving minute.
They lived full lives in that generation.

These died on April the Nineteenth:
(Here are nineteenth-century names)
George, Lord Byron, poet, 1824, Missolonghi, Greece,
Lord Gambier, 1833,
John Carne, miscellaneous writer, 1844, Penzance,
Professor Robert Jameson, naturalist, 1854, Edinburgh,
Lord Beaconsfield, 1881,
Charles Darwin, the naturalist, 1882.

For the rest on this day there also died,
King Robert II of Scotland, 1390, Dundonald Castle, Ayrshire,
Philip Melanchthon, German Protestant scholar, 1560, Wittenberg,
Thomas Sackville, Earl of Dorset, poet, Lord Treasurer of England,
1608,
Queen Christina, of Sweden, 1689, Rome,
Jean Gallois, French scholar and critic, 1707,
Nicholas Saunderson, blind scholar and mathematician, 1739,
Dr. Richard Price, calculator, 1791, Hackney.

Three have April the Nineteenth for birthday:
Edward Pellew, Viscount Exmouth, naval commander, 1757,
Sir Milsom Rees, the throat surgeon, 1866.

APRIL THE NINETEENTH IS ASSOCIATED WITH THESE
HAPPENINGS.
WILLIAM ADAMS, 'FATHER OF THE JAPANESE NAVY',
ARRIVED IN JAPAN, 1600,
EMBATTLED FARMERS FIRED AT CONCORD, 'THE SHOT
HEARD ROUND THE WORLD', 1775,
BULWER-CLAYTON TREATY, OVER THE ATLANTIC-PACIFIC
CANAL, SIGNED BETWEEN GREAT BRITAIN AND U.S., 1850,
PARLIAMENT HOUSES, QUEBEC, DESTROYED BY FIRE FOR
THE SECOND TIME, 1883,
GERMANS FIRST USED TORPEDO-CARRYING PLANES, 1917,
BRITISH SOLDIERS LANDED IN FAROES IN 1940,
GERMANS BROKE WALL OF ZUYDER ZEE, 1945.

April the Twentieth

Plough, sow, harrow, and reap
These my days in order keep
Eat, drink, endure and die
These my days—I wonder why.

April the Twentieth saw the birth of three men who died with—for them, at
any rate—the riddle and meaning of life unsolved.
Napoleon III was born on this day in 1808,
Adolph Hitler was born on this day in 1889,
Marcus Aurelius, the Roman Emperor who has been called the Christian
pagan, was born on this day in A.D. 121
None died happy men, but Marcus died with the word 'Equanimitas' on
his lips. His was—of the three—the better going.

Many millions have died on this day. These nine are noted.
Eliza Barton, 'the Maid of Kent', executed, 1534, Tyburn,
Prince Eugene of Savoy, the military commander, 1736, Vienna,
John Lewis Petit, 'in his time the most renowned surgeon in
Europe', 1760, Paris,
Dr. Abernethy, 1831,
James Wood, Gloucester banker and miser—the richest commoner
in the kingdom—aged 80—1884,
Samuel R. Crockett, 1914, the Scots novelist,
King Christian of Denmark, 1947,
George Warwick Deeping, author of many novels, 1950,
Sir Stafford Cripps, 1952.

EVENTS OF THE DAY, THESE OCCURRED,
FIRST USE OF SCENERY IN THEATRES, 1533,
COUNCIL OF STATE DISSOLVED, 1653,
FIRST STONE LAID OF NEW BETHLEHEM HOSPITAL, 1812,
IN LONDON,
CHITRAL RELIEVED, 1895, IN ONE OF BRITAIN'S LITTLE
WARS,
POSTAGE DUE STAMPS FIRST INTRODUCED, 1914,
GERMAN SHIP LANDED CASEMENT IN IRELAND, 1916,
U.S.A. WENT OFF GOLD STANDARD, 1933,
'LUTZOW' WAS SUNK BY R.A.F., 1945,
THE RADCLIFFE LIBRARY, OXFORD, CELEBRATED ITS
200TH ANNIVERSARY IN 1949.

April the Twenty-first

Tomorrow is along the way—
For those who tread it we can pray,
For them we pray—we can not stay
Single, we wish them, then, good day.

On April the Twenty-first in 1946, this was Easter Day.
On April the Twenty-first, in 1945, the soldiers of the U.S.S.R. entered
Berlin. They may be there for some time. April the Twenty-first is a
notable day in the rights of persons accused of high treason. In 1696
counsel was first permitted to be employed in their defence.

On April the Twenty-first,
Prince George of Denmark, Consort of Anne, Queen of England,
was born in 1653,
James Harris, Earl of Malmesbury, statesman, 1746, Salisbury,
Samuel Hilbert Ware, M.D., the scientific writer, 1782, Manchester,
Friedrich Wilhelm August Froebel, the German educational
reformer, was born at Oberweissbach, Thuringia, in 1792. He was
suspected of Socialism and irreligion. His theories were denounced
by the Government and he died of a broken heart.
Thomas Wright, historical and antiquarian writer, 1810,
Sir H. Barker, the great manipulative surgeon, 1869,
H.M. Queen Elizabeth, in 1926, all were born on April the
Twenty-first.

Alexander the Great died on this day at Alexandria, 323 B.C.,
Diogenes, the Cynic, 323 B.C., Corinth,
Anselm, Archbishop of Canterbury, 1109, Canterbury,
Peter Abelard, the eminent French scholar, 1142,
Jean Racine, the French dramatic poet, 1699,
Richthofen was killed in 1918, and
Robert Bridges, Poet Laureate, died, 1930.

ON THIS DAY IN 1760 THE FIRST EXHIBITION OF THE
WORKS OF LIVING ARTISTS TOOK PLACE IN LONDON. THERE
HAVE BEEN MANY EXHIBITIONS SINCE—TIME MARCHES ON.
EARTHQUAKE IN FORMOSA—3,000 KILLED AND 10,000
INJURED, 1935,
BRITISH SLOOP 'AMETHYST' FIRED ON IN YANGTZE, 1949,
INTERNATIONAL CONFERENCE ON TARIFFS AND TRADE
ENDED AT TORQUAY, 1951.

April the Twenty-second

O! shame to him who evil thinks
Who good for ill would barter
Who wickedness with virtue links
Does not deserve the garter.

The Order of the Garter was instituted on this day, April the Twenty-second, in 1348. It arose out of an embarrassing moment. The Countess of Salisbury was dancing with King Edward III. Somehow her garter fell down on the floor and the King picked it up, at once fastening it on his own leg and saying 'Honi soit qui mal y pense'. It was at a later time, when an English prime minister commenting on honours, deserved or donated, asserted, 'There is no damn nonsense about the Garter'. Some feel he is right but many more don't know.

The Royal Society was founded, in 1662, on April the Twenty-second,
The French Association was formed, in 1872, on this day,
Greek armies surrendered in 1941, on this day, to Germany,
The Bank of England ceased to issue £10 notes, in 1943, on this day.

And what of these occurrences?
The House of Commons General Warrants declared illegal, 1706,
H.M.S. *Erebus* and *Terror* abandoned in the ice, 1848,
Banns of marriage legally published for last time in U.S., 1850,
First use of poison gas, 1915, by Germany,
London Naval Conference opened, 1930,
Conference of Commonwealth Prime Ministers opened in London, 1949,
Mr. Aneurin Bevan resigned because of 'objections to many features of the budget', 1951.

These died on this day,
King Henry VII, of England, 1509, Richmond,
Antoine de Jussien, eminent French botanist, 1758,
Thomas Haynes Bailey, lyrical poet, 1839, Cheltenham.

THESE WERE BORN,
HENRY FIELDING, DRAMATIST AND NOVELIST, 1707,
IMMANUEL KANT, GERMAN PHILOSOPHER, 1724,
JAMES GRAHAME, POET, 1765, GLASGOW,
MARQUESS OF DALHOUSIE, 1812,
YEHUDI MENUHIN, NEW YORK, 1916.

April the Twenty-third

Let not a day so
Fair be without its
White chalk mark.

This is the day of Saint George.
There were saints, but what about William Shakespeare? All April is his
for that ever enlarging world of his adorers, for it was in April he was born,
fell ill and passed to his immortality. Some give April the Twenty-third as
his birthday in 1564, it was on April the Twenty-third he died in 1616. In
any calendar of days, Shakespeare must have his place. Let it be for birth
day and day of dying alike, this April the Twenty-third.

On Shakespeare's day, were born:
King Louis IX, of France, in 1215,
Julius Caesar Scaliger, eminent scholar, 1484,
George, Lord Anson, navigator, 1697, Shuckborough,
Sir Gilbert Elliot, first Earl of Minto, statesman, 1751,
James Buchanan, President of United States, in 1791,
Lt.-Gen. Sir Archibald Nye (Chief of General Staff at the age of
forty-five), Dublin, 1895.

On Shakespeare's day these died.
Pierre Danes, eminent French scholar, 1577,
Cervantes, 1616—who gave us the one and only Don Quixote
and Sancho Panza, Maurice de Nassau, Prince of Orange, 1625,
Andrew Baxter, philosophical writer, 1750,
Count de Volney, French philosophical writer, 1820,
Joseph Nollekens, sculptor, 1823, London.

TO COMPLETE THE CALENDAR FOR APRIL THE TWENTY-
THIRD,
THE FOUNDATION STONE OF THE BASTILLE WAS LAID IN
1369,
WARREN HASTINGS WAS ACQUITTED IN 1795,
FIRST MOVIE SHOWN, NEW YORK, 1896—THE WORLD
MOVES ON,
SHAKESPEARE MEMORIAL THEATRE OPENED IN 1932 AT
STRATFORD,
LETTER POSTAGE WENT UP TO 2½D., 1940,
SWEET RATIONING CEASED IN BRITAIN—1949—ONLY TO
BEGIN AGAIN!

April the Twenty-fourth

Wise then is he who come what may
Draws courage from a bygone day.

On April the Twenty-fourth, 'the knightly Allenby' was born in 1861 . . .
fated to win Palestine for the Allies in the First World War and sharing
his birthday, in 1889, is Sir Stafford Cripps, called 'Austerity Chancellor'
in 1949.

At Marnham, in Nottinghamshire, England on April the Twenty-
fourth, 1743, was born the inventor of the power loom—Edward
Cartwright; his hands in no small way made the Industrial Revolution, and
In 1815 Anthony Trollope, the great English novelist, was born as
too was Cyril Maude, 1862.

Four saints'-days all to be named. They are:
St. Mellitus, third archbishop of Canterbury, 624,
Saints Beuve and Doda, of Rheims, seventh century,
Saint Robert of Chase-Dieu, Auvergne, 1067, and
St. Fidelis, martyr, 1622.

On April the Twenty-fourth, these were gathered to their fathers,
James Beaton, Archbishop of Glasgow, 1603, Paris,
Captain Philips, last survivor of the *Vichy*, 1869,
Justin McCarthy, 1912, historian and writer, and the first Bishop
of London away back in 624.
Dr. Harold Moody, in 1947,
Franklin Thomas Grant Richards, in 1948.
Joseph Paton Maclay, first Baron, Shipping Controller in First
World War, 1951.

EARL BOTHWELL SEIZED MARY QUEEN OF SCOTS IN 1567,
'EASTER WEEK' IN DUBLIN 1916, IT WAS SIGNIFICANT,
THE SINN FEIN REBELLION BEGUN IN IRELAND IN 1919,
ON THIS DAY FIRST OFFICIAL AIR MAIL FROM AUSTRALIA,
TWENTY DAYS, 1931,
NAZIS WON PRUSSIA, BAVARIA, WÜRTTEMBERG AND HAM-
BURG, 1932, AT THE ELECTIONS,
EMPIRE FORCES WITHDREW FROM GREECE, 1941,
1945 BUDGET—NO CHANGE!
COMMUNIST TROOPS OCCUPIED NANKING, 1949.

April the Twenty-fifth

This was the 'day' foretold by yours
In whispers here and there with beery clamours—
You and your rat-hole spies and blustering crew
Of loud Potsdammers.

On April the Twenty-fifth, in 1945, the siege of Berlin began. The 'loud Potsdammers' of whom Punch *wrote in 1918, drew near to being silenced. The 1939–45 war approached its appointed end.*

On this day the Allies, English, French, Scots, Irish, Australians and New Zealanders began the Gallipoli Landings in 1915 and so ANZAC DAY became history. The plan is associated with the name of Winston Churchill who conceived it when First Lord of the Admiralty, although he was not fated to see it through. He was fated however to try once again 'the soft under-belly of Europe' and achieve victory.

Born to be King on April the Twenty-fifth in 1284 was King Edward II of England, at Carnarvon Castle;
Born to be Protector of England, Oliver Cromwell, in 1599,
Sir Mark Isambard Brunel, engineer of the Thames Tunnel, 1769,
Marconi in 1874, the genius who made radio-communication practicable, too, marks April the Twenty-fifth as a birth day, with Princess Mary, Countess of Harewood, Princess Royal, in 1897.

They died on this day.
Torquato Tasso, Italian poet, 1595, at Rome,
William Cowper, poet, 1800, East Dereham,
Maclise, the artist, in 1870,
Benedict Humphrey Summer, Warden of All Souls, Oxford, and distinguished historian, 1951.

THE CABINET COUNCIL WAS A DEVICE OF GOVERNMENT FIRST INSTITUTED IN 1670 ON APRIL THE TWENTY-FIFTH, THE ROYAL YACHT, 'VICTORIA AND ALBERT', WAS LAUNCHED IN 1843,
LAST WORD OF FRANKLIN'S PARTY, 1848, REACHED BRITAIN AND ON APRIL THE TWENTY-FIFTH, 1938, THE TREATY PORTS IN EIRE WERE GIVEN UP BY BRITAIN. THIS ACTION COST MANY LIVES AND MANY MILLIONS OF MONEY IN 1939–45.

April the Twenty-sixth

Not two strong men the enormous
*   Weight could raise;*
Such men as live in these degenerate days.

April the Twenty-sixth marks two Scotsmen.
Thomas Reid, born 1710, at Strachan, Kincardineshire, and the second is
David Hume, the friend of Adam Smith, the historian and philosopher, was
born on this day at Edinburgh, in 1711,
Alfred Krupp in 1812—a German and a man of iron—founder of Krupps
of Essen.

On April the Twenty-sixth these closed their eventful story.
Defoe in 1731, author of the *Diary of the Plague* and the immortal
Robinson Crusoe,
Sir Eyre Coote, the military commander, 1783, Madras,
Carsten Niebuhr, traveller, 1815, Meldorf in Holstein,
Artemus Ward in 1834, the American humorist,
Henry Cockburn, author of *Memorials of His Time*, 1854,
Dante Gabriel Rossetti in 1854.

April the Twenty-sixth is the
Date assigned for beginning of the Great Plague in London, 1665,
The Septennial Act, 1716,
First performance of *Samson and Delilah*, 1909,
Conscription in Britain, 1939,
Axis entered Egypt, 1941,
Capture of Bremen and Stettin, 1945,
Persian Parliamentary Oil Committee passed resolution calling
for immediate nationalization of Anglo-Iranian Oil Company,
1950.

BUT IT WAS FOR MORE THAN THESE THAT APRIL THE
TWENTY-SIXTH MAKES THE DAY FAMOUS. SHAKESPEARE
WAS BAPTIZED IN 1564. THE STORY HAS NOT BEEN RE-
PORTED BY ANY EYE-WITNESSES NOR HAS A LYTTON
STRACHEY RECONSTRUCTED THE SCENE FOR MANKIND, YET
IT WAS AN EVENT. IT OCCURRED IN 1564 IN THE PARISH
CHURCH OF STRATFORD-ON-AVON IN WARWICKSHIRE.
JOHN SHAKESPEARE AND HIS WIFE, MARY ARDEN, HAD
THEIR THIRD CHILD AND FIRST SON BAPTIZED WILLIAM
SHAKESPEARE ON THIS DAY, APRIL THE TWENTY-SIXTH.

April the Twenty-seventh

I've wandered East, I've wandered West,
Through many a weary way;
But never, never can forget
The love of life's young day.

A delicate boy (he was not the first nor will be the last) wrote on an August day in 1761 that he proposed 'to keep an exact journal of my actions and my studies: both to assist my memory and to accustom me to set a due value upon my time'. The delicate boy was Edward Gibbon who wrote in the Journal of My Life *these words—'1737—April 27th I was born at Putney in Surrey'.*
Edward Gibbon wrote The History of the Decline and Fall of the Roman Empire, *surely one of the greatest histories ever written, both in conception and execution.*

On the same day on which Edward Gibbon was born, these were also born,
Mary Wollstonecraft (Mrs. Godwin), 1759,
Samuel Finley Breese Morse, 1791,
Maria Christina, consort of Ferdinand VII of Spain, 1806, Naples,
General Grant in 1822—the victor of the American Civil War, and
Cecil Day Lewis (poet), 1904.

These died on April the Twenty-seventh,
Philip the Bold, Duke of Burgundy, 1404, Hall in Hainault,
Ferdinand Magellan, the Portuguese navigator, killed in 1521, at Isle of Matan,
Sir William Jones, poet and scholar, 1794, Calcutta,
James Bruce, traveller in Africa, 1794, Kinnaird, Stirlingshire,
Thomas Stothard, R.A., 1834, London,
Macready, the actor, 1873, amid the sage of concord,
Ralph Waldo Emerson, in 1882.

EVENTS WHICH MARK THIS DAY ARE VARIED,
ORDER OF ST. MICHAEL AND ST. GEORGE IN 1818,
FIRST STONE OF 'NEW' HOUSE OF COMMONS LAID, 1840,
QUEEN VICTORIA PROCLAIMED, BY THE GRACE OF GOD, OF THE UNITED KINGDOM OF GREAT BRITAIN AND IRELAND, QUEEN, DEFENDER OF THE FAITH, EMPRESS OF INDIA, 1876.

April the Twenty-eighth

Bliss was it in that dawn to be alive,
But to be young was very heaven.

*April the Twenty-eighth, 1945, was a day when young men drew breath
again. They had come through: they were alive. If it was not 'very heaven'
to be alive, at any rate sudden death was less imminent for them. On this
day Himmler offered his surrender: on this day Mussolini was lynched by
the mob: Europe—the civilized world—began to see an end of the war of
1939–45.*

Edward IV in 1442 was born on the Twenty-eighth of April,
Charles Cotton, the poet, at Ovingden, in 1630,
Anthony, seventh Earl of Shaftesbury, philanthropist and states-
man, in 1801,
Peter Guthrie Tait, physicist, in 1831,
General Henry Crerar in 1888, and
Val Gielgud, B.B.C. Drama Producer, in 1900.

On tombstones and other memorials, these deaths on April the
Twenty-eighth are recorded,
Thomas Betterton, actor, 1710, London,
Count Struensee, executed, 1772, Copenhagen,
Baron Denon, artist, learned traveller, 1825, Paris,
Sir Charles Bell, anatomist and surgeon, 1842, Hallow Park,
Sir Edward Codrington, naval commander, 1851, London,
Gilbert À Becket, comic prose writer, 1856, and
Sir A. C. Mackenzie, 1935.

ON THIS DAY THESE THINGS HAPPENED,
FIRST SCOTTISH DUKES, 1398,
SUPPRESSION OF THE HELL FIRE CLUBS ORDERED, 1721,
CLEMENT XII ISSUED FIRST PAPAL BULL AGAINST FREE-
MASONRY, 1738,
MUTINY ON THE 'BOUNTY', 1789,
REPEAL OF CORPORATION AND TEST ACTS, 1828,
COMMISSION APPOINTED TO INQUIRE INTO SEAWORTHINESS
OF BRITISH SHIPPING, 1873,
FIRST U.S. CONSCRIPTION BILLS PASSED BY CONGRESS, 1917,
PORTSMOUTH SEVERELY ATTACKED BY NIGHT PLANES,
1941,
KIEL RAIDED: YORK RAIDED—1942.

[123]

April the Twenty-ninth

They ran their race:
  They had their day
I follow on—
  This is my day.

He who died famed as 'The Iron Duke', the great Duke of Wellington, was born on this day in 1769. Victor at Assaye, Vimeiro, Talavera and Waterloo, none earned nor more proudly carried the title of 'The Duke' in the long history of Britain. He learned in his first campaign 'what not to do' and he never forgot the unwisdom in thinking that despatches arriving at the dinner hour could 'keep until tomorrow morning'. He learned from life. He taught his fellow countrymen.

These events occurred on this day.
Second Council of State was set up, 1683,
Kentish Petition, 1701,
Hogarth, the artist, first set up business in Little Cranbourne Alley, 1720,
The Stirling Peerage trial began (lasted four days), 1839,
Corn Law Bill received Royal assent, 1842,
Women were admitted to Oxford University examinations, 1885,
Unconditional surrender of Germans in Italy, 1945,
Dr. Mohammed Moussadek, leader of nationalization campaign, elected Persian Prime Minister, 1950.
And it was on this day, that Noah left the Ark.

These died,
Assassination of Cardinal Beaton at St. Andrews, 1546,
John Cleveland, poet, 1658, St. Michael's College Hill,
John Arbuthnot, 1667,
Michael Ruyter, Dutch admiral, 1676, Syracuse,
James Montgomery, the poet, 1854,
Field-Marshal the Marquis of Anglesey, 1854.

BORN ON THIS APRIL THE TWENTY-NINTH WERE,
KING EDWARD IV OF ENGLAND, 1414, ROUEN,
NICOLAS VANSITTART, LORD BEXLEY, ENGLISH STATES-
MAN, 1766,
SIR JAMES BROOKE, 1803, AND THE GREAT CONDUCTORS
SIR THOMAS BEECHAM, 1879, AND
SIR MALCOLM SARGENT, 1895.

April the Thirtieth

The night seems long: Man's days are brief.
Time is an open daylight thief.

George Washington, the First President of the United States of America, died in 1789 on April the Thirtieth.

These too died on this day:
Chevalier Bayard, killed, 1524,
John, Count de Tilly, military commander, 1632, Ingolstadt,
Dr. Robert Plot, naturalist, topographer, 1696, Borden,
G. Farquhar, dramatist, 1707, London,
Jean Jacques Barthelemi, 1795, Paris,
Thomas Duncan, Scottish artist, 1845, Edinburgh,
Samuel Maunder, author of books of information, 1849, London,
Sir Henry Bishop, musical composer, 1855,
Carl Rosa, 1889,
A. E. Housman, 1936,
Sir Almroth Edward Wright, pioneer in inoculation against typhoid, 1947.

Queen Mary II of England in 1662, wife of William of Orange, was born on April the Thirtieth,
Lord Avebury, 1834,
Franz Lehar, in 1870,
Vernon Bartlett, M.P., author, 1894, and
Queen Juliana of the Netherlands, 1909.

ON APRIL THE THIRTIETH THERE ARE RECORDED.
BATTLE OF FONTENOY WAS FOUGHT IN 1745,
LOUISIANA WAS SOLD TO U.S. BY FRANCE IN 1803,
NEW ZEALAND DECLARED TO BE INDEPENDENT OF NEW SOUTH WALES, 1841,
GOLD WAS DISCOVERED IN AUSTRALIA, 1851,
KANSAS ADMITTED AS A TERRITORY OF U.S., 1854,
FIRST JAPANESE AMBASSADOR ARRIVED IN BRITAIN, 1861,
ANGLO-FRENCH MILITARY CONVENTION, 1905,
GERMAN WARNING AGAINST SAILING IN 'LUSITANIA' PUBLISHED IN U.S. PRESS, 1915,
FALL OF KUT, 1916,
HITLER PRESUMED TO HAVE COMMITTED SUICIDE IN 1945,
POTATO RATIONING ENDED, 1948.

MAY

THIRTY-ONE DAYS

May the First

Awake, cheer, adorn,
Invite, inspire, assure,
The joys that praise thy morn,
The toils thy noons mature.

And soothe the eve of day
That darkens back to death
Oh! golden sun, whose ray
Our path illumineth!

Let's go a May-ing . . . . .
There is a doubt—some say it was April the Twenty-ninth—but
the balance of evidence seems to give May the First, 1769, as the
birthday of the Duke of Wellington. Certainly it was in 1814 he
was made a Duke!
Joseph Addison, the essayist, was born in 1672, and
A. V. Alexander in 1885—First Lord of the Admiralty and Minister
of Defence.

John Dryden died in 1700,
Dr. Livingstone died in 1873, and
Antonin Dvořák, the Bohemian composer, in 1904.

Public Works promoters favoured it—the better the day, the
better the deed.
In 1660, in England, Parliament voted for Government by King,
Lords and Commons,
Sir Christopher Wren laid the first stone of St. Paul's Cathedral in
1675,
The Union of Scotland and England was consummated in 1707,
The Caledonian Canal in Scotland—with hopes—was begun in
1803,
Natives of India first admitted to Magistracy in 1834,
The Great Exhibition—which became the Crystal Palace—was
opened in 1851,
The London and North Eastern Railway ran its first non-stop
train from London to Edinburgh in 1928—all on the First of May.

MAY THE FIRST IS LABOUR DAY, PROCESSIONS BY PER-
MISSION OF THE HOME SECRETARY GO ON MAY THE FIRST
TO HYDE PARK IN LONDON.
VISIT OF L.M.S. 'ROYAL SCOT' TO U.S.A., 1933.

May the Second

From past regret and present faithlessness,
From the deep shadow of foreseen distress
And for the nameless weariness that grows
As life's long day seems wearing to its close.

May the Second was the birthday of
William Camden, the English historical antiquary, 1551, London,
William, Earl of Shelburne, first Marquis of Lansdowne, states-
man, 1737,
Rev. Robert Hall, the Baptist preacher, 1764, Arnsby,
Sir John Malcolm, author of *History of Persia*, 1769,
John Galt, the Scottish novelist, 1779, born at Irvine, Ayrshire,
Jerome K. Jerome, born 1859, who delighted the Victorian days
with *Three Men in a Boat*,
R. E. S. Wyatt, Test cricketer, 1901.

On May the Second these came to their resting beds,
Leonardo da Vinci, the painter, 1519, Fontainebleau,
Lord Tilbury, a military commander, 1635, London,
Sir George Mackenzie, at one time King's Advocate for Scotland,
a miscellaneous writer, 1691, Oxford,
Antoine Yves Goguet, author of a work on the Origin of Laws, 1758,
Madame Piozzi, 1821, at Clifton, the friend of Doctor Johnson,
William Beckford, author of *Vathek*, in 1844, at Bath, and
Alfred de Musset in 1857.

MAY THE SECOND PRODUCED THE ESCAPE OF MARY, QUEEN
OF SCOTS, FROM LOCHLEVEN, IN 1568,
AUTHORIZED TRANSLATION OF BIBLE IN 1611,
HUDSON BAY COMPANY CHARTER 1670, AND A DOMINION
WAS FORESHADOWED,
MONSTER CHARTIST PETITION IN 1842,
THIRD AFGHAN WAR, 1919,
EARLDOM CONFERRED ON LORD FRENCH, 1922—ONCE
SIR JOHN FRENCH, AND ON THIS DAY CONCLUDING HIS
OFFICE AS LORD-LIEUTENANT OF IRELAND,
IRAQIS ATTACKED BRITISH IN 1941,
MAY THE SECOND MARKED THE SURRENDER OF BERLIN IN
1945, AND CIVIL DEFENCE IN BRITAIN 'STOOD DOWN',
DR. ADENAUER, GERMAN CHANCELLOR, JOINED COMMIT-
TEE OF MINISTERS FOR THE FIRST TIME, 1951.

May the Third

I remember, I remember,

On May the Third Thomas Hood died in 1845 at London. He gave mirth to the world in his verse but he took a hand at the job of trying to leave the world better than he found it. His Song of the Shirt *showed up the evils of what became known as 'sweating' and made better standards for industry possible.*

These died on May the Third, too,
Pope Benedict XIV, 1758,
James Morison, 'the hygeist', 1840,
Sir John Swanwick Bradbury, former joint permanent Secretary of the Treasury, 1950.

Among the recent events on this day it is recalled that on May the Third, Queen Mary had a motor-car accident in 1938, and
Up in Scotland it was on the same day in 1938 that His Majesty King George VI opened the Glasgow exhibition,
'The Protestation', i.e. against Rome, 1641,
The Royal Academy first opened at Burlington House, 1809,
First trolley 'bus in this country, 1913,
General Strike, 1926—
Some think the General Strike, the first in British history, was a greater disaster to Britain than has been generally recognized,
The Allies entered Rangoon, in 1945,
Foreign Ministers of the Four Powers met in London, 1949,
Ten-Power Conference in London established Council of Europe, 1949,
The Queen launched the new *Ark Royal* at Birkenhead, 1950,
From steps of St. Paul's, H.M. The King declared open the Festival of Britain.

MAY THE THIRD WAS THE BIRTHDAY OF . . .
NICOLAS MACHIAVELLI, STATESMAN AND POLITICAL WRITER, 1469, FLORENCE,
DEAN HUMPHREY PRIDEAUX, THEOLOGICAL WRITER, 1648,
WILLIAM WINDHAM, ENGLISH STATESMAN, 1750, LONDON,
AUGUSTUS FREDERICK KOTZEBUE, GERMAN POET, 1761,
PRINCE VON BÜLOW, GERMAN CHANCELLOR, 1849,
D'OYLEY CARTE, 1844,
SIR TIMOTHY C. EDEN, 1893.

May the Fourth

From the first dawn that ever brightened a human hearth or warmed a
human heart,
One generation has told another that there is a world beyond the dawn.

St. Monica—a widow—A.D. 387, and St. Godard—a bishop—1038, are
saints of May the Fourth, dying faithful to a world beyond the dawning of
today.

Born on this day were,
Archbishop Sharp, 1613,
Dr. Francis Peck, English historical antiquary, 1692, Stamford,
Sir Thomas Laurence, 1769,
John James Audubon, ornithologist, 1782, Louisiana,
W. H. Prescott, American historian, 1796,
Joseph J. Whitaker, 1820,
Sir William Currie, 1884.

There died on this day,
Edward, Prince of Wales, son of Henry VI, 1471, Tewkesbury,
Ulysses Aldovrandi, naturalist, 1605,
Louis XIII, King of France, 1643,
Dr. Isaac Barrow, eminent English divine, 1677,
Sir James Thornhill, painter, 1734,
Tippoo Sahib, Sultan of Mysore, killed at the siege of Seringapatam,
1799,
Edmond Brand, 1833,
Sir Robert Ker Porter, traveller, artist, 1842, St. Petersburg,
Horace Twiss, miscellaneous writer, 1849,

THESE EVENTS OCCURRED ON MAY THE FOURTH,
COLLECTIVE ACTION OF THE BOARD OF ADMIRALTY CON-
CENTRATED IN THE PERSON OF THE FIRST LORD, 1872,
JENNY LIND'S FIRST APPEARANCE IN THIS COUNTRY, 1873,
BRITAIN FAILED IN HER WAR DEBTS TO U.S., 1934,
BUCHAREST RAIDED, 1944,
GERMAN FORCES IN N.W. GERMANY, HOLLAND AND DEN-
MARK SURRENDERED, 1945,
ARMED JEWS ATTACKED PRISON AT ACRE AND RELEASED
OVER 200 PRISONERS, 1947,
ROYAL FAMILY VISITED SOUTH BANK EXHIBITION, OPEN-
ING DAY, 1951.

May the Fifth

David, Dante, Shakespeare, Pope,
Hitler, Roosevelt—there they be,
This hour is mine—and I have hope
They have but immortality.

There died on May the Fifth—Prince Clemens Lothar von Metternich in *1859*. History clears his reputation. Described as an ultra-reactionary in the disorder that was once Europe and the confusion which passes for a foreign policy, Metternich, the Austrian statesman, now appears as a man of skill in a difficult field of action. He was among the last of the main-tainers of tradition and ordered progress against the tumult of senseless change and bloody revolution.

Born on May the Fifth were
Emperor Justinian in 483, Tauresium, in Bulgaria,
General R. Craufurd, 1764,
Karl Marx in 1818,
Viscount Wavell, 1883, great commander and lover of letters, and
Dr. Geoffrey Fisher, ninety-seventh Archbishop of Canterbury,
1887.

Died on this day,
Paulus Aemilius, 1529, at Paris,
Samuel Cooper, 1672,
Napoleon Bonaparte, the great Emperor of the French, 1821, at
St. Helena,
Sir Robert Harry Inglis, Bart., a political character, 1855,
James Grant, the novelist, 1887, and that Luck of Roaring Camp,
Francis Bret Harte, the poet and writer, 1902.

EVENTS INCLUDE,
CHARLES I FLED TO THE SCOTS FOR PROTECTION, 1645,
LORD FERRERS, HANGED, 1760,
GARIBALDI SAILED FROM GENOA TO CONQUER SICILY,
1860,
RONALD TRUE SENTENCED FOR MURDER, 1922, AND—
WOMEN NOTE—
MISS AMY JOHNSON SET OFF FOR AUSTRALIA AND PROVED
HERSELF TO BE IN HER OWN RIGHT A QUEEN OF THE AIR
IN 1930,
ITALIAN TROOPS OCCUPIED ADDIS ABABA, 1936.

May the Sixth

A Day! An opportunity?
A tragedy? A comedy??
A tragi-comedy???
A commonplace!

On May the Sixth, 1862, Henry David Thoreau died. He was only forty-five, no man in modern times was more passionately and rationally an individualist. Concord, Massachusetts, was the scene of his practice of the art of being an entirely independent person. Walden, or Life in the Woods *is his best known writing, but his journals and his essays on* Civil Disobedience *and* Life without Principle *contain an elaboration and a statement of his belief in brave living.*

On May the Sixth there were born two generals, one poet—philosopher and a revolutionary leader—they are,
André Masséna, the French general, 1758, Nice, whom Napoleon made a Marshal—son of a tanner,
Robespierre, a revolutionary leader, 1758,
Rabindranath Tagore in 1861—a Nobel Prize winner who gave up a British knighthood, a poet-philosopher,
Lord Ironside, 1880, a man of two wars—in land and air.

These died on May the Sixth,
Charles, Duc de Bourbon, killed at Rome, 1527,
Cornelius Jansen (Jansenius), Bishop of Ypres, theologian, 1638,
Emperor Leopold I, 1705,
Andrew Michael Ramsay, author of *Travels of Cyrus*, 1743,
Sir James Young Simpson, 1870,
John Curwen, 1880,
Edward VII, King Emperor, in 1910, and
Maeterlinck, 1949.

ALL SORTS OF THINGS HAPPENED ON MAY THE SIXTH.
THE EARLIEST GAELIC CHARTER BEARS THIS DATE IN 1408,
LORD FREDERICK CAVENDISH AND MR. BURKE MURDERED
IN PHOENIX PARK, 1882,
OSCAR SLATER WAS TRIED AT EDINBURGH FOR MURDER,
1909,
SILVER JUBILEE REJOICINGS, 1935,
AIRSHIP 'HINDENBURG' BLEW UP AT NEW JERSEY, 1937,
FRUIT CROPS HEAVILY DAMAGED BY FROST, 1944.

May the Seventh

Day!
Faster and more fast
O'er night's brim, day boils at last . . .

May the Seventh, 1812, was the birthday of Robert Browning. He brought drama and human interest to English poetry. Those who read Saul *and* Fra Lippo Lippi *and* A Grammarian's Funeral *enlarge their minds and may enlarge their lives. Robert Browning married Elizabeth Barrett—one of the Barretts of Wimpole Street—a poetess six years his senior and they were happy.*

These were born on this day,
Gerard van Swieten, a physician, in 1700, at Leyden,
Johannes Brahms in 1833, in the line of Beethoven, and
Lord Rosebery in 1847, Prime Minister of Britain.

These died on May the Seventh.
Otho the Great, emperor, 973, Magdeburg,
First Bishop of Lincoln, 1092,
Jacques Auguste de Thou (Thuanus), French historian, 1617,
John Gwillim, herald, 1621,
Patrick Delany, D.D., miscellaneous writer, 1768, Bath,
William, Marquis of Lansdowne, 1805,
H. W. Bunbury, amateur artist, 1811,
Thomas Barnes, editor of *The Times*, 1841, London, and
Henry, Lord Brougham, 1868.

EVENTFUL THINGS HAVE HAPPENED ON MAY THE SEVENTH.
MAN ATE RAW FLESH IN PUBLIC, 1675,
THE SEPTENNIAL ACT WAS PASSED, 1716,
PREROGATIVES OF THE GUINEA COMPANY WERE TAKEN OVER BY THE CROWN, 1821,
ROYAL AFRICAN COMPANY ABOLISHED, 1821,
ROYAL COLLEGE OF MUSIC OPENED, 1883,
'LUSITANIA' TORPEDOED BY GERMAN U.20: 1,198 PASSENGERS DIED, 1915,
RUMANIA PACKED UP, 1918,
BANK OF INTERNATIONAL SETTLEMENT WAS ESTABLISHED, 1929,
THE ENEMY DRIVEN OUT OF BIZERTA AND TUNIS, 1943,
GERMANY SURRENDERED, 1945.

May the Eighth

Daily duty—daily done
What is lost—and what is won?

The Convention, the Revolutionary Government of France, on *May the Eighth 1794*, sent to the guillotine Antoine Laurent Lavoisier. Democracy is not always a good judge of human values.
'*Crucify Him*' in one generation is followed by '*to the guillotine*' in another. Lavoisier was one of the founders of modern chemistry and laid the foundation of chemical nomenclature: at *fifty-one* his usefulness to the world was deemed on this day to be over. It was an error of judgement.

These are the happenings in days gone by on May the Eighth.
Peace of Bretigny, 1360,
Choral Service in English first used in churches, 1559,
Cromwell refused to be King, 1657,
First performance of *School for Scandal*, 1777,
First issue of sovereigns, 1821,
Treaty of Washington, and *Alabama* claims signed (£3,229,166), 1871,
The Mont Pelée eruption, 1902,
Liberia broke with Germany, 1917,
Ramsay MacDonald's Cabinet, 1929,
VE day, 1945,
King and Queen of Denmark's State Visit, 1951.

Died on this day are recorded these names:
Dr. Peter Heylin, author of the *Life of Archbishop Laud*, 1662,
Archbishop William King, 1729, Donnybrook,
Dr. Samuel Chandler, 1766, London,
W. C. Townsend, Q.C., author of *Lives of Eminent Judges*, 1850,
Captain Barclay Allardice, noted athlete and pedestrian, 1854,
John Stuart Mill, 1873.

THESE ARE BIRTH DAYS:
DR. BEILBY PORTEOUS, BISHOP OF LONDON, 1731, YORK,
REV. WILLIAM JAY, CONGREGATIONALIST DIVINE, 1769, TISBURY,
PRESIDENT TRUMAN IN 1884,
WILLIAM YOUNG DARLING, 1885, A LORD PROVOST OF EDINBURGH, AND
SURGEON VICE-ADMIRAL SIR PERCIVAL NICHOLLS, 1877.

[135]

May the Ninth

What can I do with but one day?

When men sing marching-songs the world must take notice. There are not many marching-songs written about persons but the most famous, surely, is 'John Brown's Body Lies a-Mouldering in the Grave, but his Soul goes Marching on'.
John Brown was born on May the Ninth in 1800. On October the Sixteenth, 1859, in what looked like a disreputable raid on an arms depot at Harper's Ferry, Virginia, U.S.A., John Brown found immortality. He was hanged high for this affair, so high that men look up to him still as a martyr—as well as a fighter for freedom.

Two names never before joined together are remembered as having May the Ninth for their birth day:
Giovanni Paisiello, the Italian musical composer, 1741, Taranto, Sir P. Malcolm Stewart, 1872.

They died on May the Ninth:
Cardinal de Bourbon, 1590,
Francis, fourth Earl of Bedford, 1641,
Count Zinzendorf, founder of the sect of Moravian Brethren, 1760,
Frederick Schiller, illustrious German poet, 1805, Weimar, and
Nicholas Francis Gay-Lussac, chemist, 1850, Paris.

BUT THERE WAS MORE THAN BIRTHS AND DEATHS ON MAY THE NINTH.
CONSIDER THESE—AND THEIR IMPORT . . .
BLOOD AND THE CROWN JEWELS, 1671,
CAPTAIN KIDD TRIED FOR PIRACY, 1701,
ROYAL ASSENT GIVEN TO CANADA CLERGY RESERVES BILL, 1853,
FEDERAL PARLIAMENT WAS OPENED AT CANBERRA, AUSTRALIA, 1927,
NEW CONSCRIPTION ACT, 1939,
MINISTRIES OF TRANSPORT AND SHIPPING MERGE TO FORM WAR TRANSPORT, 1941,
RUSSIA CAPTURED SEVASTOPOL, 1944,
CHANNEL ISLANDS SURRENDERED, 1945,
END OF WAR IN EUROPE, 1945, AND
MR. T. W. WHITE, AUSTRALIAN MINISTER FOR AIR, APPOINTED HIGH COMMISSIONER IN LONDON, 1951.

May the Tenth

Day dawns—but the night cometh when no man shall work . . .

James Gordon Bennett of the New York Herald *decided to find David Livingstone, the Scots pioneer and missionary lost in darkest Africa. Henry Morton Stanley went and found him, greeting him with the words 'Doctor Livingstone, I presume'. This Stanley died Sir Henry Morton Stanley on May the Tenth, 1904, and those who want to know more of him will find it in his writings, particularly his book* In Darkest Africa.

Events which stand out on the Calendar for this day include,
Parliament order Militia to be mustered against Charles, 1642,
Pitt the younger's second Ministry, 1804,
Outbreak of Indian Mutiny, 1857,
E. M. Chantrell sentenced for wife murder, 1878,
Germany admitted to the League, 1926,
Germany burned the books, 1933,
Germans attacked Holland, 1940,
Mr. Chamberlain resigned, 1940,
Hess landed in Scotland, 1941,
House of Commons was destroyed by enemy action in 1941.

These nine met death on May the Tenth,
Mareschal de Marillac, beheaded at Paris, 1632,
La Bruyère, author of *Caractères*, 1696,
Barton Booth, comedian, 1733, Cowley in Middlesex,
Louis XV, King of France, 1774,
Caroline Matilda, Queen of Denmark, 1775, Zelle,
General de Dampierre, killed at Tamars, 1793,
Katsushuka Hokusai, greatest of Japanese artists, 1849,
A. T. Sheppard, historical novelist, 1947,
Dame Ethel Hope Becher, 1948.

AND SIX BIRTH DAYS STAND OUT,
A. R. J. TURGOT, ILLUSTRIOUS FINANCE MINISTER OF FRANCE IN 1727, AT PARIS,
SIR T. LIPTON, 1850,
VISCOUNT BRYCE, 1838,
SIR REGINALD TYRWHITT, 1870,
LT.-GENERAL SIR RALPH EASTWOOD, 1890,
JOHN DESMOND BERNAL, F.R.S., 1901.

May the Eleventh

Today I have failed,
May God forgive me
And give me a tomorrow.

In 1888, on May the Eleventh, was born one Israel Baline, whom fame knows as Irving Berlin. He was born in Russia but gave U.S.A. 'Alexander's Rag Time Band' and 'God Bless America'. The simple may reflect what harmonies he might have given to the world had he remained in U.S.S.R.: the world is fortunate in that he had a more fruitful base for his genius.

Born on May the Eleventh were:
Cardinal Pole, 1500, at Stoverton Castle, and
Peter Camper, anatomist, 1722, at Leyden.

On May the Eleventh these died,
David I, King of Scots, 1153, Carlisle,
Jacques de Molay, Grand Master of Templars, burnt at Paris, 1310,
Jules-Hardouin Mansard, architect, of Versailles, 1708,
Catherine Cockburn, poetess, 1749,
William Pitt, Earl of Chatham, 1778, Hayes,
Spencer Perceval, English Minister, assassinated, 1812, London,
Madame Récamier, 1849, her beauty lives in the famous picture,
John Brown, M.D., LL.D., who died at Edinburgh, 1882 (author of *Rab and his Friends*),
Tom Cribb, champion boxer, 1848.

THESE EVENTS WERE OF MOMENT IN THEIR DAY.
MAY THE ELEVENTH IS THEIR DATE:
LAST JUDICIAL DROWNING, 1685,
BATTLE OF FONTENOY, 1745, WHEN AN ENGLISH KING WENT INTO BATTLE,
RANGOON TAKEN, 1824,
'BLACK FRIDAY', COMMERCIAL PANIC IN THE CITY, 1860,
AFTER TWO YEARS IN VARIOUS COURTS THE TICHBORNE CASE ENTERED THE COURT OF COMMON PLEAS, 1871,
TURKEY RECOGNIZED ARMENIA'S INDEPENDENCE, 1920,
BRITISH TROOPS LAND IN ICELAND, 1940,
SIGNOR EINAUDI ELECTED PRESIDENT OF ITALY, 1948,
ISRAEL ADMITTED TO U.N. MEMBERSHIP, 1949.

May the Twelfth

The shining light that shineth more and more
Unto the perfect day.

May the Twelfth, 1937, saw the coronation of King George VI and Queen Elizabeth. It is noted that those who come to the throne of Britain come—if not reluctantly—unexpectedly. Edward VII came too late, George V after the death of the Duke of Clarence made him heir apparent, George VI after Edward VIII had renounced his crown, these came to the throne and proved that they who govern not from choice but from duty— govern best.

Born on May the Twelfth were:
John Bell, eminent anatomist, 1763, Edinburgh,
General the Hon. Sir George Cathcart, 1784,
John Russell Hind, astronomer, 1823, Nottingham,
Dante Gabriel Rossetti, poet and artist, 1828, and
The Marquess of Milford Haven, 1919.

Died—some in their beds and some on the scaffold—
These are the names:
Thomas Wentworth, Earl of Strafford, English minister, executed, 1641,
Christopher Smart, poet, 1771,
Sir Charles Barry, R.A., architect of the new Houses of Parliament, 1860,
Baron John Frederick William Herschel, 1871, astronomer,
Smetana, in 1884, and
Josef Pilsudski, first Marshal of Poland, 1935.

THERE WERE STIRRING EVENTS ON MANY A MAY THE TWELFTH IN BYGONE DAYS. HERE ARE SOME:
BUTE MINISTRY TOOK OFFICE, 1762,
WOMEN ADMITTED TO DEGREES BY UNIVERSITY OF LONDON IN 1874,
BRITISH PROTECTORATE OVER NORTH BORNEO, BRUNEI AND SARAWAK, 1888,
WEMBLEY PARK WAS OPENED, 1894,
END OF GENERAL STRIKE, 1926,
ARCOS RAIDED, 1927,
MR. CHURCHILL FORMED HIS GOVERNMENT, 1940,
BERLIN BLOCKADE LIFTED, 1949.

May the Thirteenth

What is the prize?
Mirth—and then sighs.
What is the end?
Who can pretend?
Who really knows?
Man comes—man goes.

He died on May the Thirteenth, 1930. He had sought the North Pole and explored the northern latitudes. He tried to fight for the cause of the League of Nations. He was awarded the Nobel Peace Prize in 1922. He was a great man. He was the Norwegian explorer, politician, humanitarian, statesman, whom men remembered as Fridjof Nansen.

St. John the Silent, an Armenian anchorite, 559, and
St. Peter Regalati, a confessor, 1456, found sainthood on May the Thirteenth.

Empress Maria Theresa in 1717, was born on May the Thirteenth, as was Charles, Marquis of Rockingham, statesman, 1730, and Dante, 1625, the poet of poets,
The great composer, Sir Arthur Sullivan, in 1842, and
Sir R. Ross, in 1857.

These took the ferry—as they say—on this day:
Johan Van Oldenbarneveld, Dutch statesman, beheaded, 1619,
Louis Bourdaloue, French divine, 1704, Paris,
James Basire, 1802, and
Cardinal Fesch, uncle of Napoleon Bonaparte, 1839,
Viscount Milner, 1925.

DOWN THE CENTURIES, MAY THE THIRTEENTH MARKS THESE DOINGS,
EARLIEST KNOWN ACHIEVEMENT OF ARMS KNOWN IN SCOTLAND, DOCUMENT DATED 1334,
RICHARD CROMWELL GIVEN £20,000 TO PAY HIS DEBTS AND TOLD TO LEAVE WHITEHALL WITHIN SIX DAYS, 1659,
UNITED PRESBYTERIAN CHURCH FORMED, 1847,
ALBERT MEMORIAL BEGUN, 1864,
SECOND CHURCH DISCIPLINE ACT, 1903,
SURRENDER OF AXIS FORCES AND CAPTURE OF VON ARNIM, 1943, END OF WAR IN AFRICA.

May the Fourteenth

It is beyond reason
It surpasses rhyme
It is without season
Is enduring time.

A man of many nationalities, Albert Einstein, may now be claimed as a citizen of the world. He would prefer it. His birth day is May the Fourteenth and he was born in 1879 in Germany. He first became Swiss—reverted to German nationality—revolted from German nationality—he is now a naturalized citizen of U.S.A. A Nobel Prize winner—in 1908 he set forth the theory of relativity.

On this day were born:
Gabriel Daniel Fahrenheit, 1686, Danzig,
Robert Owen, philanthropic social reformer, 1771—a socialist pioneer, and
Sir Squire Bancroft, an actor, 1841.

On May the Fourteenth these died:
Henry IV of France, assassinated at Paris, 1610,
Louis XIII of France, 1643, St. Germain-en-Laye,
Professor David Runkenius, 1798, Leyden,
Robert Burns, eldest son of the Scots poet, 1857,
Viscount Allenby, 1936.

EVENTS ON THIS DAY INCLUDE THESE:
L.D.V., LATER HOME GUARD, FOUNDED 1940,
COMMONS TOOK DATE FROM PARLIAMENT OF WINCHESTER, 1265,
DEBUT OF MME PATTI, COVENT GARDEN, 1861,
HOLLAND SURRENDERED, 1940,
AT EDINBURGH, GREATOREX AND THE BROTHERS GRIMSHAW, WERE SENTENCED FOR FORGERIES ON THE UNION BANK, 1867,
LAST PROGRAMME FROM SAVOY HILL, 1932,
CHARLES II PROCLAIMED IN IRELAND, 1660,
FIRST COMPLETE COPY OF 'REVISED' BIBLE WAS PRESENTED TO QUEEN VICTORIA, 1885,
FIRST ISSUE OF 'ILLUSTRATED LONDON NEWS', 1842,
GARIBALDI, DICTATOR OF ITALY, 1860,
DIAMONDS WERE DISCOVERED IN SOUTH AFRICA IN 1867.

May the Fifteenth

The day is over, it is dark,
The wounded soldier on his cot reclines
There is a glimmer—more a spark
The Lady of the Lamp forever shines.

Florence Nightingale was born on May the Fifteenth in 1820. She became a nurse and founded a system. She was ninety when she died, but three years before—knowing only that people were very kind—she was awarded the unique Order of Merit. Few Englishwomen have had an order of more enduring influence than Florence Nightingale, whose birthday is recalled on May the Fifteenth.

Cardinal Alberoni, Spanish minister, in 1664 at Placentia, and Constantine, Marquis of Normandy, 1797, and Pierre Curie, 1859, share this day as birth day.

On May the Fifteenth there died:
Mademoiselle Champmele, celebrated French actress, 1698,
Alexander Cunningham, historian, 1737, London,
Ephraim Chambers, 1740, London,
Dr. John Wall Callcott, musician, 1821,
Edmund Kean, tragedian, 1833,
Thomas Campbell, 1844,
Whitaker, 1895, and
W. J. Locke, 1930, famed for his *Beloved Vagabond*,
Viscount Snowden, 1937.

EVENTS WHICH THE YEARS RECORD ON THIS MAY THE FIFTEENTH INCLUDE:
EXCLUSION BILL, 1679,
FIRST PRIME MINISTER, 1730, SIR R. WALPOLE,
REGENCY BILL WAS PASSED BY PARLIAMENT, 1765,
THE FIRST BROUGHAM FINISHED BY HOOPERS, 1838—IT HAD A SWORDCASE ON THE BACK PANEL,
COIN IMPORTATION BILL CARRIED IN THE COMMONS, 1846,
'REVISED' VERSION ISSUED TO THE PRESS, 1885,
HAGUE CONFERENCE, 1922,
DUKE OF GLOUCESTER FLEW TO GERMANY TO INSPECT BRITISH REGIMENTS, 1947,
PRINCESS ELIZABETH REOPENED WINDSOR GUILDHALL AFTER ITS RENOVATION, 1951.

May the Sixteenth

Every weal hath its woe and every day hath its night.

Her maiden name is Browne. She is known as Mrs. Hemans—Felicia Dorothea Hemans. She died on this day, the Sixteenth of May in 1835. What schoolboy does not know 'Casabianca'?

> The boy stood on the burning deck,
> Whence all but he had fled.

She was beloved by the Victorians and they would be bold who would—with gift of self scrutiny—deny the Victorians showed good taste.

Saints'-days for May the Sixteenth are four in number:
St. Brendan, the Elder, 578,
St. Ubaldus, Bishop of Gubio, 1160,
St. Simon Stock, confessor of Kent, 1265, and
St. John Nepomuc, 1383.

Sir William Petty, the political economist, 1623, Romsey,
Sir Dudley North, merchant, traveller, author of *An Account of Turkey*, 1641,
J. S. Cotman, 1782,
Earl of Elgin, Indian Viceroy, 1849,
Herbert Ernest Bates, 1905,
Were born on May the Sixteenth.

On this day, these passed out of time into the pages of history.
Pope John XXI, killed at Viterno, 1277,
Samuel Bochard (history and languages), 1667, Caen, Normandy,
Dr. Daniel Solander, naturalist, 1782,
Lady Byron, 1800,
Sir William Congreve, in 1828,
George Clint, artist, 1854, Kensington, and
Professor Henslow, botanist, 1861.

EVENTS THERE WERE GALORE—ON MAY THE SIXTEENTH:
ABBEY OF WESTMINSTER BEGAN, 1220,
BATTLE OF ALBUERA, 1811,
ABRAHAM LINCOLN SELECTED AS CANDIDATE FOR THE REPUBLICANS, 1860,
SINO-JAP TREATY AGAINST RUSSIA SIGNED, 1918,
HEAVY FIGHTING NEAR BRUSSELS, 1940.

May the Seventeenth

Well or wicked be his way
Every dog must have its day.

May the Seventeenth is a day of death in the calendar of days, and these are recorded:
Heloise, 1163, Paraclete Abbey,
Botticelli, 1510,
Matthew Parker, Archbishop of Canterbury, 1575, Lambeth,
Catherine I of Russia, widow of Peter the Great, 1727,
Dr. Samuel Clarke, 1729, London,
William Louth(biblical scholarship), 1732, Buriton,
Alexis Claude Clairhaut, mathematician, 1756,
Dr. William Heberden, medical writer, 1801, Windsor,
Prince Talleyrand, 1838, Paris,
Paganini, the violinist, 1840,
The Rt. Hon. George William Forbes, P.C., 1947,
Field Marshal Lord Birdwood, 1951.

Dr. Edward Jenner, the discoverer of vaccination was born on May the Seventeenth, 1749, at Berkeley,
Henry William, Marquis of Anglesey, the statesman, in 1768 and on the same day,
Sir Algernon V. Willis in 1889.

EVENTS OF THE DAY—HERE IS A COLLECTION:
THE HOUSE OF COMMONS RIGHT TO IMPRISON FOR BREACH OF PRIVILEGE WAS CONFIRMED, 1811,
MAFEKING RELIEVED, 1900,
THE DAYLIGHT SAVING ACT WAS PASSED IN 1916,
FIRST PASSENGER ON UNDERGROUND, FOR THIRTY-ONE YEARS, WAS KILLED, 1938,
BELGIAN GOVERNMENT MOVED TO OSTEND, 1940,
KERCH WAS AGAIN IN GERMAN HANDS, 1942,
IT WAS ON MAY THE SEVENTEENTH RUHR DAMS WERE BROKEN IN 1943,
LABOUR PARTY CONFERENCE OPENED AT SCARBOROUGH WHEN MR. HERBERT MORRISON SAID NEXT GENERAL ELECTION PROGRAMME WOULD BE ONE OF CONSOLIDATION, 1948,
NORTH JERUSALEM HEAVILY SHELLED BY ARABS, ST. GEORGE'S CATHEDRAL BEING HIT, 1948.

May the Eighteenth

I pored on books at midnight
I gathered summer flowers
I traded and I bid right
There's nothing in these hours.

For the Scots of the middle of the nineteenth century this is disruption day.
On May the Eighteenth, 1843, the Free Church of Scotland was founded
and those who adhered to it marched out of the Established Church of their
fathers.
A later generation reunited but the reunited church remembers still the
disruption.
On May the Eighteenth in 1804 Napoleon was proclaimed the Emperor of
France—on this same day in 1944 the Polish Army captured Cassino, and
this day is the day of Saint Eric, King of Sweden, martyred in 1151.

Joseph Butler, in 1692, was born on May the Eighteenth as was
Christopher North (John Wilson), in 1785, at Paisley.

They died on May the Eighteenth:
Bishop Nicolas Longespee, 1297,
Bishop Herbert Croft, 1691,
Charles Perrault, miscellaneous writer, to him we owe *Cinderella*,
Sleeping Beauty, and a score more fairy tales, 1703,
Ephraim Chambers, encyclopaedist, 1740,
Dr. Erasmus Darwin, 1802,
Bishop John Douglas, 1807,
Nathaniel Hawthorne, 1864, and
George Meredith, novelist, in 1909.

THE ORDER OF THE BATH WAS REVIVED, 1725,
BRITISH NATIONALS WERE FORBIDDEN TO HELP OR TAKE
PART IN AMERICAN WAR IN 1861,
THERE WAS AN EARTHQUAKE IN NEW ZEALAND IN 1929,
THE R.A.F. BOMBED THE OIL TANKS AT BREMEN, HAMBURG,
AND HANOVER ON MAY THE EIGHTEENTH, 1940,
B.E.A. DISCONTINUED ITS SERVICE TO PRAGUE BECAUSE
OF OBSTRUCTIVE ATTITUDE OF CZECHO-SLOVAK AUTHORI-
TIES, 1951,
IN THE KOREAN WAR, ALLIES WERE FORCED BACK FROM
ALL POSITIONS HELD NORTH OF 38TH PARALLEL, 1951.

May the Nineteenth

Strive—work—and labour
Put forth your powers
Outdo your neighbour
Fill full your hours.

William Ewart Gladstone, author of The Impregnable Rock of the
Holy Scriptures, *and Prime Minister of Britain died on May the*
Nineteenth in 1898.
He founded English Liberalism as a political party—fought Disraeli—
felled trees for exercise at Hawarden—foresaw home rule for Ireland and
believed in peace, retrenchment and reform.

On this day these events find a place in the Calendar of days:
Mary, Queen of Scots, fled to England, 1568,
The Armada set sail, 1588,
Last Act of Uniformity, 1662,
England declared a Commonwealth, 1649,
Halifax Ministry ended, 1715,
Wilkes expelled from the House of Commons, 1764,
Foundation stone of Martyrs Memorial, Oxford, laid, 1841,
Fourth attempt on the life of Queen Victoria, 1849,
Last daylight air raid on London, First World War, 1918,
Epstein's memorial to W. H. Hudson unveiled, 1925,
Steamship *Winkfield* was mined in the Thames Estuary, 1941,
Fifty allied officers shot after escaping from a German prison
camp in 1944.

John Theophilus Fichte, the German philosophical writer, was
born on this day at Rammenau in 1762,
Nellie Melba, 1861.

DIED ON MAY THE NINETEENTH:
FLACCUS ALCUINUS, LEARNED THEOLOGIAN, 804, TOURS,
CHARLES APPERLEY, WRITER ON FIELD SPORTS, 1483,
ANNE BOLEYN, QUEEN OF ENGLAND, BEHEADED, 1536,
ADAM BILLAUT, FRENCH, 1662,
THOMAS GENT, PRINTER OF YORK, 1778,
JAMES BOSWELL, AUTHOR OF 'LIFE OF DR. JOHNSON', 1795,
T. E. LAWRENCE IN 1935, IN A MOTOR-CYCLE ACCIDENT,
BRITAIN WARNED PERSIA THAT REFUSAL TO NEGOTIATE
ON OIL WOULD HAVE SERIOUS CONSEQUENCES, 1951.

May the Twentieth

Fill then these hours—fill fully,
What else can serve you—say
Time is a tyrant-bully
And he will have his way.

It is May the Twentieth—and it is the day, in 1874, when Gilbert Keith Chesterton was born in Kensington. Chesterton might have been the last of the English. He denied himself that title by reviving the English spirit— its faith, its philosophy, its courage, its poetry, its patriotism and, not least, its humour. In England's darkest hours—and many doubtless await her— his spirit will shine eternally.

These, too, were born on May the Twentieth:
De Balzac, 1799, who wrote *The Human Comedy*,
John Stuart Mill, 1806, the economist and philosopher,
Louis Agassiz, 1807, the scientist, and
Sigrid Undset, 1882.

These died on May the Twentieth:
Henry VI, 1471,
Christopher Columbus, 1506, Valladolid,
Nicholas Brady, D.D., joint translator of the Psalms into English,
1726, Clapham,
Thomas Boston, a popular Scots writer on divinity, who wrote
The Four-Fold State, 1732, in Ettrick,
Mary Lamb, 1847,
William Chambers, 1883, the Scots encyclopaedist and
Sir Edward Goschen, 1924.

ON MAY THE TWENTIETH:
SECOND ACT OF OBLIVION WAS PASSED, 1690 (THE PAR-
DONING OF POLITICAL OFFENCES),
FRENCH DEFEATED ADMIRAL BYNG OFF MINORCA, 1756,
ANGLO-U.S. ANTI-SLAVERY TREATY WAS SIGNED, 1861,
LINDBERGH BEGAN HIS FLIGHT, 1927, ACROSS THE
ATLANTIC,
CRETE WAS INVADED BY AIRBORNE TROOPS, 1941,
FIVE THOUSAND AIRCRAFT BASED ON BRITAIN BOMB
TARGETS IN FRANCE AND BELGIUM, 1944,
AND OF ALL THESE THE SECOND ACT OF OBLIVION SEEMS
BEST WORTH REMEMBERING ON MAY THE TWENTIETH.

May the Twenty-first

Politicians, poets, preachers,
Their lights they never hid
And today they are our teachers
They were born—they lived—and did.

May the Twenty-first was the birth day of
Albrecht Dürer, the artist, in 1471 at Nuremberg,
Philip II of Spain, 1527, Valladolid,
Alexander Pope, the poet, 1688,
Francis Egerton, Duke of Bridgewater, promoter of canal navigation in England, 1736,
Bryan Edwards, historian of the West Indies, 1743, Westbury,
John, Lord Lyndhurst, Chancellor of England, 1772, Boston, U.S.,
Elizabeth Fry, the prison reformer, 1780,
General Sikorski, the leader of Poland in 1939, in 1881.

James Graham, the great Marquis of Montrose, on the scaffold in 1650,
Cornelius Van Tromp in 1691, at Amsterdam,
Jacques Maboul, a French preacher, 1723,
Robert Harley, Earl of Oxford, a prime minister of Queen Anne, 1724,
Sir John Hawkins, author of a *History of Music*, etc., 1789,
Dr. Thomas Warton, poet, Professor of Poetry, Oxford, 1790,
Sir George Frampton, 1928, and
Arnold Stephenson Rowntree, worker for adult education, 1951,
all died on May the Twenty-first.

EVENTS OF THE DAY—HERE ARE SOME WHICH MARK MAY THE TWENTY-FIRST:
TREATY OF TROYES, 1420,
COMMUNE OF PARIS (CITY COUNCIL) CONSTITUTION, 1791,
NEW ZEALAND PROCLAIMED A COLONY, 1840,
MANCHESTER SHIP CANAL OPENED, 1894,
LINDBERGH COMPLETED FLIGHT ACROSS THE ATLANTIC, 1927,
DUKE OF YORK, AS LORD HIGH COMMISSIONER, OPENED GENERAL ASSEMBLY, WHICH MARKED THE UNION OF THE CHURCHES IN SCOTLAND, 1929,
ARRAS AND AMIENS CAPTURED BY THE ENEMY, 1940,
DUISBERG AND HANOVER BOMBED, 1944.

May the Twenty-second

If you can fill the unforgiving minute
With sixty seconds' worth of distance run,
Yours is the earth and everything that's in it
And what is more—you'll be a man, my son.

Sir Arthur Conan Doyle was born on May the Twenty-second, 1859. He created a character in fiction as enduring as Robinson Crusoe—he founded modern detective fiction in the person of Sherlock Holmes. It would be enough for most men but Conan Doyle was a doctor, a romantic novelist, an historian, a politician and an investigator of the occult as well. He filled as few have done 'the unforgiving minute'.

The saints of the day are,
Saints Castus and Aemilius, martyrs, 250(?),
St. Basiliscus, Bishop of Comana, in Pontius, martyr, 312,
St. Conall, the abbot,
St. Bobo, confessor, 985, and
St. Yve, confessor, 1353.

On May the Twenty-second,
First Battle of St. Albans and the first battle in the War of the Roses was won, in 1455, by the Yorkists,
Baronets were instituted by James I and VI, 1611,
Battle of Ramillies was fought, 1706,
Mr. Stanley Baldwin's ministry, 1923,
Italy and Germany sign pact, 1939,
Moscow dissolved the Comintern, 1943.

They died on May the Twenty-second:
William de la Pole, statesman, 1450,
Albert Smith, the humorist, 1800,
Maria Edgeworth, the English writer, 1849,
Victor Hugo, 1885,
Most Rev. Andrew Joseph McDonald, Roman Catholic Archbishop of St. Andrews and Edinburgh, 1950.

ALEXANDER POPE, IN 1688, AT LOMBARD STREET, LONDON, WAS BORN ON MAY THE TWENTY-SECOND,
JONATHAN PEREIRA, A PHARMACOLOGIST, 1804, LONDON,
WAGNER, 1813; THAT NAME AND DATE MAKE AN EPOCH,
PRESIDENT TRUMAN SIGNED BILL FOR AMERICAN AID TO GREECE AND TURKEY, 1947.

May the Twenty-third

I met at eve the prince of sleep
His was a still and lovely face
He wandered through a valley steep
Lovely in a lonely place.

When a man is known to fame by his surname only, he has fame indeed.
There is no need for other names for Linnaeus, Mesmer and Ibsen.
They have more than fame in common, these three—for Linnaeus in 1707
and Mesmer in 1733, May the Twenty-third was the day of their birth:
for Ibsen in 1906, May the Twenty-third was the day of his death.
Thomas Hood, the English poet, too, was born on this day in 1789.

Other birth days on May the Twenty-third include those of
Elias Ashmole, antiquary, 1617, Lichfield,
Dr. William Hunter, 1718, Kilbride, Lanarkshire,
Empress Catharine of Russia, 1729, Zerbst Castle, Germany,
James Boaden, a theatrical writer and biographer, in 1762,
Douglas Fairbanks, 1883.

Death claimed these on May the Twenty-third:
Emperor Henry V, 1125, at Utrecht,
Jerome Savonarola, the religious and political reformer and
orator, burnt at Florence, 1498,
William Woollet, engraver, 1785,
Richard Lalor Sheil, poet, politician, 1851, also at Florence,
Sir Archibald Alison, the historian, 1867,
James Grant, the novelist and journalist, 1879,
J. D. Rockefeller, 1937,
Sir Wm. Macnamara Goodenough, former chairman of Barclays
Bank, 1951.

THERE WAS MORE THAN JUST BEING BORN AND DYING ON
MAY THE TWENTY-THIRD. THESE HAPPENED:
CHARLES II EMBARKED AT THE HAGUE FOR ENGLAND,
1660,
NEW ZOO AT WHIPSNADE WAS OPENED IN 1931,
CAPTAIN MAULE RAMSAY WAS ARRESTED, 1940,
AND THE FAMOUS COALITION MINISTRY, MR. CHURCHILL'S
WAR GOVERNMENT, WAS DISSOLVED IN 1945 ON THIS DAY,
CONSTITUTION FOR FEDERAL GOVERNMENT FOR WESTERN
GERMANY PROCLAIMED IN BONN, 1949.

May the Twenty-fourth

If life has any meaning
If living any flower—
This is my only gleaning
That man should live his hour.

May the Twenty-fourth is the day on which one great queen and one king were born. Queen Victoria was born on this day at Kensington in 1819 and her ancestor, George III, was born on the same day in 1738. Field-Marshal Smuts had May the Twenty-fourth for his birth day—he was born in 1870. Sir Arthur Wing Pinero who wrote The Second Mrs. Tanqueray, The Gay Lord Quex, *and many another play in Victorian and Edwardian days, was born in 1855—on May the Twenty-fourth.*
H.M.S. Hood *in 1941, on May the Twenty-fourth, was lost. It was a tragic disaster. Empire Day.*

Robert Bontine Cunningham-Graham, author, born 1852, a great Scot.

These died on the Twenty-fourth of May:
Pope Gregory VII, 1085,
David I, 1153,
Nicolas Copernicus, an astronomer, 1543, at Thorn, Prussia,
Robert Cecil, Earl of Salisbury, Minister to James I, 1612,
George Brydges, Lord Rodney, naval commander, 1792, and
Miss Jane Porter, novelist, 1850, Bristol,
Field Marshal Lord Wavell, great soldier, Viceroy of India and man of letters, 1950.

THESE EVENTS MARK THIS DAY:
RICHARD CROMWELL ABDICATED, 1659,
THE TOLERATION ACT, 1689,
WILL PROVED OF RICHARD ARKWRIGHT, 1843 (EIGHT MILLION POUNDS!),
ITALY AND AUSTRIA AT WAR, 1915,
AMY JOHNSON REACHED DARWIN, 1930 (TWENTY DAYS FLIGHT),
BERLIN BOMBED IN DAYLIGHT, 1944,
B.O.A.C. COMET JET AIR-LINER FLEW TO ROME IN 2 HOURS 13 MINUTES, 1952,
ALL ON THE QUEEN'S BIRTHDAY.

May the Twenty-fifth

I keep six honest serving men
(They taught me all I know)
Their names are What and Why and When,
And How and Where and Who.

In 1879, on May the Twenty-fifth, Max Aitken, who became Lord Beaverbrook, was born. No Canadian ever exerted more influence in Great Britain in two wars than he. His personality and his powerful newspapers are factors which cannot be ignored in the years between 1918 and the Second World War—his father was a Scots minister from West Lothian. He knows his Bible.

May the Twenty-fifth was their birth day.
John Mason Good, a medical writer, in 1764, at Epping,
John Pye Smith, D.D., a learned theologian, 1774, at Sheffield,
Edward Bulwer Lytton, 1803, who wrote *Rienzi—The Last of the Roman Tribunes*—and other novels,
Ralph Waldo Emerson, 1803, who created the Transcendentalist School of Philosophy in the U.S.A.,
Francis Edward Todleben, in 1818, Mitau, Courland,
Tom Sayers, 1826.

They died on this day:
Cardinal D'Amboise, Minister of Louis XII, 1510,
Pedro Calderón, 1681,
Dr. George Fordyce, medical writer and teacher, 1802, London,
Dr. William Paley, author of *Natural Theology*, 1805,
Edmond Malone, critical writer, 1812.

THESE HAPPENED ON THIS DAY:
CHARLES LANDED AT DOVER, 1660,
OXFORD BOAT CREW ROWED FROM DOVER TO CALAIS IN FOUR AND A HALF HOURS, 1885,
BANK HOLIDAYS ACT PASSED, 1871,
MODERN EXPRESS LETTER SYSTEM INTRODUCED, 1891,
MILITARY SERVICE ACT, 1916,
FIRST WOMAN BARRISTER, OLIVE CLAPHAM, 1922,
ANGLO-POLISH TREATY SIGNED IN LONDON, 1939,
FOUR THOUSAND TONS OF HIGH EXPLOSIVE DROPPED ON TOKYO, 1945,
ALL THESE ON MAY THE TWENTY-FIFTH.

May the Twenty-sixth

Roses have thorns
And thorns are briary
Forgetting that, he kept a diary.

*The Civil Service is often the whipping boy of both public and politicians.
It is undeserved. It has had many great men among its members. Not the
least famous is Samuel Pepys who died on May the Twenty-sixth in 1703
at Clapham. He has been acclaimed as the father of the British navy but
his reputation rests on his candour as a diarist and his honesty with himself
in all he did.*

These were death beds on May the Twenty-sixth:
Augustine, first Archbishop of Canterbury, died 604,
The Venerable Bede, historian, 735, Jarrow, Durham,
Thomas Southern, dramatist, 1746,
James Burnet, Lord Monboddo, 1799, Edinburgh,
Francis Joseph Haydn, musical composer, 1809, Vienna,
Admiral Sir Sidney Smith, G.C.B., 1840,
Curwen, inventor of tonic sol-fa, died 1880.

These were born on this day
Charles, Duke of Orleans, 1391,
John Gale, 1680, London,
Shute Barrington, Bishop of Durham, 1734 and
Her Majesty Queen Mary in 1867.

THESE MARK THE CALENDAR FOR TODAY:
HABEAS CORPUS ACT, 1679,
FIRST HANDEL FESTIVAL, 1784,
SIR JOHN FRANKLIN SAILED WITH 'EREBUS' AND 'TERROR',
1845,
LAST PUBLIC EXECUTION IN BRITAIN, 1868,
GAINSBOROUGH'S 'DUCHESS OF DEVONSHIRE' STOLEN,
1876,
GOLD WAS DISCOVERED NEAR KIMBERLEY, 1886,
ANNEXATION OF ORANGE FREE STATE, 1900,
PROFESSOR PICCARD REACHED THE STRATOSPHERE, 1931,
TWENTY-YEAR ANGLO-SOVIET TREATY SIGNED, 1942,
RUSSIA ABOLISHED DEATH PENALTY, 1947,
CONFERENCE OF COMMONWEALTH DEFENCE MINISTERS
ENDED, 1951.

May the Twenty-seventh

The Romans and the Greeks were here
Where now we stand.
They laughed aloud—held back a tear
Give me your hand.
One day like them we shall be dust,
None shall us miss.
What of it, sweet: well you can—just
Give me one kiss.

Enoch Arnold Bennett has a first place in any record of men who knew what to do with his time. He wrote a book on How to Live in Twenty-four Hours a Day. *His greatest and lasting contribution to literature is* The Old Wives' Tale. *He understood women. He was born on May the Twenty-seventh in 1877 in the Potteries—lived and worked in London and Paris and died famous as a great English novelist.*

These things happened on May the Twenty-seventh:
Accession of John to throne, 1199,
Mr. Pitt fought a duel, 1798,
Battle of Tsushima, 1905,
Ministry of Munitions created, 1915,
Bismarck was sunk in 1941, Colonel Britton's voice was heard on the radio to Europe.

Died on this day there were millions, here are the famous:
John Calvin, theologian, 1564, Geneva,
Vincent Voiture, prince of the belles-lettres of France in his day, 1648,
Archibald, Marquis of Argyle, beheaded at Edinburgh, 1661,
Charles de la Rue, eminent French preacher, one of the fabricators of the *Delphin Classics*, 1725,
Comte de Loewendhall, Marshal of France, 1755,
Henry Dundas, first Viscount Melville, statesman, 1811,
Field Marshal T. A. Blamey, 1951.

THESE—A STRANGE GALAXY—WERE BORN ON MAY THE TWENTY-SEVENTH:
CARDINAL LOUIS DE NOAILLES, 1651, PARIS,
REV. T. D. FOSBROKE, ANTIQUARIAN WRITER, 1770,
MRS. BLOOMER, THE FEMININE PIONEER, IN 1818,
ISADORA DUNCAN, 1878.

May the Twenty-eighth

They strive—they toil—their days are bright,
They would wear out—both day and night.

Five of them all have today for their birth day. They are the famous Dionne Quintuplets.
It happened on May the Twenty-eighth, 1934. George I in 1660 had the same birth day. Doctor Beneš, too, was born on this day in 1884.
Thomas Moore was born in Dublin in 1780 on May the Twenty-eighth.
'Oft in the stilly night' . . . is his best-remembered poem.

John Smeaton, the engineer, in 1724, at Ansthorpe, was born on this day as was
William Pitt, Prime Minister of George III, in 1759, and
Lord Alness, 1868 (Secretary of State for Scotland 1916–22).

These died on May the Twenty-eighth:
St. Bernard, of Savoy, 1008,
Admiral de Tourville, 1701, Paris,
Electress Sophia of Hanover, 1714,
George, Earl of Marischal, 1778, Potsdam,
Bishop Richard Hurd, 1808, Hartlebury,
William Eden, Lord Auckland, 1814,
Thomas Howard, Earl of Suffolk, 1826, Walden,
Noah Webster, American lexicographer, 1843, *Webster's Dictionary*,
William Erskine, 1852, Edinburgh,
Lord John Russell, 1878,
Sir George Grove, 1900, and
Lord Avebury, 1913, better known as Sir John Lubbock, scientist, business man and promoter of bank holidays.

THESE CLOSE THE STORY OF MAY THE TWENTY-EIGHTH:
FIRST DERBY DAY, 1779,
ON THIS DAY ALONE IN 1860, DURING A STORM ON THE
COASTS OF BRITAIN, 143 SHIPWRECKS TOOK PLACE,
SECOND COMMUNE OF PARIS SNAPS, 1871,
DANZIG MADE FREE CITY, 1919,
NAZIS WIN DANZIG ELECTIONS, 1933,
CHAMBERLAIN'S MINISTRY, 1937,
BELGIAN ARMY SURRENDERED, 1940,
PRINCESS ELIZABETH OPENED FESTIVAL EXHIBITION OF
INDUSTRIAL POWER, GLASGOW, 1951.

May the Twenty-ninth

He kept it dark—they called him good,
Perhaps the man was right.
This sure is fact—he never would
Sin, in the broad daylight.

On May the Twenty-ninth, 1911, Sir William Schwenck Gilbert died. He asked poignantly, 'Is life a boon' . . . He, with Sir Arthur Sullivan, made the names of 'Gilbert and Sullivan' part of the musical history of these times. No music was ever so popular or so endearing in its appeal.
In 1817 it was on this day that, at Malmaison, the Empress Josephine died.

May the Twenty-ninth saw:
Monarchy re-established by Monk, 1660,
Charles II, ascended 1660,
Loss of the *Royal George*, 1782,
Meeting to establish Bankers' Institute, 1818,
First Whit-Monday bank holiday, 1871,
S.S. *Empress of Ireland* sunk in St. Lawrence after collision with *Storstadt* in 1914,
Admiralty sells 119 warships at once in 1922,
Ostend, Ypres, Lille and other Belgian and French towns lost to the Germans, 1940,
British cruiser *York*, sunk, 1941.

These got away from it all, on May the Twenty-ninth:
Cardinal Beaton, assassinated at St. Andrews, 1546,
Stephen des Courcelles, learned Protestant divine, 1658,
Dr. Andrew Ducarel, English antiquary, 1785, South Lambeth,
Sir Humphrey Davy, 1829, at Geneva,
W. H. Pyne, miscellaneous writer, 1843, Paddington,
Sir Thomas Dick Lauder, Bart., miscellaneous writer, 1848,
John Henry Iles, founder of national band festival, 1951.

BORN ON MAY THE TWENTY-NINTH:
CHARLES II OF ENGLAND, 1630, LONDON,
SARAH, DUCHESS OF MARLBOROUGH, 1660,
LOUIS DAUBENTON, 1716, MONTBARD,
PATRICK HENRY, AMERICAN PATRIOT AND ORATOR—
'GIVE ME LIBERTY OR DEATH'—1736, VIRGINIA,
JOSEPH FOUCHÉ, POLICE MINISTER OF NAPOLEON I, WHO KNEW HIS BUSINESS, 1736, NANTES.

May the Thirtieth

We burn daylight.

On May the Thirtieth, in 1778, in Paris, at the age of eighty-four, there died François Marie Arouet, who called himself Voltaire. He had made a revolution—served two terms in the Bastille—became a friend of Frederick the Great—wrote Candide*—fought all his life against what he believed to be tyranny. He is placed in the foremost rank of those who stood for liberty.*

These died on the same day as Voltaire:
King Arthur, 542,
St. Hubert, 727, Ardennes,
Jerome of Prague, religious reformer, burnt at Constance, 1416,
Jeanne d'Arc, burnt at Rouen, 1431,
Charles IX of France, 1574, Vincennes,
Peter Paul Rubens, painter, 1640,
Charles Montagu, Earl of Halifax, statesman, 1715,
Alexander Pope, poet, 1744, Twickenham,
Dr. Thomas Chalmers, 1847, leader of the Disruption.

These events occurred on May the Thirtieth:
Second attempt on the life of Queen Victoria, 1842,
House of Commons met for the first time in their then 'New' Chamber, 1851,
Mutiny broke out at Lucknow, 1857,
Independence of Iraq recognized by Great Britain, 1930,
Constitution of Malta suspended, 1930,
British completed evacuation of Rhineland, 1930,
Rationing introduced into Germany, 1939,
Dunkirk, 1940.

BORN ON THIS DAY WERE:
HENRY IV, 1366,
PETER THE GREAT OF RUSSIA, 1672, MOSCOW,
JOHN CHARLES, THIRD EARL OF SPENCER, CHANCELLOR OF THE EXCHEQUER, 1782,
SAMUEL SPALDING, WRITER IN PHYSIOLOGY, THEORY OF MORALS, AND BIBLICAL CRITICISM, 1807, LONDON,
ALFRED AUSTIN, 1835, THE POET LAUREATE WHO DECLARED LIFE WAS WORTH LIVING STILL,
BY ORDER IN COUNCIL, NEW CONSTITUTION IN NIGERIA PROMULGATED BY THE KING, 1951.

May the Thirty-first

The road is before me. I travel,
Light footed, light hearted—but where,
My destiny who will unravel,
God, how shall I know when I'm there?

On May the Thirty-first, 1819, Walt Whitman was born. He was a poet who knew what he wanted and did not grudge the price. 'I loafe and invite my soul' was one of the most revealing lines in his many poems. He cared for men and the open road and freedom and the awakening United States. He leaves an abiding influence on both English and American thought and literature.

He realized three ambitions. He wedded an heiress. He won a liberal philosophy, not one of a little England but of an imperial destiny. He wrote one of the great studies of Napoleon. He died on May the Thirty-first, 1929. He was the Earl of Rosebery.

Events of the day:
Dissolution of the Beefsteak Club, 1869, but it opened again,
Naval Defence Act passed, 1890,
The Siberian Railway begun, 1891,
Treaty of Peace with Boers signed, 1902,
Union Day, South Africa, 1910,
The Battle of Jutland, 1916,
End of Battle of Crete, 1941,
Her Majesty received honorary degree at Manchester University and, with Princess Margaret, left Liverpool for Belfast, 1951,
These on the last day of May.

These died too:
Tintoretto, 1594,
Bishop Simon Patrick, 1707, Ely,
Philip, Duke of Wharton, 1731, Tarragona,
Frederick William I of Prussia, 1740,
Haydn, 1809,
Charlotte Brontë, novelist, 1855.

THESE WERE BORN ON MAY THE THIRTY-FIRST:
DR. JAMES CURRIE, MISCELLANEOUS WRITER, 1756, KIRKPATRICK-FLEMING,
LUDWIG TIECK, GERMAN POET, NOVELIST, AND DRAMATIST 1773.

JUNE

THIRTY DAYS

June the First

. . . 'Give me health and a day and I will make the pomp of emperors ridiculous' . . .

It was on the First of June that the mob collected on Blackheath to march on London. Revolutions have not gone well in London. Jack Cade, who led the one on June the First, 1450, was no more successful than his successors. London apparently even in the fifteenth century had learned to 'take it'. 'Silent' revolution is the British way. It should be watched, perhaps.

June the First is the First day of the sixth month—the year reaches its meridian—it is a time for out-door occasions. The city of Melbourne was founded on June the First in 1836,
The first cable connecting England and Ireland was opened in 1851, and, eighty-seven years later, in the same waters, in 1938, ninety lives were lost in the *Thetis* disaster.
These were out of doors in June.

Indoors, Robert Cecil, Earl of Salisbury, Minister to Elizabeth and James I, was born in 1560, and so was
John Masefield in 1878, and
Air Commodore Sir Frank Whittle, 1907.

Indoors, Gilray, the caricaturist, died in 1815,
Sir David Wilkie in 1841,
Charles Lever, the Irish novelist, 1872,
James Gordon Bennett, American journalist, in 1872, and
Sir Hugh Walpole, English novelist, in 1941, all on June the First.

FOR THE REST—AND THERE ARE MANY EVENTS—RANDOM RESEARCH RECOLLECTS THE ESTABLISHMENT OF THE BANK OF IRELAND IN 1783,
JOHN ADAMS, FIRST AMBASSADOR FROM UNITED STATES, PRESENTED HIS CREDENTIALS TO THE KING IN 1785,
PRINCE ALBERT'S MAIDEN SPEECH IN GREAT BRITAIN AT THE MEETING FOR THE ABOLITION OF THE SLAVE TRADE IN 1840,
FIRST OFFICIAL WAR MEDALS FOR THE BATTLES OF THE PENINSULAR WAR WERE ORDERED TO BE STRUCK, 1847,
CLOTHES RATIONING, A WARTIME NECESSITY, 1941,
EIGHTH ARMY CAPTURED FROSINONE, 1944,
LORD OGMORE APPOINTED MINISTER OF CIVIL AVIATION, 1951.

June the Second

Now's the day and now's the hour
See the front of battle lour . . .

Two campaigners died this day—one an Italian and the other a Devon man.
Garibaldi, who first made a shirt a uniform, died in 1882, and Buller—
Sir Redvers Buller, V.C.—who commanded in the opening stages of the
South African War, 1899 to 1902, died in 1908.
James Douglas, the Earl of Morton and Regent of Scotland, was beheaded
in Edinburgh on June the Second in 1581.

June the Second events . . .
Claimants to Scots throne appealed to Edward, 1291,
Gordon Riots began (they lasted until the Eighth), 1780,
First double flight over the Channel in 1910,
Italian Army crossed Isonzo; Austrians defeated, 1915,
Grand Fleet returned to base from Jutland, and reported ready for
sea 9.45 p.m., 1916,
Kiel Canal attacked, Berlin and Ruhr raided, 1941,
Dutch Harbour in Alaska raided by Japs, 1942,
Valmontone and Belletri captured, 1944,
Viceroy handed to Congress, Muslim and Sikh leaders Britain's
plan of procedure for transfer of power in India, 1947,
Queen Elizabeth visited the cotton mills in Lancashire in 1948,
In Korean War, United Nations advance across the 38th Parallel
—enemy casualties 100,000, 1951.

Thomas, Duke of Norfolk, executed, 1572, Tower of London,
Sir Edward Leigh, 1671, Rushall,
Hermann Darewski, composer, 1947,
Field-Marshal Sir Claude W. Jacob, corps commander, First
World War, 1948, these died on June the Second.

BORN ON THIS DAY WERE,
NICOLAS LE FEVRE, 1544, PARIS,
JAN SOBIESKI, POLAND, 1624,
THOMAS HARDY, 1840, SURELY ONE OF THE GREAT
ENGLISH NOVELISTS, AND
SIR EDWARD ELGAR, 1857, SURELY ONE OF THE GREAT
ENGLISH COMPOSERS,
MARQUIS DE SADE, 1740,
SIR GERALD WOODS WOLLASTON, M.V.O., 1874.

June the Third

Sweet childish days that were as long
As twenty days are now.

June the Third was the birth day of Sydney Smith in 1771, the brightest wit that ever shone in the Church of England. He had the advantage of sharpening his intelligence by living for a long time in Scotland. He had a low opinion of Scots sense of humour. He declared it required a surgical operation before a Scotsman could see a joke.

Birth days on June the Third include,
Dr. John Gregory, miscellaneous writer, Aberdeen, 1724,
Dr. James Hutton, one of the founders of geology, 1726,
Robert Tannahill, Scottish poet, Paisley, 1774,
Richard Cobden, the advocate of Free Trade, 1804,
Jefferson Davis, President of the United States, 1808,
Sir Flinders Petrie, 1853,
George V, 1865, and
Lord McGowan, 1874.

These died on this day,
Bishop (John) Aylmer, 1594, Fulham,
William Harvey, discoverer of the circulation of the blood, 1657,
Admiral Opdam, blown up at sea, 1665,
Jethro Tull, speculative experimenter in agriculture, 1740,
James Thomson, author of *City of Dreadful Night*, 1882.

AND THESE THINGS MEN SAW OR HEARD ON THIS DAY,
FIRST SADLER'S WELLS THEATRE, 1683,
FAMOUS PRITCHARD PRISON TRIAL OPENED IN EDINBURGH, 1865,
RULE AGAINST SERVICES SMOKING IN THE STREETS ABOLISHED, 1886,
ALBANIAN INDEPENDENCE, UNDER ITALIAN PROTECTION, PROCLAIMED, 1917,
DUKE OF WINDSOR MARRIED MRS. SIMPSON, 1937,
BRITAIN'S FIRST CONSCRIPTION IN PEACE, 1939,
GERMAN BOMBERS ATTACKED PARIS, 1940,
887 BRITISH SHIPS USED IN EVACUATION OF TROOPS FROM DUNKIRK, 1940,
INDIAN LEADERS RECEIVED FAVOURABLY BRITISH PROPOSALS FOR TRANSFER OF POWER, 1947.

June the Fourth

Some men wish they had spent their days and hours differently . . .

Casanova was what might be called a gay lad: a Lothario, a boy for the girls. On June the Fourth he died in the year 1789, and Casanova has left behind him a pattern that some wish they could follow and others feel should be at all cost avoided.

On June the Fourth there also died in their respective years:
Meret, a commentator on ancient classics, at Rome, in 1585,
Archbishop Juxon in Oxford, 1663,
In 1743 Sir Charles Wager,
In 1823 Marshal Davoust,
In Paris, in 1849, Marguerite, Countess of Blessington, novelist,
In London, in 1828, Wyon, the engraver,
F. R. Spofforth, 1926, and
Kaiser Wilhelm II of Germany, at Doorn, in 1941,
Death ends the story for persons, but events endure to build up the fabric of history.

On this day, in 1731, perjury was made a hanging crime,
One hundred years later the Reform Bill was passed in 1832,
In 1845, on June the Fourth, Mexico declared war on U.S.A.,
In 1860 the then Prince of Wales was invited to visit America,
On this day in 1867 London saw the first production in Britain of Verdi's *Don Carlos*, and going down the years with rapidity it is recalled that the Treaty with Hungary was signed in 1920, and coming nearer to today, it was on June the Fourth that the Allies entered Rome in 1944,
Lord Simon of Wythenshawe was appointed chairman of the B.B.C., 1947.

THIS JUNE THE FOURTH WAS THE BIRTH DAY OF GEORGE III OF GREAT BRITAIN IN 1738, BORN IN LONDON, AND JOHN SCOTT, EARL OF ELDON, CHANCELLOR OF ENGLAND, IN 1751,
JAMES PENNETHORNE, ARCHITECT IN WORCESTER, 1801,
VISCOUNT WOLSELEY IN 1833,
THE EARL OF HALSBURY, 1908,
THERE WERE OTHER BIRTH DAYS ON JUNE THE FOURTH, BUT THESE WILL SERVE TO REMIND US THAT EVERY DAY IS SOMEONE'S BIRTH DAY.

June the Fifth

Which day the goddess marks with a whiter stone . . .

June the Fifth is favoured as a day for the birth of philosophers.
Socrates was born, it is asserted, on June the Fifth in 468 B.C.,
Adam Smith was born at Kirkcaldy, in Scotland, on June the Fifth, 1723, and
Keynes—Lord Keynes at the end—was born in 1883.
Socrates let Plato do his writing for him,
Adam Smith wrote The Wealth of Nations,
Keynes wrote The Economic Consequences of Mr. Churchill *among others.*

These are other birth days,
Joseph de Tournefort, botanist, 1656,
Ernest Augustus, King of Hanover, 1771 and
Stravinski in 1882.

These died on June the Fifth:
Orlando Gibbons, 1625,
Rev. Dr. Henry Sacheverell, 1724,
Carl Maria von Weber, musical composer, London, 1826,
T. H. Lister, novelist, 1842, London,
George IV, 1830, and
He who is remembered as O. Henry, 1910—the 'de Maupassant' of America,
Lord Kitchener, drowned, 1916,
Sir Charles Madden, 1935.

IT WAS ON THIS DAY THAT
ST. BARTHOLOMEW'S HOSPITAL WAS FOUNDED, 1123,
A BALLOON (RAISED BY HOT AIR) MADE ITS FIRST ASCENT IN 1783,
IT WAS DECIDED WOMEN WERE TO BE HANGED, NOT BURNT, FOR COINING, 1790,
'SHANNON' AND 'CHESAPEAKE' ACTION AT SEA IN 1813,
FIRST Q-SHIP ACTION OCCURRED, 1915,
PRINCE ALBERT BECAME DUKE OF YORK, 1920,
RAMSAY MACDONALD'S SECOND MINISTRY BEGAN IN 1929,
HITLER PROCLAIMED A WAR OF TOTAL ANNIHILATION OF HIS ENEMIES, 1940,
HANDLEY-PAGE HERMES V FLEW LONDON TO PARIS IN 59 MINUTES, 1951.

June the Sixth

Be not therefore anxious for the morrow,
For the morrow will be anxious for itself.

June the Sixth, in 1944, was a day of commotion, confusion, confidence,
confirmation and the preliminary to conquest. It was a day of decision, daring,
determination, distinction, and destiny.
It was 'D' day—the beginning of the end.
Three years before to a day, 'Colonel Britton' had proclaimed over the
radio to Europe that Europe would be freed.
'D' Day was the fulfilment of that promise.

Born on this day were:
Diego Velazquez, eminent Spanish artist, 1599, Seville,
Pierre Corneille, French dramatist, 1606, Rouen,
Pushkin, 1799,
The Very Rev. W. R. Inge, 1860,
Scott of the Antarctic, 1868, and
Thomas Mann, 1875, the German novelist.

Died on this day—a vast company—these are recorded:
Ludovico Giovanni Ariosto, eminent Italian poet, 1533, Ferrara,
Memmon de Coehorn, eminent engineer, the 'Vauban of Holland',
1704, The Hague,
George, Lord Anson, eminent naval commander, 1762,
Patrick Henry, American patriot and orator, 1799,
Pope Gregory XVI, 1846,
Cavour, Italian statesman, 1861,
James E. Agate, critic and essayist, 1947.

EVENTS GALORE ON JUNE THE SIXTH—HERE ARE SOME,
FIRST CRUSADE REACHED JERUSALEM, 1099,
JAMES, DUKE OF YORK, BECAME THE FIRST LORD OF THE
ADMIRALTY, AND FIRST LORD HIGH ADMIRAL, 1660,
TRANSIT OF VENUS OVER THE SUN, 1760,
FIRST FACTORY ACT PASSED UNDER THAT NAME, 1844,
ABOLITION OF 'CLOTHING COLONELS' BY WARRANT, 1854,
STORAGE OF ELECTRICITY MADE KNOWN, 1881,
U.S. SENATE EXPRESSED SYMPATHY WITH I.R.A., 1919,
KING OF NORWAY ARRIVED IN THAMES ON A VISIT, 1951,
SOUTH AFRICAN SENATE PASSED ON THIS DAY SEPARATE
REPRESENTATION BILL, 1951.

June the Seventh

On June the Seventh in 1614 something happened to which this over-governed world may look back with a twinge of pardonable envy. It was on this day that the Addled Parliament was dissolved. During its sittings it never passed a single Act of Parliament. Some think that government which governs the least governs the best. The Addled Parliament has for these a special significance.

The birth days are,
John Rennie, engineer, 1761, Prestonkirk, Haddingtonshire,
Robert Jenkinson, Earl of Liverpool, Prime Minister of George IV, 1770,
Rev. W. D. Conybeare, geologist, 1787, London,
Sir James Young Simpson, 1811,
R. D. Blackmore, 1825,
Paul Gauguin, 1848,
Sir Landon Ronald, 1873,
The Earl of Clarendon, 1877.

Scotland's King, Robert the Bruce, died in 1329,
Augustin Daly, 1899, and
Sir Herbert Edward White, 1947.

EVENTS WHICH HAVE SURVIVED THE YEARS AND FELL ON THIS DAY ARE:
BEGINNING OF FIELD OF CLOTH OF GOLD, 1520 (LASTED UNTIL 24TH),
HENRY VIII BEGAN ON THE SMALLER ABBEYS, 1525,
PETITION OF RIGHT, 1628,
FOUNDATION OF ROYAL EXCHANGE, 1656,
VAUXHALL GARDENS OPENED, 1732,
REFORM BILL PASSED, 1832,
CANADIAN FISHERIES GRANTED TO U.S., 1854,
GLADSTONE'S FIRST HOME RULE BILL THROWN OUT, 1886,
NORWEGIAN DIET DECIDED TO SEPARATE FROM SWEDEN, 1905,
FIRST MEETING OF THE ULSTER PARLIAMENT, 1921,
BANK OF INTERNATIONAL SETTLEMENTS ESTABLISHED AT BASLE, 1929,
MR. BALDWIN'S THIRD MINISTRY, 1935,
KING GEORGE VI AND QUEEN ELIZABETH VISITED U.S.A. IN 1939.

June the Eighth

The morning sun never lasts a day.

*It was in Baltimore in 1809 that he died who said 'Mankind is my country
—to do good is my religion'. His name was Tom Paine, who wrote* The
Rights of Man, *and who wrote, too, his character into the Constitution
of the United States. He died on June the Eighth. His body was brought
to England but was lost. His soul goes marching on for all that.*

There are no happy returns for most of these birth days, but men
remember them:
Alexander Cagliostro, remarkable impostor, 1743, Palermo,
Robert Stevenson, engineer, 1772, Glasgow,
Robert Schumann, 1810,
Charles Reade, the novelist, 1814,
John Everett Millais, the Victorian painter, 1829,
Lt.-Gen. Sir Ronald Mackenzie Scobie, 1893.

They died on June the Eighth,
Emperor Nero, 68, Rome,
Mohammed, founder of the Moslem religion, 632,
Edward, 'The Black Prince', 1376, Westminster,
Sir Thomas Randolph, minister of Elizabeth, 1590,
Pulteney, Earl of Bath, statesman, 1764,
Andrew Jackson, President of United States, in 1837,
Sarah Siddons, 1831.

'ARTICLES OF RELIGION' PUBLISHED, 1536,
LIVERPOOL'S FIRST MINISTRY, 1812,
GERMANIC CONFEDERATION INSTITUTED, 1815,
OFFICE OF SECRETARY OF STATE FOR WAR DIVIDED FROM
THAT OF COLONIES, 1854,
BETTING ACT PASSED, 1874,
R.A.F. FORMED AS AN INDEPENDENT FORCE IN 1918,
THEIR MAJESTIES ARRIVED IN WASHINGTON, 1939,
ALLIES INVADED SYRIA, 1941,
INCREASED ENEMY RESISTANCE IN NORMANDY FAILED TO
HALT ALLIED ADVANCE, 1944,
VICTORY DAY CELEBRATED THROUGHOUT THE EMPIRE,
1946,

THEY ALL BEFELL ON JUNE THE EIGHTH.

June the Ninth

Night's candles are burnt out and jocund day,
Stands tiptoe on the misty mountain's top.

June the Ninth, 1672, was the birth day of Peter the Great. He learned shipbuilding and to that extent founded the industrial system which the U.S.S.R. inherits today. June the Ninth in 1781, at Wylam, in Northumberland, saw the birth of another who helped forward the industrial system which by machines has relieved men of toil. He was George Stephenson, the designer of the 'Rocket' and the creator of railways. June the Ninth saw, too, the death in 1870 of a critic of the Industrial Revolution—Charles Dickens died on this day.

They were born on June the Ninth,
Andrew M. Ramsay, author of *Travels of Cyrus*, 1686, Ayr,
John Howard Payne, American actor and dramatist, 1792, New York,
Schamyl, patriotic imam of Circassia, 1797,
Admiral Sturdee, 1859,
Sir Basil Brooke, 1888.

They died on June the Ninth,
Jeanne d'Albret, Queen of Navarre, mother of Henry IV, 1572,
Secretary Maitland, 1573, Edinburgh,
William Lily, astrologer, 1681, Walton,
Benedict Pictet, learned Protestant divine, 1724, Geneva,
Dr. William Kendrick, 1779,
Louis XVII, of France, 1795, Temple, Paris,
Dr. Abraham Rees, encyclopaedist, 1825, Finsbury,
G. P. R. James, 1866,
Rajah Brooke, 1868,
Sir Walter Besant, 1901,
Admiral Sir Henry Harwood, victor of Battle of the River Plate, 1950.

ON THIS DAY HAYMARKET AND ITS NEIGHBOURS SUFFERED FROM A SEVERE HAILSTORM—AND NOWHERE ELSE, 1803,
EDINBURGH FREE LIBRARY OPENED, 1890,
INVERNESS 'COURIER' INVENTED TERM 'LOCH NESS MONSTER', 1933,
KING HAAKON LEFT NORWAY FOR BRITAIN, 1940,
IRAQ BROKE WITH ITALY, 1941.

June the Tenth

Sixty years to eat and drink,
Sixty years to fill the scene,
Sixty years to plan and think,
Sixty years to be a queen.

It adorns and it delights. It is like nothing else that ever was on sea or land. It has been scorned by the superior but pleases the simple. It is the memorial to Prince Albert the Good, erected in Hyde Park, London, and unveiled on June the Tenth, in 1861.
Queen Victoria liked that day for in 1854 on the same day the Crystal Palace, first erected in Hyde Park, was reopened by her at Sydenham. Less auspiciously, she may have recalled that in 1840, on the same day, an attempt was made on her life.

The birth days of today are,
James, Prince of Wales, commonly called 'the Pretender', 1688,
Sir Edwin Arnold, the scholar who wrote *The Light of Asia*, 1832,
Lord Raglan, Lord Lieutenant of Monmouthshire, 1885,
Lieutenant Philip Mountbatten, 1921.

On this June the Tenth they died:
Emperor Frederick Barbarossa, 1190, Cilicia,
Camoens, Portuguese poet, 1580,
James Smith, promoter of sub-soil ploughing, 1850, Kinzean-cleuch, Ayrshire,
Rimsky-Korsakov, 1908,
Matteoli, murdered, 1924.

HISTORY RECORDS THESE EVENTS ON THIS DAY,
FIRST BOAT RACE, 1829,
EXPLOSIVES ACT (PACKING AND CONVEYANCE), 1904,
FIRST AUSTRIAN NOTE ON PEACE DRAFT PRESENTED, 1919,
ITALY INVADED FRANCE, 1940,
NARVIK EVACUATED, 1940,
CANADA AND NEW ZEALAND DECLARED WAR ON ITALY, 1940,
LIDICE, 1942,
EX-KING MICHAEL OF RUMANIA AND PRINCESS ANN OF BOURBON PARMA MARRIED IN ATHENS, 1948,
UNVEILING OF 51ST DIVISION MEMORIAL AT ST. VALÉRY-EN-CAUX, 1950.

June the Eleventh

All comes out even at the end of the day—

One thousand one hundred and eighty-four years before the Christian Era, as far as can be ascertained, it was on June the Eleventh that Troy was destroyed. It seemed an end, as events so often do, in history, but at this distance men know it was only an episode in their strange, eventful history. It is not a day of days. It was a day.
It was the day, too, on which in England the 'Mad' Parliament met at Oxford in 1258—it was the day on which the Dutch entered the Medway in 1664, it was June the Eleventh.

The occurrences with which this day is associated include:
William II landed in Ireland, 1690,
First Bishop of Liverpool consecrated, 1880,
Allies demanded abdication of Constantine of Greece, 1917,
Channel Tunnel Scheme squashed, 1930,
Russia shared in Lend-Lease, 1942,
Australians landed in British North Borneo, 1945,
South African Assembly passed Bill to curb Communism, 1951.

Died on this day,
Roger Bacon, 1292, Oxford,
James III, 1488,
Sir Kenelm Digby, 1665,
Duc de Vendôme, French commander, 1712,
George I of England, 1727, near Osnabrück, Hanover,
Dr. William Robertson, historian, 1793, Edinburgh,
Dugald Stewart, 1828, Edinburgh,
Rev. Dr. Alexander Crombie, 1842, London,
Sir John Franklin, 1847,
Rev. Professor Baden Powell, 1860, London,
Stephen L. Gwynn, Irish writer, 1950,
All famous names.

THESE WERE BORN ON THIS DAY,
GEORGE WITHER, POET, 1588, BENTWORTH, HANTS,
JAS. MARSHAL KNITT, 1696,
JOHN CONSTABLE, R.A., 1776,
MRS. H. WARD, 1851,
THE MARQUESS OF ZETLAND, 1876.

June the Twelfth

Each succeeding day is the pupil of its predecessor.

June the Twelfth was the birth day of Anthony Eden in 1897. It was the same day on which Charles Kingsley was born in 1819. It is the day on which Matthew Arnold died in 1888. It is a day when, recollecting Matthew Arnold, men may well remind themselves of his aim 'to see life steadily and see it whole'.
Winston Churchill visited the beachheads on this day in 1943, and in 1866 William Ewart Gladstone—an early Prime Minister—introduced his Reform Bill.

Harriet Martineau, novelist, historian, miscellaneous writer, 1802,
Sir Oliver Lodge, 1851,
Julia Neilson, the actress, 1869,
Anthony Eden, 1897, were born on June the Twelfth.

These died,
James III of Scotland, killed near Bannockburn, 1488,
James, Duke of Berwick, French commander, 1734, Philipsburgh,
William Collins, poet, 1759, Chichester,
General Pierre Augereau, 1816,
Edward Troughton, astronomical instrument maker, 1835,
Rev. Dr. Thomas Arnold, miscellaneous writer, eminent teacher, 1842, Rugby,
Rev. John Hodgson, author of *History of Northumberland*, 1845,
Dr. Robert Brown, eminent botanist, 1858,
All on June the Twelfth.

EVENTS WHICH MEN RECALL ON JUNE THE TWELFTH ARE: ACT OF SETTLEMENT PASSED (LIMITED THE SUCCESSION TO A PROTESTANT) 1701,
ROYAL ASSENT GIVEN TO THE BILL REPEALING DUTY ON PAPER, 1801,
PALMERSTON'S SECOND MINISTRY, 1859,
MAGNETIC NEEDLE TELEGRAPH PATENTED, 1869,
GLADSTONE RESIGNED 1885—SALISBURY SUCCEEDED,
TURKISH PEACE DELEGATION IN FRANCE, 1919,
LAMPEDUSA SURRENDERED, 1943,
OPENING OF NEW AUSTRALIAN PARLIAMENT BEGAN CELEBRATIONS OF 50TH ANNIVERSARY OF FIRST COMMONWEALTH PARLIAMENT, 1951.

[171]

June the Thirteenth

And he died in a good old age,
Full of days, riches and honour.

There is nothing so beautiful as a birth day, June the Thirteenth was the birth day of Agricola, the Roman general, who was born at Fréjus in Provence in A.D. 46. It was in 1752, the birth day, if you please, of Frances Burney as well as that of Madame d'Arblay. The Irish poet, W. B. Yeats, was born on June the Thirteenth in 1865 and the great scientist, Clerk Maxwell, was born on the same day in 1831.
There are two Thomases, Dr. Thomas Arnold was born at Cowes in 1795 and Thomas Young, the natural philosopher, was born at Melverton in Somerset in 1733, both on June the Thirteenth.

These died on June the Thirteenth,
Richard Lovell Edgeworth, writer on education, 1817, Edgeworthstown, Ireland, and
Sir Henry Segrave, a king of speed, in 1930, at Windermere.

RECORDED ON JUNE THE THIRTEENTH ARE:
SEVEN CLERGYMEN DISPOSSESSED A MAN OF SEVEN DEVILS AT BRISTOL, 1788,
THE GREAT QUEEN MADE HER FIRST RAILWAY JOURNEY, 1842,
FRENCH PARLIAMENT ADOPTED SECRET BALLOT, 1913,
DUTCH ACQUIESCE IN BRITISH CONVOY ARRANGEMENTS, 1918,
SIX THOUSAND BRITISH TROOPS SURROUNDED NEAR ST. VALÉRY AND TAKEN PRISONER, 1940,
BLACK DAY IN THE DESERT, 1942, EVACUATION OF KNIGHTSBRIDGE IN NORTH AFRICAN CAMPAIGN,
ISLAND OF LINOSA CAPITULATED, 1943,
AMERICAN TRANSPORT PLANE CRASHED INTO MOUNTAIN TOP IN WEST VIRGINIA, THE FIFTY OCCUPANTS WERE KILLED, 1947,
GERMAN FREIGHTER, SAILING UNDER ALLIED CONTROL COMMISSION ORDERS, BERTHED AT CORK, AS CAPTAIN AND CREW DID NOT WISH TO RETURN TO LONDON, 1947,
CONFERENCE ON CENTRAL AFRICA RECOMMENDED THAT NORTHERN AND SOUTHERN RHODESIA AND SOUTH NYASALAND SHOULD FEDERATE AS BRITISH CENTRAL AFRICA, 1951.

June the Fourteenth

The day has eyne,
The night has ears.

The fighting men had it almost to themselves on June the Fourteenth. In 1645 it was the day of the Battle of Naseby and Cromwell. In 1800 it was the day of the Battle of Marengo, when Napoleon defeated the Austrians and General Louis Dessaix was killed. On this day in 1662 Sir Henry Vane was beheaded in the tower of London and on the same day in 1800 General Kleber was assassinated in Cairo.
Hitler met Mussolini for the first time on June the Fourteenth, in Rome, in 1934, and, as a consequence then unseen, Franklin Delano Roosevelt, on the same day in 1942, published his 'Four Freedoms' to the world.

Thomas Pennant, naturalist, miscellaneous writer, 1723,
John Gibson Lockhart, 1797, and
Lord Strathcona, 1891, were born on this day.

Father Garasse, French Jesuit controversialist, 1631, Poitiers,
Marin Leroi, sieur de Gombertville, author of *Polexandre* and other romances, 1674,
Dr. Ralph Bathurst, 1704, Oxford,
Claude Fleury, confessor to Louis XV, 1723,
Edmund Halley, 1742,
Colin Maclaurin, mathematician, 1746,
Edward Fitzgerald, 1883, and
Mrs. Pankhurst, 1928. All died on June the Fourteenth.

THESE EVENTS ARE ASSOCIATED WITH THIS DAY,
DION BOUCICAULT'S FIRST APPEARANCE IN LONDON, 1852,
KAISER'S FLEET BILL PRESENTED TO REICHSTAG, 1912,
ALLIED ECONOMIC CONFERENCE IN PARIS, 1916,
GERMANS ENTERED PARIS, 1940,
EVACUATION OF SCHOOLCHILDREN IN GREATER LONDON
BEGAN, 1940,
OBERHAUSEN BOMBED, 1943,
GENERAL DE GAULLE IN NORMANDY, 1944,
THE KING AND QUEEN AND PRINCESSES WENT TO SAND-
HURST WHERE NEW COLOURS WERE PRESENTED, 1947,
FLYING BOAT BASE AT SOUTHAMPTON OPENED, 1948,
BRITAIN AND UNITED STATES REACHED AGREEMENT ON
SUBSTANCE OF JAPANESE PEACE TREATY, 1951.

June the Fifteenth

Hope comes with dawn: day lessens grief,
Men I've heard declare
Their troubles must be short and brief
Mine are the day's despair.

Hail Freedom on June the Fifteenth. In 1215 Magna Charta was signed on
that day.
The British Parliament—the famous Coalition Government under Winston
Churchill—was dissolved on June the Fifteenth, 1945.
There were other endings on June the Fifteenth. Wat Tyler's rebellion
ended with his death at Smithfield in 1381.
Mary, Queen of Scots, surrendered at Carberry Hill in 1567,
St. Just was guillotined in Paris in 1794, and President Polk, the least
well known of the Presidents of the U.S.A., died in 1849 on June the
Fifteenth.

This day is marked with these events,
Scots permitted to have the Bible in the vulgar tongue, 1542,
Anson arrived at Spithead with £1,600,000 worth of Spanish loot,
1744,
Graham went over Niagara Falls in a barrel and survived, 1887,
Lord Rhondda, food controller, 1917,
Alcock and Brown flew the Atlantic, 1919,
British offer of Union with France rejected, 1940,
Japan bombed by 'Super Fortresses', 1944,
Ribbentrop captured, 1945.

They left life behind them on this day,
Philip the Good of Burgundy, 1467, Bruges,
René Aubert de Vertot, French historian, 1735, Paris,
James Short, maker of reflecting telescopes, 1768,
Francis Pilatre de Rosier, killed by falling from a balloon, 1785,
near Boulogne,
Thomas Campbell, poet, 1844, Boulogne.

These were born on June the Fifteenth,
Edward 'the Black Prince', 1330, Woodstock,
Thomas Randolph, poet, 1605, Badby, Northamptonshire,
Anthony Francis de Fourcroy, eminent French chemist, 1755,
Hablot K. Browne, 1815,
Sir Charles Madden, 1906, all on the Fifteenth of June.

June the Sixteenth

If men had sense, and used their reasons,
They would not grieve nor fret,
They'd fill the hours through all the seasons
And would die—without regret.

On June the Sixteenth in 1722 died John Churchill who had become Duke of Marlborough. He was one of three greatest captains in English history— the favourite of Queen Anne and the first to make the name of Churchill famous as a soldier, statesman and captain of men.

Sir John Cheke, learned writer, promoter of the study of polite literature in England, 1514,
Henrietta Stuart, Duchess of Orleans, 1644, Exeter,
Louis, Duc de Saint-Simon, author of *Memoirs of the Court of France*, 1675, Paris,
King Gustav V of Sweden, 1858,
Lupino Lane, 1892, these were born today.

These died on June the Sixteenth,
Hugo the Great, father of Hugh Capet, head of the third series of French Kings, 956,
Sir Richard Fanshawe, accomplished cavalier, ambassador to Spain, 1666, Madrid,
Sir Tristram Beresford, 1701,
Jean Baptiste Gresset, French comic poet, 1777, Amiens,
Sir Edward Burne-Jones, 1898.

BATTLE OF STOKE WAS FOUGHT IN 1487 ON THIS DAY,
CHRISTINA OF SWEDEN ABDICATED IN 1654,
BENGAL MADE CHIEF PRESIDENCY OF BRITISH INDIA, 1775,
R.S.P.C.A. FOUNDED, 1824,
MAYNOOTH ENDOWMENT BILL PASSED THE HOUSE OF LORDS, 1845,
PASTEUR AWARDED THE ALBERT MEDAL OF THE INSTITUTE OF FRANCE, 1882,
U.S. ANNEXED SANDWICH ISLANDS, 1897,
ETNA IN ERUPTION, 1923,
MIXED BATHING PERMITTED IN THE SERPENTINE, 1930,
MAGINOT LINE EVACUATED, 1940,
BRITAIN HAD ITS FIRST BUZZ BOMB IN 1944,
ALL ON JUNE THE SIXTEENTH.

June the Seventeenth

The pages of thy book I read,
And as I closed each one
My heart—responding—ever said,
Servant of God—well done.

In 1703, at Epworth, John Wesley was born on June the Seventeenth. With him there came into England a passionate zeal to make men better—to make them see the way to goodness and mercy. He created the Wesleyan Church. Other churches are known by place names or words which describe beliefs: the church which John Wesley founded could only be called by his name.

These had their birthdays on June the Seventeenth.
Edward I in 1239,
Gounod in 1818, and
Sir Harold Gillies, 1882.

They died on June the Seventeenth.
John Sobieski, at Warsaw, in 1696,
Joseph Addison, poet and essayist, at Holland House, in 1719,
Louis Hector, Duke de Villars, illustrious French commander, at Turin, 1734,
Selina, Countess of Huntingdon, in 1791,
Lord William Bentinck, statesman, in 1839,
Richard H. Barham, comic poet, at Amen Corner, in 1845.

ON THIS DAY, EDWARD III RENOUNCED ALL PRETENSIONS TO SOVEREIGNTY OVER SCOTLAND IN 1328, AND ON THIS DAY THESE EVENTS ARE REPORTED . . . .
THE BATTLE OF BUNKER HILL IN 1775,
THE 'GREAT EASTERN' LEFT THE NEEDLES ON HER MAIDEN VOYAGE ACROSS THE ATLANTIC IN 1860,
THE LAST GERMAN AIR RAID ON BRITAIN IN THE 1914–18 WAR, 1918,
THE END OF THE GENEVA CONFERENCE ON TRADE IN ARMS IN 1925,
MR. BEVIN FLEW TO PARIS TO CONSULT THE FRENCH PREMIER, 1947,
H.M. THE QUEEN AND PRINCESS MARGARET ATTENDED SERVICE AT ST. PAUL'S TO COMMEMORATE 250TH ANNIVERSARY OF FOUNDING OF SOCIETY FOR PROPAGATION OF THE GOSPEL, 1951.

June the Eighteenth

No day at all it is for me
If I have not my liberty.

June the Eighteenth is such a day as Englishmen may dwell on because two
of the most characteristic of their race died on that day, albeit nearly two
centuries lay between.
John Hampden died in 1643, William Cobbett died in 1835.
Many love and have loved England—none surely have loved her in their
way more than these men who were both patriots and politicians.

On this day these occurred,
Hampton Court Palace finished, 1525,
Charles I crowned at Edinburgh,
United States declared war against Great Britain in 1812,
Waterloo, 1815,
Waterloo Bridge was opened, 1817,
Last Annual Waterloo Banquet, Apsley House, 1851,
Statue of Liberty arrived in New York, 1881,
Crathie Parish Church, Balmoral, dedicated, 1895,
Anglo-German Naval Pact, 1935,
This was our finest hour, 1940.

In 1492 on Eighteenth June, at Orleans, Joan of Arc led French-
men to independence and defeated the chivalry of England.

On June the Eighteenth in 1815 at Waterloo the ambitions of
Napoleon and France were shattered by Wellington and Blücher.

On this June the Eighteenth these died,
Caliph Othman, assassinated at Medina, 655,
Bishop Thomas Bilson, 1616,
A. Philips, poet, 1749, near Vauxhall, London,
General Sir Thomas Picton, 1815, Waterloo,
William Coombe, novelist and comic poet, 1823, London,
John Roby, author of *Traditions of Lancashire*, drowned 1850,
Sir George Russell Clerk (Ambassador in Paris), 1951.

FOR THESE, JUNE THE EIGHTEENTH WAS BIRTH DAY,
ROBERT STEWART, MARQUIS OF LONDONDERRY, MINISTER
OF GEORGE IV, 1769, LONDON,
CAPTAIN WEBB, 1848,
EARL OF GLASGOW, 1874.

June the Nineteenth

His life was short but in his day
He with his fellows had his way
He cared not for the passing hour
Unless it yielded sovereign power.

Lord Acton died on June the Nineteenth, 1902. He was one of that select few whose names are made memorable because of some enduring sentence. Lincoln's name is joined to 'Government of the people, by the people, for the people', Acton's great dictum is less well known but it declared a truth men would do well to remember: 'Power corrupts', he said, 'and absolute power corrupts absolutely'.

June the Nineteenth was the day on which
President Madison declared war on Britain, 1812,
Sir Robert Peel's Police Act was passed, 1829,
Alabama was sunk, 1864,
King abolished foreign titles in British Royal Family, 1917,
U.S.A. went off Gold Standard in 1933,
Mr. Churchill was in America in 1942.

They died on this day:
St. Romauld, 1027, Ancona,
Piers Gaveston, favourite of Edward II, executed, 1312,
Dr. William Sherlock, Dean of St. Paul's, Master of the Temple, theologian, controversialist, 1707, Hampstead,
Nicolas Lemery, one of the fathers of true chemistry, 1715, Paris,
John Brown, D.D., Scots dissenting divine, author of the Self-Interpreting Bible, 1787, Haddington,
Sir Joseph Banks, naturalist, 1820, Spring Grove,
Emperor Maximilian, shot in Mexico, 1867,
Sir J. M. Barrie, 1937.

THEY WERE BORN ON JUNE THE NINETEENTH:
JAMES THE SIXTH OF SCOTLAND AND FIRST OF GREAT BRITAIN, 1566, EDINBURGH CASTLE,
BLAISE PASCAL, FRENCH RELIGIOUS WRITER, 1623, CLERMONT,
REV. C. H. SPURGEON, 1834,
EARL HAIG, 1861,
VISCOUNT ADDISON, 1869, AND
W. R. HAMMOND, 1903.

June the Twentieth

What is there left of yesterday?
What gifts are these of fate's?
I've had my life: I've gone my way:
And leave a list of dates.

He died on June the Twentieth in 1527. He gave his name to a policy which is supposed to embody craft, guile, sophistry, subtlety, deception, insincerity, tortuosity, corruption, false witness, and all unrighteousness. He would be surprised if he knew, for he served faithfully by the light which was vouchsafed to him. His name was Niccolo Machiavelli.

These, too, died today:
Wiliam Cavendish, Second Earl of Devonshire, 1628, Derby,
Henrietta Stuart, Duchess of Orleans, 1670, St. Cloud,
Charles Coffin, French poet, 1749,
Charles Frederick Abel, musical composer, 1787,
William IV, King of Great Britain, 1837, Windsor,
James C. Mangan, poet, 1849,

Born on this day were:
Dr. George Hickes, Dean of Worcester, learned theologian and controversialist, 1642, Newsham, Yorkshire,
Dr. Adam Ferguson, historian, 1723, Logierait, Perthshire,
Anna Letitia Aiken, 1743, Knibworth,
Earl de la Warr, 1900.

THESE ARE RECORDED ON JUNE THE TWENTIETH:
BISHOPRIC OF MORAY FOUNDED, 1107,
BLACK HOLE OF CALCUTTA, 1756,
ACT PASSED IMPOSING TEA DUTY ON AMERICA, 1767,
ARRIVAL OF FIRST STEAMER FROM U.S., 'SAVANNAH', 1819,
ACCESSION OF QUEEN VICTORIA, 1837,
DUKE OF CUMBERLAND ASSUMED SOVEREIGNTY OF HANOVER, 1837,
NEW ARMY ENLISTMENT ACT (LIMITED SERVICE), 1867,
FOUNDATION OF TOWER BRIDGE LAID, 1886,
INTERNATIONAL AIR CONVENTION GREAT BRITAIN, 1922,
THE KING VISITED MALTA, 1943,
PERUGIA CAPTURED, 1944,
GOVERNMENT REJECTED APPLICATION OF PRINCIPLE OF EQUAL PAY IN CIVIL SERVICE BECAUSE OF EXPENSE, 1951.

June the Twenty-first

The better the day,
The better the deed,
The harder the way
God . . . .
The greater my need!

Scapa Flow is east of Scotland—the base of the Grand Fleet in two wars
against Germany. From Scapa, Kitchener sailed to die: to Scapa was
brought the German Fleet after its surrender to Beatty in the Firth of
Forth in 1919.

It seemed the end. The British had won. The Fleet of the enemy
was in their hands. There was still a card to play. On June the
Twenty-first, in Scapa Flow, the crews of the German Fleet
opened the cocks and scuttled their ships. It was a victory, but not
the one expected.

Born on June the Twenty-first were:
William Aytoun, 1813,
Offenbach, 1819,
General Auchinleck, 1884.

Died on this day,
Edward III of England, 1377, Sheen, Richmond,
John Skelton, poet, 1529,
Captain John Smith, colonizer of Virginia, 1631,
Sir Inigo Jones, architect, 1652,
William Beckford, Lord Mayor of London, 1770,
Gilbert, first Earl of Minto, statesman, 1814,
Mrs. Mary Anne Clarke, 1852,
Froebel, 1852.

ON JUNE THE TWENTY-FIRST IN DAYS GONE BY THESE
THINGS HAPPENED:
UNIONS AMONG JOURNEYMAN WORKMEN FORBIDDEN BY
LAW, 1799,
BATTLE OF VITTORIA, 1813,
ARMY SERVICE ACT WAS PASSED, 1847,
NEW ST. THOMAS'S HOSPITAL OPENED, 1871,
QUEEN VICTORIA'S JUBILEE CELEBRATION, 1887,
OPENING OF KIEL CANAL, 1895.

June the Twenty-second

Alas! Three whole days to wait
But she will surely come:
She will come when it is late,
But is she coming home?

On June the Twenty-second in the year 1772 it was decreed that a slave who set foot on the Isle of Britain so set himself free. It was a great moment in the history of human rights and it is inalienably to Britain that this honour belongs. It is true that it was on the same day in 1904 that the first of the Chinese indentured labourers arrived in Transvaal—that seemed a falling back—but there was worse to come. Hitler invaded U.S.S.R. on this day in 1941. The great debate continues.

This June the Twenty-second recalls:
Re-abdication of Napoleon, 1815,
Enormous London fire, 1861,
Diamond Jubilee of Queen Victoria, 1897,
Salaries of M.P.s raised from £400 to £600, 1937,
France signed armistice on German terms, 1940,
Mulheim heavily bombed, 1943.

Bishop John Fisher, beheaded on Tower Hill, 1535,
Henry Hudson, 1611,
Catherine Philips, poetess, 1664, Fleet Street, London,
Matthew Henry, biblical commentator, 1714,
R. B. Haydon, artist, 1846, London,
Howard Staunton, the chess player, 1874,
Sir Henry Wilson, murdered 1922—all died on this day.

ROBERT NELSON (WORKS OF DIVINITY), 1656, LONDON,
JACQUES DELILLE, FRENCH POET, 1738,
THOMAS DAY, AUTHOR OF 'SANDFORD AND MERTON', 1748,
MAZZINI, 1805,
SIR H. RIDER HAGGARD, 1856,
PUCCINI, 1858,
PROFESSOR JULIAN SORELL HUXLEY, 1887—ALL WERE
BORN ON THIS DAY.

BRITAIN'S APPLICATION FOR INTERIM MEASURES OF
PROTECTION IN PERSIAN OIL PROBLEM SUBMITTED TO
INTERNATIONAL COURT OF JUSTICE AT THE HAGUE, 1951.

[181]

June the Twenty-third

These were the days and I was there,
But neither long remained,
I lost my friends—I ceased to care—
And now I am disdained.

On June the Twenty-third in 1646 (some say July the Sixth) Gottfried
Wilhelm Leibnitz was born at Leipzig. The birth of a philosopher is of
more moment to men than the crowning of a king. With Leibnitz a light
came into the world. It grows. It is undimmed today.

To take two birth days,
Bishop John Fell, 1625, Longworth, and
The Duke of Windsor, 1894—will serve. They were both born on
June the Twenty-third.

Death claimed these this day:
Louis I of France, 840,
Mary Tudor, Duchess of Suffolk, 1533,
Mark Akenside, poet, 1770,
Catherine Macaulay, historian, 1791, Bingfield,
James Mill, author of the History of India, 1836, at Kensington,
(father of John Stuart Mill),
Lady Hester Stanhope, 1839, Lebanon,
Patrick Chalmers, Scots antiquary, 1854.

EVENTS OF MOMENT ON JUNE THE TWENTY-THIRD:
BATTLE OF PLASSEY, 1757,
FIRST ENGLISH REGATTA, 1775,
FIRST CHARTER OF THE ROYAL ACADEMY OF MUSIC, 1830,
SHELLEY GOT HIS PUBLISHER TRIED FOR BLASPHEMY,
1841,
GREAT NAVAL REVIEW AT SPITHEAD BEFORE THE QUEEN
AND ALBERT, 1845,
PUBLIC INAUGURATION AT EDINBURGH OF THE DUKE OF
WELLINGTON STATUE, 1851,
GENERAL GORDON GAZETTED TO R.E.S, 1852,
THE VOLUNTEER REVIEW IN HYDE PARK, 1860,
SALISBURY'S FIRST MINISTRY, 1885,
SOVIET FORCES OPENED OFFENSIVE ON CENTRAL FRONT,
1944,
THESE—AND OTHERS UNCOUNTED FILLED THIS DAY IN
YEARS GONE BY.

June the Twenty-fourth

This day, in truth a holiday to me,
Shall banish gloomy cares
Reckless to spend and scatter is to be—
One day I'll reap my tares.

They are a tenacious and indomitable people. They have given more to the world than they have received. They have proved themselves to be terrible in battle, unshaken in defeat, staunch in friendship. They glorify the Battle of Bannockburn, fought and won on June the Twenty-fourth in 1314. It was a great victory over the Norman English. It was a victory for the Scots which gave them their independence and their freedom. It made Scotland a nation and her nationhood endures.

The Twenty-fourth of June had other occasions, some very odd:
Order of the Garter, 1348,
John Cabot reached North America in 1497,
Hawkers and pedlars licensed, 1697,
Laws against witchcraft repealed, 1736,
French retook Newfoundland, 1762,
First stone laid of Abbey Craig memorial, Stirling, to Wallace, 1861,
First Act of Preservation of Birds passed, 1869,
General Nobile rescued by aeroplane from Arctic one month after disaster in 1928,
Italian armistice signed, 1940.

These too died on this day,
Vespasian, Emperor of Rome, 79, Cutilia,
John Hampden, illustrious patriot, 1643, Thame,
Dr. Thomas Amory, English Presbyterian divine, miscellaneous writer, 1774.

THESE WERE BORN ON THIS DAY,
JOHN CHURCHILL, DUKE OF MARLBOROUGH, 1650, ASHE,
DR. ALEXANDER ADAM, EMINENT CLASSICAL TEACHER, 1741,
DEODATUS DE DOLOMIEU, MINERALOGIST, 1750,
JOSEPHINE, EMPRESS OF THE FRENCH, 1763, MARTINICO,
REAR-ADMIRAL SIR JOHN ROSS, ARCTIC NAVIGATOR, 1777,
ALEXANDRE DUMAS, FRENCH NOVELIST, 1803,
HENRY WARD BEECHER, A FIGHTING PREACHER, 1813.

June the Twenty-fifth

That was your first day,
This was your last:
This I would durst say
Bury the past!

In days when democracy seemed to be on the ascendant it turned to the aristocrat as the architect of its achievements. It found in its direst need a Churchill and he was not alone. It found many aristocrats to uphold its cause and not least of these he who became the Earl Mountbatten of Burma. He was born on June the Twenty-fifth, 1900.

John Horne Tooke, a political character, author of the *Diversions of Purley*, was born on this day, in 1736, at Westminster, Sir Ernest Benn born 1875.

On June the Twenty-fifth there died:
Edward V, 1483,
John Marston, poet, 1634,
Roger Gale, learned antiquary, 1744, Scruton, Yorkshire,
General Custer, 1786,
Charles Barbaroux, Girondist politician, guillotined, 1793,
William Smellie, naturalist, miscellaneous writer, 1795,
Thomas Sandby, R.A., 1798,
J. C. L. de Sismondi, historian, 1842, near Geneva,
Louis Bonaparte, ex-king of Holland, 1846,
Alma Tadema, 1912, the painter.

CONSECRATION OF FIRST BISHOP OF BRISTOL, 1542,
REMONSTRANCE AGAINST TUNNAGE AND POUNDAGE, 1628,
PUBLIC DINNER TO DICKENS, EDINBURGH, 1841,
THIRD READING OF CORN IMPORTATION BILL IN THE LORDS, 1845,
ROYAL COMMISSION ON RAILWAY GAUGES APPOINTED, 1845,
ORDER OF THE STAR OF INDIA INSTITUTED, 1861,
SALISBURY'S THIRD MINISTRY, 1895,
CORONATION OF KING GEORGE V AND QUEEN MARY, 1911,
LONDON HAD FIRST AIR RAID WARNING SINCE FIRST WEEK OF WAR, 1940,
KOREAN WAR STARTED, 1950,
THESE WERE THE DOINGS ON THIS DAY.

June the Twenty-sixth

For though the day be never as long,
At last the bells ringeth to even songe.

Nature abides, some want to be remembered among those who loved their fellow men but there are others. On June the Twenty-sixth in 1793 there died at Selborne the Reverend Gilbert White, that gentle naturalist who turned men's minds from their uneasy selves to the works of nature to seek and find therein the calm soul of all things. These too, the lovers of nature, serve and solace the world, and die gratefully remembered.

Born on this bright day were:
Dr. Philip Dodridge, eminent English Nonconformist divine, 1702, London,
George Morland, the English artist, in 1763, at Haymarket, and
The great scientist Lord Kelvin in 1824.

Died on this bright day—these—
Julian, emperor, slain near Samara, upon the Tigris, 363,
Archbishop Robert Leighton, 1684, Warwick Lane, London,
Ralph Cudworth, English latitudinarian divine, author of the *True Intellectual System of the Universe*, 1688, Cambridge,
Samuel Crompton, inventor of 'The Mule' (spinning machine), 1827,
George IV of England, 1830, Windsor,
William Smyth (historical writings, poetry, &c.), 1849, Norwich,
Ford Madox Ford, 1939, who was born 'Hueffer', a competent critic and a fine novelist,
Howell Arthur Gwynne, editor of *The Morning Post* for twenty-six years, 1950,
Peter Cheyney, 1951.

AND WHAT OF THESE—THEY FELL ON THIS DAY:
SAID TO BE THE DATE OF THE PIED PIPER INCIDENT, 1284,
CHARTER GRANTED TO CHRIST'S HOSPITAL (BLUE COAT SCHOOL), 1553,
FIRST STONE OF LONDON DOCKS LAID, 1802,
FIRST DISTRIBUTION OF THE VICTORIA CROSS, 1857,
COURT OF SESSION, EDINBURGH, GAVE AWARD IN BREADAL-BANE CASE, CAMPBELL V. CAMPBELL, CAMPBELL WON, 1866,
U.S. TROOPS LANDED IN FRANCE, 1917,
WORLD SECURITY CHARTER, SAN FRANCISCO, 1945.

June the Twenty-seventh

I began my life a-squalling,
And I have sailed the seas,
And I can't help recalling
Some most strange memories.

I've spent my nights in madness
I've followed wicked ways
But for all their vice and badness
These nights were worth the days.

On June the Twenty-seventh in the year 1844 died one of the pioneers of the United States in the covered-wagon days. His life has been the subject of controversy but Salt Lake City and the State of Utah are memorials of Joseph Smith who founded the Mormon Church and, with his brother, was murdered by a mob on this day.

These, too, died on June the Twenty-seventh:
Nicholas Tindal, historian, 1774, Greenwich Hospital,
Dr. William Dodd, executed at Tyburn, 1777,
John Murray, the eminent publisher, 1843, London,
Harriet Martineau, 1876,
Ernest Bramah in 1942, who wrote about Kai Lung,
Rt. Hon. Richard B. Bennett, P.C., K.C., Architect of the Ottawa Agreements, 1947.

Born on this day were two Kings of France,
Louis XII ('the Just') in 1462 at Blois,
Charles IX, 1550, St. Germain, and one of Sweden,
Charles XII in 1682, and also
C. S. Parnell in 1846.

EVENTS WERE MANY ON THIS DAY DOWN THE YEARS—HERE ARE A FEW:
CADE'S MOB ENTERED LONDON, 1450,
BATTLE OF DETTINGEN, 1743,
FRENCH EVACUATED EGYPT, 1801,
GERMANS REACHED SPANISH FRONTIER, 1940,
THE V SIGN, 1941,
FIVE-YEAR TRADE TREATY WITH ARGENTINA SIGNED 1949,
ALL ON JUNE THE TWENTY-SEVENTH.

June the Twenty-eighth

This night, me thinks, is but the daylight sick,
Life a nightmare—and time a dirty trick.

He died on this day. He led us in pastures green. He delighted his genera-
tion. He was a master of an art peculiarly English. He would have had
little fame in any other land. He died on June the Twenty-eighth in 1915.
He played the game. He played cricket. His name was Victor Trumper.

These things occurred on June the Twenty-eighth,
First crossing of the Channel. A Captain Boynton floundered
across in a patent swimming-suit, 1875,
Kelly gang mopped up near Melbourne, 1880,
The murder, 1914—Archduke Francis Ferdinand and his consort
assassinated at Sarajevo,
Battle of Gully Ravine, Gallipoli, 1915,
Germans signed Peace Treaty, 1919,
Labour Party rejected affiliation with Communism, 1922,
W.A.A.F. founded, 1939,
De Gaulle recognized by British Government, 1940,
Signor Enrico de Nicola elected first President of Italian Republic,
1946,
British and U.S. aircraft began 'Air Lift' into Berlin, 1948,
Yugoslavia expelled from Cominform, 1948.

Death certified these men on June the Twenty-eighth:
Alphonso V of Aragon, 'the Magnanimous', 1458,
Thomas Creech, translator of Roman poems into English verse,
1701, Oxford,
Maurice, Duc de Noailles, French commander, 1766,
Francis Wheatley, R.A., 1801,
Charles Mathews, comedian, 1835, Plymouth,
James Henry Fitzroy, Lord Raglan, British commander, 1855,
Marshal Balbo, Italian Governor General of Libya, 1940.

FOR
HENRY VIII OF ENGLAND, 1491, GREENWICH,
JEAN JACQUES ROUSSEAU, 1712, GENEVA,
CHARLES MATHEWS, COMEDIAN, 1776, LONDON
PIRANDELLO, THE PLAYWRIGHT, 1867, AND
QUEEN VICTORIA'S CORONATION, 1838,
THIS DAY WAS THE BEGINNING.

June the Twenty-ninth

When I was only twenty-one,
I was my father's favoured son,
But now that I am seventy-seven
My father prays for me in heaven.

'Thank God, no more Aurora Leighs,' thundered Edward Fitzgerald. He said this of the author of Aurora Leigh, *one of the greatest tales in verse in any language. It was written by Elizabeth Barrett Browning, the wife of Robert Browning—the poet who on this day, June the Twenty-ninth, died at Florence in 1861. Something of her early days and her elopement and her dog is recalled in the famous contemporary play* The Barretts of Wimpole Street.

Sir Henry Yelverton, an eminent English judge, was born on this day, in 1566, at Islington—so was
Peter Paul Rubens in 1577, and
Rev. John Williams, the Apostle of Polynesia, 1796.

Margaret Beaufort, Countess of Richmond (mother of King Henry VII), 1509,
Pierre de Marca, Archbishop of Paris, historian, 1662,
Bishop Zachary Pearce, 1774,
Valentine Green, eminent mezzotint engraver, 1813, London,
J. A. Hansome, inventor of the famous cab, 1882,
Thomas Henry Huxley, 1895,
I. J. Paderewski, New York City, 1941—these finished their strange eventful history on June the Twenty-ninth.

WESTMINSTER ABBEY COMPLETED, 1285,
TRIAL OF THE SEVEN BISHOPS BEGAN, 1688,
FLEET MARRIAGES, 1723,
NATIONAL REGISTRATION BILL INTRODUCED, 1915,
SIR ROGER CASEMENT SENTENCED, 1916,
CANADA HOUSE IN TRAFALGAR SQUARE WAS OPENED IN 1925,
LAST FOREIGN TROOPS LEFT GERMAN SOIL, 1930,
FIRST GERMAN TROOPS ENTERED BRITISH SOIL (CHANNEL ISLES), 1940,
NUREMBERG TRIAL OF NAZI WAR LEADERS ENDED 1946,
A LOT OF THINGS HAPPENED—BESIDES THESE—ON JUNE THE TWENTY-NINTH.

June the Thirtieth

They had their days of heat and dust,
They were not very long,
These days of passion—days of lust,
Of sorrow and of song.
Days of rest and days of riot,
Now they lie so very quiet.

On June the Thirtieth, these took reluctant leave of the world. They should have died hereafter, but men willed it otherwise.
In 1685, in Edinburgh, Archibald Campbell, the ninth Earl of Argyll, was beheaded on this day. In 1797 at the Nore, Richard Parker, who was charged with leading the mutiny, was hanged, and on this day in 1825 the Reverend Henry Kett was drowned.

Born on this day—a poet and an artist—
Alfred Austen in 1835, and
James Gunn in 1893.

They died on June the Thirtieth:
Bishop Gavin Dunbar, 1547,
Cardinal Baronius, eminent ecclesiastical writer, 1607, Rome,
Alexander Brome, poet, 1666,
Sir Thomas Pope Blount, miscellaneous writer, 1697, Tittenhanger,
Dr. Thomas Edwards, learned divine, 1785, Nuneaton,
Sultan Mahmoud of Turkey, 1839,
Sir James Macadam, originator of the famous road system, 1851.

DAY GIVEN FOR INTRODUCTION OF PRINTING INTO ENGLAND, 1477,
GREENWICH HOSPITAL FOUNDED, 1696,
FOUNDATION OF SUNDAY SCHOOLS, 1780,
MRS. SIDDONS'S FAREWELL, 1812,
USE OF PILLORY OFFICIALLY ABOLISHED, 1837,
THE MADELINE SMITH TRIAL OPENED IN EDINBURGH, 1857,
FIRST CHINESE RAILWAY OPENED, 1876,
JESUITS EXPELLED FROM FRANCE, 1880,
TOWER BRIDGE OPENED, 1894,
HITLER 'BLOOD PURGES' BEGAN, 1934,
BASIC RATION OF PETROL FOR PRIVATE CARS DISCONTINUED, 1942,
UNITED STATES ATOM BOMB TESTS AT BIKINI, 1946.

JULY

THIRTY-ONE DAYS

July the First

... 'So here hath been dawning another blue day' ...

July the First is the crown of the year and promoters of great occasions have found it a great day for their purposes.

The Scots first used the St. Andrew's Cross as a National Flag on this day in 1385,
The Battle of the Boyne was fought in 1690,
The first steamboat sailed on the Thames in 1801,
Louis Bonaparte of Holland abdicated in 1816,
Victoria was declared a separate Colony of Australia in 1851,
It was the first day of the Gettysburg Battle, 1863,
It is Dominion Day in Canada since 1867,
Colorado was admitted into the United States of America in 1876,
The Dominion of South Africa was legally established in 1910,
The London Passenger Transport Board assumed responsibility for the metropolitan migrating millions in 1933.

These births are recorded on July the First :
Bishop (Joseph) Hall, 1574, Bristow Park, Leicestershire,
Jean Baptiste, Comte de Rochambeau, 1725, Vendôme, and
Adam, Viscount Duncan, the admiral, in 1731, at Dundee.

These were great events, pregnant with possibilities for human happiness, but the First of July was not always so fortunate a day. These died . . .
Edgar, King of England, 975,
The Admirable Crichton, assassinated at Mantua, 1582,
Frederick, the Duke Schomberg, at the Battle of the Boyne, 1690,
Edward Lloyd, antiquary, 1709, Oxford, and
Henry Fox, Lord Holland, in 1774.

ABSENTING ONESELF AGAIN FROM FELICITY AWHILE, UNCOUNTED THOUSANDS WILL RECOLLECT, THE BATTLE OF THE SOMME ON JULY THE FIRST, 1916, WHERE, IN THE WORDS OF THE GREATEST OF OUR GENERATION, BY 'KITCHENER'S ARMY', 'UNCONQUERABLE EXCEPT BY DEATH, WHICH THEY HAD CONQUERED, WAS SET UP A MONUMENT OF NATIVE VIRTUE WHICH WILL COMMAND THE WONDER, THE REVERENCE AND THE GRATITUDE OF OUR ISLAND PEOPLE AS LONG AS WE ENDURE AS A NATION AMONG MEN'.

July the Second

Things bad—must surely be better,
The worst—it can never hold sway,
The wet—it can not be wetter
The best becomes better each day.

He taught that 'Every day and in every way I am becoming better and
better': he proclaimed that imagination—the poetic dreaming creative
faculty—could do more for men's happiness than the will to be well or
indeed the will to live. He did not cure. He taught men to cure themselves.
He was Emile Coué and he died on July the Second, 1926.

On this day these events are recorded,
Cromwell victor at Marston Moor, 1644,
Legislative Union of Great Britain and Ireland effected, 1800,
Union Jack adopted,
Anti-Corn Law League dissolved, 1846,
Trotman's 'Anchor' won the Trials, 1851,
First meeting at Wimbledon of the National Rifle Association,
1860,
Demolition of Northumberland House begun, 1874,
Peace proclaimed at St. James's Palace and in City, 1919,
Women over twenty-one entitled to vote for the first time, 1928.

On this day there were born:
Christian II, King of Denmark, 1480,
Archbishop Cranmer, 1489, Aslockton, Notts,
Frederick Theophilus Klopstock, German poet, 1724, Saxony,
Henry, third Marquis of Lansdowne, statesman, 1780,
Adm. Cradock, 1862,
Mr. Lewis Douglas, in 1948 U.S. Ambassador to Britain, 1894.

ON THIS DAY THERE DIED,
HENRY I, EMPEROR OF GERMANY, 936,
MICHEL NOSTRADAMUS, 1566, SALON,
JEAN JACQUES ROUSSEAU, 1778, ERMENONVILLE,
DIONYSIUS DIDEROT, PHILOSOPHICAL WRITER, 1784,
PARIS,
DR. HAHNEMANN, ORIGINATOR OF HOMEOPATHY, 1843,
PARIS,
SIR ROBERT PEEL, STATESMAN, 1850, LONDON,
WILLIAM BERRY (WORKS ON HERALDRY), 1851, BRIXTON.

July the Third

The years they come,
The years they go,
Man travails—joy and pain
All have their share
The high and low
The far saints—they remain.

The far saints of July the Third are here:
St. Phocas, martyr, 303,
St. Gunthiern, abbot in Brittany, sixth century,
St. Bertran, Bishop of Mans, 632,
St. Guthagon, recluse at Ostkerk, eighth century.

But July the Third was a day of great events,
Champlain founded Quebec, 1567,
Mauritius was captured in 1810,
The third attempt was made on the life of Queen Victoria in 1842,
Commodore Parry, of the United States, arrived in Japan in 1853,
Cerera's fleet destroyed off Santiago, Cuba, by U.S. ships, 1898,
Arandora Star torpedoed, 1940,
It was on this day that the French warships joined the Allies at Oran in 1940,
The world heard from Germany the claim that the U.S.S.R. was defeated, 1941,
Palmyra and Debra Tabor surrendered to Allies, 1941,
Minsk captured, 1944,
Arab States rejected Count Bernadotte's proposals for solution of Palestine problem, 1948.

There died on this day,
Mary de Medici, mother of Louis XIII of France, 1642, Cologne,
Ferdinand, Duke of Brunswick, 1792, and
Lord Rhondda, 1918, who made a great reputation for himself as the first Minister of Food in the 1914–18 war.

JULY THE THIRD IS A DAY OF MANY BIRTHDAYS.
THREE ARE SELECTED FOR RECOLLECTION,
LOUIS XI OF FRANCE, 1423, BOURGES, AND
HENRY GRATTAN, IRISH PARLIAMENTARY ORATOR, 1746, DUBLIN,
W. H. DAVIES, A POET, 1871.

July the Fourth

Of course you've had it—fear ye not
The worst you now have seen
You've seen men die—you've seen men rot
At any rate . . . you've been.

Pittsburgh, Pennsyvlania, U.S.A., honours the name of Stephen Collins Foster who was born there on July the Fourth, 1826. Who was he? He wrote 'Nelly Bly', 'My Old Kentucky Home', and the undying 'Old Folks at Home'. He died tragically and had his share of the unhappiness which often companions pure genius.

There was born,
Christina Gellert, the German poet and fabulist, in 1715, in Saxony,
The American novelist, Nathaniel Hawthorne, 1804, whose book, the *Scarlet Letter*, is still read as a classic, and
Garibaldi, on this day, in 1807.

There died on this day many famous men . . .
William Byrd, English composer of sacred music, 1623,
Henry Bentinck, first Duke of Portland, 1726, Jamaica,
Richard Watson, Bishop of Llandaff, 1816,
John Adams, second President of the United States, 1826,
Thomas Jefferson, third President of the United States, 1826,
Sir Henry Montgomery Lawrence, English soldier, 1857,
Mme Curie, the scientist, 1934,
General Sikorski, 1943, and
Sir Francis Norie-Miller in 1947.

ON JULY THE FOURTH THE BAREBONES PARLIAMENT WAS SUMMONED IN 1653,
IT WAS INDEPENDENCE DAY IN THE UNITED STATES IN 1776,
FIRST GOVERNOR-GENERAL OF INDIA TOOK OFFICE, 1828,
FIRST OMNIBUS IN LONDON, 1829,
DENMARK ALSO GUARANTEED BY THE 'SCRAP OF PAPER' TREATY, 1850,
FRANCE GAVE U.S. STATUE OF LIBERTY, 1883,
BRITISH AND AMERICANS WENT INTO ACTION TOGETHER, 1918,
ITALIANS CROSSED SUDAN BORDER, 1940,
THE PHILIPPINES WERE LIBERATED IN 1945.

July the Fifth

Life is mostly sin and sorrow
And at last it ends in dust
So they chant it—Let tomorrow
Mind itself—today I must!

Cecil John Rhodes was born in 1853; no single man has left a greater im-
print upon the history of the British Empire than this splendid Englishman
who, seeking health in Africa, founded a foundation and founded an empire.
He was a man of great generosity of spirit, and bequeathed the greater
part of his fortune to provide scholarships to enable men of the United
States, Germany and other countries to complete their education at Oxford
and so serve the British way of life in their native countries on their return.

Born on this day were,
Étienne de Silhouette, French Finance Minister, 1709,
Mrs. Sarah Siddons, tragic actress, 1755,
G. Barrow, 1803,
The Great Barnum, 1810,
B. Creighton, 1843,
W. T. Stead, 1849.

There died on this day:
Queen Magdalen of Scotland, 1537,
Sir Robert Strange, the 'prince of British line-engravers', 1792,
Mrs. Dorothea Jordan (*née* Bland), comic actress, 1816, St. Cloud.

AMONG THE EVENTS WHICH HISTORY ASSOCIATES WITH
JULY THE FIFTH ARE,
THE STAR CHAMBER WAS ABOLISHED IN 1641,
SOVEREIGNS WERE FIRST ISSUED, 1817,
DANIEL O'CONNEL WAS ELECTED TO PARLIAMENT FROM
CLARE (FIRST ROMAN CATHOLIC SINCE THE REVOLUTION),
1828,
THOMAS COOK'S FIRST EXCURSION (LEICESTER TO LOUGH-
BOROUGH), 1841,
SALVATION ARMY FOUNDED, 1865,
COURT OF QUEEN'S BENCH SAT FOR LAST TIME AS INDE-
PENDENT COURT, 1875,
WILLIAM BOOTH STARTED HIS CHRISTIAN MISSION IN
LONDON, 1865,
POLLING DAY GENERAL ELECTION, 1945.

July the Sixth

One day brings the punishment
Which many days demand
Men dare not ask the Gods
To stay the avenging hand.

July the Sixth saw the birth of Paul Jones in 1747, who was destined to become a great figure in the naval history of the United States and give his name to a popular dance.
There are less happy lots than his apportioned by Fate. John Flaxman, the sculptor, had the same birthday. He was born at York in 1755. July the Sixth was the birthday of Reginald McKenna in 1863, once a Chancellor of the Exchequer, Member of the Asquith-Lloyd George Government and latterly Chairman of the Midland Bank and
Brigadier-General the Earl of Gowrie, V.C., 1872.

There died on this day,
Henry II of England, 1189, Chinon Castle,
Edward VI of England, 1553, Greenwich,
Archbishop Grindal, 1583, Croydon,
Michael Bruce, poet, 1767, Kinneswood, Kinross-shire,
George Augustus Elliot, Lord Heathfield, military commander, 1790,
Granville Sharpe, philanthropist, 1813, Fulham,
Sir Thomas Munro, 1827, Madras,
D. M. Moir, poet and miscellaneous writer, 1851, Musselburgh,
Andrew Crosse, electrician, 1893,
Samuel Lover, 1868,
Guy de Maupassant, 1893,
Admiral Sir Colin R. Keppel, a Serjeant-at-Arms, House of Commons, 1947,
Field Marshal Philip Walhouse Chetwode, famous leader in First World War, 1950.

THESE EVENTS ARE RECORDED,
BATTLE OF SEDGEMOOR, 1685,
KINGDOM OF GREECE WAS FOUNDED IN 1827,
CHANNEL TUNNEL SCHEME BLOCKED, 1882,
CANADIAN COMMONS PASSED CONSCRIPTION BILL, 1917,
C25 ATTACKED BY PLANES, 1918,
CHANCELLOR OF THE EXCHEQUER ANNOUNCED STANDSTILL IN DOLLAR EXPENDITURE, 1949.

July the Seventh

For who hath despised the day of small things?

On this day the author of Jew Süss *was born at Munich in 1884—Lion Feuchtwanger. His most important work depicts life in Germany in the eighteenth century.*
The Emperor Nicholas of Russia was born in 1796 on this day.
These were beginnings.
For John Huss, the reformer. . . He was burned on this day in 1415 at Constance.
Sir Thomas More, Chancellor of England and author of Utopia, *was beheaded this day in 1535.*

Thomas, Earl of Arundel, collector of ancient sculptures, was born on this day in 1592.

There died on this day,
Edward I of England, 1307, Burgh-on-Sands,
Bishop Compton, 1713,
Dr. Thomas Blacklock, 'the blind poet', 1791, Edinburgh,
Richard Brinsley Sheridan, 1816, London,
Sir Arthur Conan Doyle, novelist and creator of the most famous detective in fiction, Sherlock Holmes, 1930,
Commissioner David Lamb, veteran of Salvation Army, 1951.

THESE EVENTS ARE RECORDED,
'MOURNING' FIRST BECAME GENERAL IN SCOTLAND, 1537,
REVIEW OF THE VOLUNTEERS AT EDINBURGH, 1860,
FIRST USE OF ELECTRIC CHAIR, NEW YORK, 1890,
FIRST DAYLIGHT RAID ON LONDON, 1917,
SINO-JAPANESE WAR BEGAN, 1937,
U.S. FORCES ARRIVED IN ICELAND, 1941,
SOUTHAMPTON ATTACKED BY GERMAN BOMBERS, 1941,
SUPER FORTRESSES BOMB SASEBO IN JAPAN, 1944,
COMMUNAL RIOTS IN CALCUTTA—45 KILLED—1947,
THEIR MAJESTIES AND PRINCESS MARGARET TOURED THE ROYAL SHOW OF YORK, 1948,
THE FREEDOM OF THE CITY OF EDINBURGH WAS CONFERRED UPON THE RIGHT HON. ANDREW FISHER, PRIME MINISTER OF THE COMMONWEALTH OF AUSTRALIA AND THE RIGHT HON. SIR EDWARD PATRICK MORRIS, K.C., PRIME MINISTER OF NEWFOUNDLAND, 1911.

July the Eighth

On a good day good things are to be spoken.

July the Eighth saw the end of that golden mind which shed its radiance over his own and succeeding generations. It was in 1822 on this day that Percy Bysshe Shelley died.
Edmund Burke died on the same day in 1797 at Beaconsfield—a great House of Commons man—an orator—a political philosopher and a states-man who, had he had his way, might have prevented the separation of Britain from the American colonies.

Born on this day were:
Lafontaine, 1621,
Joseph Chamberlain, 1836,
Count von Zeppelin, 1838,
Rockefeller, 1839,
Sir John Anderson, 1882.

There died on this day,
Peter the Hermit, preacher of the first Crusade, 1115,
The Black Prince, 1376,
Pope Gregory XV, 1623,
Second Marshal Villeroi, 1730,
Jean Pierre Niceron, useful writer, 1738, Paris,
Jean Baseillac (Frère Come), eminent French lithotomist, 1781,
Sir Henry Raeburn, 1823,
Duke of Cambridge, 1850,
Phiz (Hablot K. Browne), 1882,
Havelock Ellis, 1939.

THESE EVENTS ARE RECORDED:
ACCESSION OF EDWARD II, 1307,
A HILL DISAPPEARED—BULKELEY HILL IN CHESHIRE—
1657,
ROYAL BANK OF SCOTLAND CHARTERED, 1727,
'THE KING BATHED.' THE ROYAL SPLASH WAS GREETED BY
'GOD SAVE THE KING' PLAYED BY A WAGON-LOAD OF
FIDDLERS, 1789,
DISCOVERY OF THEFT OF STATE REGALIA—DUBLIN
CASTLE, 1907,
DECLARATION OF LONDON RESCINDED, 1916,
COLOGNE RAIDED, 1943.

July the Ninth

One of those heavenly days that cannot die,
But live in memory—a wistful sigh.

July the Ninth is a day which recalls some diverse happenings. On this day
in 1860 the then Prince of Wales, travelling as Lord Renfrew, left for a
tour of Canada and the United States. In 1900, this was the day of the
Commonwealth of Australia Constitution Act. In 1915, on July the Ninth,
what was then called German South West Africa surrendered to British and
South African forces.
Germany ratified the Peace Treaty in 1919 on this day.
Tea rationing began in Britain on July the Ninth in 1940, and in 1944 the
Allies entered Caen.
Kaye Don set up a world speed-boat record of 110.28 m.p.h. at Lake
Garda, Italy, 1931.

These were born:
Thomas Butler, Earl of Ossory, 1634, Kilkenny Castle,
Alexis Piron, 1689, Dijon,
Anne Radcliffe, novelist, 1764, London,
Henry Hallam, historian, 1777, Windsor,
Sir Harold Bowden, 1880.

Died on this day,
Archbishop (Stephen) Langton, 1228,
Emperor Leopold III of Austria, killed Sempach, 1386,
John Oldmixon (English history), 1742, Bridgewater,
General Braddock, killed at Du Quesne, North America, 1755,
William Strachan, publisher, 1785,
Zachary Taylor, President of the United States, 1850,
Dr. Keith Johnson, the geographer, 1871,
Hill Burton, 1881.

ON JULY THE NINTH IN 1709, THE POWER OF RUSSIA WAS
ASSERTED WHEN PETER THE GREAT DEFEATED CHARLES
XII OF SWEDEN AT THE BATTLE OF PULTOWA,
GENERAL DENTZ, HIGH COMMISSIONER IN SYRIA, ASKED
FOR ARMISTICE TERMS, 1941,
GERMAN BATTLESHIP 'TIRPITZ' TORPEDOED BY RUSSIAN
SUBMARINE, 1942,
BETROTHAL OF PRINCESS ELIZABETH TO LIEUTENANT
PHILIP MOUNTBATTEN, 1947.

July the Tenth

The prosperous day dawns, be propitious with your tongues and thoughts; now on this happy day happy words are to be said.

Who of these, think you, made most of their lives?
John Calvin, the theologian, born at Noyon, Picardy, in 1509, or Sir William Blackstone, born in Cheapside in 1723, and writer on the Law, or Frederick Marryat, the novelist for boys especially, born in London in 1792, or—going back into the fifteenth century—James the Third of Scotland, born in 1451, or Mrs. Aphra Behn, an early woman writer, born in 1640, or Robert Chambers, the Scots encyclopaedist, in 1802, or Lord Gort, born on this day in 1886. They had all this in common, that July the Tenth was their birth day.

These died,
Emperor Adrian, 138,
Pope Benedict VII, 938,
Pope Benedict VIII, 1024,
Henry II of France, 1559,
William, first Prince of Orange, assassinated at Delft, 1584,
Louis Moréri (*Historical and Critical Dictionary*), 1680, Lyons,
François Eudes de Mezerai, historian, 1683,
Bishop Fell, 1686, Oxford,
Dr. Alexander Munro, professor of anatomy, 1767, Edinburgh,
David Rittenhouse, astronomer, 1796, Philadelphia, U.S.,
Daguerre, 1851.

THESE EVENTS ARE RECORDED:
'ORATOR' HANLEY BEGAN TO TALK, 1726,
COCK LANE GHOST CONSPIRATORS CONDEMNED TO PILLORY AND IMPRISONMENT, 1762,
NIGER COMPANY CHARTERED, 1886,
FRENCH OCCUPIED FASHODA, 1898,
FORTH MADE NAVAL BASE OF HOME FLEET, 1903,
HOWARD HUGHES FLEW ROUND THE WORLD IN UNDER FOUR DAYS, 1938,
FIRST BIG DAYLIGHT BATTLE OVER SOUTH-EAST COAST, 1940,
THE ALLIES CAME BACK TO EUROPE, 1943 (SICILY).

July the Eleventh

Yoked in knowledge and remorse,
Now we come to rest,
Laughing at old villainies, that
Time has turned to jest.

Place aux dames—it might be said more often than it is said in history books. Historians are at small pains to put women and children first as is the rule, when ships are sinking. Gertrude Bell died on July the Eleventh in 1926, and every woman should know her story. A middle-class English woman of proper upbringing—the sister of Sir Hugh Bell—she became a power in the Middle East—'between the desert and the sown'—and takes her place among the most remarkable of Englishwomen.

Born on this day were:
Robert I of Scotland, 1274, Lochmaben,
Lalande, French mathematician, 1732, Bourg en Bresse,
John Quincey Adams, sixth President of United States, 1767,
Lord Tedder, 1890.

Died on this day,
Jack Cade, leader of a peasant rebellion in England, killed near Lewes, 1450,
Charles Macklin, comedian, 1797, London,
General Alexander Hamilton, American politician, killed in a duel, 1804,
William Ernest Henley, 1903. 'I am the captain of my soul,' he wrote,
Dr. Campbell Dodgson, 1948.

THESE THINGS OCCURRED ON JULY THE ELEVENTH.
BATTLE OF OUDENARDE, 1708,
WATERLOO STATION WAS OPENED, 1848,
FIRST PERFORMANCE IN BRITAIN OF GOUNOD'S 'ROMEO AND JULIET', 1867,
H.M.S. 'BACCHANTE' SAW 'THE FLYING DUTCHMAN', 1881,
BOMBARDMENT OF ALEXANDRIA, 1882,
LORD SALISBURY RESIGNED, 1902,
REPORTED DISCOVERY OF CANCER GERM, 1925,
BOMBERS RAIDED DANZIG AND FLENSBURG, 1942,
TEN SICILIAN TOWNS TAKEN, 1943,
ROYAL PROCLAMATION OF A STATE OF EMERGENCY, 1949.

July the Twelfth

Look thy last on all things lovely,
Every hour. Let no night
Seal thy sense in deathly slumber
Till to delight
Thou hast paid thy utmost blessing:
Since that all things thou wouldst praise
Beauty took from those who loved them
In other days.

He was just one of the Smiths. He became the Smith—the artificer of his own fortune. Lawyer, sportsman, politician, soldier, hunter, statesman, orator—F. E. Smith, who became Lord Birkenhead and Lord Chancellor of England, was born on July the Twelfth in 1872. He hurled himself like a fiery comet against the dull drabness of his contemporaries, castigating his enemies and enlightening, enlivening and inspiring all his friends who came within his orbit.

Born on this day were:
Caius Julius Caesar, 100 B.C.,
Jonas Hanway, 'Umbrella Man', 1712,
H. D. Thoreau, 1817,
Sir William Osler, 1849.

Died on this day:
Desiderius Erasmus, scholar, 1536, Basel,
General St. Ruth, killed, Aghrim, Ireland, 1691.
Titus Oates, 1704,
Christian G. Heyne (illustrator of ancient writings), 1814,
Mrs. Tonna ('Charlotte Elizabeth'), controversial writer, 1846,
Robert Stevenson, engineer of Bell Rock lighthouse, etc., 1850,
Colonel Dreyfus, 1935.

THESE EVENTS ARE RECORDED:
ACRE WAS TAKEN BY RICHARD, 1191,
EVACUATION OF CRIMEA, 1856,
MR. BALFOUR'S MINISTRY BEGAN IN 1902,
TWENTY PER CENT DUTY IMPOSED ON I. F. STATE IMPORTS
TO MAKE GOOD UNPAID 'ANNUITIES', 1932,
BREMEN HEAVILY BOMBED, 1941,
TURIN HEAVILY BOMBED, 1943.

July the Thirteenth

Once all earth proclaimed the glory
The glory of the skies
Alas, now in mankind's story
The heavens are shot with sighs.

To be the son of the greatest man in Europe—to succeed him in the highest office of the State—to resign that office—return to private life and die in peace, is no small achievement. Richard Cromwell—son of the great Protector—achieved it, dying on this day, July the Thirteenth, in 1712 at Cheshunt.

Born on this day were:
Richard Cumberland, Bishop of Peterborough, 1632,
Regnier de Graaf, 1641, Schoenhaven in Holland, and
Lord Passfield, 1859,
Sir Kenneth McKenzie Clark (art critic), 1903.

There died on this day:
Pope John III, 573,
Emperor Henry II, 1024,
Du Guesclin, Constable of France, illustrious warrior, 1380,
Sir William Berkley, 1677, Twickenham,
Elijah Fenton, poet, 1730, Easthampstead,
Bishop John Conybeare, 1755, Bristol,
Dr. James Bradley, astronomer, 1762,
Jean Paul Marat, French Revolutionary leader and writer, 1793,
Henry Card, Duke of York, 1807,
Rev. John Lingard, author of a history of England, 1851, Hornby,
near Lancaster,
W. W. Armstrong, 1947.

THESE EVENTS ARE RECORDED ON THIS DAY,
ROCKINGHAM'S MINISTRY, 1765,
NEW BUILDINGS OF BUCKINGHAM PALACE WERE OCCUPIED
BY QUEEN VICTORIA, 1837,
REFORM ACTS FOR IRELAND AND SCOTLAND, 1868,
THE EMS TELEGRAM, 1870,
DISQUALIFICATION OF BANKRUPT PEERS, 1871,
BERLIN TREATY, 1878 (PEACE WITH HONOUR),
GERMANS MADE SECOND VICTORY CLAIM OVER RUSSIA,
1941.

July the Fourteenth

I made the breakfast: swept the house
Watered the plants and darned some socks:
I fed the poultry: killed a mouse:
Its my destiny that mocks—
This is my sure appointed way,
I live my life: I have my day.

July the Fourteenth is a great day for the French. It was on this day, in
1789, that the Bastille fell in Paris, and on the same day, in 1919, the
peace celebrations for the 1914–18 war were held.
It is said by some that Parisians are cynical. It is difficult to believe it of
them generally, when one reflects on these events and their sequels.

On this day there were born:
Cardinal Mazarin, 1602, Pescina, in Abruzzo,
John Hunter, eminent surgeon, 1728, Long Calderwood,
John Frederick Lewis, R.A., painter, 1805,
Lieut.-General Sir Robert Grice Sturges, D.S.O., 1891.

On this day there died:
Philip Augustus of France, 1223, Nantes,
Dr. William Bates, eminent physician, 1699, Hackney,
Dr. Richard Bentley, editor, controversialist, 1742, Cambridge,
Baroness De Staël Holstein (*née* Anne Necker), 1817, Paris,
Lady Duff Gordon, authoress of *Letters from Egypt, 1863–65*, 1869,
Brendon Finucane, air ace of the Second World War, 1942,
Sir Andrew Caldicott, 1951,
Sir Herbert Edward Morgan, expert in publicity, 1951.

THESE THINGS OCCURRED ON THIS DAY,
SUBMARINE CABLE WAS COMPLETED BETWEEN BRITAIN
AND DENMARK, 1859,
COMPLETION OF FRENCH ATLANTIC CABLE, 1869,
ATTORNEYS SOLICITORS ACT WAS PASSED, 1870,
NATIONAL REGISTRATION ACT, 1915,
ATTACK ON LONGUEVAL (SOMME) BY 11TH ROYAL SCOTS,
1916,
SCOTTISH WAR MEMORIAL, EDINBURGH CASTLE, OPENED,
1927,
L.D.V. BECAME HOME GUARD, 1940,
ALLIES OCCUPIED SYRIA, 1941.

July the Fifteenth

Sweet day, so cool, so calm, so bright,
The bridal of the earth and sky:
The dew shall weep thy fall tonight:
For thou must die.

Things happen every day—every diarist knows it—but July the Fifteenth has its full share of happenings. Some may be recalled. On this day, in 1099, the City of Jerusalem fell in the First Crusade. On this day, in 1917, to the despair of the democracies fighting on the Western Front, Russia's Revolution began. The democracies had to go on without her aid. On this day in 1839, there were Chartist Riots in Birmingham and in 1925 Amundsen crossed the Pole . . .

There were, too, born on this day:
Inigo Jones, 1573,
Rembrandt, 1606,
Henry Edward Manning, Cardinal, 1808, Totteridge, Hertfordshire,
Gerard Langbaine, the Younger (bibliography of the English drama), 1856, Oxford.

These died on this day,
Anne of Cleves, consort of Henry VIII, 1576, Chelsea,
James, Duke of Monmouth, executed on Tower Hill, 1685,
John Wilson, botanist, 1751,
Bryan Edwards, author of *History of the West Indies*, 1800, Southampton,
Thomas Dermody, peasant-poet, 1802,
Winthrop Mackworth Praed (comic poetry) contributor to the *Etonian and Quarterly Magazine*, 1839,
Prince Adam Czartoryski, Polish patriot, 1861, Paris,
Gustav Rose, German chemist, 1873,
General Pershing, 1948.

THESE EVENTS ARE RECORDED,
FIRST PRISON HULKS, 1776,
CONVENTION OF LONDON, 1840,
RE-ESTABLISHMENT OF TEMPORAL POWER OF THE POPE
PROCLAIMED AT ROME, 1848,
GENERAL MIHAILOVITCH SENTENCED TO DEATH, 1946.

July the Sixteenth

Of all the days that are in the week,
I dearly love but one day:
And that's the day that comes betwixt
A Saturday and a Monday.

What of July the Sixteenth?
The Atomic age may be said to begin on this day.
The test bomb was exploded in New Mexico in 1945 on July the Sixteenth.
This day is the anniversary of the flight of Mohammed in A.D. 622—of the
crowning of Richard II of England in 1377 with King's Champion in
attendance—of Lord Melbourne's first ministry in 1834—of the Battle of
Cawnpore in 1857 and of the Reform Bill read on this July the Sixteenth for
the first time in 1867. A goodly list of events—but there is one more—who
*shall say not more significant—*Punch *was first published on July the*
Sixteenth in 1842.

These were born,
Carneades, founder of the 'New Academy' school of philosophy,
217 B.C., Cyrene,
Sir Joshua Reynolds, celebrated painter, 1723, Plympton,
Rev. James O. Hannay, 1865,
Trygve Lie, 1896.

THESE DIED ON JULY THE SIXTEENTH:
ANNE ASKEW, MARTYRED AT SMITHFIELD, 1546,
TOMMASO ANIELLO (BY CONTRACTION MASANIELLO),
CELEBRATED REVOLUTIONARY LEADER BY THE POPULACE
AT NAPLES, 1647,
FRANÇOIS LE TELLIER, MARQUIS DE LOUVOIS, CHANCELLOR
OF FRANCE, 1691, PARIS,
DR. THOMAS YALDEN, POET, 1736,
PETER III, CZAR OF RUSSIA, HUSBAND OF THE EMPRESS
CATHARINE, STRANGLED, 1762,
JEAN LOUIS DE LOLME, WRITER ON THE BRITISH CONSTI-
TUTION, 1806,
MARGARET FULLER OSSOLI, AMERICAN AUTHORESS, 1850,
NICHOLAS II, MURDERED, 1918,
R.A.F. MADE FIRST DAYLIGHT RAID ON THE RUHR, 1942,
HOUSE OF COMMONS APPROVED BILL TO RECTIFY OMISSION
FROM CIVIL LIST ACT OF ANNUITY OF £6,000 TO PRINCESS
MARGARET ON REACHING AGE OF 21, 1951.

July the Seventeenth

If there be good in what I wrought,
Thy hand compelled it, master, thine—
Where I have failed to meet thy thought
I know, through Thee, the blame was mine.

From sudden death, good Lord deliver us.
These who gave up their lives on July the Seventeenth were not so delivered.
Jacques Arteveldt, a brewer of Ghent and a leader of the people, was slain on this day in 1344.
Janet, Lady Glamis, was on this day burned as a witch in 1537, on the Castle Hill at Edinburgh.
The murderer of Marat, Charlotte Corday, was guillotined on July the Seventeenth in 1793.
The Right Honourable Joseph Westwood, Secretary of State for Scotland, died in a road accident in 1948 on this day.
On this day died Adam Smith, in 1790, who left the world The Wealth of Nations.

Born on this day were,
Dr. Isaac Watts, well-known divine and writer of hymns, 1674, Southampton,
Adrian Reland, Oriental scholar and author, 1676,
Anton Krupp, 1787.

These, too, died this day:
Robert Guiscard the Norman, Duke of Apulia, 1085, Corfu,
Sir William Wyndham, noted Tory orator, 1740, Wells, Somerset,
Dr. John Roebuck, founder of the Carron Ironworks, 1794,
Charles, second Earl Grey, Prime Minister to William IV, 1845,
Whistler, 1903.

ON THIS DAY THESE EVENTS ARE RECORDED,
BATTLE OF CASTILLON ENDED ENGLISH DOMINATION OF FRANCE, 1453,
AFTER THIS DAY SCOTTISH DOCUMENTS MUST BE SIGNED AND WITNESSED, 1525,
HOUSE OF LORDS REJECTED BILL TO ADMIT JEWS INTO PARLIAMENT, 1851,
WAR BETWEEN FRANCE AND PRUSSIA, 1870,
ROYAL HOUSE ASSUMED THE NAME OF WINDSOR, 1917,
FIRST BRITISH PLANES BOMBED JAPAN, 1945.

July the Eighteenth

To think of time—of all that retrospection—
To think of today and the ages continued henceforward.

July the Eighteenth is the anniversary of the death of Jane Austen. She died in 1817 and left behind her successive generations of admirers of her novels. She is as fresh and characteristic as the English climate and her memory is fragrant, although a century and more has passed since she quitted the English scene.
In 1872, on this day, the Baroness Burdett Coutts received the freedom of the City of London—the first woman recipient: and July the Eighteenth is the day of Saint Symphorosa and her seven sons—a blessed martyr in the year 120.

There were born on July the Eighteenth:
Dr. John Dee, astrologer and mathematician, 1527, London,
Saverio Bettinelli, Italian author, 1718, Mantua,
Gilbert White, naturalist, 1720, Selborne,
Thackeray, 1811,
Dr. Grace, 1848.

These died on July the Eighteenth,
Pope John XVIII, 1009,
Godfrey of Bouillon, King of Jerusalem, 1100,
Francesco Petrarc (Petrarch), great Italian poet and sonnetteer, 1374, Arque, near Padua,
Thomas Sherlock, Bishop of London, 1761, Fulham,
Paul Jones, 1792,
Dean Stanley, 1881,
Sir George Granville Leveson-Gower, 1951.

THESE EVENTS ARE RECORDED:
PAPAL AUTHORITY EXTINGUISHED BY ROYAL ASSENT IN ENGLAND, 1536,
FIRST CHAIN BRIDGE IN ENGLAND ACROSS THE TWEED, 1820,
FIRST CUNARDER ARRIVED AT NEW YORK, 1840,
PAPAL INFALLIBILITY DECREED, 1870,
THE BALLOT ACT (AUTHORIZING PARLIAMENTARY VOTING BY BALLOT BOX) 1872,
CIVIL WAR BROKE OUT IN SPAIN, 1936,
ROYAL ASSENT GIVEN TO INDIA INDEPENDENCE BILL, 1947.

July the Nineteenth

It was there this morning,
And now, alack! it's gone,
I need no gipsy's warning,
Time—it marches on!

July the Nineteenth was the day on which peace was officially declared in
1919—the day on which the Franco-Prussian war began in 1870—the day
on which the first convention on Women's Rights was held in 1848—the
day on which Lady Jane Grey was deposed in 1553 to be succeeded by many
—the day on which Sir Henry Irving, the first actor-knight, received
congratulations at the Lyceum Theatre in 1895—the day of Peel's Bank
Charter Act in 1844 and the day on which Rome had its first air raid in 1943
—July the Nineteenth was that day.

These were born on this day,
Conrad Vorstius, or Vorst, celebrated German divine, 1569, Cologne,
Gilbert Sheldon, Archbishop of Canterbury, erector of the Sheldon Theatre at Oxford, 1598, Staunton, Staffordshire,
John Martin, celebrated painter, 1789, Haydon Bridge,
Lord Airedale, 1882.

There died on this day,
Dr. John Caius, physician and author, founder of Caius College, 1573,
William Somerville, author of *The Chase*, 1742, Edstone,
Nathaniel Hooke, author of the Roman History, 1764, Hedsor,
Captain Matthew Flinders, Australian explorer, 1814,
Professor John Playfair, writings in natural philosophy, geology, etc., 1819, Edinburgh,
Tom Hayward, the cricketer, 1939.

THESE EVENTS ARE RECORDED,
PHILIP OF SPAIN ARRIVED IN ENGLAND FOR THE 'SPANISH MARRIAGE', 1554,
HAVING DRIVEN THE NEAPOLITANS OUT OF SICILY, GARIBALDI LANDED ON THE MAINLAND, 1860,
MISS FOSTER WON KING'S PRIZE, 1930,
DEDICATION OF FREEMASONS' HALL BY DUKE OF CONNAUGHT, 1933,
MILITARY TARGETS IN ROME BOMBED, 1943.

July the Twentieth

Sixty is past—what is there left
For he who is of time bereft
He needs must limit all his hours,
His last request—perhaps—'no flowers'.

On July the Twentieth died William Scrope in 1852 in London. He was of
the angling fraternity—a kindly sort—a follower of Izaak Walton. His work
is still sought for—it is entitled Days and Nights of Salmon Fishing.
Andrew Lang—the Scots poet, critic, essayist, author and scientist—died on
this day in 1912. As, too, did Catherine Anne Southey, the poetess and
novelist, at Buckland, near Lymington, in 1854, and John Prideaux, the
scholarly Bishop of Worcester, in 1650, at Bredon.
On July the Twentieth Marconi died in 1937, and in 1939, on the same
day, Sir Dan Godfrey died.

Born on this day were:
Petrarch, Italian poet, 1304 (O.S.), Arezzo in Tuscany,
James Harris, author of *Hermes*, 1709, Salisbury,
Sultan Mahmoud II, 1785,
Sir James Phillips Kay-Shuttleworth, noted for his exertions in
promoting education, 1804,
John Sterling, poet and essayist, 1806, Kames Castle, Bute,
Santos-Dumont, 1873.

These died on July the Twentieth:
Robert the Wise, King of France, 1031, Melun,
Peter Lombard, Bishop of Paris, 1164,
Thomas Randolph, Earl of Moray, 1332, Musselburgh,
Talbot, Earl of Shrewsbury, distinguished warrior, 1452,
Sir Richard Wallace, 1890.

THESE EVENTS ARE RECORDED:
ARMADA ARRIVED OFF THE LIZARD, 1588,
FIRST BRANCH OFFICE OF THE BANK OF ENGLAND OPENED,
GLOUCESTER, 1826,
LONDON AND BIRMINGHAM RAILWAY OPENED FROM
EUSTON TO BOXMOOR, 1837,
EXTRADITION TREATY, AMPLIFYING THAT SIGNED IN
1842, BETWEEN GREAT BRITAIN AND UNITED STATES,
1886,
ATTEMPT ON HITLER'S LIFE, 1944.

[211]

July the Twenty-first

Every man has his ill day.

On July the Twenty-first Saint Zoticus—a bishop—was martyred in 204. In the fourth century Saint Victor of Marseilles was martyred—and so, too, was Saint Barhadbeschiabas in 354. It was on this day that King Darius the Third of Persia was murdered by Bessus in 330 B.C., and it was on the same day that William, Lord Russell, was beheaded in Lincoln's Inn Fields in 1683. On this day Robert Burns died in 1796 at Dumfries, and Ellen Terry died in 1928.

On July the Twenty-first, in 1588, the fight with the Armada began, and in 1941, the first raid in history by Germany on Moscow took place.

These are the saints of the day:
St. Praxedes, virgin, second century,
St. Arbogastus, Bishop of Strasburg, confessor, about 678.

On this day was born:
Mathew Prior, English poet, 1664, Wimborne, Dorsetshire.

Died on this July the Twenty-first were:
Pope Nicholas II, 1061,
James Butler, Duke of Ormond, 1688,
Peter Thelusson, celebrated millionaire, 1797, Plaistow, Essex,
Daniel Lambert, 1809 (weighed fifty-three stones),
Viscount Lee of Fareham—donor of Chequers—1947,
Sir Herbert Barker, 1950.

THESE ARE THE EVENTS OF THE DAY:
FIRST ARCHBISHOP OF YORK CONSECRATED, 625,
BATTLE OF CHALGROVE, 1643,
FEMALE CHARACTERS FIRST PLAYED BY WOMEN, 1662,
ACT OF UNION WITH IRELAND PUBLISHED, 1801,
BELGIAN INDEPENDENCE DAY, 1831,
SCOTTISH BANKING ACT PASSED, 1845,
A SOLEMN MEMORANDUM (THE VERY FIRST) PERMITTED
THE ARMY TO GROW A MOUSTACHE, 1854,
COBDEN CLUB INSTITUTED, 1866,
ALLIED FORCES CAPTURED ENNA IN SICILY, 1943,
OSTROV TAKEN BY RUSSIANS, 1944,
NORTH ATLANTIC TREATY RATIFIED BY U.S. SENATE, 1949,
DUKE OF EDINBURGH FLEW TO LONDON ON COMPLETING
SERVICE WITH MEDITERRANEAN FLEET, 1951.

July the Twenty-second

Things bad must surely be better,
The worst it can't always hold sway,
Wet—it can't always be wetter
The best becomes better each day.

In 1875 Samuel Plimsoll, whose bust stands in the Embankment Gardens in
London, made his great stand in the House of Commons, on July the
Twenty-second.
In 1921, after a continuous run of five years, 'Chu Chin Chow', the
popular musical play, finished its run on July the Twenty-second.
On this day in 1298 the Battle of Falkirk was fought and the Scottish
patriot, Sir John Graham, was killed in action and, on this day in 1812, too,
was fought in the Peninsular War the Battle of Salamanca.
Margarine rationing commenced in Britain on July the Twenty-second in
1940.

On this day was born
Anthony Ashley Cooper, first Earl of Shaftesbury, celebrated
politician in the reign of Charles II, 1621, Wimborne, Dorsetshire,
Mendel, Austrian botanist, 1822,
Lord Lyle of Westbourne, politician and sugar magnate, 1882.

There died on this day:
Sir Henry Percy (Hotspur), King of France, 1403, Meun in Berry,
Henry Carey, Lord Hunsdon, 1596, London,
Gerbrant Vander Eexkhout, Dutch painter, 1674,
Francis, Lord Gardenstone, Scottish judge, miscellaneous writer,
1793,
Marie François Xavier Bichat, eminent French anatomist, 1802,
Dr. George Shaw, naturalist, 1813, London,
Joseph Piazzi, eminent astronomer, 1826, Palermo,
Rt. Hon. William Lyon Mackenzie King, Prime Minister of
Canada for twenty-one years, 1950.

THE EVENTS ARE:
FOUNDATIONS LAID OF GUILDFORD CATHEDRAL, 1936,
NAPLES ATTACKED BY R.A.F., 1941,
THE EIGHTH ARMY IN EGYPT ATTACKED ON ALL FRONTS,
1942,
BREAD RATIONING IN BRITAIN, 1946,
BRITISH H.Q. IN JERUSALEM BLOWN UP, 1946.

[213]

July the Twenty-third

My days are swifter than a weaver's shuttle.

These were born on July the Twenty-third:
Godfrey Olearius, the Younger, German divine, in 1672, at Leipzig,
The poet, Coventry Patmore, in 1823, and
The soldier, Viscount Alanbrooke, in 1883.

These died on this July the Twenty-third:
St. Bridger of Sweden, 1372,
Sir Robert Sherley, English military adventurer in Persia, 1627,
Duke of Buckingham, assassinated by Felton, 1628,
Richard Gibson, artist, 1690,
Gilles Menage, grammarian and versifier, 1692, Paris,
Vicomte Alexandre de Beauharnais, first husband of the Empress Josephine, guillotined, 1794,
Jean François Vauvilliers, eminent French scholar, 1800, St. Petersburg,
Arthur Wolfe, Lord Kilwarden, murdered by the populace in Dublin, 1803,
Mrs. Elizabeth Hamilton, authoress of *The Cottagers of Glenburnie*, 1816, Harrogate,
S. T. Coleridge, 1834,
General Grant, 1885, and
James Maxton, 1946—the last of the Independent Labour Party.

THESE EVENTS FILL OUT THE CALENDAR:
JENNY GEDDES THREW A STOOL IN ST. GILES, 1637,
CHARLES EDWARD STUART LANDED IN THE HIGHLANDS, 1745,
FIRST APPEARANCE OF THE BLOOMER, 1851,
OATH OF ALLEGIANCE COMBINED WITH STATUTES RE-QUIRING OATHS OF SUPREMACY AND ABJURATION, 1858,
JEWISH RELIEF ACT (POWER TO MODIFY ABOVE TO ENABLE JEWS TO SIT IN PARLIAMENT), 1858,
ALEXANDRA PARK OPENED, 1863,
'GREAT EASTERN' STARTED OFF ON HER FIRST CABLE-LAYING ATTEMPT, 1865,
BOARD OF AGRICULTURE CREATED, 1889,
AUSTRIAN ULTIMATUM TO SERBIA, 1914,
INCOME TAX COLLECTED AT SOURCE, 8s. 6D. IN THE £, 1940, BUT ON ITS WAY UP.

July the Twenty-fourth

Is today nothing?
Is the beginningless past nothing?
If the future is nothing
They are as surely nothing.

There is a very jostling of saints on July the Twenty-fourth; from that great company these may be recalled:
St. Christina, virgin and martyr, beginning of fourth century,
St. Declan, first Bishop of Ardmore, Ireland, fifth century,
St. Lupus, Bishop of Troyes, confessor, 478,
Saints Romanus and David, patrons of Muscovy, martyrs, 1010,
St. Kinga or Cunegundes of Poland, 1292.

On this day were born:
Roger Dodsworth, eminent antiquary, 1585, at Newton Grange in Yorkshire,
Rev. John Newton, evangelical divine, 1725, London, and
John Philpot Curran, distinguished Irish barrister, 1750,
Alexandre Dumas the Elder in 1802,
Lord Cardwell, 1813, the army reformer.

On July the Twenty-fourth these men died:
Caliph Abu-Bekr, first successor of Mohammed, 634, Medina,
Don Carlos, son of Philip II of Spain, died in prison, 1568,
Alphonse des Vignoles, chronologist, 1744, Berlin,
George Vertue, eminent engraver and antiquary, 1756, London,
John Dyer, poet, author of *Grongar Hill*, 1758, Coningsby,
Dr. Nathaniel Lardner, author of *Credibility of the Gospel History*, 1768, Hawkhurst, Kent,
Armand Carrel, French political writer, died in consequence of wounds in a duel, 1836.

THESE WERE THE EVENTS OF THE DAY:
BATTLE OF HARLAW, NEAR ABERDEEN—DEFEAT OF CELTS BY LOWLANDERS, 1411,
MARY, QUEEN OF SCOTS, FORCED TO ABDICATE, 1567,
GIBRALTAR CAPTURED, 1704,
FIRST ROAD-TRAMWAY, 1801,
WINDOW TAX REPEALED, 1851,
PUBLIC OFFICES SITE ACT, 1882,
THE KING VISITED HIS TROOPS IN ITALY, 1944.

[215]

July the Twenty-fifth

In the day of prosperity be joyful
But in the day of adversity consider:
And in the day of prosperity
Or in the day of adversity
Be not righteous overmuch.

July the Twenty-fifth is the anniversary of the consecration of Buckfast Abbey by Cardinal Bourne in 1932.
It is the day of the death of Thomas à Kempis, in 1471, at Mount St. Agnes near Zwolle, who is the reputed author of the Imitation of Christ.
It is the day of the death, in 1694, at Rotterdam, of Robert Fleming, the author of The Fulfilling of the Scripture.
It is the day of the death of Philip Beroaldus—the Elder—the classic commentator, in 1505 at Bologna: of Charles Dibdin, who wrote 'The Songs of the Sea', at Camden Town in 1814, and of William Savage in 1844 at Kennington, who wrote the The Dictionary on the Art of Printing.
Herr Dollfuss, the gallant Chancellor of Austria, was murdered, 1934.

Born on this day were:
Rev. William Burkitt, author of *Expository Notes on the New Testament*, 1650, Hitcham, Northamptonshire,
Mrs. Elizabeth Hamilton, authoress of *The Cottagers of Glenburnie*, 1758, Belfast,
Earl of Balfour, K.G., O.M., 1848.

There died on this day:
Ferdinand I, Emperor of Germany, 1564, Vienna,
William Romaine, eminent divine, 1795, London,
William Sharp, engraver, 1824, Chiswick,
James Kenney, dramatic writer, 1849, London,
Sir James Mitchell, former Premier and Governor of Western Australia, 1951.

THESE EVENTS ARE RECORDED:
CALTON HILL OBSERVATORY, EDINBURGH, FOUNDED, 1776,
HANGING IN CHAINS ABOLISHED, 1834,
ELECTRIC TELEGRAPH EXPERIMENT BETWEEN EUSTON SQUARE AND CAMDEN TOWN, 1837,
BLÉRIOT FLEW THE CHANNEL, 1909,
MUSSOLINI RESIGNED, 1943.

July the Twenty-sixth

Day is pushed out by day,
And each new moon hastens to its death.

George Bernard Shaw was born on July the Twenty-sixth, 1856. He wrote Man and Superman *and* The Intelligent Woman's Guide to Socialism.

George Borrow died on July the Twenty-sixth in 1881. He wrote The Bible in Spain *and* Lavengro.

In Ireland on this day the Irish Church was disestablished in 1869, the rising took place in Dublin in 1914, and in 1939 the British Government condemned the Irish Republican Army.

The Bank of England was founded on July the Twenty-sixth in 1694, and on the same day, in 1945, the Labour Government came to power in Britain.

Born on this day were:
Henry VII of England, 1456, Pembroke, South Wales,
André Charlot, 1882,
Aldous Huxley, famous novelist and critic, 1894.

There died on this day:
King Roderick of Spain, killed in battle with the Moors, 711,
Ladislaus I, King of Poland, 1102,
Pope Paul II, 1471,
Jacopo Bonfadio, historian and poet, executed at Genoa, 1560,
Armand de Gontaut-biron, Marshal of France, killed at siege of Epernai, 1592,
Charles Emmanuel the Great, Duke of Savoy, 1630,
John Wilmot, Earl of Rochester, noted debauchee and poet, 1680,
Thomas Osborne, Duke of Leeds, statesman, 1712,
Dr. John Freind, eminent scholar, 1728,
John Emery, comic actor, 1822,
Baron Gourgaud, distinguished general under Napoleon, 1852.

THESE ARE RECORDED:
BRITISH COLUMBIA JOINED CANADIAN CONFEDERATION, 1871,
THE 'WARATAH' SAILED, 1909,
HAMBURG BOMBED, 1943,
AFTER FURTHER MEETINGS NEGOTIATORS AGREED ON AGENDA FOR ARMISTICE, 1951 (KOREAN WAR).

July the Twenty-seventh

The great, the important day, big with fate,
For Cato and for Rome.

On July the Twenty-seventh in 1935, it was announced that eleven million six hundred and forty thousand persons had signed the 'Peace Ballot'. It was a significant event for Britain and went not unnoticed in Germany.

These were born on July the Twenty-seventh:
Isaac Maddox, Bishop of Worcester (Vindication of Government &c., of Church of England), 1697, London,
Thomas Campbell, poet, who was he? (*Pleasures of Hope*), 1777, Glasgow,
George Biddell Airy, Astronomer Royal of England, 1801, Alnwick,
Vladimir de Pachmann (pianist), 1848,
Hilaire Belloc, 1870.

These died on this day:
James I, King of Aragon, 1276, Xativa,
Henri, Maréchal de Turenne, killed near Salzbach in Alsace, 1675,
Viscount Dundee, 1689,
Pierre Louis de Maupertuis, natural philosopher, 1759, Basel,
Samuel Gottlieb Gmelin, naturalist, 1774, Achmetkent in the Caucasus,
George Burnet, Scottish painter, 1816,
Dr. John Dalton, eminent chemist, 1844, Manchester.

THESE EVENTS ARE RECORDED,
KILLIECRANKIE, 1689,
BANK OF ENGLAND RECEIVED ITS CHARTER, 1694,
RUSSIAN AMBASSADOR IMPRISONED FOR DEBT, 1708,
END OF REIGN OF TERROR, 1794,
PORT OF ADELAIDE FOUNDED BY COLONEL LIGHT, 1836,
ATLANTIC CABLE COMPLETED, 1866,
WILLIAM II'S 'HUNS' SPEECH AT BREMERHAVEN, 1900,
CAPTAIN CHARLES FRYATT, BRITISH SAILOR, EXECUTED CONTRARY TO INTERNATIONAL CODES OF JUSTICE BY THE GERMANS, 1916,
ROSTOV EVACUATED BY THE RUSSIANS, 1942,
TOBRUK HEAVILY ATTACKED BY ALLIED BOMBERS, 1942,
LVOV, DVINSK AND BIALYSTOK CAPTURED, 1944.

July the Twenty-eighth

Not a day passes, not a minute or second without an accouchement,
Not a day passes, not a minute or second without a corpse.

Born on this day were:
Jacopo Sannazaro, Italian poet, 1458, Naples,
Joseph I, Emperor of Germany, 1678, Vienna,
Sir Hudson Lowe, 1769,
John Stuart Blackie, 1809.

There died on this day,
Theodosius the Younger, Roman emperor, 450, Constantinople,
Thomas Cromwell, Earl of Essex, beheaded on Tower Hill, 1540,
John Speed, historical writer, 1629, Cripplegate, London,
Richard Corbet, Bishop of Norwich, humorous poet, 1635,
Abraham Cowley, metaphysical poet, 1667, Chertsey, Surrey,
Sir John Cope, 1760,
George Bubb Dodington, intriguing politician, 1762,
Maximilian Isidore Robespierre, terrorist autocrat, guillotined at
Paris, 1794,
Giuseppe Sarti, musical composer, 1802, Berlin,
Sultan Selim III, assassinated at Constantinople, 1808,
Marshal Mortier, Bonapartist general, killed at Paris by Fieschi's
'infernal machine', 1835,
Joseph Bonaparte, ex-King of Sardinia, 1849, Oporto,
Hans C. Andersen, 1875,
Mortimer Collins, poet and novelist, contributor to *Punch*, and
author of *Sweet Anne Page*, &c., 1876,
Bismarck, 1898.

THESE EVENTS ARE RECORDED,
BEGINNING OF THE ARMADA FIGHT, 1588,
FOUNDATION STONE OF ROYAL HIGH SCHOOL OF EDIN-
BURGH LAID BY VISCOUNT GLENORCHY, 1825,
THE 'ALABAMA' SAILED, 1862,
SOURCE OF NILE DISCOVERED BY SPEKE, 1862,
FIRST WOMAN LICENSED TO PRACTISE MEDICINE (MISS
GANET), 1865,
CONVICTION ON JAMESON RAIDERS, 1896,
AUSTRIA DECLARED WAR ON SERBIA, 1914,
FASCIST PARTY DISSOLVED IN ITALY, 1943.

July the Twenty-ninth

O, that a man might know
The end of this day's business ere it come!
But it sufficeth that the day will end,
And then the end is known.

July the Twenty-ninth was a day of endings.
The Spanish Armada was finally dispersed on this day in 1588,
The Eighth Army was disbanded on this day in 1945.

There were birthdays on July the Twenty-ninth.
Benito Mussolini was born on this day in 1883,
Max Nordau was born in 1849 as was also the great de Tocqueville in 1805,
July the Twenty-ninth is stated to be the birthday of Albert I, Emperor of Germany, in 1248.

There died on this day:
Philip I, King of France, 1108, Melun,
Sebastian, King of Portugal, killed near Tangier, 1578,
Thomas Stukeley, adventurer, 1578,
Pope Urban VIII, 1644,
Andrew Marvell, poet and politician, 1678, London,
Benjamin Robins, celebrated mathematician and experimenter on projectiles, 1751, Madras,
Augustus William Ernesti, editor of Livy, 1801, Leipzig,
Anna Selina Storace, favourite singer, 1814, London,
William Wilberforce, philanthropist, 1833, London,
Schumann, 1856,
Dr. Thomas Dick, author of various scientific works, 1857, Broughty Ferry, Forfarshire,
Sir Cresswell Cresswell, first judge of the Divorce Court, 1863,
Vincent van Gogh, famous Dutch artist, 1890.

THESE EVENTS ARE RECORDED,
FINAL ATTEMPT AT LAYING ATLANTIC CABLE BEGAN, 1858,
MARY, QUEEN OF SCOTS, MARRIED HER SECOND HUSBAND, DARNLEY, 1565,
'YOUNG IRELAND' PARTY FORMED, 1846,
FIRST IMPERIAL DEFENCE CONFERENCE, 1904,
BAR OF GOLD RECOVERED FROM 'LUTINE', 1938.

July the Thirtieth

A poet and a banker,
What a happy man was he,
He lived life without rancour,
He did not have to hanker
The poet, not the banker
Wrote Pleasures of Memory.

Samuel Roger who wrote The Pleasures of Memory, *was born on July the Thirtieth in 1763 at Stoke Newington, near London. He was a poet and a banker but it is as a poet he is remembered. This fact may be a warning to bankers.*
Lord Haldane, who created Britain's Territorial Army, was born, too, on July the Thirtieth in 1856, and another creator of power shares that day. Henry Ford was born in 1863, Mr. 'Ebby' Edwards, 1884.

These died on July the Thirtieth:
Ladislaus I, King of Hungary, 1095,
Maria Theresa, queen of Louis XIV, 1683,
William Penn, colonizer of Pennsylvania, 1718,
John Sebastian Bach, eminent composer, 1750, Leipzig,
Thomas Gray, poet, 1771,
Fred Muntz, M.P., 1857,
Sir C. Hastings, founder of the British Medical Association, 1866,
Walter Pater, 1894,
Sir Joseph Cook, P.C., a Prime Minister of Australia, 1947,
Madame Guilhermina Suggia, famous Portuguese 'cellist, 1950,
Admiral Sir Max Kennedy Horton, submarine commander in First World War, 1951.

THESE EVENTS ARE RECORDED:
CHATHAM'S MINISTRY, 1766,
LAST PUBLIC PENANCE RECORDED, 1882,
MR. CLEISHER ATTRIBUTED CHOLERA AT BETHNAL GREEN TO A PECULIAR BLUE MIST. HE STATED THAT ELSEWHERE SCARLATINA WAS DUE TO A YELLOW MIST, 1866,
RUMANIAN OIL WELLS BOMBED, 1940,
RUSSO-POLISH AGREEMENT, 1941,
KASSEL AND REMSCHIED BOMBED, 1943,
SUBSTANTIAL INCREASES IN RETIRED PAY AND PENSIONS OF ARMED FORCES ANNOUNCED, 1951.

July the Thirty-first

It awaits you—all down the days,
The chance to do—the hope of praise,
It is all there—it all awaits,
The sure unfolding of our fates.

A tinker in the army of Cromwell, inspired by a vision of the Holy City,
wrote a book in Bedford Jail. The book is part of all English thought and
speech ever since. It is The Pilgrim's Progress, *and John Bunyan wrote it.*
He died on July the Thirty-first in 1688.
Another great inspirer of men's faith in God died, too, on July the Thirty-
first. It was in 1556 at Rome and his name was Ignatius Loyola, who
founded the Society of Jesus.

There died, too, on July the Thirty-first:
Charles de Gontaut, Duc de Biron, favourite commander of Henri
IV, beheaded in Bastille, 1602,
Martin Harpertzoon Van Tromp, Dutch Admiral, killed in an
engagement near Texel, 1653,
John V, King of Portugal, 1750,
Denis Diderot, French encyclopaedist, 1784, Paris,
William T. Lowndes, bibliographer, 1843,
Liszt, 1886,
Owen Nares, 1943.

Princess Augusta of Brunswick was born on this day in 1737.

THESE EVENTS ARE RECORDED:
BENJAMIN DISRAELI BAPTIZED (ST. ANDREW'S, HOLBORN),
1817,
INTERNATIONAL COPYRIGHT ACT WAS PASSED, 1836,
NEWLY MADE HALF CROWNS AND FLORINS DECLARED
LEGAL TENDER, 1849,
ARTISANS AND LABOURERS DWELLINGS ACT, 1868,
ARREST OF CRIPPEN, 1910, ST. LAWRENCE,
GUARDS DIVISION CONSTITUTED, 1915,
ARRANGEMENTS FOR BRITISH WITHDRAWAL FROM ARCH-
ANGEL AND MURMANSK, 1919,
BRITISH FLEET MOBILIZED, 1939,
RUSSIANS RESISTING PRESSURE IN THE DON ELBOW, 1942,
ALLIES CROSSED THE SOMME AND THE MEUSE, 1944.

AUGUST

THIRTY-ONE DAYS

August the First

. . . Out of eternity
This new day is born
Into eternity
At night will return . . .

First place is given to death in this record of August the First. 'Die thou at the right time,' wrote Frederick Nietzsche.

Cavour was born in 1810.

Queen Anne died in 1714,
Admiral Sir John Leake, naval commander, in 1720,
Savage, the poet and Samuel Johnson's friend, died in 1743,
Mrs. Inchbald, the actress, in 1821,
The Rev. Robert Morrison, D.D., first Protestant Missionary to China, 1834.

Roads and railways claim a place:
The new London Bridge in 1831,
The Thames Tunnel was opened in 1842,
The Royal Border Bridge at Berwick-on-Tweed in 1850,
The North Eastern Railway began working over the North British Railway to Edinburgh in 1869, and
The Glasgow Central Station was opened in 1879.

Looking backward over travelled roads,
Montgomery took up his command in 1942,
Hitler became Head of the German Reich in 1934,
Germany declared war on Russia in 1914 . . .
these are all in living memory.

FOLDED UP IN AN UNRETURNING PAST, AUGUST THE FIRST HOLDS THE ANNIVERSARIES OF:
ON THE WATERS OF THE THAMES, THOMAS DOGGETT ESTABLISHED HIS FAMOUS ROWING MATCH IN 1716,
THE DAY WHEN ENGLISH SOLDIERS FOUGHT WITH ROSES IN THEIR HATS, 1759,
THE BATTLE OF ABOUKIR IN 1798,
WELLINGTON'S ENTRY INTO SPAIN IN 1832,
QUEEN VICTORIA LEAVING, IN 1849, FOR HER FIRST VISIT TO IRELAND,
THE INAUGURATION OF PARCEL POST, 1883.

August the Second

The day may be defined as consisting of from sunrise to sunset.

Between the sunrise and sunset on August the Second,
William Rufus was shot in the New Forest in the year 1100,
The tax on gloves was repealed in 1795,
The Tower subway, the first tube railway, was opened in 1870.

On August the Second, 216 B.C., the Battle of Cannae was fought,
and on the same day in 1704 the Battle of Blenheim was fought.
Merrily, between London and Bristol, ran the first Mail Coach on
this day in 1774.

There was a lot doing.
On the Second of August, in 1914, the Opposition offered its
support to the Government in the National Emergency:
Germany demanded right of way through Belgium on that day,
and, simultaneously, Germany invaded France and Poland while
Russia crossed the frontier into East Prussia.

In 1916 the Italian battleship *Leonardo da Vinci* blew up,
August the Second, in 1937, marked the setting up of a new record
for the Atlantic passage—3 days 22 hrs. 7 min.,
August the Second was U.S.S.R.'s first Navy Day in 1939,
The Food Defence Bill went through the House of Commons in
the same year,
Britain extended blockade to Finland on August the Second, 1941,
The three envoys had two-hour talk with Generalissimo Stalin
and Mr. Molotov, 1948.

There were born on August the Second,
Pope Leo XII, 1760,
Cardinal Wiseman, 1802,
Marion Crawford, the author of *Barlasch of the Guard*, 1854,
Ethel M. Dell, 1881.

DEATH HAD, TOO, ITS CONQUEST ON AUGUST THE SECOND,
THOMAS GAINSBOROUGH, THE PAINTER, DIED IN 1788,
JOHN PALMER, THE ACTOR, IN 1798,
IN 1921 THE VOICE OF ENRICO CARUSO WAS STILLED
FOREVER,
VON HINDENBURG DIED IN 1934 (AND HITLER BECAME
PRESIDENT) AND MASCAGNI IN 1945.

August the Third

What's a day for but to do?

Few have known what to do with days better than Lord Beaverbrook. On August the Third, 1941, he was appointed a member of the Cabinet. He, doubtless, was unaware that this was the day of destiny, but none the less it was so.

On August the Third in 1916 Sir Roger Casement was hanged,
It was the anniversary of the Moratorium in 1914,
It was the day of British mobilization,
It was the day on which Belgium rejected the German ultimatum and Germany declared war on France,
This day saw the second air raid in the 1914–18 war. It occurred over Luneville, the first having been over Vienna,
Long, long before these days, James the Second of Scotland was killed before Roxburgh Castle in 1460, and a cobbler, so the records show, was whipped from Holloway to London for criticizing the government in 1715,
On this day in 1939 the Bank of International Settlements released Czech gold to Germany and two years later in 1941 Marshal Pétain rejected the demand of Germany to be allowed to 'protect' Dakar, Casablanca and other bases in North Africa,
Rennes occupied, 1944,
Dutch military action in Indonesia ended, 1947,
In message to the Persian Government, Britain recognized principle of nationalization of Persian oil industry, 1951.

These died on August the Third,
Stephen Dolet, eminent scholar and typographer, burned, 1546,
In 1772 Sir Richard Arkwright, inventor of the spinning jenny, left behind him the seeds of an industrial revolution,
Pierce Egan (Boxiana), 1849,
Eugene Sue, the novelist, in 1857,
Joseph Conrad in 1924, and
Dr. A. F. Pollard, F.B.A., 1948.

HOPEFULLY ON AUGUST THE THIRD, WERE BORN:
THE EARL BALDWIN IN 1867,
KING HAAKON OF NORWAY IN 1872,
RUPERT BROOKE, POET, 1887,
LESLIE HENSON, 1891.

August the Fourth

So keep right on to the end of the road,
And grin if you cannot smile
The lighter the heart—the lesser the load,
It shortens the longest mile.

Scotland has produced many solemn men—the grim John Knox, the dyspeptic
Thomas Carlyle, that solemn King James the Sixth who was called 'the
wisest fool in Europe'—but it has had its brighter and lighter moments, too:
such a moment was August the Fourth, 1870, when Sir Harry Lauder was
born. He is one of the immortal comedians with that touch of pathos which
makes us 'all John Tamson's bairns'.
August the Fourth was the birthday of Her Gracious Majesty Queen
Elizabeth in 1900.

Percy Bysshe Shelley in 1792,
Edward Irving, 1792.

On this day there died,
William Cecil, Lord Burleigh, 1595,
Admiral Duncan in 1804,
Hans C. Andersen in 1875,
'Gipsy' Smith, evangelist, 1947.

On this day these events were recorded,
Christopher Columbus set sail in 1492 (according to Chambers it
was a Friday and the hour eight),
The shrine of Our Lady of Walsingham was dissolved, 1538—the
most famous shrine in medieval England,
Admiral Vernon shattered the moral of the navy by introducing
grog—water–rum—1740,
East India docks were opened, 1806.

FIRST TIME THE TERM C.-IN-C. OF THE GRAND FLEET USED,
WHEN ADMIRAL JELLICOE TOOK OVER ITS COMMAND FROM
ADMIRAL CALLAGHAN, 1914,
GERMANY INVADED BELGIUM, BRITAIN DECLARED WAR
IN 1914,
THE TURKISH ATTACK ON SUEZ CANAL IN 1916,
TRANSATLANTIC AIR MAIL RESUMED BY BRITAIN, 1940,
GANDHI'S ORIGINAL DOCUMENT FORESHADOWING ALLI-
ANCE WITH JAPAN, 1942.

August the Fifth

Neither tyranny nor time can we abide,
We pilgrims fear not neither wind nor tide.

The hour had come. A continent awaited them. The impulse was upon them. They could not have foreseen what they did—these early pioneers who on August the Fifth set sail from England to lay the first Atlantic Cable to the United States of America. There is a tide in the affairs of men. They did not fear it—they availed themselves of it.

Two of the famous men born on this day were:
Kinglake, author of *Eothen*, 1809,
Guy de Maupassant, the world's greatest writer of short stories, 1850.

There died:
John, Earl of Gowrie, slain at Perth in the curious Gowrie House Conspiracy, 1600,
Frederick, Lord North, statesman, 1792,
Lord Howe, victor of the 'Glorious First of June', 1799,
Empress Frederick of Germany, 1901,
Hon. Herbert Asquith, barrister, poet and novelist, 1947.

These events are recorded:
Accession of Henry I, 1100,
The first attempt to lay the Atlantic cable commenced, 1857,
Atlantic cable finished, 1858,
Supreme Court of Judicature Act passed, 1873,
War Council formed at 10 Downing Street, 1914,
Kitchener appointed War Secretary in place of Mr. Asquith, 1914,
Austria-Hungary declared war on Russia, 1914,
Edith Cavell arrested in Brussels, 1915,
Last Zeppelin raid on England. Captain Strasser, German airship ace, lost, 1918.

TEMME SWAM CHANNEL IN 14 HOURS 29 MINUTES, 1927,
BRITAIN AGREED TO BEAR HALF THE COST OF ACCOMMO-
DATION IN CANAL ZONE. A MERE £6,000,000, 1938,
BYELGOROD CAPTURED BY RUSSIANS, 1943,
CATANIA FELL TO EIGHTH ARMY, 1943,
AMERICANS REACHED BREST, 1944,
FIRST ATOMIC BOMB, 1945, HIROSHIMA.

August the Sixth

And ye shall die before your thrones are won,
Yours the doubtful dawn, theirs the risen sun.

Herbert George Wells died in London at Regent's Park in 1946. Born in Victorian England, the son of a professional cricketer, this man made himself and was one of the architects of the modern world. Politics, sociology, economics were his main interest, but his enduring place will be as one of the greatest writers of his time. He knew and depicted the 'little man', and Kipps *and* The History of Mr. Polly *are his monuments.*

Born on this day were,
Fénelon, author of *Télémaque*, born 1651,
Dr. William Wallaston, chemist, 1766,
Tennyson, poet laureate, 1809,
General Sir W. J. Slim, 1891.

There died on this day,
St. Dominic de Guzman, founder of Dominican Order, 1221,
Anne Hathaway, 1623,
Ben Jonson, 1637,
Velazquez, famous Spanish painter, 1660.

THESE EVENTS ARE RECORDED:
CHEVALIER D'EON MADE FIRST APPEARANCE IN LONDON, DISGUISED AS A WOMAN, 1777,
DISSOLUTION OF HOLY ROMAN EMPIRE, 1806,
LOUIS NAPOLEON ATTEMPTED TO INCITE INSURRECTION AT BOULOGNE, 1840,
OPENING OF THE RAILWAY GAUGE COMMISSION, 1845,
H.M.S. 'DAEDALUS' SIGHTED A SEA SERPENT, 1848,
ROYAL ASSENT TO SCOTTISH EDUCATION BILL, 1872,
MR. PLIMSOLL'S MOTION BECAME LAW, 1875,
SURPRISED LANDING AT SUVLA BAY, 1915,
MINING DISASTER NEAR BARNSLEY, FIFTY-SEVEN DEATHS, 1936,
GERMANS ATTACKED RUSSIANS NEAR KHOLM, 1941,
GERMANS ADVANCED TOWARDS THE CAUCASUS, 1942,
MUNDA TAKEN BY THE ALLIES, 1943,
FAMILY ALLOWANCE FIRST PAID IN UNITED KINGDOM, £1,000,000 WEEKLY, 1945,
NEW SOUTH AFRICAN PARLIAMENT OPENED, 1948.

[229]

August the Seventh

The day is done and the darkness
Comes down on the wings of night.

On August the Seventh, 1914, Kitchener called for his new army. He demanded the first hundred thousand and got them—the largest voluntary army in British history. They died for the King and Country that called them on all the battlefields of the First World War, but principally in the first Battle of the Somme in 1916.

There were born on August the Seventh:
Princess Amelia, daughter of George III of England, 1783,
John Ayrton Paris, 1785,
Sir Granville Bantock, 1868.

There died on August the Seventh:
Henry IV, surnamed 'The Great', of Germany, 1106,
Caroline of Brunswick, consort of George IV, 1821,
Lady Tree, the famous actress, 1937.

THESE EVENTS ARE RECORDED:
SHIP MONEY DECLARED ILLEGAL, 1641,
FACULTY OF PHYSICIANS ENABLED TO GRANT DEGREES, 1840,
OTTAWA NAMED AS CAPITAL OF THE NEW DOMINION OF CANADA, 1858,
THAMES EMBANKMENT BILL RECEIVED ROYAL ASSENT, 1861,
BRITISH EXPEDITIONARY FORCE BEGAN TO EMBARK, 1914,
FIRST ISSUE OF 'BRADBURYS', 1914,
SUMMERTIME MADE PERMANENT, 1924,
NORTHERN RHODESIA GOVERNMENT REFUSED TO ACCEPT JEWISH REFUGEES, 1938,
BRITISH TRANSATLANTIC AIR MAIL SERVICE OPENED BY THE ARRIVAL AT NEW YORK OF FLYING BOAT 'CARIBOU', 1939,
FIRST RUSSIAN RAID ON BERLIN, 1941,
EXPLOSION IN BRITISH SHIP 'MAHIA' IN DOCK AT MELBOURNE, KILLED TEN MEN AND VESSEL SANK, 1947.
IN 1588 IN AND AROUND THIS DAY, AUGUST THE SEVENTH, SPAIN ALLIED WITH THE POPE AND THEIR ARMADA WAS DEFEATED IN THE ENGLISH CHANNEL BY LORD HOWARD OF EFFINGHAM AND SIR FRANCIS DRAKE.

August the Eighth

Twice in our time they tell the story,
Today's defeats become tomorrow's glory.

August the Eighth, in 1918, was, in Ludendorff's words, 'the black day of the German Army'—but it did not so appear to those who battled in the line in France and Flanders on that day.
August the Eighth, in 1940, was the beginning of the Battle of Britain. German massed air squadrons struck, it seemed irresistibly, to the fearless few of the Royal Air Force. August the Eighth carried in it the certainty of victory.

There died on this day,
Pope Alexander VI, probably the worst pope, 1503,
Duke de Plessis, captor of Minorca, 1788,
George Canning, statesman, 1827,
Sir Daniel Wilson, 1892,
General Anton Denikin, 'White' commander in Russian Civil War, 1917.

These events are recorded,
Coronation stone sent to England, 1296,
First edition of the poems of Burns published, 1786,
First locomotive run in the U.S., 1829,
English Poor Law Act passed, 1834,
Natal annexed, 1843,
Grand Naval Review at Spithead, 1853,
Algeciras Conference, 1904,
H.M.S. *Dunraven*, mystery ship, fought a magnificent losing fight against U.71, 1917,
Second Battle of Amiens, 1918,
Mr. Cordell Hull made a great Declaration on Peace and World Recovery, forty nations adhere, 1937,
Germany began on the West Wall, 1938,
Russia advanced into Manchuria, 1945,
Delhi and Karachi became capitals of India and Pakistan, 1947.

THESE WERE BORN ON THIS DAY:
SIR G. KNELLER, 1648,
JACQUES BASNAGE, PREACHER, ROUEN, 1653,
FRANCIS HUTCHESON, 1694,
SIR FRANCIS RAYMOND EVERSHED, 1899.

August the Ninth

At length the man perceives it die away,
And fade into the light of common day.

He was born on August the Ninth in 1593: he became an ironmonger and
wrote The Compleat Angler: *his name was Izaak Walton. He was born*
on August the Ninth in 1631: he became a poet and a satirist and wrote
Absolom and Achitophel: *his name was John Dryden. He was born*
on August the Ninth in 1757: he began life as a stonemason and before
he died built thousands of miles of roads, bridges and canals: his name was
Thomas Telford.
George Payne Rainsford James, an English author, son of Pinkstan James,
the well-known physician, was born 1799,
Born, too, was Isidore de Lara, 1858.

These events are recorded:
Ashburnham and Washington treaty signed with U.S., 1842,
Act legalizing meeting of Parliament in six days after proclamation, 1870,
Heligoland ceded to Germany, 1890,
Nigeria was annexed, 1899,
U.15 rammed and sunk by H.M.S. *Birmingham*, 1914,
First British troops landed at Boulogne, 1914,
Anglo-Persian agreement signed at Teheran, 1919,
Admiralty decided to have control of Fleet Air Arm. New post
Assistant Chief Naval Staff (Air) formed, 1937,
Queen Mary beat *Normandie*'s record for Atlantic crossing, 1937—
time: 3 days, 21 hours, 48 minutes, 1938,
Gandhi and all members of the Congress Working Committee
arrested after they had guilelessly passed a resolution in Congress
demanding the surrender of all power by Britain in India, 1942,
Mannheim and Ludwigshafen raided, 1943,
Second atomic bomb—Nagasaki—1945.

THESE DIED ON THIS DAY:
SIMON OCKLEY, AUTHOR OF 'HISTORY OF THE SARACENS',
1720,
CAPTAIN MARRYAT, 1848,
MADAME VESTRIS (MRS. CHARLES MATHEWS), FAMOUS
SINGER AND ACTRESS, 1857,
LEONCAVALLO, 1919,
GRAHAM WALLAS, 1932.

August the Tenth

The heavens hold more than mere delight
Praise not the day—before the night.

These events are recorded:
Battle of Otterburn, 1388,
Greenwich Observatory was commenced by Charles II, 1675,
The Paris mob stormed the Tuileries in 1792,
Dingwall and Skye Railway opened to Strome Ferry, 1870,
Criminal law amendment bill passed, 1885,
Boundaries of Gambia settled, 1889,
House of Commons payment of members resolution, 1911,
Peace Treaty with Turkey signed at Sèvres, 1920,
Luftwaffe machine-gunning of civilians started in Britain, 1940,
American forces landed in the Solomon Islands, 1942,
Mr. Attlee broadcast an appeal for a united front to regain economic freedom and declared Government were resolved on equality of sacrifice, 1947,
Capt. W. P. Odom's solo world flight record—73 hours, 5 minutes, Chicago, 1947,
Britain agreed plans for economic co-operation, Marshall Plan, 1948.

These were born on August the Tenth:
Bernard Nieuwentyt, eminent Dutch mathematician, 1654,
Sir Charles Napier, conqueror of Sind, 1782,
Dr. J. Scott-Lidgett, 1854,
Laurence Binyon, 1869,
Herbert C. Hoover (President, U.S.A.), 1874.

THESE DIED ON AUGUST THE TENTH,
MAGNENTIUS, USURPER OF ROMAN EMPIRE, 353,
HENRIETTA MARIA, QUEEN OF CHARLES I, 1669,
BROTHERS DE WITT, MURDERED BY THE MOB, 1672,
CARDINAL DUBOIS, INTRIGUING STATESMAN, 1723,
DR. BENJAMIN HOADLY, AUTHOR OF 'SUSPICIOUS HUS-BAND', 1757,
FERDINAND VI OF SPAIN, 1759,
JOHN WILSON CROKER, TORY POLITICIAN AND REVIEWER, 1857,
SIR GEORGE THOMAS STAUNTON, 1859.

August the Eleventh

Our days on the earth
Are as a shadow.

He knew the shadow: he knew the pride and the garish day as well as the encircling gloom:
He died on this day, August the Eleventh, 1890: John Henry Newman, who became a cardinal and gave men for their guidance one of the finest of English hymns: 'Lead kindly light amid the encircling gloom, lead thou me on'.

These were born on this day,
Betterton, the actor, 1635,
Dr. Mead, the distinguished physician, 1673,
Nollekens, the sculptor, 1737,
Moreau, French Republican general, 1763,
General Hill, of Peninsular fame, 1772,
Charlotte Young, 1823,
Denis William Brogan, Professor of Political Science, Cambridge, author, broadcaster, 1900.

These events are recorded:
First Bishop of Nova Scotia consecrated, 1787,
Religious wars of Switzerland ended by Treaty of Aarau, 1712,
Austrian Empire formed, 1804,
Last gibbeting in this country, 1832,
Hungarian rebellion against the Austrians, 1849,
'Abandonment of Railways' Act passed, 1869,
British Press Bureau formed, 1914,
Montenegro at war with Germany, 1914,
Fight between German aircraft and British coastal motor boats, 1918,
Salvador withdrew from the League of Nations, 1937,
Battle of Britain flared up: sixty-two of the raiders being claimed against a loss of twenty-six, 1940,
Atlantic Charter signed, 1941,
Mr. Jinnah elected President Pakistan Assembly, 1947.

THESE DIED ON THIS DAY:
GENERAL SIR SAMUEL AUCHMUTY, 1812,
JAMES WILSON, 1860,
STEPHEN EARLY, SECRETARY TO ROOSEVELT, 1951.

August the Twelfth

Today is yours—
From lives and boors,
From facile fools,
From rigid rules,
From cranks and crooks,
From shearing hooks,
  Good Lord, deliver you.

August the Twelfth is the day on which grouse shooting commences.
Pope Gregory the Ninth died on this day in 1241,
Pope Innocent the Eleventh died on this day in 1689,
George the Fourth was born on this day in 1762—and Robert Southey, the poet, was born on this day in 1774.
On this day in 1746—following the 'Forty-five'—highland dress was forbidden in Scotland—and on the same day in 1840, the Glasgow, Paisley, Kilmarnock and Ayr Railway was completed.

These were born on August the Twelfth:
Thomas Bewick, the engraver, 1753,
Francis Horner, 1778,
Cyril E. M. Joad, 1891, philosopher,
Viscount Templeton, 1894.

There died on this day:
Nahum Tate, Poet Laureate and versifier of the psalms, 1715,
George Stevenson, engineer, 1848,
William Longman, the publisher, 1877,
Arthur Griffith, 1922.

THE EVENTS OF THE DAY ARE:
HAVANA CAPITULATED TO THE BRITISH, 1762,
FIRST COMMERCIAL USE OF STEAM LOCOMOTIVES, MIDDLETON COLLIERY, A RACK RAILWAY, 1812,
FIRST AMERICAN RAILWAY COMPLETED, 1830,
BUFFER SPRINGS INVENTED FOR USE ON RAILWAY WAGONS BY JOHN BROWN, 1848,
BRITAIN DECLARED WAR ON AUSTRIA-HUNGARY, 1914,
FLORENCE IN ALLIED HANDS, 1944,
FLOODS IN SOUTH-EAST SCOTLAND AND NORTH-EAST ENGLAND ISOLATED VILLAGES AND DELAYED TRAINS, BRIDGES BEING SWEPT AWAY, 1948.

August the Thirteenth

Sunset and day's end puts the hours away,
But these hours will lend much—for another day.

On August the Thirteenth Queen Adelaide, the consort of King William the Fourth, was born in 1792.
On August the Thirteenth Florence Nightingale died in 1910.
It was on this day, the Thirteenth of August, in 1704, that the British, under Marlborough, won the Battle of Blenheim.
On August the Thirteenth The Times *reported that a mechanical device had been introduced at the Zoo by which, for 6d. placed in a slot, a joy horn was sounded, bringing sea lions to the fore, and a fish was then thrown into the water, 1932.*

Born on this day were:
Dr. William Wotton, 1666,
Sir George Grove, 1820,
Sir A. L. Liberty, 1843.

On this day there died:
Jeremy Taylor, 1667,
Dr. Gilbert Stuart, 1786,
Robert Plumer Ward, novelist, 1866,
Millais, 1896,
Lord Runciman, the shipping magnate, 1937,
H. G. Wells, 1946,
Cecil B. Harmsworth, journalist, 1948,
These events are recorded:
Titus Oates created a panic with one of his bogus popish plots, 1678,
Cape of Good Hope finally ceded to Britain, 1814,
Royal Naval Reserve established, 1859.

AGRICULTURAL HOLDINGS ACT PASSED, 1875,
BRITISH FLY FIFTY-SIX MACHINES ACROSS THE CHANNEL TO LAND AT AMIENS, 1914,
BRITISH GOVERNMENT REFUSED PASSPORTS TO THE LABOUR DELEGATES TO THE STOCKHOLM CONFERENCE, 1917,
CZECHOSLOVAKS RECOGNIZED AS ALLIES, 1918,
GERMANY EXPERIENCED HEAVY LOSSES IN THE BATTLE OF BRITAIN, 1940.

August the Fourteenth

There's not much in it, friend, I see,
When all is said and done,
There's food and drink and you and me,
And bed at set of sun!

The Essay on the Constitution of Man in Relation to External Objects *was an important work of the nineteenth century. It is still worth reading. Its author was George Combe, a scientist, a philosopher, and particularly a phrenologist, died on August the Fourteenth at Moor Park in Surrey in 1858.*

On August the Fourteenth, the Secretary for Scotland Act was passed in 1885, first secretary Duke of Richmond and Gordon, and on the same day in 1948, the plot to overthrow the newly established Government in Burma was frustrated.

Born on August the Fourteenth were:
Dr. Meric Casaubon, eminent Protestant divine, 1599, Geneva,
Dr. Charles Hutton, distinguished mathematician, 1737,
John Galsworthy, 1867.

There died on this day:
John I of Portugal, 1433,
Edmund Law, Bishop of Carlisle, editor of Locke, 1787,
Thomas Sheridan, author of the *Pronouncing Dictionary*, and father of the dramatist, 1788, Thanet,
George Colman (the elder), dramatist, 1794, Paddington,
Rev. Henry Francis Cary, translator of Dante, 1844, London,
Sir Landon Ronald, 1938.

THESE ARE THE EVENTS OF THE DAY.
VLADIVOSTOK SQUADRON DEFEATED—RUSSO-JAP WAR, 1904,
BRITISH TRANSPORT, 'ROYAL EDWARD', SUNK, 1915,
THE 'QUEEN MARY' GAINED 'BLUE RIBAND' OF ATLANTIC—WEST TO EAST CROSSING, 3 DAYS, 20 HOURS, 42 MINUTES, 1938,
THIRTY-ONE ENEMY PLANES SHOT DOWN OVER BRITAIN, 1940,
JAPAN SURRENDERED, 1945,
DOMINIONS OF INDIA AND PAKISTAN—MIDNIGHT—1947,
LORD MOUNTBATTEN ADDRESSED PAKISTAN ASSEMBLY AND READ KING'S MESSAGE, 1947.

August the Fifteenth

Take therefore no thought for the morrow:
For the morrow shall take thought for the things of itself.
Sufficient unto the day is the evil thereof.

August the Fifteenth is memorable for much but not least for its birth days.
These were born on this day:
In 1599, Admiral Blake,
In 1613, Jeremy Taylor, author of Holy Living and Holy Dying,
In 1688, Frederick William I of Prussia,
In 1769, Napoleon Bonaparte,
In 1771, Sir Walter Scott, who wrote, in addition to his poems and romances,
a life of Bonaparte,
In 1785, Thomas de Quincey, who wrote the Confessions of an Opium
Eater, *and who is buried in St. Cuthbert's churchyard, Edinburgh,*
In 1845, Walter Crane, socialist and artist craftsman, and—place for a
lady—today is the birthday of the famous actress, Ethel Barrymore, in 1879.

On this day there died:
James, Earl of Douglas, 1388,
Joe Millar, the comedian, 1738,
Thomas Tyrwhitt, editor of Chaucer, 1786,
Hawker of Morwenstow, 1875.

THESE ARE THE EVENTS:
FAMILY COMPACT CONCLUDED BETWEEN FRANCE AND
SPAIN, 1761,
FOUNDATION STONE OF SIR WALTER SCOTT MONUMENT,
1840: INAUGURATED 1846,
ROYAL ASSENT GIVEN TO REFORM BILL, 1867,
JAPANESE ULTIMATUM TO GERMANY, 1914,
PANAMA CANAL INAUGURATED, 1914,
BRITISH NATIONAL REGISTER TAKEN, 1915,
H.M.S. 'FURIOUS' LAUNCHED, LATER TO BECOME AIR-
CRAFT CARRIER, 1915,
FIRST U.S. TROOPS IN LONDON, 1917,
SEVENTH CENTENARY OF THE FOUNDATION OF CITY OF
BERLIN, 1937,
GERMAN LOSSES IN BATTLE OF BRITAIN—180 AGAINST 34,
1940,
VJ DAY, 1945,
PRINCESS ANNE OF EDINBURGH, BORN THIS DAY, 1950.

August the Sixteenth

The supreme day has come and the inevitable hour.

An important anniversary on August the Sixteenth is the introduction of gas as an illuminant into London in 1807, on this day, too, Bunsen—Robert Wilhelm von Bunsen—died in 1899. His researches in many fields included gas and his name is remembered in the Bunsen Burner, a device which moves air and gas before ignition producing heat without luminosity in the flame. His name is also associated with the carbon-zinc electric cell.

Born on this day were:
Ralph Thoresby, antiquary, 1658,
Catherine Cockburn, dramatist and moral writer, 1679,
Frederick, Duke of York, 1763,
Col. D. Clifton Brown (Speaker) 1879,
Lawrence of Arabia, 1888.

These events are recorded:
Halfpennies and farthings first coined by Government, 1672,
So-called 'Peterloo massacre', 1819,
Houses of Parliament were burned, 1834,
Imprisonment for debt abolished, 1838,
German pill-boxes first encountered, 1917,
Davies scheme accepted by London Conference. Ruhr evacuation agreed to 1924.
Details of National Registration in the event of war issued, 1939,
Battle of Britain reached the outskirts of London. It cost the Germans seventy-five planes against twenty-two, 1940,
Russians reported evacuation of Maikop, oil centre of Caucasus, 1942.

THESE DIED ON THIS DAY:
DR. THOMAS FULLER, 1661, AT COVENT GARDEN,
MARVELL 1678,
DR. MATTHEW TINDAL, FREETHINKING WRITER, 1733,
EUGENE ARAM HANGED, 1759,
JOHN PALMER, REFORMER OF THE POST SYSTEM, 1818,
LORD STRATFORD DE REDCLIFFE, 1880,
FRED R. J. ROE, PORTRAIT, HISTORICAL AND GENRE PAINTER, 1947,
THE RIGHT HON. DOUGLAS M. H. HAILSHAM, P.C., A FORMER LORD CHANCELLOR, 1950.

August the Seventeenth

This happy day to be enrolled
In rubric letters and in gold
I tell a tale forever told
Which generations yet will hold.

In 1839, on August the Seventeenth, the penny postage act was passed. It
was on August the Seventeenth, 1949, two and a half times more costly to
send a letter than it was in 1839—a challenge to those who tell of the
progress of the twentieth century!
On this day, in 1794, Astley's amphitheatre was totally destroyed by fire.
On this day in 1836, the Dissenters Marriage Act was passed,
On this day in 1901, the Royal Titles Act was passed.

There were born on this day:
Stothard, the artist, 1755,
Dr. William Carey, 1761,
Richard Lalor Shiel, politician, 1791,
Wilfrid Scawen Blunt, 1840,
Sir William Edward Rootes, 1894.

There died on this day:
John Gower, early English poet, 1408,
Edward V and his brother, the Duke of York, smothered in the
Tower, 1483,
Admiral Robert Blake, 1657,
Madame Anne le Fevre Dacier, translator of Homer and other
classic authors, 1720,
Frederick II, the Great, of Prussia, 1786,
Mathew Boulton, engineer and partner of Watt, 1809,
Dr. Edward Pearson, Armenian Champion, 1811,
Balzac, 1850,
Wilhelm Heinrich Bleek, philologist, Berlin, 1875,
Winston Joseph Dugan, Baron Dugan of Victoria, 1951.

THESE EVENTS ARE RECORDED:
REFORMATION ADJUSTED IN SCOTLAND, 1560,
DANISH POSSESSIONS ON THE COAST OF AFRICA CEDED TO
GREAT BRITAIN, 1850,
100 BOMBERS ATTACK BREMEN AND DUISBURG, 1941,
END OF AXIS RESISTANCE IN SICILY, 1943.

August the Eighteenth

Last night I watched the setting sun
And felt how little I had done
I turned to God to praise and pray:
My prayer is answered: here's today.

August the Eighteenth in 1940 was a day of days in the history of the Island of Britain.
In high summer, over her coasts, hundreds of the Luftwaffe sought her destruction, but, when night fell, it was recorded that one hundred and forty-four German planes had been destroyed while the defenders lost—too many alas!—but still only twenty-two. The Battle of Britain was being won by the Royal Air Force.

These were born on this day,
Brook Taylor, mathematician, 1685,
John, Earl Russell, Prime Minister of Great Britain 1846–52, 1792.

These died on this day:
Empson and Dudley, ministers to Henry VII, executed on Tower Hill, 1510,
Earl of Kilmarnock and Lord Balmerino, executed for High Treason, 1745,
Francis I, Emperor of Germany, 1765,
Dr. James Beattie, the poet, 1803,
Sir William Fairbairn, engineer, 1874.
W. H. Hudson, 1922.

THESE EVENTS ARE RECORDED:
PEACE OF ABO, BETWEEN SWEDEN AND RUSSIA, 1743,
ROYAL ASSENT TO BILL FOR STANDARD RAILWAY GAUGE, 1845,
THE QUEEN'S YACHT, WITH HER MAJESTY ON BOARD, WAS CONCERNED IN AN ACCIDENT, AND WAS CENSURED BY A BRITISH JURY IN 1874,
BRITISH MOTOR BOAT RAID ON CRONSTADT, 1919,
BRITISH AIRWAYS LINER STRUCK BY LIGHTNING, 1939,
N.F.S. FORMED, 1941,
FIRST ALL-AMERICAN DAYLIGHT BOMBING RAID, ROUEN, 1942,
LIEUTENANT-GENERAL MONTGOMERY BECAME COMMANDER OF THE EIGHTH ARMY, 1942.

August the Nineteenth

Wait till night before
Saying it had been a fine day.

August the Nineteenth finds Scotland prominent in the calendar. That great Scotsman who became Lord Haldane of Cloan was born on this day in 1856, and so was Elizabeth Stuart. She was born in 1596, the daughter of James the Sixth of Scotland and First of England, and became in due course Electress-Palatine of the Rhine and Queen of Bohemia. Another Scottish Queen, Mary, Queen of Scots, landed on this day in 1561 at Leith to take up her throne in Scotland. James Watt, one of the prime creators of the Industrial Revolution and one of the greatest of Scots inventors, died on this day in 1819.

These were born on this day:
John Flamsteed, astronomer, 1646,
Antonio Salieri, composer, 1750,
Jean Pierre de Béranger, 1780,
James Nasmyth, engineer, 1808,
Orville Wright, 1871,
Mr. Bernard Baruch, U.S. financier and friend of Mr. Churchill, 1870.

There died on this day:
Timothy Bright, shorthand inventor, 1615,
Blaise Pascal, 1662,
Sir Benjamin Thomson, Count Rumford, 1814,
Robert Bloomfield, poet, 1823,
Sir Martin A. Shee, President of the Royal Academy, 1850.
Dame Rosalind Paget, the first Queen's Nurse, 1948.

THESE EVENTS ARE RECORDED:
BEGINNING OF QUEEN CAROLINE'S TRIAL, 1820,
BARALONG CASE, 1915,
CURIOUS DIPLOMATIC ROW BETWEEN PORTUGAL AND CZECHOSLOVAKIA OVER THE NON-FULFILMENT OF AN ARMS ORDER, 1937,
THE WHOLE OF GREAT BRITAIN MADE A 'DEFENCE AREA', 1940,
BRITISH FORCED OUT OF SOMALILAND, 1940,
THE DIEPPE RAID, 1942,
DAY OF NATIONAL THANKSGIVING, 1945.

August the Twentieth

How many minutes are there mine
In all this day of many hours?
Let me turn ten to some design
Enduring—worthy of my powers.

Winston Churchill reviewed, in unforgettable words, on this day in 1940,
what history calls the 'Battle of Britain'. Of the achievements of the
Royal Air Force he said: 'Never was so much owed by so many to so few',
and the battle continued.
It was on this same day, August the Twentieth, in 1914, that the German
armies entered Brussels: it was on this same day in 1915 that Italy declared
war on Turkey and it was on this same day that the American Army
reached Versailles in 1944.
Convertibility of sterling into dollars temporarily suspended, 1947.

These were born on this day.
Robert Herrick, 1591,
George Villiers, Duke of Buckingham, 1592,
Louis Bourdaloue, celebrated preacher, 1632,
Thomas Simpson, 1710,
George Eden, Earl of Auckland, Governor-General of India, 1784,
Raymonde Poincaré, 1860.

These died on this day:
Martin Opitz, poet and philologist, 1639,
Lord Herbert of Cherbury, philosophical writer, 1648,
Sir Charles Sidley, poet, 1701,
Tom Spring, last of the old-style pugilists, 1851,
John Thomas Quekett, eminent microscopist, 1861.

WILLIAM MILLAR, THE 'NURSERY POET', 1872,
ELLEN TREE, THE ACTRESS, 1880,
GENERAL BOOTH, 1912,
TROTSKY ASSASSINATED, 1940,
DR. NORMAN MCLEAN, FORMER MASTER OF CHRIST'S COL-
LEGE, CAMBRIDGE, 1947,
ADMIRAL SIR GEORGE H. LYON, COMMANDER-IN-CHIEF AT
THE NORE, 1947,
THE RT. REV. JOHN WHITE, FIRST MODERATOR OF THE
UNITED CHURCH OF SCOTLAND, 1951.

MARTIAL LAW PROCLAIMED THROUGHOUT BURMA, 1948.

August the Twenty-first

My days are gone a-wandering.

August the Twenty-first is the birthday of Princess Margaret Rose: she was born in 1930.
On this day in 1939, the Pope appealed—in vain—for peace on earth and the local authorities in Britain were called on to set up their Civil Defence organization, on the same day in the same year, to meet the near contingency of war damage on houses and factories.
In 1485 on August the Twenty-first, Henry VII of England ascended to the throne,
In 1553, on this day, the Duke of Northumberland was beheaded.

These were born on this day:
The Admirable Crichton, 1561,
St. Francis de Sales, Catholic divine and mystic, 1567,
William IV, King of Great Britain, 1765,
Henry White, 1785,
Jules Michelet, Paris, 1798, French historian,
Henry Ainley, the actor, 1879.

On this day there died,
Lady Mary Wortley Montague, 1762,
William Maginn, scholar, 1842.

THESE EVENTS ARE RECORDED:
WEST INDIA DOCKS OPENED, 1802,
CANADIANS ENTER LENS, 1917,
THE BATTLE OF BAPAUME, 1918,
GENERAL BYNG OPENED A STRONG OFFENSIVE NORTH OF THE ANCRE, AND BY NIGHT HAD CAPTURED BEAUCOURT, BACQUOY, ABLAINYEVILLE AND COURCELLES, 1918,
GREAT BRITAIN ANNEXED THREE ISLANDS ALMOST MIDWAY BETWEEN NEW ZEALAND AND SOUTH AMERICA—HENDERSON ISLAND, DUCIE AND OENO ISLANDS, 1937,
GERMAN-SOVIET NON-AGGRESSION PACT ANNOUNCED, 1939,
KISKA ISLAND OCCUPIED, 1943,
U.S. TROOPS OVER SEINE. TOULON CAPTURED, 1944,
GOVERNMENT ANNOUNCED PLAN TO INCREASE HOME FOOD PRODUCTION BY £100,000,000 BY 1951–2, ON THIS DAY IN 1947.

August the Twenty-second

Is there a recorder
Over death's dark border?
O what, I wonder, will he say
Of how I spent my yesterday!

In 1914 on August the Twenty-second, Britain knew she was at war with
Germany . . . the armies clashed for the first time in modern warfare on this
day at Le Cateau, near Mons. The first British aeroplane was shot down
on this day and to balance the account the French destroyed the first Zeppelin
in Alsace on August the Twenty-second.
On August the Twenty-second, Richard III of England was killed on
Bosworth Field in 1485.
Thomas Percy, the Earl of Northumberland, was beheaded at York in
1572, and
On the same day with an Indian Empire largely of his creation behind him,
there died in England in 1818 Warren Hastings, one-time Governor-General
of India.

Born on this day were:
Thomas Tredgold, engineer, 1788,
De Bussy, 1862,
Lord Citrine, 1887.

On this day there died:
William Whitson, translator of Josephus, 1752,
Dr. Franz Gall, founder of the 'Ten Hours Movement', 1861,
Shillibeer, 1866,
Lord Salisbury, 1903,
Sir Oliver Lodge, 1940.

THESE EVENTS ARE RECORDED:
QUEEN VICTORIA SENT A MESSAGE TO PRESIDENT BUCHANAN
OVER THE NEW ATLANTIC CABLE, 1858,
SANTOS DUMONT MADE THE FIRST LONGISH EUROPEAN
FLIGHT, 1906,
'LA GIOCONDA' STOLEN FROM LOUVRE, 1911,
GERMAN LONG-RANGE GUNS OPENED FIRE IN SURPRISE
ATTACK ON AN UP-CHANNEL CONVOY, WITHOUT RESULT:
THAT AFTERNOON DOVER WAS SHELLED, 1940,
LIBERATION OF PARIS, 1944.

August the Twenty-third

Who goes there in highest summer?
I come . . . I am death's loud drummer.

William Wallace, Scotland's warrior for Scotland's independence, was
executed on August the Twenty-third in 1305.
The Duke of Buckingham was assassinated in 1628 on August the Twenty-
third.
The Battle of Mons began on August the Twenty-third in 1914, but the
'contemptible little army' survived to win immortality.
Japan declared war on Germany on this day in 1917, and in 1945 the
Charter of the United Nations was approved by Parliament.

On this day were born:
Louis XVI, King of France, in 1764,
Sir Astley Cooper, surgeon, in 1768,
William Frederick I, King of Netherlands, in 1772,
Sir Henry Acland, 1815,
William Ernest Henley, Gloucester, 1849, a patriot and a poet,
and a brave man,
Geoffrey Faber (the publisher) in 1889,
Brigadier Sir George Harvie Watt, 1903.

There died on this day:
Roy Chadwick, 1947,
Sir Clive Forster Cooper, F.R.S., Director of National History
Museum, 1947.

THESE ARE SOME OF THE EVENTS OF THE DAY:
CHARTER OF INCORPORATION GRANTED TO LONDON
PHYSICIANS, 1518,
NEW MEXICO WAS ANNEXED TO UNITED STATES, 1846,
GERMANY UNDERTOOK ARMY MANŒUVRES OF QUITE UN-
NECESSARY PRETENTIOUSNESS, 1938,
BRITISH GUNS RETURNED FIRE ON THE FRENCH COAST,
1940,
GERMAN-SOVIET PACT SIGNED BY VON RIBBENTROP, 1939,
KHARKOV RECAPTURED, 1943,
RUMANIA SURRENDERED, 1944.
SIXTY LIVES, INCLUDING THIRTY-EIGHT CHILDREN UNDER
SIX YEARS OF AGE, WERE LOST WHEN A LIBERATOR AIR-
CRAFT CRASHED IN FLAMES AT FRECKLETON, LANCS, 1944.

August the Twenty-fourth

The law of the past can not be eluded
The law of the present and future can not be eluded,
The law of the living can not be eluded,
It is eternal.

On August the Twenty-fourth Lend-Lease—'the most unselfish contract ever made between two nations'—ended in 1945.
In 1572 this day saw the Massacre of St. Bartholomew's Eve.
In 1662, the passing of the Act of Uniformity, and
In 1867, the last diet of the German Confederation.
August the Twenty-fourth in 1500, saw the end of Papal authority over Scotland.
In 1814, the capture of Washington by the British forces,
In 1875, the first swimming of the English Channel, by Captain Webb,
In 1921, the wreck of the aircraft R38 over the Humber,
Thomas Chatterton—'that marvellous boy who perished in his pride'—died on this day in 1770.

Born on this day were:
Letizia Ramolini, mother of Napoleon, 1750,
William Wilberforce, 1759,
Lord Woolton, 1883.

On this day there died:
Alphonso V of Portugal, 1481,
Admiral Coligny, murdered, 1572,
Colonel Thomas Blood, the man who tried to steal the Crown Regalia, 1680,
Theodore Hook, the novelist, 1841.

THESE ARE THE EVENTS OF THE DAY:
BISHOP ATTERBURY SENT TO THE TOWER AS A JACOBITE, 1722,
BARTHOLOMEW FAIR, EXISTING FOR SEVEN AND A HALF CENTURIES, CEASED IN 1855,
GERMANY PLACED RESTRICTION ON HER U-BOAT COMMANDERS, 1915,
THIRD UNITED STATES REGISTRATION, 1918,
DANZIG SENATE FLOUTED THE WHOLE IDEA OF THE DANZIG CONSTITUTION BY ELECTING FORSTER, LOCAL NAZI LEADER, AS HEAD OF THE STATE, 1939.

August the Twenty-fifth

While the sun shines it is day.
Shall I work or shall I play?
Shall I go or shall I stay?
Shall I owe or must I pay?

On August the Twenty-fifth, his mind clouded with confusion, Frederick Nietzsche died in 1900. He wrote Beyond Good and Evil *and* Thus Spake Zarathustra, *and inspired a generation. His was the philosophy of the Super-man—'What was that life? Up once again'—it found strange disciples. Some think it made the two world wars as well as giving a new direction to human thought and purpose.*

There were born on this day:
Charles Etienne Louis Camus, 1699,
Henry Fawcett, 1833,
Francis Bret Harte, 1839.

There died on this day:
Louis IX, St. Louis, 1270,
Margaret of Anjou, queen of Henry VI of England, 1482,
David Hume, the philosopher and historian, 1776,
Michael Faraday, 1867,
William Herschel, astronomer, 1882,
The Duke of Kent, killed in air crash in Scotland, 1942,
Colonel Frederic Hugh Page Creswell, 1948.

THESE ARE THE EVENTS RECORDED ON THIS DAY:
HONOURABLE ARTILLERY COMPANY INCORPORATED, 1537,
FORTY THOUSAND SCOTTISH VOLUNTEERS REVIEWED BY
QUEEN VICTORIA, EDINBURGH, 1881,
NATIONAL GOVERNMENT FORMED, 1931,
PACT OF MUTUAL ASSISTANCE SIGNED BETWEEN GREAT
BRITAIN AND POLAND, 1939,
MR. NEVILLE CHAMBERLAIN VISITED HITLER, 1939,
JAPAN BREAKS AWAY FROM ANTI-COMINTERN PACT, 1939,
FIRST BOMBS DROPPED ON BERLIN, 1940, R.A.F.,
IRAN ENTERED BY BRITISH AND RUSSIAN TROOPS, 1941,
GERMANS BROKE INTO STALINGRAD, 1942,
SOLOMONS BATTLE IN FULL SWING, 1942,
DUKE OF GLOUCESTER OPENED 'ENTERPRISE SCOTLAND'
EXHIBITION AT EDINBURGH, 1947.

August the Twenty-sixth

A day of battle! All I know
Too hot for me—I had to go!

August the Twenty-sixth saw the English bowmen defeat the French at the Battle of Crécy in 1376. It was the day chosen in 1943 for the recognition by the Allies, Britain, U.S.A., and U.S.S.R., of the French Committee for National Liberation.

In 1940, on the same day, Italy began to campaign against Yugoslavia and Greece.

German bombs fell on a creamery in County Wicklow on the same day in the same year and the first all-night raid over London, in 1940, gave a foretaste of what was to come.

Born on this day were:
Sir Robert Walpole, Earl of Orford, 1676,
Prince Albert, consort of Queen Victoria, 1819,
The Sultan of Zanzibar, 1879,
Prince Richard, 1944.

There died on this day:
Archbishop Bradwardine, 'The Profound Doctor', 1349,
De la Vega, Spanish dramatist, 1635,
Franz Hals, 1666,
Lord George Sackville, commander and statesman, 1785,
Karl Theodore Körner, Kiplingish song writer, killed at Gadebusch, 1813,
Dr. Adam Clarke, eminent divine and author, 1832,
Louis Philippe, ex-king of France, 1850.

THESE ARE THE EVENTS:
BOMBARDMENT OF ALGIERS, 1826,
TREATY OF PEACE CONCLUDED WITH CHINA, 1842,
MENDELSSOHN'S 'ELIJAH' PERFORMED FOR FIRST TIME, 1846,
'COUNTRY COURTS ACT' RECEIVES ROYAL ASSENT, 1846,
KRAKATOA ERUPTION, 1883,
ANGLO-EGYPTIAN TREATY SIGNED IN LONDON, 1936,
JAPANESE PLANES WOUNDED BRITISH AMBASSADOR TO CHINA NEAR SHANGHAI, 1937,
BAN ON THE 'DAILY WORKER' LIFTED, 1942,
BULGARIA OUT OF THE WAR, 1944.

August the Twenty-seventh

Each creature has its sure two days,
For this let's give unmeasured praise:
Thanks for the day, our first full breath,
Thanks for the day we close in death.

August the Twenty-seventh was the day in which Titian died in 1576,
Pope Sixtus in 1590,
James Thomson—the poet of 'The Seasons'—in 1748,
Dr. John Jortin, critic, 1770,
John Leyden in 1811,
Countess Craven (née Louisa Bruton), once a favourite actress, 1860,
J. H. Foley, R.A., eminent sculptor, 1874, and
Sir Rowland Hill in 1879.

August the Twenty-seventh was the day on which the Marquis of
Salisbury was born in 1893, and
William Woollett, engraver, 1735,

August the Twenty-seventh was the day on which, in 55 B.C., the
Emperor Julius Caesar landed in Britain,
On the same day in 1914, the marines landed at Ostend.

THESE ARE OTHER EVENTS OF THE DAY,
MILTON'S BOOKS AGAINST THE STUART MONARCHY PUB-
LICLY BURNT BY REQUEST OF THE HOUSE OF COMMONS,
1660,
PELHAM'S MINISTRY, 1743,
FIRST ASCENT OF THE MONTGOLFIER BALLOON, 1782,
LAST EXECUTION FOR ATTEMPTED MURDER, 1861,
WALLACE MONUMENT, STIRLING, INAUGURATED, 1869,
BRITISH ASSOCIATION HELD ITS FIRST MEETING ABROAD
(MONTREAL), 1884,
PEACE PACT SIGNED, 1928,
LONDON BECAME A ZONE OF 'SILENCE', 1934,
HERR HITLER COMMUNICATED WITH M. DALADIER,
DURING WHICH COMMUNICATION HE DESPAIRED OF
POLAND, 1939,
GOVERNMENT OF TCHAD TERRITORY, FRENCH EQUATORIAL
AFRICA, JOINED THE ALLIES, 1940,
KING GEORGE OF THE HELLENES RETURNED TO GREECE,
1946.

August the Twenty-eighth

Before this day its course has run
Please God, a little—little—fun!

August the Twenty-eighth is the birth day of many famous men . . .
Goethe was born on this day in 1749, Tolstoy in 1828, and Burne-Jones in
1833. Let these three suffice!

There is a long list of famous men who died on this day . . .
Saint Augustine in 430,
Sir Francis Vere, distinguished military commander and author,
1608,
Grotius in 1645,
Oxenstierna—the Swedish Chancellor in 1654,
Charles Boyle, Earl of Orrery, 1731,
Leigh Hunt, the poet and critic, in 1859,
William Lyon Mackenzie, leader in the Canadian Rebellion of
1837, in 1861,
General Botha in 1919,
Charles Evans Hughes in 1948.

These are solemn and important names—but life is not always
solemn—on August the Twenty-eighth in 1856 Gilbert Abbott
à Becket—a descendant of the father of St. Thomas à Becket—
died a barrister, a magistrate, and a life-long contributor to the
immortal *Punch*.

THESE EVENTS ARE RECORDED.
LORD HOOD CAPTURED TOULON IN 1793,
THE ABOLITION OF NEGRO SLAVES, 1833, IN BRITISH
COLONIES BILL PASSED,
THE EGLINTON TOURNAMENT, 1839,
SUBMARINE CABLE LAID BETWEEN ENGLISH AND FRENCH
COASTS, 1850,
ALBERT BRIDGE, CHELSEA, OPENED, 1873,
BRITISH NAVAL VICTORY OF HELIGOLAND BIGHT, 1914,
AUSTRIA DECLARED WAR ON BELGIUM, 1914,
GRAF ZEPPELIN REACHED LOS ANGELES FROM JAPAN IN
SIXTY-EIGHT HOURS IN 1929,
HOLLAND MOBILIZED, 1939,
RUSSIANS DESTROYED THE DNIEPER DAM, 1941.

August the Twenty-ninth

Philosophy does the going, and wisdom is the goal.

August the Twenty-ninth was a birth day of philosophers.
John Locke, who wrote the Essay of Human Understanding, *was born on this day in 1632,*
John Henry Lambert, 1728,
Oliver Wendell Holmes in 1809—The Professor at the Breakfast Table,
John Leech, 1817, and
In 1862, Maurice Maeterlinck, the Belgian poet-philosopher all saw the light on August the Twenty-ninth.

On this day, in the nineteenth century, Queen Victoria embarked for her first visit to Scotland in 1842, and in 1894 on August the Twenty-ninth the Government declared Uganda a Protectorate. In the twentieth century, on this day in 1910, Japan annexed Korea. In 1921 the I.R.A. cut the Atlantic Cable and the Graf Zeppelin circled the world in twenty-one days (flying only twelve days) in 1929.

These died on this day:
St. John the Baptist, beheaded A.D. 30,
John Lilburne, zealous parliamentarian, 1657,
Edmund Hoyle, author of the book on games, 1769,
Joseph Wright, historical painter, 1797,
Pope Pius VI, 1799,
Sir Charles Napier, 1853,
William Brockedon, painter, 1854,
Brigham Young, 1877,
Queen Astrid of Belgium, 1935.

THESE EVENTS ALSO ARE RECORDED:
NEW YEAR'S DAY OF THE OLD CAESAREAN CALENDAR BEGINNING, 30 B.C.,
THE LOSS OF 'THE ROYAL GEORGE', 1782,
A RUSSIAN PURGE . . . THIS TIME THE KOMSOMOL OR YOUNG COMMUNISTS LEAGUE, TOOK PLACE IN 1937,
ALASKAN HIGHWAY—ALBERTA TO FAIRBANKS—WAS OPENED, 1942,
CONSTANZA WAS TAKEN IN 1944,
AMERICANS TOOK SOISSONS, 1944.

August the Thirtieth

Blossoms, bees, and butterflies,
And soft falling summer rain,
Nothing beauty me denies—
But, will summer come again?

They died, they fell asleep, they passed over, they took the ferry . . . men
have sought to soften the fact of death and its finality. These died on
August the Thirtieth:
Hervey, first Bishop of Ely, 1131,
Pope Alexander III, 1181,
Louis XI, King of France, 1483,
Soliman II, 'The Magnificent', 1566,
Francis Baily, astronomer, 1844,
John Camden Neild—a miser who had the roof of his parish church
repaired with strips of painted calico, and who left his fortune of £500,000
to Queen Victoria—1852,
Sir John Ross, Arctic explorer, 1856,
John Francis, sculptor, 1861.

Birthdays for August the Thirtieth are:
Dr. Hartley, author of *Observations on Man*, 1705,
William Paley, author of *Evidences of Christianity*, 1743,
J. M. Dent, the publisher of Everyman's Library, 1849,
Lord Rutherford, 1871,
The Duke of Sutherland, 1888,
Mr. Raymond Massey, 1896.

AUGUST THE THIRTIETH IS THE ANNIVERSARY OF THE
BATTLE OF TANNENBERG IN 1914, WHEN THE RUSSIAN
ARMIES MET DISASTER, AND IT WAS ON THE SAME DAY, IN
THE SAME YEAR, THAT PARIS FIRST HAD AN AIR RAID
FROM THE GERMANS.
CONVENTION OF CINTRA, 1808,
PEEL'S SECOND MINISTRY, 1841,
FIRST TRAM RAN IN ENGLAND, 1860,
SECOND BATTLE OF BULL RUN, 1862,
METROPOLITAN POLICE STRIKE, 1918,
RUSSIA CAPTURED TAGANROG, 1943,
BRITISH NAVY RETURNED TO HONG KONG, 1945,
BEAUVAIS AND GOURNAY CAPTURED, 1944.

August the Thirty-first

Summer, summer, summer, summer,
The soundless footsteps on the grass
Where is the noiseless drummer?
Time's sands are running in its glass.

John Bunyan died on August the Thirty-first in 1688. It may well have seemed to him to be a good day for a pilgrim. He was literally a jail-bird but no jail could imprison the spirit which found winged words to write 'The Pilgrim's Progress from this world to that which is to come'.

August the Thirty-first is a soldiers' day. The Guards Division was formed in 1915 on this day;
The Allies crossed both Somme and Meuse on this day in 1944;
Eighty-eight enemy planes were shot down in 1940 on this day, and August the Thirty-first was the official ending of the First World War in 1921.

Queen Wilhelmina was born on this day in 1880—her sixty-eighth birthday and the golden jubilee of her reign was celebrated throughout the Netherlands on August the Thirty-first in 1948;
Caius Caesar Caligula, Roman emperor, born at Antium, A.D. 12.

There died on this day:
Henry V, 1422,
Dr. James Currie, biographer of Burns, 1805,
Charles Lever, the Irish novelist, 1806,
Baudelaire, 1867,
William Holman Hunt, 1910,
Andrei Alexandrovitch Zhadanov, Stalin's chief adviser, 1948.

THESE EVENTS ARE RECORDED:
FIRST LAW REGULATING EMIGRATION PASSED, 1835,
HEALTH OF TOWNS ACT, FIRST IMPORTANT SANITARY LEGISLATION, 1847,
GRAND FLEET HAD TO LAND HALF ITS S.A.A. TO HELP ARMY, 1914,
BRITISH FLEET MOBILIZED, 1939,
EGYPTIAN FIGHTING RECOMMENCED, 1942,
GENERAL MONTGOMERY PROMOTED FIELD-MARSHAL, 1944,
BUCHAREST ENTERED, 1944,
BRITAIN TEMPORARILY CEASED TO BUY FOOD FROM U.S., 1947.

SEPTEMBER

THIRTY DAYS

September the First

. . . The innocent brightness of a new born day . . . is lovely yet.

September the First begins, for most of us, the turn of the year. It is an event, but there were others, too.
For Adrian the Fourth, an English Pope, it was the day of his election in 1159, as it was the day of accession for Henry the Sixth in 1422.

Louis the Fourteenth—who thought 'it would last his time'—died in 1715,
Sir Richard Steele in 1729,
Sir Richard Westmacott, the sculptor, 1856, and
W. W. Jacobs in 1943.

On this day Queen Victoria arrived at Granton on her first visit to Scotland in 1842,
The Prince of Wales was elected Past Grand Master of Freemasons, 1869,
It was the day of the inauguration of the official Home Rule for Ireland Movement in 1870, and
The annexation, albeit only temporarily, of the Transvaal in 1900.
The name of St. Petersburg was changed to Petrograd on this day, the prelude to other mightier events in 1914. Australians captured Péronne in 1918,
Great earthquake in Japan, Tokio and Yokohama in ruins, 1923,
The Dawes Plan was announced in 1924,
The National Service (Armed Forces) Act was passed (men eighteen to forty-one) on the eve of the war in 1939,
Germany invaded Poland and the evacuation of women and children from London began in 1939,
Gothic Line penetrated, 1944,
Dieppe was captured by the Canadians in 1944 and
Communal rioting broke out in Calcutta in 1947.

THESE WERE BORN,
EDWARD ALLEYN, FOUNDER OF DULWICH COLLEGE, 1566,
MARGARET, COUNTESS OF BLESSINGTON, NOVELIST, 1789,
KNOCKBRIT, NEAR CLONMEL,
LORD METHUEN, 1845,
REX BEACH, AUTHOR, 1877,
AIR CHIEF MARSHAL SIR FREDERICK BOWHILL, 1880.

September the Second

Fear no more—take heart—enjoy,
Now you can challenge Nemesis.
All you have you must employ—
There never was a day like this!

In 1685, on this September the Second, Alice Lisle was executed for—it was said—sheltering a rebel. It was on the self-same day in 1792 that Maria Thérèse, Princess de Lamballe, was murdered by the mob of the Revolution, and in 1813 at the Battle of Dresden, on this day, General Jean Victor Moreau was wounded mortally. September the Second is an anniversary of battles—the Battle of Actium, which settled the fate of the Roman world in 31 B.C.—the Battle of Sedan in 1870 and the Eighth Army's victory in the Gothic Line in 1944.

On this day were born:
John Howard, philanthropist, 1726, Hackney,
Sir Robert Bruce Lockhart in 1887.

There died on this day:
Thomas Telford, 1834,
Joseph Livesey, 1884,
Hon. Dame Edith Lyttelton, writer, 1948,
Professor Tancred Borenius, art historian, 1948,
The Rt. Hon. John Albert Beasley, High Commissioner for Australia in London, 1949.

THESE ARE THE EVENTS OF THE DAY:
FIRST GREAT FIRE OF LONDON STARTED ON THIS NIGHT, 1666, AND LASTED UNTIL THE SIXTH,
HERRING FISHERY PERMANENTLY ESTABLISHED, 1750,
ASTLEY'S AMPHITHEATRE BURNT, 1803,
STATISTICAL SOCIETY FORMED AT MANCHESTER, FIRST IN ENGLAND, 1833,
FIRST FREE LIBRARY, MANCHESTER, OPENED, 1852,
FIRST SECRETARY OF STATE FOR INDIA, 1858,
FIRST ZEPPELIN BROUGHT DOWN AT CUFFLEY, 1916,
EIRE ANNOUNCED NEUTRALITY, 1939,
SUMY CAPTURED BY THE RUSSIANS, 1943,
JAPANESE SIGNED SURRENDER TERMS, 1945,
INTERIM INDIAN GOVERNMENT IN OFFICE, 1946,
GREECE POLLS FOR MONARCHY, 1946.

[257]

September the Third

All through the year there is a day
It's ever drawing nigh,
It is the day on which I say
This day I am to die.

September the Third was a day of fate for Oliver Cromwell. It was on September the Third in 1650 that he won the Battle of Dunbar: it was on September the Third in 1651 that he won the Battle of Worcester: it was on September the Third in 1658 that the great Protector died. Richard I of England ascended to the throne on this day, and another Richard, Richard Cromwell, succeeded his father on this day in 1658. On September the Third in 1783, a peace treaty was signed with the United States of America by Great Britain, and in 1939 Great Britain declared war again on Germany. The Athenia *was sunk by Germany on the same day in 1939.*

These were born on September the Third,
Matthew Boulton, the partner of James Watt, in 1728, at Birmingham,
Prince Eugène de Beauharnais, the Empress Josephine's boy, stepson of Napoleon Bonaparte, in 1781, at Paris.

There died on this day:
Richard Tarleton, celebrated comedian, 1588,
Sir Edward Coke, the lawyer, 1634,
George Lillo, dramatist, 1739,
John Rennie, the engineer, 1874,
I. S. Turgenev, the novelist, 1883 (Russian),
Dr. Eduard Beneš, former President of Czechoslovakia, 1948.

THE EVENTS OF THE DAY ARE:
COCKER'S ARITHMETIC LICENSED, 1677,
ABBAYE MASSACRES IN PARIS, 1792,
'PRINCESS ALICE' WRECK IN THE THAMES, 1878, OVER SEVEN HUNDRED LIVES LOST,
BRITISH EAST AFRICA COMPANY CHARTER GRANTED, 1888,
AMERICA GOT THE BASES, WE GOT THE DESTROYERS, 1940,
EIGHTH ARMY LANDED IN ITALY, 1943,
BRITISH IN BRUSSELS, 1944,
MR. EVAN DURBIN, M.P., PARLIAMENTARY SECRETARY TO MINISTRY OF WORKS, DROWNED WHILE HELPING ONE OF HIS CHILDREN NEAR BUDE, 1948.

September the Fourth

What is life for but living,
For what may man life barter,
Man gives his all in giving
And dies a blessed martyr.

Three of the saints for September the Fourth are
Saint Marcellus and St. Valerian, martyrs in 179,
St. Ultan, first Bishop of Ardbraccan, in Meath, 656.

These died on this day:
John Corvinus Huniades, Hungarian general, 1456, Zemlin,
Robert Dudley, Earl of Leicester, the one time favourite of Queen Elizabeth, 1588,
J. J. Heidegger, Master of Revels to George II in 1794.
Barry Cornwall (B.W. Proctor), poet, 1874,
Charles Townshend, orator and statesman, 1767,
W. G. Robertson, playwright, 1948.

The events of the day include:
Royal assent to a bill for keeping a seamen's register, 1844,
France declared a republic, 1870,
First night plane raid on London, 1917,
R.A.F.'s first leaflet raid; attack on German warships; advance parties of B.E.F. in France, 1939,
Cease fire in Finland, 1944,
Royal Family attended Braemar Gathering, 1947,
T.U. Congress gave overwhelming vote in support of Mr. Bevin's foreign policy and urged immediate steps to stamp out Fascist activities in Britain, 1947,
The *Brabazon I*, world's largest air liner, made its first flight at Filton, 1949.

PINDAR, THE LYRIC POET, WHO GAVE POETRY THE PINDARIC ODE, WAS BORN ON SEPTEMBER THE FOURTH, 518 B.C.
ALEXANDER III OF SCOTLAND, AT ROXBURGH, IN 1241,
THE DUKE OF MILAN, FOUNDER OF THE CATHEDRAL, IN 1402,
CHATEAUBRIAND, THE NOBLE MAN OF FRANCE, WHO IS REMEMBERED AT RESTAURANTS, WAS BORN ON SEPTEMBER THE FOURTH IN 1768.

September the Fifth

There till the vision he foresaw,
Splendid and whole arise,
And unimagined empire draw
To council 'neath his skies.

He had the vision and the dream
Beyond the living hour,
As things may be—not as they seem,
Gave him compelling power.

In an uncertain wavering world, he was sure of man's chief end. He wrote and devised the positive philosophy—his name was Auguste Comte—his English disciples were many and his influence still persists. He died in Paris on September the Fifth, 1857.

These had September the Fifth as birth days,
Cardinal Richelieu in 1585,
Louis XIV of France, 1638,
Robert Fergusson, Scottish poet, born in Edinburgh in 1750.

On this day died:
Catherine Parr, Queen of Henry VIII, 1548,
Bishop Bonner in the Marshalsea Prison, 1569,
James Wyatt, architect, 1813,
Dr. Patrick Neill, author of works on natural history, in 1851,
Dr. William Macgillivray, distinguished naturalist, 1852,
Sir John Kennedy, Vice-chairman British Red Cross Society, 1948.

EVENTS OF NOTE WHICH OCCURRED ON SEPTEMBER THE FIFTH INCLUDE:
FIRST AMERICAN CONGRESS SAT AT 'PHILADELPHIA', 1774,
FIRST CONSCRIPTION LAW PASSED, 1798,
BRITISH TOOK MALTA, 1801,
SHEERNESS DOCKS OPENED, 1823,
COPYRIGHT CONVENTION AT BERNE, 1887,
AMERICANS FORBADE EXPORT OF PLANES TO ANYBODY, 1939,
AIR-RAID ALARMS BECAME 'ALERTS', 1940,
RUSSIA DECLARED WAR ON BULGARIA, 1944,
MR. MORRISON AND OTHER MINISTERS MET REPRESENTATIVES OF FEDERATION OF BRITISH INDUSTRIES TO DISCUSS GOVERNMENT STEPS TO MEET THE CRISIS OF 1947.

September the Sixth

Faith, hope and eternity—never say
They will not usher in a nobler day.

September the Sixth is a day of comings and goings—Scottish Jacobites
came to rebellion in 1715—September the Sixth was the last day of the
Great Fire of London in 1666—French troops cautiously entered Germany
in 1939 and, with equal caution, Germany put her first air raid over
Britain on the same day.
In 1844, on this day, Queen Victoria crossed the Tay on the occasion of her
second visit to Scotland—this was the day of the Battle of the Marne in
1914—and this was the exact day on which, so it is asserted, the Pilgrim
Fathers set out from Plymouth in 1620.

Marquis de la Fargette, in 1757,
John Dalton, in 1766, and
Sir Walford Davies, 1869, were born on September the Sixth as
were Sir Norman Birkett, barrister, 1883 and Sir Edward Victor
Appleton, 1892.

These died on this day:
Pope John XIII in 972,
Jean Baptiste Colbert, French statesman, in 1683,
James II and VII in 1701,
Sir John Fielding in 1780,
George Alexander Stevens, song and burlesque writer, in 1784,
John Bird Sumner, Archbishop of Canterbury, author of *Records*
of Creation and other works, 1862,
Sir Gilbert Parker, 1932.

IN 1766, ON SEPTEMBER THE SIXTH, THERE WAS COMMO-
TION IN THE CITY OF LONDON, THE LORD MAYOR WAS
'HELD UP'—AND, ON THE SAME DAY, IN 1658, RICHARD
CROMWELL WAS PROCLAIMED PROTECTOR AT OXFORD,
IN 1909 A DESPATCH WAS PUBLISHED CLAIMING THE
DISCOVERY OF THE NORTH POLE BY COMMANDER PEARY,
IN 1911 T. W. BURGESS SWAM THE CHANNEL.

THE SAINTS'-DAYS FOR SEPTEMBER THE SIXTH ARE:
ST. MACCULINDUS, BISHOP OF LUSK, 497,
ST. ELEUTHERIUS, ABBOT, ABOUT 585,
ST. BEGA OR BEES, VIRGIN, SEVENTH CENTURY.

[261]

September the Seventh

On dials and watches and on clocks,
Time taps and ticks and chimes and knocks,
It has a measured beat like rhyme,
But where is he who would beat time?

At Greenwich Palace on the Thames, on September the Seventh, in 1533,
was born to Henry VIII and his second wife, Anne Boleyn, a daughter
whom history calls the Virgin Queen.
The most English of English queens, Queen Elizabeth led and fed what
has been called the exuberance of England and laid the foundations of the
British Empire.

These share this day as birthday:
Count de Buffon, the naturalist, in 1707,
Arthur Young, the agricultural writer, in 1741,
Sir Henry Campbell Bannerman, the Liberal leader, in 1836,
Lieut.-Gen. Sir Brian Horrocks, 1895.

Died on September the Seventh,
Dr. Armstrong in 1779,
Mrs. Hannah More, the poetess, in 1833, and
John Greenleaf Whittier, the poet, in 1892.

September the Seventh marks the day on which, in 1838, Grace
Darling rescued the survivors of the *Forfarshire*,
The day on which the *Great Eastern* set out on her maiden voyage
in 1859.
This day saw the first voyage of the *Lusitania* in 1907, and
In 1929, Britain won the Schneider Trophy outright.

PORTEOUS LYNCHED BY EDINBURGH MOB, 1736—SEVEN-
TEEN OR EIGHTEEN PEOPLE KILLED OR WOUNDED,
LOSS OF H.M.S. 'CAPTAIN', 1870,
LORD PROVOST OF EDINBURGH, ANNOUNCED THAT EDIN-
BURGH FREE LIBRARY GIFT OF £25,000 HAD BEEN EN-
LARGED TO £50,000, 1886,
TREATY WITH TIBET SIGNED AT LHASA, 1904,
POLISH GARRISON AT WESTERPLATTE SURRENDERED, 1939,
THREE MONTHS ASSAULT ON LONDON BEGAN, 1940,
VICHY SET UP A WAR CRIMINAL TRIBUNAL, 1941,
MR. BEVIN AND SIR STAFFORD CRIPPS VISITED WASHING-
TON, 1949.

September the Eighth

Three hundred and sixty-five days
They're yours to make a year—
A primrose path—a road—a maze
A course that you must steer.

A plot to cultivate—a chance—a task
What more from fate and fortune dare you ask?

In 1853, at Stockholm, on September the Eighth, George
Bradshaw died. He was born in 1801 and was the inventor of the
railway time tables. It was a better contribution than many more
notable men have made to the affairs of mankind.
In 1803, on this day, the Battle of Delhi was fought,
Sevastopol was taken in 1855, and
Italy surrendered unconditionally in 1943.

On September the Eighth, Thomas, Duke of Gloucester was mur-
dered at Calais, 1397,
Amy Robsart died in 1560,
Francis Quarles, poet, in 1644,
Princess Elizabeth, daughter of Charles I, 1650, and
Bishop Joseph Hall, author of *Contemplations and Satires*, at Higham,
near Norwich, in 1656.

Born on September the Eighth were:
Richard I, 1157,
Ludovico Ariosto, Italian poet, in 1474,
Princess de Lamballe, 1749,
A. W. Schlegel, German author, 1767,
John Leyden, 1775, and,
Antonin Dvořák, composer, 1841.

THESE EVENTS ARE RECORDED:
BRITISH ASSEMBLY HELD ITS FIRST MEETING AT EDIN-
BURGH IN 1834,
MALAKOFF AND REDAN STORMED, 1855,
LORDS REJECTED HOME RULE BILL, 1893,
RUSSIA MOBILIZED IN 1939,
SPITZBERGEN WAS RAIDED IN 1941,
STALINO TAKEN BY THE RUSSIANS, 1943,
BULGARIA DECLARED WAR ON GERMANY IN 1944.

September the Ninth

Of hours each day I've twenty-four,
The richest man he has no more:
The poorest man he has his grief,
May justice come to his relief.
Rich beyond dreams he well may be
In hours—he is the same as me.

In 1087 there died at Rouen, on September the Ninth, in great agony,
William the First of England, surnamed the Conqueror, born the bastard
son of Robert, surnamed the Devil, by Herleva, the daughter of a tanner.
He was buried at Caen, to which the English, whom he helped to fashion,
came in battle in 1945.
In 1513 another king died on this day—
James the Fourth of Scotland was killed at the Battle of Flodden Field
when 'the floo'ers o' the forest were a' wede awa'.'

Galvani in 1737,
Richard Chenevix Trench, Dean of Westminster, the etymologist,
in 1807, and
The Earl of Harewood, in 1882, were born on this day as was, too,
James Agate, 1877.

There died on this day:
Sir Humphrey Gilbert, navigator, in 1583,
Charles de St. Evremond, wit and letter writer, 1703,
Robert Wood (Palmyra Wood), 1771,
John Brand, the antiquarian, 1806,
Bulmer, the typographer, in 1830.

EVENTS WITH WHICH SEPTEMBER THE NINTH IS ASSOCIATED:
BEAR-BAITING PROHIBITED, 1835,
MUNICIPAL CORPORATIONS ACT WAS PASSED, 1835,
VAUXHALL GARDENS SOLD BY AUCTION FOR £22,000,
1841,
'ALABAMA' INDEMNITY PAID AT WASHINGTON, 1873,
BRITISH ARMY CROSSED THE MARNE, 1914,
IRISH FREE STATE PARLIAMENT MET, 1922,
BATTLE OF WARSAW BEGAN, 1939,
ALLIES LANDED AT SALERNO, 1943,
HOSTILITIES CEASED BETWEEN BULGARIA AND RUSSIA,
1944.

September the Tenth

The high gods—can they unsay—
That we have lived our life today?

September the Tenth was the day on which the Atlantic cable was completed in 1874.
Mary Wollstonecraft Godwin died on September the Tenth in 1797 after giving birth to Mary Godwin, who became the wife of Percy Bysshe Shelley, on August the Thirtieth.
Mary Wollstonecraft Godwin was the author of The Vindication of the Rights of Women—*and a pioneer of the view that if women are not educated up to the standard of men there will be no progress of knowledge, for 'truth must be common to all', and these, too, died on September the Tenth...*

Louis d'Outremer, King of France, killed 954,
John, Duke of Burgundy, murdered at Montereau, 1419,
Dr. Edward Pococke, traveller and oriental scholar, 1691,
Dr. Thomas Sheridan, Irish scholar, translator of Persius, 1738,
The Empress Elizabeth, assassinated, 1898,
Ex-King Ferdinand of Bulgaria, 1948,
The Rt. Hon. Bernard A. W. P. Hastings Forbes, eighth Earl of Granard, former Master of the Horse, 1948,
The Rt. Hon. Hamar Greenwood, first Viscount, President of the Pilgrims, 1948.

Sir J. R. Seely, Professor of Modern History at Cambridge, and author of *The Expansion of England*, was born on this day, 1834, Robert Young, biblical scholar, Edinburgh, 1882, and
Sir J. Soane, 1753.

THIS DAY SAW THESE:
BATTLE OF PINKIE, 1547,
PROTECTORATE OF BECHUANALAND FORMED, 1884,
'DISCOVERY' RETURNED TO SPITHEAD FROM ANTARCTIC, 1904,
COMMERCIAL TREATY BETWEEN BRITAIN AND RUSSIA, 1922,
NOYON PACT (SUBMARINES IN MEDITERRANEAN), 1937,
CANADA DECLARED WAR ON GERMANY, 1939, AND B.E.F. ARRIVED AT CHERBOURG,
BELGIAN GOVERNMENT RETURNED TO BRUSSELS, 1944,
QUISLING SENTENCED TO DEATH AT OSLO, 1945.

September the Eleventh

Who are they dare to play?
Duty calls on us today.

September the Eleventh records many and diverse birthdays.
Chuter Ede, the Home Secretary of the 1945 Socialist Government, was born
on this day in 1882,
D. H. Lawrence, the novelist, in 1885,
Lord Byng of Vimy in 1862,
Sir James Jeans, the astronomer, in 1877,
In 1700, on the same day, James Thomson, the poet of 'The Seasons' was
born, and
In the eighteenth century, Arthur Young, the traveller, was born on Septem-
ber the Eleventh in 1741,
The Marshal of France, Henri de la Tour d'Auvergne Turenne, the ideal
army leader, was born on September the Eleventh in 1611,
Aldrovandus, the naturalist, in 1522,
So much for birth days.

On September the Eleventh:
The Battle of Malplaquet was fought in 1709,
Wallace Monument at Stirling was handed over to Stirling Town
Council in 1809,
Buckingham Palace was hit in 1940 and unexploded bombs fell
on St. Paul's,
The Americans entered Germany in 1944.

These departed this life on September the Eleventh,
Michel Eyquem de Montaigne, 1592,
James Harrington, the author of *Oceana*, in 1677,
Robert Craw, known as the Mad Vegetarian, in 1680,
John Augustus Ernesti, classical editor, 1781,
David Ricardo, political economist, 1823,
Captain Basil Hall, author of books of voyages and travels, 1844,
Mrs. Fitzwilliam, the actress, in 1845,
H. E. Mahomed Ali Jinnah, Governor-General of Pakistan, 1948,
Field-Marshal Rt. Hon. Jan Christian Smuts, O.M., C.H., F.R.S.,
1950.

THE SAINTS'-DAYS FOR SEPTEMBER THE ELEVENTH ARE,
SAINTS PROTUS AND HYACINTHUS, MARTYRS,
ST. PAPHNUTIUS, BISHOP AND CONFESSOR.

September the Twelfth

All starry-eyed we can say,
Ours too is the milky way.

'Aequanimitas' might be the word for him and his long life of public service. H. H. Asquith—later to become Lord Oxford and Asquith—who was born on September the Twelfth in 1852, was Prime Minister in Britain in 1914.

These too were born on this day:
Francis I of France, 1494,
Sir William Dugdall, the antiquary, 1605,
Jean-Philippe Rameau, a writer of operas, 1683, at Dijon,
H. L. Mencken, 1880, the American writer and critic,
The Reverend Prebendary Hubert Harold Treacher, 1891.

Died on this day, these are recorded,
Pope Innocent VI, 1362,
Griffith Jones, miscellaneous writer, 1786,
William Tytler, writer, Edinburgh, 1792,
Von Blücher, the German general, 1819,
Lord Metcalfe, statesman, 1846,
James Fillans, sculptor, 1852, Glasgow,
Sir James Stephen, historical and miscellaneous writer, 1859,
F. P. G. Guizot, the historian, 1875.

The events include:
Sack of Drogheda in 1694,
Switzerland adopted a new constitution in 1848,
Cleopatra's needle re-erected on the Victoria Embankment, London, 1878,
Argentina handed German ambassador his passport, 1917,
Battle of St. Mihiel, 1918,
New London barrage, 1940,
Germans reached the gates of Stalingrad, 1942,
Le Havre surrendered, 1944.

THE SAINTS'-DAYS FOR SEPTEMBER THE TWELFTH ARE:
ST. ALBEUS, BISHOP AND CONFESSOR, 525,
ST. EANSWIDE, VIRGIN AND ABBESS, SEVENTH CENTURY, AND
ST. GUY, CONFESSOR, ELEVENTH CENTURY.

September the Thirteenth

Can I these hours betray,
This is my lucky day.
These hours—all things are mine
A fortune to combine.

September the Thirteenth is birth day for the politicians and the generals.
Lord Burleigh in 1520 and Arthur Henderson in 1863 were born on this day.
General Pershing who commanded the American Army in 1918, and Lord
Birdwood who commanded the Anzacs in Gallipoli in 1915 were born
on this day—the first in 1860 and the second in 1865—and Sir Ralph
Cockayne Assheton, too, had it for a birthday in 1860.

Generals died on this day,
Charles Nicolas Oudinot, Duke of Reggio and Marshal of France,
died on September the Thirteenth in 1847, and it was on this day
in 1759 that General Wolfe died on the Plains of Abraham.

Titus, Roman emperor, A.D. 81,
Sir John Cheke, eminent Greek scholar, 1557,
William Farel, coadjutor of Calvin, 1565,
John Buxtorf the Elder, eminent Hebrew scholar, 1629,
Charles James Fox, in 1806, died on September the Thirteenth
and so, too, did Saverio Bettinelli, the Italian writer, on September
the Thirteenth in 1808 at Mantua, also
Sydney Webb, 1947.

THESE WERE SOME OF THE THINGS THAT HAPPENED ON
THIS DAY,
CAPTURE OF QUEBEC, 1759,
FRENCH AND BRITISH COMBINED IN GOVERNMENT OF
CANADA, 1842,
CONGRESS PASSED A BILL PERMITTING OWNERS TO FOLLOW
ESCAPED SLAVES INTO FREE STATES, 1850,
GERMANS CROSSED THE VISTULA, 1939,
ITALIANS INVADED EGYPT, 1940,
PATROLS PENETRATED ROMMEL'S REAR BASE AT BENGHAZI
AND BARCE, INFLICTING HEAVY DAMAGE, 1942,
HEAVY FIGHTING AT SALERNO, 1943,
GREAT BRITAIN, U.S.A., AND U.S.S.R. SIGNED ARMISTICE
WITH RUMANIA, 1944,
LOMZA CAPTURED, 1944.

September the Fourteenth

Does time fall from Heaven,
Or is it that it grows?
An enlarging leaven
That flowers and fruits and flows?

September the Fourteenth saw many of the captains and the kings—as well as the lesser sorts—depart. The great Duke of Wellington died on this day in 1852,
Sir Arthur Wauchope, one-time High Commissioner of Palestine, in 1947, and
In 1583, too, on September the Fourteenth, Wallenstein died,
In 1321, on September the Fourteenth, Dante died,
In 1769, on this day, Humboldt died,
Charles Rollin, the historian, died on September the Fourteenth, 1741, in Paris.
On September the Fourteenth, Thomas G. Masaryk—the founder of Czechoslovakia—died in 1937,
Place aux dames—in 1927, on this day, Isadora Duncan, the famous dancer of the U.S.A., died, and
In 1935, Madge Kendal, the English actress, died.
It was a less graceful and gracious world for their going.

These were born on this day:
Henry Cornelius Agrippa, alchemist and author, 1486, Cologne,
Browne Willis, antiquary, 1682, Blandford, Dorsetshire,
Lord William Henry Cavendish Bentinck, Governor-General of India, 1774,
Sir William Robertson, Chief of the Imperial General Staff, 1860,
Sir David Kelly, 1891.

EVENTS OF THE DAY INCLUDE:
OLDEST TOWN CHARTER EXTANT, 1338, DATED SEPTEMBER THE FOURTEENTH,
BURNING OF MOSCOW, 1812,
CHARTIST NATIONAL CONVENTION DISSOLVED, 1839,
ALLIED ARMIES LANDED IN THE CRIMEA, 1854,
FINDINGS OF 'ALABAMA' CLAIMS COMMISSION ANNOUNCED, 1872,
WESTERN POLAND INVADED BY GERMANS, 1939,
SALAMAUA CAPTURED FROM THE JAPANESE, 1943,
PRAGA CAPTURED, 1944.

September the Fifteenth

Now autumn's fire burns
Slowly along the woods
And day by day
The dead leaves fall and melt.

On September the Fifteenth these were born:
Jean Sylbain Bailly, a distinguished astronomer, 1736, Paris,
James Fenimore Cooper, American novelist, 1789, Burlington,
New Jersey,
John, Lord Campbell, Chancellor of England, 1779, at Cupar in
Fife, Scotland, and
General Sir Bernard Paget, 1888.

These died on this day:
Philip of Austria, father of Charles V, 1506,
Sir Thomas Overbury, poisoned in the Tower, 1613,
Lady Arabella Stuart, 1615,
Richard Boyle, Earl of Cork, the eminent statesman, 1643,
Sidney, Earl of Godolphin, Premier to Queen Anne, at St.
Albans, 1712,
Abbé Terrasson, translator of *Diodorus Siculus*, 1750,
General Lazare Hoche, French commander, 1797,
William Huskisson, distinguished politician and economist, killed
at the opening of the Liverpool and Manchester Railway, 1830,
Isambard K. Brunel, eminent civil engineer, 1859, Westminster.

THESE THINGS HAPPENED ON THIS DAY:
LIVERPOOL AND MANCHESTER RAILWAY OPENED, 1830,
FOUNDATION STONE OF CHARING CROSS HOSPITAL LAID,
1831,
TANKS FIRST USED BY BRITAIN, 1916,
RUSSIA PROCLAIMED A REPUBLIC, 1917,
FRENCH OCCUPIED RUHR, 1921,
CHAMBERLAIN FLEW TO MUNICH, 1938,
END OF BATTLE OF BRITAIN, 1940,
OF WHICH PERHAPS SOME WOULD SAY THE MOST MOMEN-
TOUS WAS THE OVERTHROW OF THE CZAR IN 1917—AND
THE PRODUCTION OF THE KERENSKY REPUBLIC,
BOTH HOUSES OF CONGRESS PASSED LEGISLATION APPOINT-
ING GENERAL GEORGE MARSHALL SECRETARY OF DEFENCE,
1950.

September the Sixteenth

O day and night, but this is wondrous strange.

On September the Sixteenth
Henry V was born in 1387,
Bonar Law, the Scots-Canadian Prime Minister, in 1858, and
Alfred Noyes, the English poet, in 1880.

Many died on September the Sixteenth—here are eight:
Pope Martin I, 665,
Pope Victor II, 1087,
Torquemada, 1498,
Fahrenheit, 1736,
Blackwood, the publisher, 1834, and *Blackwood's Magazine* lives today,
Edward Bouverie Pussey, 1882,
Sir James Jeans, mathematician and astronomer, 1946,
Sir Ronald Ross, 1932.

THESE OCCURRED ON SEPTEMBER THE SIXTEENTH:
IN CANADA, A GREAT DARKNESS FELL AT QUEBEC IN 1785,
IN SOUTH AFRICA, IN 1795, THE BRITISH CAPTURED THE
CAPE OF GOOD HOPE,
IN 1816 ON THIS DAY THE GREAT MACREADY MADE HIS
FIRST APPEARANCE,
IN ENGLAND, SHAKESPEARE'S HOUSE WAS BOUGHT BY THE
SHAKESPEARE COMMITTEE FOR £3,000 IN 1847, AND
IN LONDON, TOO, IN 1861, ON SEPTEMBER THE SIXTEENTH,
SAVINGS BANKING THROUGH THE GENERAL POST OFFICE
WAS SET UP,
IN THE FAR EAST, RUSSIA AND JAPAN STOPPED FIGHTING
IN 1939,
IN 1947, ON THIS DAY, THE PRINCESS MARGARET
LAUNCHED A TANKER ON THE CLYDE.
SO MUCH FOR SEPTEMBER THE SIXTEENTH.

THE SAINTS'-DAYS FOR SEPTEMBER THE SIXTEENTH ARE:
ST. CORNELIUS, POPE AND MARTYR, 252,
ST. EUPHEMIA, VIRGIN AND MARTYR, ABOUT 307,
ST. NINIAN OR NINYAS, BISHOP AND CONFESSOR, AND
APOSTLE OF THE SOUTHERN PICTS, 432,
ST. EDITHA, VIRGIN, 984.

September the Seventeenth

Where are the lads of yester year
Who tossed their tankards—swigged their beer,
Some in Burma—some in Greece,
I wonder what they think of peace.
I wonder if that humour stays
That salted—sweetened—those old days?

'He strove with none for none was worth his strife—nature he loved and,
next to nature, art'—so wrote Walter Savage Landor, the English poet,
who died on September the Seventeenth in 1864.
This day was the day, too, on which Doctor Tobias Smollett died in 1771,
who not only left his mark in English literature but, some claim, opened out
for the English a vista of the charms of the Riviera.

On September the Seventeenth:
Bonnie Prince Charlie entered Edinburgh, 1745,
The trial of Robert Emmett began in 1803,
Brazil was declared independent in 1822,
Edward Terry, the actor, made his first appearance in London
in 1867,
Russia entered Poland in 1939,
H.M.S. *Courageous* was the first warship to be sunk in the Second
World War, with a loss of 515 lives, 1939,
Streets in the West End of London bombed, 1940,
The R.A.F. went into action in Russia, 1941,
Briansk captured, 1943,
The airborne armada landed in Holland, 1944, and
Trade agreement signed with the Argentine, 1946.

On this day were born,
Jean Antoine, Marquis de Condorcet, Picardy, 1743,
Samuel Prout, painter, London, 1783.

THERE DIED ON SEPTEMBER THE SEVENTEENTH:
CARDINAL BELLARINE IN 1621,
FRÉDÉRIC CHOPIN IN 1849,
VIOLLET LEDUC, THE ARCHITECT, IN 1875,
COUNT FOLKE BERNADOTTE, UNITED NATIONS MEDIATOR
IN PALESTINE, 1948,
DAME LILIAN BRAITHWAITE, D.B.E., DISTINGUISHED
ACTRESS, 1948.

September the Eighteenth

Thou art a day of mirth
And, where the week-days trail upon ground
Thy flight is higher.

On September the Eighteenth Samuel Johnson was born in 1709. None who loves life and literature lives fully who has not marched with Samuel Johnson's mind and opinions . . . an intellectual journey made possible by the faithful interpretation and records of a curious Scotsman called James Boswell. English literature owes much to the Scots generally, but its greatest debt is to James Boswell.

Bishop Burnet, the churchman and historian, was born on this day in 1643,
William Collins, artist, born 1787,
Sir Owen Seaman, the poet and editor of *Punch* was born on this day in 1861,
Fay Compton, 1894.

Hugo van der Goes, Flemish painter, 1684,
Matthew Prior in 1721,
Leonard Euler in 1783,
Olaf Swartz, eminent botanist, 1817,
William Hazlitt, the critic and essayist, in 1830,
Joseph Locke, eminent engineer, 1860, and
Tin Tut Maung U, one of the founders of independent Burma 1948 . . . these died on this day.

ON SEPTEMBER THE EIGHTEENTH:
GEORGE I LANDED IN ENGLAND IN 1714,
THE ANTI-CORN LAW LEAGUES FORMED AT MANCHESTER IN 1838,
SOVIET RUSSIA WAS ADMITTED TO THE LEAGUE OF NATIONS AND TO A SEAT ON THE COUNCIL IN 1934,
RUSSIANS AND GERMANS MET AT BREST-LITOVSK IN 1939,
8,000-LB. BOMBS WERE BEING USED IN 1942,
YORK AIRCRAFT LOADED WITH SUPPLIES FOR BERLIN CRASHED, CREW BEING KILLED, 1948,
SIR STAFFORD CRIPPS BROADCAST THE NEWS OF THE DEVALUATION OF THE POUND, 1949.

September the Nineteenth

Happiest of all mankind
My dearest darling died
With timeless thought and dateless mind
O! innocence quite undenied.

On September the Nineteenth President Garfield died of wounds at the hand of an assassin in 1881. He was one of the three presidents of the United States of America who died in this fashion, Lincoln and McKinley being the others.
One English king was executed: none died by assassination, seeming to substantiate the claim that kingship is safer in a democracy than a presidency.
Doctor Barnardo died on this day in 1905—a great benefactor of the neglected children of Britain.
William Joyce, the Fascist, was sentenced to death, 1946.

Born on this day were:
Rev. William Kirby, entomologist, 1759, Witnesham Hall, Suffolk,
George Cadbury, the business pioneer and philanthropist, 1839,
Lord Carnock (ambassador to Russia), 1849,
Kajos Kossuth, 1802.

Died on this day:
Charles Edward Poulett Thomson, Lord Sydenham, Governor of Canada, 1841,
Professor John P. Nichol, author of *The Architecture of the Heavens*, 1859, Rothesay.
Sir William A. Russell, K.C.M.G., of the Colonial Legal Service, 1948.

THE EVENTS OF THE NINETEENTH OF SEPTEMBER INCLUDE:
BATTLE OF POITIERS, 1356,
HEIGHT OF THE GREAT PLAGUE IN LONDON, 1666,
BARROW-IN-FURNESS DOCKS WERE OPENED IN 1867,
MR. DE VALERA AND THREE OF HIS MINISTERS FLEW TO LONDON AND DISCUSSED ECONOMIC MATTERS WITH MR. ATTLEE AND MEMBERS OF THE BRITISH CABINET, 1947,
DELEGATES FROM BRITISH WEST INDIES AT CONFERENCE AT MONTEGO BAY PASSED RESOLUTIONS APPROVING PRINCIPLE OF BRITISH CARIBBEAN FEDERATION AS STEP TOWARDS A DOMINION, 1947.

September the Twentieth

Count the hours and watch your days,
Do your work—look not for praise.

The records are obscure and in contradiction of each other, but there is some agreement that it was on September the Twentieth, in 356 B.C., that Alexander the Great was born.
He was the first in history to conceive a world state imposed by power, but inspired by the principles of order and justice. The great dream died with Alexander, but it lives again in others who by differing means still seek the same end.

Prince Arthur, elder brother of Henry VIII, 1486, was born on September the Twentieth,
Mungo Park, the Scots explorer, in 1771, as, too, was Maria Paulina, in 1780, the sister of Napoleon who became the Princess Brighese.

Owen Glendower died on this day in 1415,
Nelson's Hardy, captain of the *Victory*, died on this day in 1839,
Sir Denison Ross died on this day in 1840,
Jacob Grimm died on this day in 1863,
Fiorello la Guardia, a Mayor of New York, died on this day in 1947.

THESE HAPPENED ON SEPTEMBER THE TWENTIETH:
ETON WAS FOUNDED BY HENRY VI IN 1440,
AT VALMY ON SEPTEMBER THE TWENTIETH, 1792, THE FRENCH, UNDER KELLERMAN, DEFEATED THE ALLIES, UNDER THE DUKE OF BRUNSWICK, IN ONE OF THE DECISIVE BATTLES OF HISTORY.
COVENT GARDEN THEATRE WAS BURNT IN 1808,
THE BATTLE OF ALMA WAS FOUGHT IN 1854,
DELHI DAY, 1857,
THE LORD CHIEF JUSTICE CLERK COMMITTED SUICIDE IN 1869,
THE FIRST ELECTRIC TRAM RAN IN PARIS IN 1870,
THE POPE'S TEMPORAL POWER ENDED IN 1870,
THE FIRST INTERNATIONAL PRESS ASSOCIATION CONFERENCE TOOK PLACE IN 1909,
THE HATRY GROUP CRASHED IN 1929,
EMPEROR HAILÉ SELASSIÉ FLEW TO GENEVA, 1936.

September the Twenty-first

Born obscurely yet born bold
You may seek new worlds for old.

Born obscurely in the domestic sphere of the lower class in England, he sought to find new and better worlds for old. His name was Herbert George Wells and he was born on September the Twenty-first, 1866. He was shop assistant, school teacher, student, journalist and author. He was one of the creators of modern English Socialism but may be more kindly and lastingly remembered as the author of The History of Mr. Polly, *of* Love and Mr. Lewisham, *and of* Kipps.

Girolamo Savonarola, preacher and reformer, in 1452,
John Loudon McAdam, improver of roads, 1756,
Louis Bonaparte, King of Holland, 1778,
James Gordon Bennet in 1841,
Sir Edmund Gosse in 1849,
Field-Marshal Lord Chetwode, 1869.

These died on this day:
Edward II in 1327,
Sir Walter Scott in 1832,
Lord George Bentinck in 1848,
De Quincey in 1859,
Arthur Schopenhauer in 1860,
Sir Kingsley Wood in 1943.

THESE EVENTS OCCURRED ON THIS DAY:
SCOTS SURRENDERED CHARLES I, 1646,
BATTLE OF PRESTONPANS, 1745,
NATIONAL CONVENTION, 1792,
LONDON–BRIGHTON RAILWAY OPENED, 1841,
GREAT BRITAIN ABANDONED GOLD STANDARD, 1931,
RUSSIA AND GERMANY CARVED UP POLAND, 1939,
FIRST FIRE-WATCHING ORDER, 1940,
REPORTED FROM VICHY THAT 5,000 MEN WERE ARRESTED IN PARIS EITHER FOR THROWING BOMBS OR EVADING CURFEW, 1942,
'BATTLE OF BRITAIN' THANKSGIVING SERVICE IN WESTMINSTER ABBEY, 1947,
GENERAL MAO TSE-TUNG PROCLAIMS PEOPLE'S REPUBLIC OF CHINA, 1949.

[276]

September the Twenty-second

Joy—O! that was gala day
Trout and Tarts and fine Tokay.

September the Twenty-second is an anniversary of war and warriors. On this day, in 1914, the first British air raid took place over Germany, on Düsseldorf, and Lord Kitchener heard it on his birthday. He was born on September the Twenty-second in 1850.
In 1586 the Battle of Zutphen was fought on this day, the battle which saw the death of the Elizabethan hero, Sir Philip Sidney, and down the years, in 1944, on the same day, Rimini and Tallinn were captured by the Allied armies, and Boulogne fell to the Canadians.

Dr. Busby in 1606,
Lord Chesterfield in 1694,
John Hume, of 'Douglas' fame, 1722,
Faraday, the scientist, 1791,
Theodore Hook, 1788,
Sir George Stapledon in 1882 . . . all these great and famous men had September the Twenty-second as their birth day.

Virgil in 19 B.C. died on this day,
Major Bernardi in 1736,
John Bartram, botanist, 1777,
Princess Augusta of England, 1840,
Mrs. Sherwood, the authoress, in 1851,
Sir Charles Santley in 1922, died, too, on September the Twenty-second.

These are the saints of the day,
St. Maurice and his companions, martyrs, 286, and
St. Emmeran, Bishop of Poitiers, and patron of Ratisbon, martyr, 653.

ON THIS DAY, IN 1638, THE GENERAL ASSEMBLY WAS CALLED AT GLASGOW,
ANNOUNCEMENT OF 'PAY AS YOU EARN' INCOME TAX TO BEGIN APRIL 1944–5,
2,500 MILES COMPLETED IN TWELVE HOURS BY PILOTLESS AUTOMATIC PLANE FROM UNITED STATES TO BRIZE NORTON, 1947,
COMMONS TOLD WESTERN POWERS AGREED ON CONTINUATION OF BERLIN AIR LIFT, 1948.

September the Twenty-third

I die daily—so it's said—
But one day soon I will be dead.

Paracelsus died on September the Twenty-third in 1541,
John Morley, who became Viscount Morley, was in his long life critic,
essayist, historian, biographer, politician and statesman. He was the
author of the Life of Gladstone *and a pillar of post-Gladstonian Liberalism.*
He died on this day in 1923 and that kind of liberalism which he repre-
sented died then, too.
William Wilkie Collins who won fame with his book The Woman in
White, *died on September the Twenty-third in 1889.*

These events occurred on this day:
Physicians College incorporated, 1518,
Paul Jones and Flamborough Head, 1779,
Wellington's first victory, Assaye, 1803,
Discovery of planet Neptune, 1846,
First balloon post from Paris, 1870,
Andrew William Mellon, American financier and statesman,
bought $800,000 worth of Old Masters from Soviet Russia, 1930,
Abyssinian delegation admitted to League meeting, 1936,
Petrol and butter stocks commandeered in Britain, 1939,
George Cross and George Medal instituted, 1940,
Forty Japanese ships and 375 aircraft destroyed in a two-day
attack near Manila, 1944,

Octavius Caesar Augustus, first Roman emperor, 63 B.C.,
Dr. Jeremy Collier, celebrated author of *A View of the Stage*, etc.,
1650,
William Archer, the critic and playwright, was born in 1856,
Lord Boyd Orr in 1880.

BISHOP JEWEL, EMINENT PRELATE, 1571,
HERMANN BOERHAAVE, DISTINGUISHED PHYSICIAN, 1738,
DR. MATTHEW BAILLIE, EMINENT PHYSICIAN, 1823,
WILLIAM UPCOTT, COLLECTOR OF HISTORICAL MANU-
SCRIPTS, 1845,
EDWARD WEDLAKE BRAYLEY, TOPOGRAPHICAL AND
ANTIQUARIAN WRITER, 1854, AND
PROSPER MÉRIMÉE, FRENCH AUTHOR, DIED IN 1870
ON SEPTEMBER THE TWENTY-THIRD.

September the Twenty-fourth

On yester night I was on edge,
Today my mind is clear
Today I neither dodge nor hedge
I feel no fear of fear.

'Manners maketh man' was his faith and belief and practice, and to give
enduring influence to his conviction William of Wykeham founded
Winchester School. He died on September the Twenty-fourth in 1404.
Eight episodes associated with this day appear in the records:
In 1693 the bayonet was adopted by the English army,
In 1850, the bishops of the Catholic Church were re-established in Britain,
Allied air raid on Krupp's works at Essen, 1916,
In 1918 Kaiser Wilhelm at Kiel told submarine commanders they could
win the war,
Gordon-Bennett balloon race ended disastrously, five lives and three
balloons being lost in 1923,
In 1928 both first- and third-class sleepers were inaugurated on the railways
of Great Britain,
Japanese troops entered Indo-China, 1940,
The R.A.F. delivered its first saturation raid in 1945, and
United States Marines began main attack on Seoul and met fierce resistance,
1950 (Korean War).

Three birth days are recalled,
Horace Walpole, essayist and critic, in 1717,
Sharon Turner, the historian, poet and playwright, in 1768,
Sir A. P. Herbert, 1890.

These died on September the Twenty-fourth,
Michael III, Greek emperor, assassinated 867,
Pope Innocent III in 1143,
Henry, Viscount Hardinge, Governor-General and Commander-
in-Chief in India, 1856,
Eliza Cook, the poetess, in 1889,
The Dowager Marchioness of Milford Haven, grand-daughter of
Queen Victoria, 1950.

SAINTS'-DAYS FOR SEPTEMBER THE TWENTY-FOURTH ARE:
ST. RUSTICUS OR ROTIRI, BISHOP OF AUVERGNE,
ST. GERMER OR GEREMAR, ABBOT, 658,
ST. GERARD, BISHOP OF CHONAD, MARTYR, 1046.

September the Twenty-fifth

All through the day and all the night,
I watched trunks and their tossing boughs.
It was a soothing, soaring sight,
My roots stand firm: I keep my vows.

On September the Twenty-fifth in 1630 the Italian general, Spinola, died—
It was the day on which Samuel Pepys drank, in 1660, his first cup of tea.
September the Twenty-fifth is Lucknow Day, commemorating 1857—
It is the anniversary of the Battle of Loos in 1915—
It is the date, in 1915, on which the British armies first used lethal gas in war—
It is the day of the Dakar endeavour in North Africa with General de Gaulle in 1940—and
It is the day on which, in 1943, the Russians captured Smolensk.

William Romaine, eminent divine, was born on September the Twenty-fifth in 1714,
Christian Gottlob Heyne, classical editor at Chemnitz, Saxony, in 1729,
Abraham Gottlob Werner, geologist, 1750,
Mrs. Hemans was born on this day in 1793, and
Sir Charles Cochran, 1872.

These died on this day:
Lancelot Andrews, eminent prelate and writer, in 1626,
Samuel Butler in 1680,
Robert Dodsley, author and publisher, in 1764,
Richard Pococke, Bishop of Ossory, oriental traveller, 1756,
Johann Strauss, the elder, 1849,
Joseph Greenwood, Principal of Owen's College, Manchester, 1894,
Sir Norman F. W. Fisher, former Secretary to the Treasury, 1948,
Admiral Sir James Startin, a brave and fearless sailor, 1948.

THIS DAY SAW THE
BEGINNING OF HUNGARIAN WAR OF INDEPENDENCE IN 1848,
FOUNDATION STONES OF POST OFFICE AND CHAMBERS STREET MUSEUM, EDINBURGH, LAID, 1861,
THE CASABLANCA INCIDENT, 1908,
INTRODUCTION OF RATIONING IN GERMANY IN 1939.

September the Twenty-sixth

Today I will go and ramble
And I will go round—
Walk the hills—and scramble—
And see what can be found.

Lord Collingwood, not the least of Nelson's admirals, was born on this day
in 1750,
Charles Bradlaugh was born on this day in 1833—the first professed
atheist to be elected to the House of Commons,
Mr. William J. McKell, Governor-General of Australia, in 1891.

There died on September the Twenty-sixth:
Pope Clement VII, 1534,
Cooke, the actor, 1812,
Richard Colley, Marquis Wellesley, statesman, and eldest brother
of the Duke of Wellington, 1842, Kingston House, Brompton,
Thomas Clarkson, the anti-slavery champion, in 1846,
Béla Bartók, Hungarian composer, 1945.

There is room to remember the saints of the day
Saints Cyprian and Justina, martyrs, 304,
St. Eusebius, pope and confessor, 310,
St. Colman Elo, abbot and confessor, 610, and
St. Nilus, the Younger, abbot, 1005.

THERE WERE MANY EVENTS IN THE PAST WHICH MAKE
SEPTEMBER THE TWENTY-SIXTH MEMORABLE—
WILLIAM RUFUS SUCCEEDED WILLIAM THE CONQUEROR ON
THIS DAY IN 1087,
THE BRITISH ASSOCIATION FOR ADVANCEMENT OF SCIENCE
WAS FOUNDED IN 1831,
DOMINION DAY—NEW ZEALAND, 1907,
PRINCE ITO, JAPANESE STATESMAN, ASSASSINATED BY A
KOREAN, 1909,
BATTLE OF THE MEUSE BEGAN, 1918,
TRADE TREATY BETWEEN CANADA AND AUSTRALIA, 1924,
FIRST DIVE-BOMB ATTACK ON WARSHIPS, 1939,
EIGHTH ARMY FORMED, 1941,
ESTONIA WHOLLY OCCUPIED BY RUSSIAN FORCES, 1944,
DR. RALPH BUNCHE, ACTING U.N.O. MEDIATOR, ORDERED
JEWS AND ARABS TO STOP FIGHTING IN PALESTINE, 1948.

September the Twenty-seventh

Night will fall—time will not tarry
Hate and rancour—love and marry
Of this at least be sure that still
Time marches on—and ever will.

These things befell on September the Twenty-seventh:
Order of Jesuits established by Papal Bull, 1540,
The Africa, or Guinea, Company founded, 1672,
Rome surrendered to the British Navy, 1799,
Bombardment of Algiers, 1816,
Stockton and Darlington Railway opened, 1825,
British Association established, 1825,
Independence of Norway, 1905,
Battle of Cambrai, 1918,
Constantine of Greece abdicated, 1922,
The Queen Elizabeth, *world's largest liner, launched by H.M.* Queen
Elizabeth *at Clydebank, 1938,*
Income Tax 7s. 6d. in the pound, 1939,
Warsaw surrendered, 1939,
Axis Pact, 1940,
Foggia was taken by Allied forces, 1943,
Allied landing in Albania and withdrawal of Arnhem troops, 1944.

Louis XIII of France in 1601,
Jacques B. Bossuet, preacher and controversialist, 1627,
Samuel Adams, U.S. patriot and statesman, in 1722,
George Cruikshank, 1792,
Sir Ronald Hugh Campbell, 1883, were all born on this day.

THESE DIED ON SEPTEMBER THE TWENTY-SEVENTH,
MARCO GIROLAMO VIDA, AUTHOR OF LATIN POEMS, ETC.,
1566, ALBA,
POPE INNOCENT XII, 1700,
DR. THOMAS BURNET, AUTHOR OF 'THE SACRED THEORY
OF THE EARTH', 1715,
JAMES BRINDLEY, CELEBRATED ENGINEER, 1772, TURN-
HURST, STAFFORDSHIRE,
FRANK CELLIER, ACTOR, 1948,
THE RT. REVEREND H. H. HENSON, D.D., A BISHOP OF
DURHAM, 1947.

September the Twenty-eighth

Time is the only enduring theme.

A great cavalry soldier and a French doctor, who one time practised in New York, are joined by destiny on this day. Sir John French, who became Lord French of Ypres, and Georges Clemenceau, who became President of the French Republic, were both born on September the Twenty-eighth—the first in Edinburgh in 1852—the second in 1841. They met in France in 1914.

These, too, were born on this day,
Sir William Jones, Oriental scholar, 1746, London,
Richard Owen, 1804,
F. T. Palgrave, 1824,
John Denton Pinkston French, 1st Earl of Ypres, 1852,
The Earl of Listowel in 1906.

There died on September the Twenty-eighth:
George Buchanan, 1582,
John Byron, poet, 1763,
Thomas Day, 1789,
Granville Penn, miscellaneous writer, 1844, Stoke Park, Bucks,
Dr. Karl Ritter, distinguished geographer, 1859, Berlin,
Louis Pasteur, French chemist, 1895.

On this day, Twenty-eighth September, 490 B.C., 10,000 Greeks under Miltiades overthrew 100,000 Persians under Darius at Marathon,
Siege of Sevastopol opened, 1854,
The first line in the world to be run on hydro-electric power, the Giants' Causeway railway, 1883, was inaugurated,
Turks defeated at Kut-el-Amara, 1915,
British Navy mobilized, 1938,
Genoa bombed 1941,
Russia agreed to supply Germany with raw materials, 1939,
Mr. J. G. N. Strauss elected to succeed Field-Marshal Smuts as leader of South African United Party, 1950.

HERE ARE SOME OF THE SAINTS OF THE DAY:
ST. ESTOCHIUM, VIRGIN, 419,
ST. LIOBA, ABBESS, 779,
ST. WENCESLAS, DUKE OF BOHEMIA, MARTYR, 938.

September the Twenty-ninth

Men have found misery in machinery
Who was the devil who invented the clock?

This is the day of
St. Michael and All Angels.

Tintoretto (Jacopo Robusti) in 1518,
John Tillotson, Archbishop of Canterbury, 1630,
Robert Clive in 1725, and
Nelson in 1758—two of the greatest of Englishmen—were born
on this day,
Mrs. Gaskell in 1810,
Sir J. Lyons in 1848, and
Lord Barnby, the Yorkshire wool magnate, 1884, these, too, were
born on September the Twenty-ninth.

Gustavus Vasa, King of Sweden, 1560,
Rachel Russell, heroic wife of William, Lord Russell, 1723,
Marshal St. Arnand in 1854,
Émile Zola in 1902, died on this day.

THESE EVENTS ARE RECORDED:
DUKE WILLIAM THE CONQUEROR, LANDED AT PEVENSEY,
1066, AND CONQUERED ENGLAND,
NEW POLICE TOOK OVER, 1829,
REGULAR GOVERNMENT ESTABLISHED IN VICTORIA, 1836,
ITALY DECLARED WAR ON TURKEY AND SEIZED TRIPOLI,
1911,
PALESTINE MANDATE CAME INTO FORCE, 1923,
TERMS OF 'SUCCESSFUL WOMEN' APPEARED FOR FIRST
TIME IN HIGHER CIVIL SERVICE EXAMINATION, 1925,
MUNICH AGREEMENT—CHAMBERLAIN, DALADIER, HITLER
AND MUSSOLINI, 1938,
'NATIONAL REGISTER' NIGHT IN BRITAIN, 1939,
ARMISTICE TERMS SIGNED BY ITALY, 1943,
BRITAIN, UNITED STATES AND FRANCE ASKED SECURITY
COUNCIL, UNITED NATIONS, TO CONSIDER BLOCKADE OF
BERLIN WHICH CREATED THREAT TO PEACE, 1948,
THE SEVENTH EARL OF HAREWOOD MARRIED MISS MARION
STEIN, 1949,
ALL THESE ON SEPTEMBER THE TWENTY-NINTH.

September the Thirtieth

We go forward clockwise—round and round—and never break out of the circle.

The English called Napoleon Bonaparte 'Boney'. The English called another great warrior 'Bobs'. He was Lord Roberts, the inspirer of the armies of 1914, with whom he died. He was born on this day in 1832.

William Hutton in 1723,
Jacques Necker, financier to Louis XVI, 1734, at Geneva, and
Air Chief Marshal Sir Richard Peirse, 1892, were born on September the Thirtieth.

These died on this day:
Sir Fulke Greville, Lord Brooke, poet, murdered in 1628,
John Reinhold Patkul, Livonian statesman, broken on the wheel, 1707,
John Dollond, the optician, 1761,
George Whitefield, celebrated preacher, in 1770,
Bishop Percy, 1811,
Thomas Horatio Nelson, fourth earl, inheritor of Trafalgar Estate, 1947,
Mrs. Theodore Roosevelt, widow of the twenty-sixth President of the United States, 1948.

WHICH OF THESE MATTER MOST TO MEN TODAY?
THEY WERE GREAT OCCURRENCES IN THEIR TIME. THEY ARE ALL CONNECTED WITH SEPTEMBER THE THIRTIETH.
RICHARD II DEPOSED, 1399, ACCESSION OF HENRY IV,
PRECEDENCY BRAWL BETWEEN FRENCH AND SPANIARDS IN LONDON, 1661,
FIRST PERFORMANCE OF 'THE MAGIC FLUTE', 1781,
CONGRESS OF VIENNA, 1814,
FOUNDATION STONE LAID OF NELSON'S MONUMENT, 1840,
FIJI CEDED TO GREAT BRITAIN, 1874,
FOUNDATION STONE OF FORTH BRIDGE LAID, 1878,
BULGARIA GRANTED CONDITIONS OF PEACE, 1918,
SOVIET BALLOON 'STRATOSTAT SSSR' REACHED 19,000 METRES, 1933,
POLISH GOVERNMENT SET UP, 1939,
POLTAVA EVACUATED BY THE RUSSIANS, 1941,
CALAIS SURRENDERED TO CANADIANS, 1944.

OCTOBER

THIRTY-ONE DAYS

October the First

. . . And if I drink oblivion of a day . . .
. . . So shorten I the stature of my soul . . .

Governments like October the First.

The Battle of Arbela, in which Alexander the Great defeated Darius and his Persians, made October the First a fateful and bloody day, 301 B.C.

Charles Kean made his first appearance in London in 1827, ten years before Victoria ascended the throne,

Postcards for a halfpenny and communications in unsealed envelopes at the same price were introduced in 1870—the Paper Duty was abolished in 1861 and—not less important—Money Orders were made exchangeable between the United Kingdom and British India in 1872,

The Passengers Act came into force in 1885 on this day, and Sixpenny telegrams were introduced.

Second-class carriages went out in 1923,

The Peace of Amiens was signed in 1801, on October the First,

The same day in 1939 saw the Germans enter Warsaw, and in 1943 the not yet victorious Allies entered Naples on their way to Rome and Berlin—and victory,

New austerity measures—petrol restricted, currency controlled for foreign travel—were announced in 1947.

These were born:
Henry III, in 1207,
William Beckford, writer, 1760,
George Colman, playwright, 1762,
Mrs. Annie Besant, theosophist, 1847,
Lord Stravordale, born 1905.

THERE DIED ON OCTOBER THE FIRST:
PIERRE CORNEILLE IN 1684,
SIR EDWIN LANDSEER IN 1873,
GREGORIO MARTINEZ SIERRA, THE SPANISH PLAYWRIGHT, IN 1947.
ON OCTOBER THE FIRST—THESE—
BAYEUX TAPESTRY SAFE IN THE LOUVRE, 1944,
VERDICT AND SENTENCES ON NAZI LEADERS ANNOUNCED, 1946.

October the Second

O! are there yet for me more days for laughter, love and gracious ways,
For time to see and time to know, time to see Spring's blossoms blow,
Time to eat and time to drink, time to ponder deep and think,
Time to see the Autumn sheaves, and all the reddening of its leaves,
Time to comfort and to aid the things and creatures that I've made,
Time to bar and time to bless, time for fullest happiness . . .
O! are there yet for me some days the Lord of Life to thank and praise?

October the Second was the birth day of Marshal Foch who was born in
1851. His statue stands near Victoria Station in London—soldiers of the
1914–18 war remember him as the architect of the final victory. Mahatma
Gandhi, doomed to die at the hand of the assassin, was born on October the
Second in 1869.
Cordell Hull, the U.S.A. statesman, was born on this day in 1871.

Other birthdays include:
Richard III in 1452,
Chevalier d'Eon in 1728,
Graham Greene, author, 1904.

There died on this day:
Major André, in 1780, executed as a spy for Britain,
Samuel Adams, the American patriot and statesman, in 1803,
Miss Biffin, painter without hands or arms, in 1850,
Thomas Thomson, the Edinburgh antiquary, 1852,
Sir John Jarvis, financial expert and former M.P., 1950.

It was on October the Second that the acts of attainder on
James II were cancelled and publicly burned in 1695,
The first British mines were laid in North Sea, 1914,
The Allied troops evacuated Constantinople, 1923, and
The Royal Indian Navy was inaugurated, 1934.
Hitler and Mussolini met on the Brenner Pass, 1940.

IT IS THE ANNIVERSARY OF THE BATTLE OF LARGS, 1263,
IN SCOTLAND, TOO, ON THIS DAY IN 1878, WAS ANNOUNCED
THE FAILURE OF THE CITY OF GLASGOW BANK, A GREAT
DISASTER FOR A SMALL COUNTRY, IN WHICH THOUSANDS
WERE RUINED,
RUSSIA RECOGNIZED NEWLY ESTABLISHED CHINESE
PEOPLE'S REPUBLIC, 1949.

October the Third

Tomorrow is the goal to which
All mankind sets its eyes.
Tomorrow I will be great and rich
Tomorrow knows no sighs.

This is the day of Saint Dionysius the Areopagite, Bishop of Athens and a martyr in the first century.
This is the day on which Neville Chamberlain, Prime Minister of Britain, on October the Third in 1940, resigned his high office.
This is the day on which, in 1896, William Morris, poet and socialist, died.

On October the Third, these were born,
Richard Boyle, the Earl of Cork, in 1566,
Giovanni Baptista Beccaria, the natural philosopher, in 1716 at Mondovi,
William Crawford Gorgas (eradicator of yellow fever, Canal Zone) at Panama in 1854,
Eleonora Duse, 1859, and
Lord Irwin in 1912.

On this day died:
John Lyon of Harrow in 1592,
G. F. A. Belcher, the artist, in 1947, and
Sir Percy Carter Buck, musician and instructor, in 1947.

The two Ewalds, the martyrs, about 695, and
St. Gerard, an abbot in 959, are three of the Saints of the day.

In 1870, on October the Third, President Buchanan of the United States of America entertained the Prince of Wales at White House.
In 1935 this day marked the outbreak of the war between Italy and Abyssinia.

HENRY VI WAS RESTORED TO THE THRONE IN 1470, AND EDWARD IV DEPOSED, 1470, ON THIS DAY,
TREATY OF LIMERICK, IN 1691, BELONGS TO THIS DAY,
PASSING OF MANCHESTER SHIP CANAL BILL, 1885, TOOK PLACE ON THIS DAY,
FRENCH CAPTURED ST. QUENTIN, 1918,
HEAVY JAPANESE LOSSES ON MANCHUKUO AND MONGOLIAN BORDER, 1939,
KASSEL RAIDED, 1943.

October the Fourth

That self-same day shall be the ending of us both.

It was journey's end for two of the greatest of men on October the Fourth.
On this day in 1226, Francis of Assisi, died into immortality.
On this day in 1669, Rembrandt and all he painted, passed into the possession of a still wondering world never wholly blind to beauty.

These four were born on October the Fourth:
Richard Cromwell in 1626,
Edmond Malone, 1741,
Maréchal Niel, 1802, and
Admiral Lord Keyes in 1872.

These five died on this day:
Cardinal Bellermine in 1542,
Henry Carey, musician, in 1743,
John Rennie in 1821,
John Vandenhoff, tragedian, in 1861, at London,
Professor Max Planck, famous German physicist, in 1947.

History lists these events on October the Fourth,
Loss of the first *Victory*, 1744,
Battle of Germantown, 1777,
Perceval's Ministry, 1809,
Belgian independence proclaimed, 1830,
First power-driven flight, balloon propelled by screw, 1863,
Date of Queen Victoria's signed letter to Negus of Abyssinia, 1866,
Ferdinand of Bulgaria, abdicated, 1918,
Germany proposed armistice, 1918,
Geneva Protocol, 1922,
British steamer *Clement* sunk in South Atlantic by an armed raider, 1939,
Hitler and Mussolini met on the Brenner Pass, 1940,
Corsica in Allied hands, 1943.

SOME OF THE SAINTS WHO, WITH ST. FRANCIS HAVE
OCTOBER THE FOURTH AS THEIR DAY—
AMMON, A HERMIT IN THE FOURTH CENTURY,
EDWIN, KING OF NORTHUMBERLAND, 633,
AUREA, VIRGIN AND ABBESS, 666.

October the Fifth

The daytime grows,
The cold grows, says the fisherman,
And this day knows,
Woes and woes, says the fisherman.

October the Fifth, 1535, is a great day for the English-speaking peoples. It was the day on which—it may be said—they were born again into a world they were destined to rule, for it was on this day that the first English Bible was published in print. The English Bible has long held the record of being the book with the largest circulation in the world.

On October the Fifth,
Jonathan Edwards in 1703,
Denis Diderot, French philosopher, 1713,
Horace Walpole in 1717,
John Addington Symonds in 1840, and
Sir Waldron Smithers, 1880, were born.

On October the Fifth,
Offenbach in 1789 died,
Lord Cornwallis in 1805,
William Heinemann, the publisher, in 1920, and, too,
Dr. Montague John Randall, former Headmaster of Winchester,
1950.

What can we make of these—
Ça Ira first heard, 1789,
Fanny Kemble's first appearance in London, 1829,
Allied troops landed at Salonika, 1915,
Lord Derby, Director of Recruiting, 1915,
Locarno Conference on Security Pact, 1925,
R. 101 disaster, 1930,
First trans-Pacific non-stop flight, 1931,
Revolution broke out in Spain, 1934,
Italian lira devaluated, 1936,
Beginning of the Battle of Moscow, 1941,
British landed in Greece, 1944.

THEY HAVE LITTLE IN COMMON, EXCEPT THAT THESE
EVENTS IN THEIR SUCCESSIVE YEARS ALL HAPPENED ON
OCTOBER THE FIFTH.

October the Sixth

If you can count up the sunny and cloudy days in a complete year,
You will find that the fine day has come more often.

He was a patriot whom fortune treated badly: he died on October the Sixth
in 1891: his name is part of Ireland's unhappy history: he was Charles
Stewart Parnell. He was a poet and a patriot and a Poet Laureate: his life
was long: his melodies sweet: his poetry an inspiration and a consolation to
the Victorians. He died on October the Sixth, 1892, and his name was
Alfred Lord Tennyson.

Dr. John Key, founder of Caius College, Cambridge, was born on
this day in 1510 . . . and these, too—
Neville Maskelyne, 1732,
Madame Campan, biographer of Marie Antoinette, 1752, Paris,
Sir Isaac Brock, 1769,
Jenny Lind in 1820,
Lord Cullen of Ashbourne, 1912.

Charles the Bald, King of France, in 877, died on this day,
William Tyndale, the protestant martyr, was burned at the stake
on this day in 1536,
Sir John Young, Baron Lisgar, Governor-General of Canada in
1868, died on October the Sixth, 1876.

WHICH OF THESE EVENTS WAS OF MOST MOMENT TO MEN?
MEETING OF 'THE ILLITERATE' PARLIAMENT (NO
HANGERS), 1404,
BRITISH TOOK MANILA IN THE PHILIPPINES, 1762,
JOHN WILKES WAS CHOSEN LORD MAYOR, 1772,
THE LORDS OF THE ADMIRALTY (OUT FOR A SAIL) COL-
LIDED WITH A LIGHTER, 1877,
THE INNER CIRCLE OPENED FOR PASSENGER TRAFFIC,
1884,
AUSTRO-GERMANS INVADED SERBIA, 1915,
CHIANG KAI-SHEK ELECTED PRESIDENT OF CHINA, 1928,
EVACUATION OF MADRID BEGAN, 1936,
R.A.F. BOMBED DOCKS AT AMSTERDAM, ROTTERDAM AND
FLUSHING, 1940,
GERMANS ATTACKED MOSCOW, 1941,
HAMBURG AND BERLIN BOMBED, 1944,
CONTROL OF ENGAGEMENTS ORDER, 1947.

October the Seventh

O day most calm, most bright,
The fruit of this, the next world's bud,
Th' endorsement of supreme delight,
Writ by a friend, and with his blood.

October the Seventh was a day of battles.
In 1571, they fought at Lepanto on this day,
In 1777, they fought at Saratoga on this day,
In 1813, Wellington entered France on this day,
In 1916, the Battle of the Somme continued its carnage on this day.
The corn is rich on the battle fields, but men are not yet at peace.
The great fire at Chicago, which lasted four days, began on this day in 1861,
The Japanese occupied the Marshall Islands on October the Seventh in 1914,
British forces were in action in Palestine, 1936,
German troops entered Rumania, 1940,
Stuttgart raided, 1943,
American pilotless plane flew from England to Newfoundland by radio
control, 14 hours 11 minutes, 1947.

Archbishop Laud, in 1573, was born on this day,
Sir Ralph Abercromby, in 1734, was born on October the Seventh,
Lord Tenterden, the eminent naval and mercantile jurist, 1762, at Canterbury, and
W. H. L. Lister, Lancashire cricket captain from 1936–40 was born 1911, on October the Seventh.

These went the way of all flesh on this day:
Margaret, Maid of Norway, 1290,
Sir Thomas Chaloner, statesman and writer, 1565,
Nicholas Heinsius, scholar and critic, 1681,
Antonio Sacchini, composer, 1786, Paris,
Dr. John Brown, 1788,
Dr. Thomas Reid, eminent Scottish metaphysician, 1796, Glasgow,
Edgar Allan Poe, 1849,
Oliver Wendell Holmes, 1894,
Marie Lloyd, 1922,
Charles Ricketts, 1931,
C. R. W. Nevinson, artist, 1946.

October the Eighth

God gave all men all earth to love,
But since our hearts are small,
Ordained for each one spot should prove,
Beloved over all.

October the Eighth, in 1831, saw the Reform Riots—they were uneasy,
restless times in England, but not less so one hundred years and ten later, for
on the same day, in 1941, the Government took over from the British
Broadcasting Corporation the publication of news for the duration of the
war. It was an essential step for public order and morale.
On October the Eighth, in 1838, Lord Rowton was born. His life's work was
the provision of homes for the homeless, and Rowton Houses to this day in
London recall his achievement.

Doctor John Hoadly, the dramatist, was born on this day in 1711,
Alison Cockburn was born in 1713, and
John Hay, American historian, was born on October the Eighth
in 1838.

There died on this day:
Mrs. Cromwell, 1672 (The wife of the Great Protector),
Sir Richard Blackmore, the poet, 1729,
Henry Fielding, novelist, 1754,
Vittorio Alfieri, the Italian dramatist, 1803,
Charles Fourier, the Socialist pioneer, 1837, Paris,
Johann H. Dannecker, German sculptor, 1841, Stuttgart,
Archbishop Whately, 1863.

THESE ARE SOME OF THE EVENTS OF THE DAY:
JUDICIAL COMBAT BETWEEN MEN AND DOG CAME BEFORE
THE COURTS IN 1361,
EDDYSTONE LIGHTHOUSE WAS COMPLETED IN 1759,
SECOND WINDOW TAX BEGAN TO OPERATE IN 1766,
WILLIAM I OF HOLLAND ABDICATED, IN 1840, ON THIS DAY,
THE COOK ISLANDS WERE ANNEXED ON THIS DAY IN 1900,
WAR DECLARED AGAINST TURKEY BY MONTENEGRO, 1912,
THE FORMATION OF THE EAGLE SQUADRON ANNOUNCED
IN 1940,
R.A.F. BOMBERS RAIDED BERLIN MILITARY OBJECTS, 1940,
DIEPPE PRISONERS MANACLED BY THE GERMANS IN 1942,
RUSSIANS CROSSED THE DNIEPER, 1943.

October the Ninth

We are such stuff as time is laid on
'Tis what we do that we are paid on . . .
'Tis what we make of hours and days
That brings us blame or earns us praise.

In 1547, on October the Ninth, light broke on the eyes of Cervantes, who was born on this day to give in due time, out of much trial and tribulation, the immortal tales of Don Quixote and Sancho Panza. The same day, in the same century, saw Henry VIII granted the title of Fidei Defensor *by Papal Bull in 1521.*

This day shows these events in the pattern of history,
Battle of Tunis, 732,
Parliament abolished bishops, 1646,
Russians took Berlin, 1760,
The Elder Pitt retired on a pension of £3,000 a year, 1761,
Congress of Aix-la-Chapelle, 1818,
Prince of Wales at Philadelphia, 1860,
Municipal Corporations Act, 1835,
William II of Germany abdicated, 1918,
Churchill and Eden were in Moscow, 1944,
A shower of meteors from comet Giacobini-Zinner entered earth's atmosphere, 1946,
Tudor IV arrived at London airport after a successful flight of 6,500 miles to South America and back, 1947.

On October the Ninth these finished their diverse labours:
Pope Clement II, 1047,
Claude Perrault, architect, 1688,
Barbara Villiers, Duchess of Cleveland, mistress of Charles II, 1709,
Dr. James Johnson, medical and miscellaneous writer, 1845.

ON THIS DAY WAS BORN:
JACOB AUGUSTUS THUANUS (DE THOU), HISTORICAL WRITER, 1553,
BISHOP GEORGE TOMLINE, THE AUTHOR OF 'REFUTATION OF CALVINISM', IN 1753,
CHARLES, COMTE D'ARTOIS, LATER CHARLES X, 1757,
EDWARD, DUKE OF KENT, GRANDSON OF KING GEORGE V, 1935.

October the Tenth

A miser he recounted out the gold,
He knew that time was wealth indeed—untold,
He made of every day he had to live—
To his last minute—a preparative.

Lord Reading was born on October the Tenth in 1870. He was many things in his crowded life—he sailed before the mast—knew something of the City of London and finance—became Rufus Isaacs, a King's Counsel, a Member of Parliament, a Member of the Crown and Viceroy of India. He made his mark on the nineteenth century and added to his fame in the twentieth.

These, too, were born on October the Tenth:
Duke of Argyll, 1680,
Cavendish, the chemist, 1731,
Benjamin West, the painter, 1738,
John Abercrombie, the physician, 1780,
Hugh Miller, the Scots geologist, who wrote *The Testimony of the Rocks*, in 1802,
Giuseppe Verdi, Italian opera composer, in 1813,
Fridjof Nansen, Norwegian explorer, in 1861,
Viscount Nuffield born, 1877.

These occurred on this day:
Boer War began 1899,
Canada announced to be training ground for Empire Air Training Scheme for British airmen, 1939,
Chiang Kai-shek reinaugurated President of China, 1943.

SIX WRITERS DIED ON THIS DAY:
ARCHBISHOP JOHN POTTER, AUTHOR OF 'GRECIAN ANTIQUITIES,' 1747, CROYDON,
DR. WILLIAM WILKIE, AUTHOR OF 'THE EPIGONIAD', 1772,
HENRY BROOKE, NOVELIST, 1783, DUBLIN,
JEREMIAH JAMES OBERLIN, 1806, STRASBURG,
VARNHAGEN VON ENSE, EMINENT GERMAN WRITER, 1858,
A COMPOSER DIED ON THIS DAY IN 1708—HE WAS DOCTOR JOHN BLOW.
AT TOURS, ON THE TENTH OCTOBER, A.D. 732, THE MOSLEM INVASION OF EUROPE WAS CHECKED BY CHARLES MARTEL ('THE HAMMER') IN ONE OF THE DECISIVE BATTLES OF THE WORLD.

October the Eleventh

He dreams—he dawdles—yes he dines,
It is day still while the sun shines.

On October the Eleventh, in 1851, the Great Exhibition closed,
Its successor was held a hundred years later,
In London, too, on this day in 1879, the then existent Waterloo Bridge was
lit by electric light,
The Transvaal war against the Boers began on this day in 1899,
This was the day of the Battle of Camperdown, in 1797,
This was the day when Lord Derby launched his recruiting plan in 1915, and
In 1399, the most Noble Order of the Bath was instituted on October the
Eleventh.

Philip Astley, in 1742, was born on this day,
Sir Bernard Partridge, in 1861, was born on this day to make
famous *Punch* cartoons,
Mrs. Eleanor Roosevelt, wife of the late President of the United
States, in 1884.

Ulrich Zwingli, the Swiss reformer, died on this day in 1531,
Sir Thomas Wyatt was executed in 1542,
Mary, Queen of Scots, was sentenced in 1586 on October the
Eleventh,
Lord Caldecott, former Lord Chancellor and Chief Justice, and
Rt. Hon. William Brace, P.C., former miners' leader, both died on
October the Eleventh in 1947.

On October the Eleventh
Partition Treaty between England, France and Holland, 1699,
Waterloo Bridge begins, 1811,
Gamelin made C.-in-C. of Allied forces, 1939.

FOR OCTOBER THE ELEVENTH THE SAINTS ARE:
TARACHUS, PROBUS AND ANDRONICUS, MARTYRS, 304,
CANICUS OR KENNY, ABBOT IN IRELAND, 599,
ETHELBURGE, ABBESS, ABOUT 664,
GUMMAR, CONFESSOR, 774.

ON OCTOBER THE ELEVENTH IN 1777 THE ARMY OF THE
AMERICAN STATES DEFEATED THE BRITISH ARMY AT
SARATOGA. IT WAS THE END OF AN EPOCH IN THE
RELATIONS OF BRITAIN AND THE AMERICAN COLONIES.

October the Twelfth

Uprouse ye, then, my merry men!
It is our opening day.

October the Twelfth, 1492, is the reported day on which Christopher Columbus landed in the American continent. He was really looking for India and he found America—a good example of planning which turned out better than the planners proposed. Mankind may draw encouragement from the event.

Two kings have this day for birth day:
Edward VI in 1537, and
Pedro I, Emperor of Brazil, in 1798.
Hugh Miller, the geologist, was born on this day in 1802, and
Dr. Ralph Vaughan Williams, 'the Grand Old Man of British Music', on the same day in 1872.

These died on this day:
Pope Honorius I in 638,
Pope Boniface VIII in 1303,
Maximilian II, Emperor of Germany, in 1576,
Mrs. Fry, the philanthropic quakeress, in 1845,
Robert Stephenson, engineer, in 1859, and
Edith Cavell—a nurse from Norwich—was shot in Germany on the morning of October the Twelfth in 1915. Her statue stands overlooking Trafalgar Square in London, flanking the church of St. Martins-in-the-Fields. Inscribed on it are words to be remembered—her words—'Patriotism is not enough',
Sir Joseph Burn, 1950.

ON OCTOBER THE TWELFTH:
RIGHTS OF MAGDALEN COLLEGE, OXFORD, RESTORED, 1688,
GENERAL ROBERTS OCCUPIED CABUL IN 1879,
THE GERMAN LINER 'CAP NORTE' WAS CAPTURED IN 1939,
ON THIS DAY, IN 1942, MR. WINSTON CHURCHILL, RECEIVING THE FREEDOM OF THE CITY OF EDINBURGH, ENDED HIS SPEECH WITH HARRY LAUDER'S 'KEEP RIGHT ON TO THE END OF THE ROAD'—AND HARRY LAUDER LED THE SINGING.
AGREEMENT REACHED BETWEEN BRITAIN AND UNITED STATES ON AID TO FIRST STAGE OF BRITAIN'S REARMAMENT PROGRAMME, 1950.

October the Thirteenth

Who counts the minutes, if a hundred ages,
In the sight of eternity, are as a moment gone?

On October the Thirteenth, 1706, the Parliament of Scotland met for the last time. It was 'the end of an auld sang' said a contemporary sadly, and some of that regret still lingers. Parliament House in Edinburgh still stands and is used in association with the Law Courts of Scotland. Some think in Scotland it shall be used again for a National Assembly of the Scots.

These died on October the Thirteenth:
Pope Gregory XII, 1417,
Pope Pius III, 1503,
Sir Isaac Brock, 1812,
Joachim Murat, King of Naples, shot, 1815,
Sir Henry Irving, the actor, 1905,
Anatole France, the French author and satirist, 1924,
Lord Passfield (Sidney Webb), 1947,
Admiral the Hon. Sir Algernon Douglas Edward Harry Boyle, one of the commanders at Zeebrugge, 1949.

On October the Thirteenth in 1797, Sir Benjamin Hammet was fined £1,000 for refusing to serve as Lord Mayor of London,
Queen Victoria visited Aberdeen to unveil statue of Prince Consort, 1863,
On this day Charles Stewart Parnell, the Irish leader, arrested, 1881,
Greenwich Time was universally adopted in 1884,
Forty Allied aeroplanes raided the Mauser works at Oberndorf and dropped four tons of bombs, 1916,
Italy—renouncing her Axis alliance—declared war on Germany in 1943,
Russian troops captured Riga, the capital of Latvia, 1944,
Muslim League accepted Viceroy's invitation to join interim government, 1946.

THESE WERE BORN ON OCTOBER THE THIRTEENTH:
SOPHIA, ELECTRESS OF HANOVER, MOTHER OF GEORGE I, 1630, MAYENCE,
MARSHAL SAXE, 1693,
FERDINAND VII, KING OF SPAIN, 1784,
MRS. LANGTRY, 'THE JERSEY LILY', 1852,
SIR GEOFFREY VICKERS, V.C., BORN IN 1894.

October the Fourteenth

Other days will come—
They will not be yours—
You dead—dead and dumb—
Will not know the hours.

This day saw other wars and battles.
On October the Fourteenth, 1939, His Majesty's ship Royal Oak *was sunk and, in 1944, this day saw the British troops enter Athens. On the same day the world learned that four thousand five hundred tons of bombs had been dropped by the R.A.F. on Duisburg in twenty-five minutes in what was called a 'saturation' raid.*
For citizens of the United States this day recalls the birth of William Penn in 1644—author of Fruits of Solitude *and from whom the State of Pennsylvania takes its name, and, less personal but not less notable, it is the anniversary of the Declaration of Rights by the U.S.A. in 1774.*

These called October the Fourteenth their birth day:
James II, 1633,
Eamon de Valera, Prime Minister of Eire, 1882,
Katherine Mansfield, a great short story writer, 1888,
Gen. Dwight D. Eisenhower, 1890.

These on this day died:
Pierre Gassendi, mathematician and philosopher, 1655, Paris,
'Orator' Henley, 1756,
Marshal Keith, killed, 1758,
Curran, the Irish patriot, 1817,
Admiral of the Fleet Sir Osmond Brock, 1947,
George Daggar, M.P., and Barbara Ayrton Gould, M.P., 1950.

AT HASTINGS ON THIS DAY THE FOURTEENTH OCTOBER IN 1066, WILLIAM THE NORMAN SLEW HAROLD, THE LAST OF THE SAXON KINGS, AND SEIZED THE THRONE OF ENGLAND. FOR THE REST—ON THIS DAY—
GRAFTON'S MINISTRY, 1768,
CLEOPATRA'S NEEDLE ABANDONED IN BAY OF BISCAY, 1877,
WOMEN GRADUATES ADMITTED FOR FIRST TIME TO DEGREES IN OXFORD UNIVERSITY, 1920,
GERMANY WITHDREW FROM DISARMAMENT CONFERENCE, 1933,
B.B.C. WAS INTERRUPTED BY A VOICE, 1941.

October the Fifteenth

Sick with sadness,
Struck with madness,
His life reached its end.
The passing hours,
Once wreathed with flowers,
Could no light of reason lend.

The flickering light of genius that was Friedrich Nietzsche burnt itself out on October the Fifteenth, 1844, but Thus Spake Zarathustra *and* Beyond Good and Evil *still live to make his name memorable among the philosophers who did not despair of the destiny of man.*
Two poets knew October the Fifteenth:
Virgil was born on this day in 70 B.C., and
Allan Ramsay, who wrote The Gentle Shepherd, *in 1686.*

Frederick William IV, King of Prussia, 1795, and
Phyllis Neilson Terry, the distinguished English actress, in 1892, were born on October the Fifteenth.

These died on October the Fifteenth:
Pope Gregory XIV, 1591,
Dr. James Anderson, author of works on political economy, etc., 1808, London,
Marie Tempest, the most charming of light comedy actresses, 1942,
Pierre Laval, French statesman, executed, 1945,
Rommel, Hitler's North African general, 1944.

THESE WERE GREAT OCCURRENCES ASSOCIATED WITH OCTOBER THE FIFTEENTH:
GREGORIAN CALENDAR INTRODUCED, 1582,
FIRST DISARMING OF THE HIGHLANDERS, 1725,
PITT RESIGNED OVER THE AMERICAN QUESTION, 1768,
FIRST MEETING OF THE METEOROLOGICAL SOCIETY, 1823,
FIRST AVIATION WEEK IN GREAT BRITAIN OPENED, 1909,
BRITAIN BEGAN REPAYMENT OF WAR DEBTS TO U.S., 1922,
CAPTAIN DREYFUS ARRESTED, 1894,
GERMAN FORCES ENTERED OSTEND, 1914,
GERMAN AIRSHIP CROSSED ATLANTIC, 1928,
COLOGNE RAIDED, 1942,
HUNGARY ASKED FOR ARMISTICE TERMS, 1944,
WILHELMSHAVEN AND HAMBURG BOMBED, 1944.

October the Sixteenth

Before their time they died,
They forfeited their hours,
They left unpluck't their flowers,
They left their tears undried.

Bishop Latimer and Bishop Ridley were burnt at the stake on October the
Sixteenth, at Oxford, in 1555,
Marie Antoinette, the Queen of France, was executed on this day in 1793,
In 1946, this day saw the hanging which followed the Nuremberg trials of
National Socialist war criminals,
Napoleon was sent to Elba on October the Sixteenth in 1815,
He did not stay long—his Waterloo awaited him.
October the Sixteenth, in 1859, saw John Brown's foray at Harper's Ferry,
an incident that played its part in causing civil war.

These figures of eighteenth and nineteenth centuries were born on
October the Sixteenth:
Dr. Albert Von Haller, distinguished physiologist, 1708,
John George Sulzer, writer on the fine arts, 1720,
Noah Webster, American lexicographer, 1758,
Austen Chamberlain, politician, 1863,
Oscar Wilde, Irish poet, playwright, 1854,
Eugene O'Neill, 1888,
These figures of eighteenth and nineteenth centuries were born on
this day.

On this day these died—
Robert Ferguson, Scottish poet, 1774,
John Hunter, the anatomist, 1793,
Joseph Strutt, the antiquary, 1802,
Henry Martyn, oriental missionary, 1812, Tokat, Asia Minor,
Thaddeus Kosciusko, Polish patriot, 1817, Soleure in Switzerland,
Sharman Crawford, Irish political character, 1861.

ON OCTOBER THE SIXTEENTH,
A LODGE OF FREEMASONS ATTACKED BY AN AMSTERDAM
MOB, LED TO THE MOVEMENT BEING BANNED IN 1735,
THE HOUSES OF PARLIAMENT WERE BURNED, 1834,
THE FIRTH OF FORTH RAID, 1939,
PRINCESS MARGARET LAUNCHED THE 'EDINBURGH CASTLE'
AT BELFAST, 1947.

October the Seventeenth

There's not much in it, friend, I see,
When all is said and done—
There's food and drink and you and me,
And bed at set of sun!

On October the Seventeenth, 1705, died Ninon de Lenclos, the memory of whose beauty still lingers in history. She was born in 1616 and she was ninety years of age when she took farewell of the world which she had decorated by her wit and her charm. She had many lovers, from the great generals to the men of literature. By modern standards she was a wicked woman, but the world has often been more interested, alas! in the wicked than in the virtuous.

These, too, died on this day,
Sir Philip Sidney, the hero of Zutphen, 1586,
Sir Edmund Godfrey, murdered, 1678,
Dr. John Ward, rhetorician, 1758,
Chopin, the musician, 1849.

And what of these occurrences:
They have place on this day . . .
Charles II sold Dunkirk, 1662,
Charter granted to Thomas Coram for the Foundling Hospital, 1739,
General Burgoyne surrendered Saratoga to the Yankee Rebels, 1777,
Agra captured, 1803,
Several lives lost when vats burst in a brewery, 1814,
Bessemer steel process patented, 1855,
Irish National League founded, 1860,
Treaty giving independence to Burma, signed at 10 Downing Street, 1947,
Le Creusot armament works bombed, 1942.

THIS IS THE BIRTH DAY OF
JOHN WILKES, IN 1727, AND
WILLIAM SCOTT, BARON STOWELL, GREAT CONSISTORIAL
LAWYER, 1745,
JEAN ANTOINE, MARQUIS DE CONDORCET, DISTINGUISHED
MATHEMATICIAN, 1743,
SAMUEL PROUT, PAINTER IN WATER-COLOURS, 1883.

October the Eighteenth

Oh, don't the days seem lank and long
When all goes right and nothing goes wrong?
And isn't your life extremely flat
With nothing whatever to grumble at?

All seemed to go wrong and nothing to go right for the three Scandinavian kings and the President of Finland when they met at Stockholm on October the Eighteenth, 1939, to discuss Russia's demands on Finland.

It is a day of varied events and much activity:
The Battle of Leipzig was fought on this day in 1813,
The last English lottery was held in 1826,
Kate Terry married Arthur Lewis in 1867, and
The United States took over Alaska on the same day and year,
The Provisional Government of Czechoslovakia was recognized by the Allies in 1918,
President Roosevelt closed United States waters to belligerent submarines in 1939,
Hanover was bombed in 1943, and
The Russians crossed the Prussian border in 1944,
The Queen opened Loch Sloy Power Station and first major project of N. of S. H. E. Board came into operation, 1950.

Prince Eugen was born on this day, in 1663, and shares his birthday with
Beau Nash, the exquisite, in 1674,
Peter Frederik Suhm, Danish archaeologist, in 1728,
Thomas Phillips, portrait painter, in 1770,
C. E. Mudie, bookseller and librarian, in 1818,
Henri Bergson, French philosopher, in 1859 and
Emanuel Shinwell in 1884.

On October the Eighteenth these famous men and women died:
John Ziska, Hussite commander, in 1424,
Sarah Jennings, Duchess of Marlborough, in 1744,
Lord Palmerston in 1865,
James Truslon Adams in 1878,
Gounod, the composer, in 1893.

ST. LUKE THE EVANGELIST, COMPANION AND BIOGRAPHER OF ST. PAUL, HAS OCTOBER THE EIGHTEENTH FOR HIS DAY.

October the Nineteenth

Love reckons hours for months, and days for years,
And every little absence is an age.

Dean Swift died on October the Nineteenth, 1745, literature, politics, the Church and love made his life full, but probably unhappy. He was not as gullible as his own immortal Gulliver and suffered for it. He is among the underrated figures in English literature; as great, certainly, as Doctor Johnson, he found no Boswell, but Gulliver's Travels *secured his immortality.*

King John of England died, 1216,
Sir Thomas Browne, whose *Religio Medici* is bought by every young doctor if he does not receive it as a gift from an encouraging relative, was born on this day in 1605, and died on the same day in Norwich, in 1682,
William Ged, the first stereotyper, died on October the Nineteenth in 1749,
Henry Kirke White, youthful poet, 1806,
In 1826 on this day, too, died Francis Joseph Talma, the French tragedian, in Paris, and
Sir Charles Wheatstone died on October the Nineteenth in 1875.

These five had the same birthday:
James Butler, Duke of Ormond, commander and statesman, 1610,
James Gronovius, scholar and author, 1645,
John Adams, distinguished American statesman, 1735,
Leigh Hunt, poet, 1784,
Harold Gimblett, the English cricketer, 1914.

THESE ARE REMEMBERED ON THIS DAY:
WILLIAM OF ORANGE, DRIVEN BACK, SET SAIL AGAIN FOR ENGLAND, 1688,
FIRST APPEARANCE OF GARRICK (GOODMAN'S FIELDS), 1741,
LEEDS CANAL OPENED, 1774,
YORKTOWN CAPTURED, 1781, IN AMERICAN WAR,
BRADSHAW'S RAILWAY TIME-TABLE FIRST PUBLISHED, 1839—A GREAT EVENT,
ITALY AND BULGARIA AT WAR, 1915,
PRESIDENT EBERT DISSOLVED GERMAN REICHSTAG, 1924,
STUTTGART BOMBED BY 1,000 PLANES, 1944.

October the Twentieth

Does time fall from Heaven,
Or is it that it grows?
An enlarging leaven
That flowers and fruits and flows?

A veritable galaxy of greatness emerges into the world on October the Twentieth.

These were born on this day:
Sir Christopher Wren, in 1632—St. Paul's is his monument,
Viscount Palmerston, Queen Victoria's 'Pam', in 1784,
Sir Colin Campbell, Lord Clyde, in 1792, the hero of the Crimea,
John Dewey, in 1859, a great American,
Jean Arthur Rimbaud, French poet, 1854,
Stanislaus Leczinski, King of Poland, 1677.

And, if a galaxy of greatness entered the world on October the Twentieth, a like loss befell it on this day.
These died . . .
James Anthony Froude, historian, 1894,
Duke of Marlborough, 1758,
Grace Darling, 1842,
Sir Richard Burton, traveller, 1890,
Sir Standen Leonard Pearce, D.SC., engineer-designer of Battersea Power Station, 1947.

AND THINGS HAPPENED . . .
THERE WERE GREAT OCCURRENCES, EVENTS, EPISODES—
JOHN WILKES WAS ELECTED MEMBER OF PARLIAMENT FOR MIDDLESEX ON OCTOBER THE TWENTIETH IN 1774,
BATTLE OF NAVARINO—BRITISH, FRENCH AND RUSSIANS BEAT TURKISH AND EGYPTIAN FLEETS, 1827,
PRINCE OF WALES EMBARKED AT PORTLAND, OREGON, FOR HOME, 1860,
ALASKA FRONTIER WITH CANADA SETTLED, 1903,
D.S.M. ESTABLISHED, 1914,
FIRST BATTLE OF YPRES, 1914,
RHINE REPUBLIC PROCLAIMED: BAVARIA DEFIED THE REICH, 1923,
AMERICANS LANDED ON PHILIPPINES, 1944,
CAPITULATION OF ULM, 1805.

October the Twenty-first

On dials and watches and on clocks,
Time taps and ticks and chimes and knocks,
It has a measured beat like rhyme,
But where is he who beat time?

October the Twenty-first is Trafalgar Day.
'Here and here did England help me, How can I help England, say'—so
wrote Robert Browning of October the Twenty-first, 1805, of that day when
Nelson declared to his men that England expects no more and no less of
Englishmen than that they do their duty. It was a moving moment in 1805
. . . it still moves in recollection millions of Englishmen everywhere.

Edmund Waller, poet, 1687, Beaconsfield, near Windsor,
Charles E. Horn, musical composer, 1849, Boston, U.S.,
Sir Dudley Pound, a great English Admiral, died on this, Nelson's
Day, in 1943.

George Coleman, the younger, was born on October the Twenty-
first in 1762,
Samuel Taylor Coleridge, who wrote *The Ancient Mariner* was
born on this day in 1772,
Alfred Nobel, the founder of the Nobel Peace Award, was born on
October the Twenty-first in 1833, and
Major-General Sir Ernest Swinton, great soldier and writer of
military text-books, 1868.

ON THIS DAY—LIGHT CAME MORE ABUNDANTLY TO THE
WORLD ON OCTOBER THE TWENTY-FIRST WHEN—
URBAN VI WAS ELECTED AT AVIGNON IN 1378,
THE FOUNDATION STONE LAID OF OLD NORTH BRIDGE,
EDINBURGH, IN 1763,
TELEGRAPHIC COMMUNICATION BETWEEN LONDON AND
ADELAIDE BEGAN IN 1872,
EDISON INVENTED INCANDESCENT LAMP IN 1879,
THE DOGGER BANK INCIDENT OCCURRED, 1904,
THE 'DISCOVERY II' LEFT ENGLAND ON AN ANTARCTIC
EXPEDITION, 1933,
THE FIRST REGISTRATION FOR NATIONAL SERVICE (ARMED
FORCES ACT) TOOK PLACE, 1939,
FOUR GERMAN PLANES WERE SHOT DOWN DURING AN
UNSUCCESSFUL ATTACK ON A NORTH SEA CONVOY, 1939.

October the Twenty-second

The days of our age are three score years and ten;
And though men be so strong
That they come to four score years;
Yet is their strength then
But labour and sorrow;
So soon passeth it away, and we are gone.

These died on this day:
Sir Cloudesley Shovell, British admiral, 1707,
William Wollaston, 1724,
Dr. Arnold, the composer, 1802,
Thomas Sheraton (cabinet maker), 1806,
Lord Holland, statesman and man of letters, 1840,
Louis Spohr, celebrated composer, 1859,
Captain Mayne Reid, novelist, 1883,
William E. H. Lecky, the historian, 1903.

This day is remembered for these events:
Revocation of the Edict of Nantes, 1685,
First parachute descent from balloon, 1797,
Genoa bombed, 1942,
Kassel heavily bombed, 1943,
One thousand one hundred bombers attacked Hamm, Munster, Brunswick and Hanover, 1944,
King George VI unveiled statue to King George V, outside Westminster Abbey, 1947,
Moslems rebelled in Kashmir against Hindu Maharaja in favour of Pakistan, 1947.

Three men of mark were born on October the Twenty-second— famous in their day and generation:
John Reinhold Forster, traveller and naturalist, 1729, Dirschau, West Prussia,
Dr. Alexander Murray, distinguished Orientalist, 1775, Dunkitterick, Kirkcudbright,
Franz Liszt, Hungarian pianist and composer, 1811.

THE SAINTS OF OCTOBER THE TWENTY-SECOND INCLUDE:
ST. MARK OF THE SECOND CENTURY,
ST. PHILIP OF THE FOURTH CENTURY,
ST. DONATUS OF THE NINTH CENTURY.

October the Twenty-third

Every man hath his ill day.

The scholars say that the world began on Sunday, October the Twenty-third, 404 B.C. . . . At least some scholars so asserted.
There are here events associated with this day:
Lord Derby died in 1869,
Picasso was born on this day in 1881,
Cézanne died on this day in 1906, and
W. G. Grace—Doctor Grace—England's famous cricketer, died, too, on October the Twenty-third in 1915.
October the Twenty-third, 1942, marks the opening of the Allied offensive in Egypt.

Events which occurred on this day include:
University of Heidelberg chartered, 1385,
Outbreak of Irish rebellion, 1642,
First Parliament of Great Britain, 1707,
'John Doe' and 'Richard Roe' officially abolished in Great Britain, 1852,
Decided in Glasgow law courts that a student may publish his lecture notes, 1885,
Bonar Law Ministry, 1922,
Congress of India decided not to aid Britain in the war, 1939,
. . . these, in historical sequence, are joined together in that they shared the same day, if not the same deed.

Born on this day were:
Francis Jeffrey, who founded the *Edinburgh Review* and died Lord Jeffrey, in 1773,
George Saintsbury, in 1845, who wrote much good literary criticism but most acceptably *Notes on a Cellar Book.*

SARAH BERNHARDT—SHE WAS BORN ON OCTOBER THE TWENTY-THIRD, 1845. IT IS SAID SHE WAS NEVER OLD. IT IS SAID SHE NEVER DIED. CERTAINLY SARAH BERNHARDT HAS IN THE WORLD OF THE STAGE A SURE IMMORTALITY.
LOUIS RIEL, BORN ON THIS DAY IN 1844—WAS FATED TO LEAD A REBELLION IN CANADA AND WAS HANGED AT REGINA AS A CONSEQUENCE. TO MANY OF THE CANADIANS OF HIS DAY, HE WAS A HERO AND A MARTYR.

October the Twenty-fourth

The fairest day must set in night;
Summer in winter ends;
So anguish still succeeds delight,
And grief our joy attends.

Sir Moses Haim Montefiore was born on October the Twenty-fourth, 1784. He married a Rothschild and secured a fortune by the time he was forty. He was a pioneer of Zionism and in 1838 had plans for the colonization of Syria. He died in 1885 at Ramsgate where he had built, on his estate, a college with ten rabbis in residence, a synagogue and a tomb for his wife and himself.
On October the Twenty-fourth, in 1896, another Jewish philanthropist, Sir Albert Abdullah David Sassoon, died at Brighton:
Sir Moses Montefiore was born at Leghorn,
Sir Albert Sassoon was born at Baghdad,
Both made Britain their home.

Dr. James Beattie, poet, was born 1735,
Sir James Macintosh was born on this day in 1765,
George Stanley Faber, theological writer, in 1773, and
Sir Horace Plunkett, 1854.

Tycho Brahe, the great Danish astronomer, died on October the Twenty-fourth, 1601, after many vicissitudes and much travelling. It has been said of him, however, 'His eyes were ever on the stars'. The Irish politician, Daniel Webster, died on this day in 1852, Miss Susan Lawrence, one of the first Socialist Ministers in Britain, died on this day in 1947.

HERE TOO ARE OTHER HAPPENINGS ON THIS DAY.
BENEFIT OF CLERGY TAKEN FROM MURDERERS, 1513,
TERM 'KING OF GREAT BRITAIN' FIRST ADOPTED, 1604,
PRESBYTER OF EDINBURGH CITED SCOTCH BISHOP, 1638,
TREATY OF WESTPHALIA, 1648,
FIRST MEETING OF BRITISH ASTRONOMICAL SOCIETY, 1890,
GERMAN HIGH SEAS FLEET PUT TO SEA FOR THE FIFTH AND LAST TIME, 1915,
ZINOVIEV LETTER PUBLISHED, 1924,
SOUTH AFRICAN FLAG AGREED TO, 1927,
MILAN RAIDED BOTH BY DAY AND NIGHT, 1942.

October the Twenty-fifth

It was there this morning,
And now alack! it's gone,
I need no gypsy's warning,
Time—it marches on!

October the Twenty-fifth is a day of battles:
In 1415 on this day the English fought the French at Agincourt: and on this
day in 1854, the English and French fought, as Allies, the Russians at
Balaclava in the Crimea:
October the Twenty-fifth is a day on which poets are remembered.
Chaucer died on this day in 1400,
Thomas Babington Macaulay was born on this day in 1800, and
Robert Bridges, who became Poet Laureate, was born in 1844 on October
the Twenty-fifth.
Trotsky, who with Lenin made the Bolshevist revolution, was born on
October the Twenty-fifth in 1877, and
Rear-Admiral Richard Byrd, the famous Antarctic explorer, was born in
1888.

Two English kings died on this day:
Stephen in 1154 and George II in 1760, and
One emperor abdicated, Charles as Emperor of Germany, 1555.

William Hogarth, the painter, died in 1764 on October the
Twenty-fifth,
Lieut.-Gen. Sir Harold Fawcus, K.C.B., C.M.G., D.S.O., 1947, and
Victor Alexander Bulwer-Lytton, K.C., P.C., G.C.S.I., second Earl
and former Governor and League of Nations leader, 1947.

THIS DAY MARKED:
BISHOPS RESTORED, 1660,
FIJI ISLANDS ANNEXED, 1874, AND
IN 1911 THE LAST HORSE-DRAWN BUS WAS SEEN IN LONDON
ON THE LONDON BRIDGE—MOORGATE STREET ROUTE.
IN 1921 THE HOUSE OF LORDS DELIVERED JUDGEMENT
THAT LOSER OF A BET ON A HORSE RACE WHO PAID BY
CHEQUE COULD RECOVER HIS LOSSES AT LAW UNDER THE
GAMING ACT OF 1835,
FIVE-DAY WEEK BEGAN IN FORD PLANTS, 1926,
MR. WALTER ELLIOT ELECTED RECTOR OF GLASGOW
UNIVERSITY, 1947.

October the Twenty-sixth

Dear friend, had I the power,
Time would stand still:
I'd halt this very hour,
Had I my will!

Some die for their country—some live for it—and some write its songs.
Caroline Oliphant, who became Lady Nairne, was in the latter category.
Few have done more to endear the Scots and the Scots tongue than she.
'The Laird o' Cockpen', 'Charlie is my Darling' and the plaintive,
touching song 'The Land of the Leal', are her legacy. She died in 1845.
Some die for their country and some would say that Georges Jacques
Danton, who was born on this day in 1759, died for France. His was a bold
spirit—to him the world owes the words 'Toujours de l'audace'.

There were born, too, on this day:
Henry Cockburn in 1779,
Viscount Sankey of Sankey Report fame in 1866,
The Shah of Iran (Persia) in 1919.

Sir Godfrey Kneller died on this day—the pupil of Rembrandt
and the portrayer of Kings—in 1723,
Dr. Philip Doddridge, eminent divine and author, 1751.

FROM 1277 TO 1947, THINGS HAPPENED ON OCTOBER THE
TWENTY-SIXTH. HERE ARE SOME OF THEM:
FOUNDING OF MERTON COLLEGE, 1277,
ROYAL MARINES FORMED, 1664,
SOCIETY OF ANTIQUARIANS INAUGURATED AT LONDON,
1751,
FIRST APPEARANCE IN ENGLAND OF ASIATIC CHOLERA,
1831,
PROFESSOR SIMPSON PRESENTED WITH FREEDOM OF CITY
OF EDINBURGH, 1869,
ITALY INFORMED THE POWERS THAT SHE HAD ANNEXED
TRIPOLI, 1911,
PRINCE OF WALES SAILED IN 'RENOWN' FOR INDIA, 1922,
KHARKOV CAPTURED BY THE GERMANS, 1941,
JAP NAVAL DEFEAT OFF PHILIPPINES, 1944,
WITHDRAWAL OF BRITISH ARMY FROM IRAQ COMPLETED,
1947.

October the Twenty-seventh

O day of wrath.

An English sea captain who added much to the British Empire in the eighteenth century was born on this day in 1728. He became Captain Cook—discovered the Sandwich Islands and other parts in the Antipodes and was murdered there in 1779.
On October the Twenty-seventh, in the year 42 B.C., Marcus Brutus came to Philippi to die after his part as conspirator in the murder of Julius Caesar.

On October the Twenty-seventh in the year 901 Alfred the Great died. He not only united his people but instructed them, translating for them Augustine and Bede.

James Macpherson, whom Doctor Johnson thought was a scoundrel but who wrote *Ossian*, one of Napoleon's favourite books, was born on October the Twenty-seventh in 1796 in Inverness. He made a fortune and helped, inadvertently, to create the Romantic Revival in European literature.
Dr. Andrew Combe, the eminent physiologist who wrote *The Constitution of Man*, was born on this day in 1797, at Edinburgh, Theodore Roosevelt, President of the United States, was born on this day in 1858, and
Lieut.-Gen. Sir Oliver Leese in 1894.

John Thomson, the landscape painter, died on October the Twenty-seventh, 1840.
Lascelles Abercrombie, the poet, died on this day in 1938.

EVENTS WHICH MARK OCTOBER THE TWENTY-SEVENTH INCLUDE:
NAPOLEON ENTERED BERLIN, 1806,
CONSCRIPTION PROPOSED IN CONGRESS BY MONROE, 1814,
NEW YORK'S FIRST SUBWAY WAS OPENED, 1904,
NORWAY RECOGNIZED AS INDEPENDENT OF SWEDEN, 1905,
AUSTRIA SUED FOR PEACE, 1918,
FASCIST COUP IN ITALY, 1922,
GREECE REJECTED ITALIAN ULTIMATUM, 1940,
HITLER AND MUSSOLINI MET IN FLORENCE, 1940,
SKODA WORKS IN CZECHOSLOVAKIA BOMBED, 1940,
SHELL STORE EXPLOSION NEAR BURTON ON TRENT, 1944.

October the Twenty-eighth

You turn these pages, read this book,
Is that for you enough?
You are not here to long and look,
Life you will find is rough—
Take up your task: take up your toil—
Make this day a battle royal.

October the Twenty-eighth is Saint Jude's day—a carpenter and a blessed martyr, shot to death by arrows. It is, too, the feast day of St. Simon, who was a fishmonger. These two disciples of Christ are joined together in this day of our Lord.

Erasmus was born on this day in 1467,
Dr. Nicholas Brady in 1659,
Sir David Dalrymple in 1726,
Puccini, the Italian composer, was born on this day in 1858,
Admiral Lord Mountevans, 1881.

John Locke—the most English of philosophers—whose principal work was his *Essay on Human Understanding*—died on October the Twenty-eighth in 1704,
Prince George of Denmark, Queen Anne's husband, 1708,
Grant Allen, who wrote on science and wrote light magazine fiction with equal skill, died on October the Twenty-eighth in 1899, and Meredith Farrar Titterington, Labour M.P. for South Bradford, 1949.

EVENTS STARRY AND WONDERFUL ARE REPORTED AS
HAVING OCCURRED ON THIS DAY:
ACCESSION OF HENRY III, 1216,
HARVARD UNIVERSITY, 1636,
TREATY CONCLUDED BETWEEN GREAT BRITAIN AND
PERSIA, 1841,
NEW ROYAL EXCHANGE OPENED, 1844,
BROWNING SOCIETY FORMED BY DR. FURNIVALL, 1881,
ELECTRICALLY CONTROLLED M.T.B. HIT MONITOR, H.M.S.
'EREBUS', 1917,
FIRST WAR CABINET ENDED, 1919,
COLLAPSE OF NEW YORK STOCK EXCHANGE, 1928,
ITALY AND GREECE AT WAR, 1940,
BULGARIA SIGNED ARMISTICE WITH ALLIES, 1944.

October the Twenty-ninth

Love reckons hours for months, and days for years;
And every little absence is an age.

It was on October the Twenty-ninth, or a date very near—there is a dispute on the matter—that John Keats was born in 1795, the son of a livery stable proprietor. He wrote, in one magic year—1820—the 'Odes' to a nightingale, to a Grecian urn, and to melancholy, and much beside. He died in Italy. 'Here lies one whose name is writ in water.' It was written none the less immortally.

James Boswell, who discovered one of the great stars in literature —who might have been called the Great Bear—was born on this day in 1740, and
William Hayley, poet and biographer of Cowper, 1745.

Sir Walter Raleigh was beheaded on this day in 1618—the greatest of the Elizabethans to die at the hand of the first of the Stuarts. He was a man of great quality; soldier, courtier, explorer, scientist, philosopher and historian—he deserved a better fate than befell him.

There died on October the Twenty-ninth:
James Shirley, dramatist, 1666, London,
Edmund Calamy, eminent Puritan divine, 1666, London,
Admiral Edward Vernon, 1759,
Jean D'Alembert, encyclopaedist, 1783,
John Leech, humorous artist, 1864.

THESE OCCURRENCES ARE RECORDED ON THIS DATE:
FIRST BARRIER TREATY BETWEEN GREAT BRITAIN AND HOLLAND, 1709,
FIRST PERFORMANCE OF 'DON GIOVANNI', 1787,
ALDERMAN SOLOMONS ELECTED LORD MAYOR OF LONDON, 1856,
CONSERVATIVE BANQUET GIVEN TO MR. DISRAELI IN THE CORN EXCHANGE, EDINBURGH, 1867,
OPENING OF NEW ROYAL INFIRMARY, EDINBURGH, 1879,
TREATY OF CONSTANTINOPLE—INTERNATIONAL AND NEUTRAL SUEZ CANAL ZONE, 1889,
BRITISH 'JOURNAL OF ASTROLOGY' CEASED, 1939,
BRITISH LANDED IN GREECE, 1940,
BREDA, HOLLAND, CAPTURED, 1944.

October the Thirtieth

Tomorrow we will believe, today not at all.

Mikhailovich Dostoevski wrote Crime and Punishment *and* The Brothers of Karamazov. *He was born on this day in 1821 and received and gave impulse from and to the Russian Revolution. He had the ill health that almost invariably accompanies genius—was transported for his political opinions and missed death by a miracle. His work and life show a passionate sympathy with the weak, foolish, sick, ineffectual and incompetent. Only the infinite pity, he seems to suggest, is equal to the infinite pathos of human existence.*

Among the great, these were born on October the Thirtieth:
Cardinal Caesar Baronius, historical writer, 1538,
George II, King of Great Britain and Ireland, in 1683,
John Adams, second President of the United States, in 1735,
R. Brinsley Sheridan, the dramatist, 1751, and
John Perry, editor of the *Morning Chronicle*, 1756.

These died on this day:
James Sturmius, Protestant champion, 1553,
The Rev. John Whitaker, historical writer, 1808,
Allan Cunningham, the writer of many songs including 'A Wet Sheet and a Flowing Sea', 1842,
Thomas Cochrane, Earl of Dundonald, in 1860, an Admiral of the Fleet,
John Chubb, inventor of the safe, 1872,
Bonar Law, a Scots-Canadian Prime Minister, 1923.

In Scotland on this day, Princess Elizabeth launched the *Caronia* at Clydebank, 1947,
Consecration of St. Mary's, Edinburgh, 1879, and
Freedom of Edinburgh conferred on Benjamin Disraeli, 1867.

AND THERE WERE OTHER DOINGS . . .
HENRY VII FORMED YEOMEN OF THE GUARD, 1485,
NEW GUINEA BECAME A COLONY, 1888,
FISHER SUCCEEDED BATTENBERG, 1914,
ARMISTICE WITH TURKEY SIGNED, 1918,
KING OF ITALY ASKED MUSSOLINI TO FORM CABINET, 1922,
MIXED CLAIMS COMMISSION IN N.Y., 1938,
COLOGNE AND BERLIN BOMBED, 1944.

[317]

October the Thirty-first

Flow'rs and food and larks and linnets—
A tree—a hill—a lovely bay—
O Lord, let me fill my minutes,
Give me, I pray, one perfect day!

Among the bravest recorded words in history, surely these have a high place:
'Here I take my stand:
I can do no other
So help me God,
Amen.'
Martin Luther wrote these words on October the Thirty-first, 1517, nailed
them to the door of the church at Wittenberg where he was a professor. He
was excommunicated—his writings were publicly burned—but he wrote
defiant hymns. His most famous is 'A mighty fortress is our God'—'Ein' feste
Burg ist unser Gott'—which Germans admire even more than the English.

Hallowmass—or Hallowe'en—is October the Thirty-first.

October the Thirty-first saw the end of what is called the Battle of
Britain, in 1940. It was a stage—but there was a long road to
travel before Winston Churchill could write 'The Beginning of the
End'.
In the First World War, this day saw the British Army get steel
helmets in 1915—they called them 'Tin Hats', and in 1918
Hungary—disjoined from Austria—became a republic.

These, too, are recorded on this day:
Five Mile Act, 1665,
First stone of first Blackfriars Bridge laid, 1760,
On the Kentish coast the tide rose three times in two hours, 1827.

John Bradshaw, presiding judge at the trial of Charles I, died in
1659,
Jean Pierre Brissot, distinguished Girondist, was guillotined in
1793,
Mrs. Black, Byron's 'Maid of Athens', died, aged 76, in 1875,
Max Reinhardt, the theatrical and film producer, died in 1943.

THE BIRTHS RECORDED INCLUDE:
JOHN EVELYN, AUTHOR, 1620,
JAN VAN VERMEER, DUTCH ARTIST, 1632,
CHRISTOPHER ANSTEY, AUTHOR OF 'THE NEW BATH
GUIDE', 1724.

NOVEMBER

THIRTY DAYS

November the First

I have considered the days of old: and the years that are past . . .

The old Bank of Scotland began business in 1695, on this day,
William of Orange set sail the second time in a 'Protestant Wind' in 1688,
Of great moment, perhaps, but who can assess such things—
On this day there was in 1755 the great earthquake at Lisbon,
In 1763, for public safety, a horse patrol was established round the Metropolis,
War against Russia was declared in 1856,
The Honourable East India Company came to its end—not without glory—on November the First, 1858, and
The Irish Viceroy was proclaimed on this day.
The purchase of commissions in the British Army was discontinued in 1871,
And—a melancholy but proud remembrance—it was on November the First, 1914, that the Battle of Coronel and Falkland Islands was fought to the death and deathless glory.
Greeks repel Italian attacks, 1940,
Russians cut retreat of Germans from the Crimea, 1943,
H.M.S. Amethyst arrived in Plymouth, 1949.

On November the First, Charles the Second of Spain died in 1700,
Dr. John Radcliffe, the good physician in the days of William the Third and Queen Anne, died in 1714 at Carshalton, leaving behind him gifts to medical science as well as a reputation as a Member of Parliament,
Alexander Cruden—of *Concordance* fame—died in 1770,
Edward Shuter, the comedian, died on this day in 1776,
Lord George Gordon—whom Dickens remembered in *Barnaby Rudge*—died in 1793, and
Alfred Mynn in 1861.

THE BOOKS OF BIOGRAPHY RECORD AS HAVING BEEN BORN ON THIS DAY:
IN 1597, DENZIL HOLLIS, A REFORMING PATRIOT,
IN 1609, SIR MATTHEW HALE, THE EMINENT JUDGE,
IN 1730, THE EXPOSITOR OF THE BIBLE, BISHOP HORNE.
DR. ALEXANDER ALEKHINE, CHESS CHAMPION OF THE WORLD, MOSCOW, 1892,
LORD BALFOUR OF INCHYRE, 1897,
NOVEMBER THE FIRST IS ALL SAINTS' DAY.

November the Second

He sighed, Ah, me! Alas! Alack!
Time sweeps me forward in his track.

There was born on this day,
Marie Antoinette, in 1755, Queen of France, consort of Louis XVI. She
had beauty and charm, knew imprisonment, and died by the guillotine on
October the Sixteenth in 1793.
November the Second was the birthday of:
Dr. William Vincent, a scholar and miscellaneous writer, in 1739,
Father Radetzky, as he was called by the Austrian Army, in 1766,
Edward, Duke of Kent, the father of Queen Victoria, in 1767,
The Hon. Rupert Beckett, 1870,
Victor Trumper, 1877.

On this day there died,
Dr. Richard Hooker, the scholarly defender of the Church of
England, in 1600,
Richard Bancroft, Archbishop of Canterbury, in 1610, at Lambeth,
Sophie Dorothea, consort of George I of England, 1726,
Alexander Menzikoff, Russian statesman and general, 1729,
Princess Amelia, daughter of George III, 1810,
Sir Alexander Brunes, the British diplomatist who was murdered
at Cabul in 1841,
Jenny Lind in 1887,
Bernard Shaw, 1950 (aged 94).

WITH THESE EVENTS AND OCCURRENCES THIS DAY IS
ASSOCIATED,
COMMONS PASSED BILL EXCLUDING DUKE OF YORK, 1680,
BILL OF RIGHTS PASSED, 1689,
SOCIETY OF ANTIQUARIAN'S CHARTER GRANTED, 1751,
OPENING OF FIRST SESSION OF NEW SUPREME COURT OF
JUDICATURE AND HIGH COURT OF JUSTICE, 1875,
HAILÉ SELASSIÉ WAS CROWNED KING OF ETHIOPIA, 1930,
BUTTER RATIONING ANNOUNCED, 1939,
A LARGE-SCALE TANK BATTLE IN PROGRESS IN EGYPT,
1942,
BELGIUM FINALLY CLEARED OF GERMANS, 1944,
AMERICANS LANDED ON BOUGAINVILLE, 1945.

THESE THINGS ARE ALL RECORDED ON THIS DAY.

November the Third

Yesterday I was—and will be
'I have everything', said Trilby.

On November the Third, the name of Karl Baedeker should be remembered. It is the birthday of this German printer who was born on this day in 1801. He wanted all the world to be an open book—he published *Baedeker* with good intentions but these were turned to an evil purpose when what were called Baedeker Raids—raids on famous towns—became a feature of German National Socialist bombing in the Second World War.
Fortunately Karl Baedeker died in 1859.
The earliest of the great American poets, William Cullen Bryant, was born on November the Third, 1794, famous as the author of *Thanatopsis*.

The first Act of Supremacy was passed on this day in 1534,
Drake returned on this day in 1580,
The Long Parliament met on this day in 1640,
First attempt to launch *Leviathan* (*Great Eastern*) failed in 1857,
Yarmouth was bombarded in 1914,
Mr. Roosevelt was re-elected President, 1936.

Died on this day, these famous men,
Pope Leo the Great in 461,
James II, King of Aragon, 1327, at Barcelona,
Thomas de Montacute, Earl of Salisbury, killed in France in 1428,
Bishop Robert Lowth, biblical writer, 1787, Fulham,
John Gilbert Winant, a former United States Ambassador to Britain, 1947.

THESE WERE BORN ON THIS DAY:
LUCAN, WHO WROTE THE EPIC ON THE CONFLICT OF POMPEY AND CAESAR AND WHO DIED BY HIS OWN HAND, A.D. 39,
BENVENUTO CELLINI, ARTIST CRAFTSMAN OF FLORENCE, WRITER OF ONE OF THE MOST ENTERTAINING AUTOBIOGRAPHIES IN LITERATURE, 1500,
IAN MACLAREN IN 1850—WHO BECAME A MINISTER OF THE CHURCH OF SCOTLAND AND WROTE BOOKS OF THE 'KAILYAIRD' SCHOOL.
THE EARL OF MEATH IN 1910.

November the Fourth

O was it tragedy or jest
These hours, the loveliest and best?
'O you must say who made the rhyme'
'I give you all'—said Father Time.

Francis Auguste Rodin, the greatest of French sculptors, was born on this day in 1840. His work is preserved privately and in public galleries all over the world. 'Marble moved', it has been said, 'under his chisel.'

This day, too, was the birth day of
William of Orange, who became William III, in 1650,
Augustus Toplady, Calvinist divine, author of 'Rock of Ages cleft for me' and other noted hymns, 1740,
James Montgomery in 1771,
Sir F. R. Benson, the English Shakespearian actor, in 1858,
Eden Phillpotts, Poet Laureate, 1862.

Admiral Benbow, on this day, in 1702,
Charles Churchill died on this day in 1765,
Josiah Tucker, D.D., Dean of Gloucester, political economist, in 1799,
Mendelssohn on this day in 1847, and
Paul Delaroche, celebrated painter, at Paris in 1856,
The Hon. Sir Arthur Stanley, formerly head of the British Red Cross Society, 1947,
These died on November the Fourth.

ON THIS DAY:
SCOTCH COMPANY EFFECT A LANDING ON DARIEN IN 1689,
BEGINNING THE NATIONAL DEBT IN 1690,
NELSON COLUMN, TRAFALGAR SQUARE, COMPLETED IN 1843,
ABRAHAM LINCOLN WAS ELECTED PRESIDENT A SECOND TIME IN 1864,
FIRST TURBINE SHIP LAUNCHED IN 1894,
AUSTRIA SIGNED ARMISTICE, 1918,
STANLEY BALDWIN'S SECOND MINISTRY, 1924,
U.S. NEUTRALITY ACT PASSED IN 1939,
EL ALAMEIN, 1942,
ISERNIA CAPTURED BY THE EIGHTH ARMY, 1943,
COUNCIL OF FOREIGN MINISTERS MET IN NEW YORK, 1946.

November the Fifth

Across the world the wind it blows,
Below the bridge the water flows,
And man he thinks, and thinks he knows,
But man he merely comes and goes.

The Fifth of November is Guy Fawkes Day in England—because on that day in 1605, Guy Fawkes, an English Catholic who had soldiered in the Low Countries, under the direction of Robert Catesby and other plotters, planned to destroy King James and both Houses of Parliament. Informers told the King—arrests were made—the plot was scotched—Guy Fawkes was tried for treason and was executed on January the Thirty-first, 1606.

Less well remembered are the saints of the day:
Saints Vitalis and Agricola, martyrs, about 304,
St. Joannicius, abbot, 845,
St. Clarus, martyr, 894, and
St. Brinstan, Bishop of Winchester, 934,
These enjoy no such ardent followers as Guy Fawkes on November the Fifth, but they too have a place in history.

James Clark Maxwell—great man of science—died on this day in 1879,
Maria Angelica Kaufmann, a portrait painter, unique in her range, died on November the Fifth in 1807, at Rome.

On this day:
William of Orange landed, in 1688, in England,
Society of Antiquaries (formed 1572) was reconstituted in 1707,
The abandonment of royal title to France was announced in 1800,
Battle of Inkerman, in the Crimean War, was fought in 1854,
Britain and Turkey at war in 1914, the prelude to Gallipoli,
Poland declared an independent state by Germany and Austria, 1916,
Ex-Kaiser married at Doorn to Princess Hermine of Reuss in 1922,
The *Jervis Bay* fought it out—hopelessly but most gloriously—in 1940.

HANS SACHS, THE GERMAN POET, IN 1494, AT NUREMBERG, AND DR. JOHN BROWN, AN INTERESTING MISCELLANEOUS WRITER, IN 1715, AT ROTHBURY, NORTHUMBERLAND, AND SIR PERCY LORAINE IN 1880, WERE BORN ON NOVEMBER THE FIFTH.

November the Sixth

Time like an ever rolling stream
Invades your life today.
What will you do—despair—or dream?
For you it's judgement day.

Beat the drum, sound the trumpet for November the Sixth, 1854. It was the day on which John Philip Sousa was born. In that day U.S.A. had not yet learned to beat the big drum, perhaps Sousa, in a world deafened with jazz, has not got the place, as a pioneer, he deserves, not only of music but all things American. Anyway those who heard and saw him conduct Stars and Stripes Forever *will always cherish a great memory of the world's greatest band conductor.*

These were born on November the Sixth:
Julian, Roman emperor, 331, Constantinople,
James Gregory, inventor of the reflecting telescope, 1638, Aberdeen,
Colley Cibber, dramatist, 1671, London.
Richard Jeffries, 1848.

These died on November the Sixth,
Sir John Falstaff, 1400,
Pope Innocent VII, 1406,
Prince James, died on this day in 1612, the first recorded case of typhoid fever in English history,
Gustavus Adolphus, 1632,
William Hore, the antiquarian and politician, 1842.

Other events which are recalled on November the Sixth include—
'Égalité' Orleans executed, 1793,
Abraham Lincoln elected President of the United States of America, 1860,
Bishop Colenso awarded judgement against Mr. Gladstone and others, 1866,
A new Blackfriars Bridge opened, 1869,
Suez Canal shares purchased 1875, at instigation of Mr. Disraeli,
Italy joins Anti-Comintern Pact, 1937.

THESE SAINTS OF LONG CENTURIES AGO LOOK DOWN ON
NOVEMBER THE SIXTH AS THEIR DAY.
ST. LEONARD A HERMIT AND CONFESSOR, SIXTH CENTURY,
ST. ILTUTUS, AN ABBOT, AND
ST. WINOC, AN ABBOT OF EIGHTH CENTURY.

November the Seventh

Time there was, and—when I'm gone—
Without pause—time marches on—

Poland has given much to the world—much in martyrdom—much, too, in healing and science. On November the Seventh no name in the calendar is more deserving of recollection than that of the Polish scientist Marie Sklodowska Curie who was born on this day in 1867. Madame Curie, with her husband, Pierre Curie, discovered radium and was awarded a Nobel Prize. Her life story has been beautifully and movingly told by her daughter in a faithful biography.

These entered the world on November the Seventh:
William Stukeley, the antiquarian, 1687, Holbeach, Lincolnshire,
Leopold Frederick, Count Stolberg, miscellaneous writer, 1750, Bramstedt, Holstein,
James Abercrombie, the politician, 1776.

These left the world on November the Seventh,
Caius Cilnius Maecenas in 8 B.C.,
Gaspar Tagliacozzi, the surgeon, 1599,
Sir Martin Frobisher, 1594,
John Kyrle, 'The Man of Ross', 1724,
Jean André Deluc, geologist and natural philosopher, 1817,
Sir George Augustus Stutton, Bt., of Britain, prominent figure in newspaper world, 1947.

The first gazette was published in England in 1665 on this day at Oxford.

OTHER EVENTS ASSOCIATED WITH NOVEMBER THE
SEVENTH INCLUDE:
COVENT GARDEN THEATRE BUILT, 1732,
LAST EXECUTION AT TYBURN, 1783,
DECISION IN THE CELEBRATED CASE OF MRS. MANNING, 1849,
BATTLE OF GAZA, 1917,
GERMAN ATTACHÉ MURDERED IN PARIS, 1938,
A CODE OF SOMEWHAT VAGUE WAR AIMS OF BRITAIN WAS
PRODUCED ON THIS DAY BY LORD HALIFAX IN 1939,
SOMEBODY BOMBED THE VATICAN, 1943,
GEORGE VI NAMED A NEW RESERVOIR AT STAINES AND
STARTED THE FLOW OF WATER, 1947.

November the Eighth

My heart is teased with time—
Its measured pulsing rhyme—
Its relentless motion,
Comes it from some ocean
Unplumbed, brimmed with power
To drown my little hour?

Hail on November the Eighth, Edmund Halley, who was born on this day in 1656. He was a searcher of the heavens and identified the returning comet which bears his name. He was among the greatest of English astronomers and a friend of the great Isaac Newton whose scientific work was made public by his generosity. Of him it has been truly said he sought and found the wider horizons for men.
Sir Arnold Bax, born 1883.

Events which men note on this day include,
Oxford's world-famous Bodleian Library opened, 1602,
Admiralty put into commission, 1710,
Slidell and Mason, Confederate Commissioners, were taken off the British steamer *Trent* in the Civil War in 1861,
The Canadian Pacific Railway marks this day in 1895,
P. and O. liner *Arabia* sunk, 1916,
Hitler's *coup d'état* failed, 1923,
The Allies landed in North Africa, 1942,
Bomb explosion in Munich Beer Hall—after Hitler left—1939,
H.M. King George VI visited United States warship *Columbus* at Portsmouth and inspected crew and their quarters, 1949,
Pandit Nehru arrived in London on an official visit, 1949,
United States protested in Security Council against invasion of Chinese Communists in Korea, 1950, on this day.

Pope Boniface II in 532 died on November the Eighth,
Duns Scotus in 1308 died on this day,
Cardinal Ximenes, governor of Spain during minority of Charles V, in 1517 died on this day,
Thomas Bewick, the engineer, in 1828.

JOHN MILTON, THE ENGLISH PURITAN POET WHO BECAME A POLITICIAN—WHO WROTE 'AREOPAGITICA'—MARRIED THREE TIMES—DIED BLIND ON THIS DAY IN 1674.

November the Ninth

Yesterday returneth not
Perchance tomorrow cometh not
Thine is today,
Misuse it not.

November the Ninth was the birthday of Edward the Seventh in 1841,
The day in which Neville Chamberlain, Prime Minister of Britain, died
in 1940—and the day on which Kaiser Wilhelm abdicated in 1918.
Ivan Turgenev was born on November the Ninth in 1818. He greatly
influenced Russian literature and is a symbol of the impact of western ideas
on the mentality of the Slav. His great work is Fathers and Sons, *pub-*
lished in 1862.

Mark Akenside, author of the *Pleasures of Imagination*, was born on
November the Ninth, 1721,
William Sotheby, who founded the famous bookshop in Bond
Street, London, was born on this day in 1757, and
Sir Giles Gilbert Scott, architect of Liverpool Cathedral, born
in 1880.

These died on this day:
William Camden, scholar author of *Britannia*, 1623,
Archbishop Sheldon, founder of the Sheldon Theatre, Oxford,
1677,
Paul Sandby, founder of an English school of water-colour painting,
1809,
Marshal Count de Bourmont, distinguished French commander,
1846.

THESE ARE SOME OF THE EVENTS ON NOVEMBER THE
NINTH:
PROCLAMATION AGAINST FIRING OFF GREAT GUNS, 1681,
JOHN WILKES ELECTED LORD MAYOR, 1774,
THE FRENCH DIRECTORY WAS OVERTHROWN IN 1799,
FLOGGING VIRTUALLY ABOLISHED IN THE ARMY, 1859,
D.S.O. INSTITUTED, 1886,
THE CRUISER 'EMDEN' WAS DESTROYED IN 1914,
RAPALLO CONFERENCE, 1917,
CONVENTION BETWEEN POLAND AND DANZIG AGREED,
1920,
POTATO RATIONING IN BRITAIN BEGAN IN 1947.

November the Tenth

What's Time?
Leave now for dogs and apes!
Man has forever.

November the Tenth is a great anniversary for birth days. A flock of famous men descended on the world on this day.
Mahomet was born on this day at Mecca in 570,
Martin Luther was born on this day in 1483,
Robert Devereux, Earl of Essex, Queen Elizabeth's favourite, 1567.

In the seventeenth century, George II was born on November the Tenth in 1683,
In 1697, William Hogarth, the painter and engraver, was born on this day—destined to show vice and—so showing it—shame it.

These were born on this day—
Oliver Goldsmith in 1728,
Granville Sharp in 1734,
Frederick Schiller in 1759,
Jacob Epstein, the sculptor, born 1880.

Ladislaus VI of Hungary, killed at Varna, 1444,
Pope Paul III (Farnese) died 1549, and
On this day, too, died a less famous Mr. Brighton of Maldon, Essex, in 1755. He was aged twenty-seven and weighed forty-four stones.
Isidore Geoffrey St. Hilaire, zoologist, in 1861,
Prince Leopold George Frederick, King of Belgians, in 1865,
Sir Frank Henry Bowater, Bt. (Lord Mayor of London in 1938), 1947.

These are the events recorded:
Proceedings against Queen Caroline abandoned in 1820,
Mr. Stanley met Dr. Livingstone 'I presume' in 1871,
H.M.S. *Cossack* sunk, 1941,
Naples and Brindisi bombed, 1941,
General de Gaulle became President in 1943,
Forli captured 1944.

THERE ARE TWO CONFESSOR SAINTS:
ST. JUSTUS, ARCHBISHOP OF CANTERBURY, 627, AND
ST. ANDREW AVELLINO, 1608.

November the Eleventh

'Never the time and the place,
And the loved one all together.'

On the eleventh hour of the eleventh day of the eleventh month of 1918, the First World War ended. November the Eleventh is Remembrance Day for millions who lived through and served in the years of 1914–18.
On this day, too, in the same year, Karl of Austria abdicated, and the kingdom of Albania became a republic.
In the Second World War, this day saw the Italians in the air over London in 1940, and the British attacking at Taranto. The Axis entered Vichy on November the Eleventh in 1940.

These knew November the Eleventh as birth day:
John Albert Fabricius, scholar and editor, 1668, Leipzig, ·
Firmin Abauzit, celebrated man of learning, 1679,
de Bougainville, 1729,
Dr. Abercrombie, physician, 1781,
Dostoevski, the Russian writer, in 1821, and
Arthur Deakin in 1890.

On this day these died—at the appointed time:
Canute the Dane, King of England, 1035, Shaftesbury,
Thomas, Lord Fairfax, Parliamentary general, 1671,
Jean Sylvain Bailly, eminent astronomer, guillotined 1793,
Joshua Brookes, eccentric clergyman, 1821, Manchester.

THESE OCCURRENCES ARE IN THE RECORDS OF NOVEMBER THE ELEVENTH:
MAILS FIRST CARRIED BY TRAIN, 1830,
THE BURNING OF 'THE SARAH SANDS', 1857,
EDWARD SOTHERN CREATED 'LORD DUNDREARY', 1861,
THOMAS CARLYLE ELECTED RECTOR OF EDINBURGH UNIVERSITY, 1865,
LONDON AND NORWICH ON THE TELEPHONE, 1878,
'BOYCOTTING' BEGAN, 1880,
BARNUM AND BAILEY OPENED AT OLYMPIA, 1889,
WAR COMMITTEE FORMED, 1915,
THE CENOTAPH WAS UNVEILED AND THE UNKNOWN WARRIOR BURIED IN WESTMINSTER ABBEY IN 1920,
CANADIAN LEGATION IN WASHINGTON, AND THE UNITED STATES LEGATION IN OTTAWA BECAME EMBASSIES, 1943.

November the Twelfth

How soon hath time, the subtle thief of youth,
Stol'n on his wing my three-and-twentieth year.

This is the day of St. Augustine, one of the four Fathers of the Church of Christ. He lived fully—a youth of philandering with pleasure—a manhood of hard thinking, hard labour and hard living. He was honest with all men and honest with himself. His 'confessions', written almost two thousand years ago, is the living proof of his relentless self examination and criticism. He was born on November the Twelfth in A.D. 313 and died Bishop of Hippo and author of The City of God.

These were born on November the Twelfth:
Richard Baxter in 1615,
Admiral Vernon in 1684,
Amelia Oppie, the novelist, 1769, and
Admiral Harold R. Stark, Commander of the U.S. Naval Forces in Europe from 1942 to 1945, born in 1880.

There died on this day:
Pope Boniface III, 606,
Stephen Gardiner, Bishop of Winchester, 1555,
Sir John Hawkins, 1595,
Charles Kemble, the actor, 1854,
Mrs. Gaskell, 1865,
Baroness Orczy, author of *The Scarlet Pimpernel*, 1947.

EVERY DAY HAS ITS EVENTS—BUT HOW FEW DO MEN TROUBLE TO REMEMBER!
FROM THE PAGES OF HISTORY—THESE STAND OUT:
THE AMERICANS TOOK MONTREAL, 1775,
FIRE WATCHERS FIRST ESTABLISHED IN LONDON, 1791,
FIRST APPLICATION OF CHLOROFORM BY PROFESSOR SIMPSON IN EDINBURGH, 1847,
MR. GLADSTONE ELECTED RECTOR OF EDINBURGH UNIVERSITY, 1859,
ROYAL ARMY SERVICE CORPS ESTABLISHED, 1869,
CAPTAIN SCOTT'S BODY FOUND IN THE ANTARCTIC, 1913,
FIRST AUTOMATIC TELEPHONE EXCHANGE OPENED IN LONDON, 1927,
AXIS DRIVEN OUT OF EGYPT BY THE BRITISH, 1942,
SINKING OF THE 'TIRPITZ', BY THE BRITISH, 1944.

November the Thirteenth

The bird of Time has but a little way,
To fly—and lo! the bird is on the wing.

On this day, in Edinburgh in 1850, Robert Louis Balfour Stevenson was born. He loved his native city—wrote for it a guide-book which reads like an original story—dreamed of it all his life and died hankering for the long line of gas lamps flickering in its Princes Street. He wrote romances for boys —poems for children—tales for fathers and grandfathers—essays for all. He was forty-four years of age when death took him in Samoa—this Tusitala—'The Teller of Stories'.

On this day:
The Battle of Sheriffmuir was fought in 1715,
Capture of Beaumont Hamel by 51st (Scottish) Division, 1916.
The first bomb on British soil fell in the Shetlands on this day in 1939 and killed a rabbit,
Sinking of *Ark Royal*, 1941,
Tobruk in 1942, marks the calendar of the Second World War for the British,
Zhitomir captured, 1943, and
Mr. Dalton resigned Chancellorship, Sir Stafford Cripps succeeded him, 1947,
Two British scientists were awarded Nobel Prizes for physics and chemistry, 1947.

These died on November the Thirteenth,
Justinian, a Roman emperor, 565,
Malcolm Canmore, 1093,
Thomas May, poet, 1650,
George Fox, the Quaker, 1690,
William Etty, the painter, 1849,
Sir John Forbes, an eminent physician and medical writer, 1861,
Rossini, the Italian composer, 1868.

THESE COUNTED NOVEMBER THE THIRTEENTH THEIR BIRTHDAY:
PELAGIUS, 354,
EDWARD III, 1312,
PHILIP BEROALDUS, THE ELDER, SCHOLAR AND CRITIC, 1450, BOLOGNA, AND
SIR JOHN MOORE, 1761—DESTINED TO DIE AT CORUNNA.

November the Fourteenth

What is this life, if full of care,
We have no time to stand and stare.

November the Fourteenth, in 1831, saw in Berlin the death of George William Frederick Hegel. He was born in 1771—a follower of that Scoto-German, Kant—the philosopher of the Absolute—the foundation of a German philosophical system which half the world fails to understand and the other half fears.
The same day, in 1716, Leibnitz died—another German philosopher who, the critics asserted, believed that in the long run everything was for the best in the best of all possible worlds. He may be right.

On this day too, these died:
The Earl of Elgin, of 'Elgin Marbles' fame, in 1841,
John Abercrombie, the physician, in 1844,
Lord Roberts of Kandahar in 1914,
Mrs. Belloc Lowndes, novelist, in 1947,
May Sinclair, novelist, 1946,
Manuel de Falla in 1946.

On November the Fourteenth:
First bishop was consecrated in America in 1784,
It was discovered that Army officers' daughters were attempting to earn a living by making shirts at 1½d. each in 1842 . . . this report made the 'Hungry Forties' seem a reality,
First London to Brighton motor race took place in 1896,
Labour Party left the Coalition in 1918,
Statute of Westminster was passed in 1938,
The Coventry raid in 1940 stiffened, rather than weakened, British resolution,
U.S. Neutrality Act, amended on this day in 1941, made American sympathy seem less sentimental and more serviceable.

THERE WERE BORN ON THIS DAY:
BENJAMIN HOADLEY, BISHOP OF BANGOR, EMINENT WHIG PRELATE, 1676,
ADAM GOTTLOB OEHLENSCHLAGER, DANISH POET, 1779,
SIR CHARLES LYELL, GEOLOGIST, 1797, KINNORDY,
JOHN CURWEN, 1816,
PANDIT JAWAHARLAL NEHRU, INDIAN STATESMAN, IN 1889,
PRINCE CHARLES OF EDINBURGH, 1948.

[333]

November the Fifteenth

Who was the man who made the clock?
He gave poor fools like me a knock.
I never want to serve my time,
Nor live by reason or by rhyme.

William Pitt, the Elder, who died Lord Chatham, was born on November the Fifteenth in 1708. He was among the foremost of British statesmen and in his closing years begged the Commons to 'beware lest they break those ties, which light as air yet strong as iron, bound the colonies to the Motherland'. These were the words of Burke, but Pitt stood with him, and with a great body of opinion against the policy which led to the withdrawal of the American colonies from the British Empire.

Two great English poets were born on November the Fifteenth—
Andrew Marvell, the Cromwellian poet, in 1620,
William Cowper, the author of *John Gilpin*, in 1731,
Sir William Herschel, the great astronomer, was born on this day in 1738,
Johanan K. Lavater, the Swiss theologian, 1741,
Averell Harriman in 1891, and
Rt. Hon. Aneurin Bevan, M.P., Minister of Health, 1897.

On November the Fifteenth these died:
Albertus Magnus, the German scholar, 1280,
John Kepler, 1630,
Thomas Parr, 'Old Parr', supposedly 115 years old, died on this day in 1634,
The Duke of Hamilton and Lord Mohun killed each other in a duel in 1712,
Christopher Gluck, the composer, in 1787.

THESE EVENTS MEANT MUCH WHEN THEY HAPPENED ON THIS DAY IN YEARS GONE BY,
DOMESDAY BOOK COMPLETED, 1087,
DRAKE SET SAIL, 1577,
WELLINGTON RESIGNED PRIME MINISTERSHIP, 1830,
POPE ESCAPED IN DISGUISE FROM ROME, 1848,
CHURCH BELLS WERE RUNG IN BRITAIN TO CELEBRATE VICTORY IN EGYPT, 1942,
GENOA RAIDED, 1942,
AMERICAN FORCES CAPTURE METZ FORTS, 1944.

November the Sixteenth

My love and I lay on the grass,
Time fell asleep and let us pass
Contented hours of utter bliss
Why are not all our hours like this?

On November the Sixteenth, 1812, John Walter died. He made his mark in his own day as an enterprising publisher and journalist. In 1785 he founded a paper called the Universal Register *which became some few years later* The Times, *today the uniquely English newspaper in its special field of affairs—the name of Walter is still associated with this famous newspaper.*

John Bright, the opponent of the Corn Law, was born on this day in 1811,
Tiberius, Roman emperor, was born in 42 B.C.,
Freinshemius, scholar and critic, at Ulm, in 1608,
Jean le Rond d'Alembert, encyclopaedist, at Paris, in 1707,
Francis Danby, artist, at Wexford, in 1793,
Gen. Sir Montagu George North Stopford, soldier in two world wars, born 1892.

St. Margaret died on this day in 1093,
Henry III died on November the Sixteenth in 1272,
Pierre Nicole, logician of Port Royal, in 1695,
James Ferguson, astronomer, 1776,
Wombwell (Circus), died 1850.
Two executions took place in England on this day:
Perkin Warbeck in 1499, and
Jack Sheppard in 1724.

THESE ARE THE EVENTS OF THE DAY:
PRETENDER'S PROCLAMATION ORDERED TO BE BURNT BY THE COMMON HANGMAN, 1722,
WESTMINSTER BRIDGE OPENED, 1750,
FIRST TREATY OF COMMERCE WITH ABYSSINIA, 1841,
CAPTAIN COOK TOOK POSSESSION OF NEW ZEALAND FOR BRITAIN IN 1869,
BRITISH BECHUANALAND ADDED TO CROWN COLONIES, 1895,
CLEMENCEAU BECAME PREMIER OF FRANCE, 1917,
GERMANS CAPTURED KERCH, 1941,
BRITISH RAIDED ROMMEL'S HEADQUARTERS, 1941,
BATTLE OF DERNA, 1942.

November the Seventeenth

Of course, of course, of course, you love me,
You've shown it today,
But you, my lord, are far above me
You hold me in sway.

The wars, the wars, the wars, they call you,
The eagles are flown.
What, O! what, O! what, shall befall you,
And I am here alone.

November the Seventeenth is a notable day. On it in A.D. 9 the Emperor
Vespasian was born. He was chosen for the purple by his own soldiers of
the Legion.
On November the Seventeenth, in 1887, Bernard Montgomery was born.
He became, acclaimed by those who served under him, Lord Montgomery of
Alamein and the British general who accepted the surrender of the German
armies in the field in 1945.
Marshal Macdonald, who became Duke of Tarentum, one of Napoleon's
marshals, was born on this day in 1765.
Simon Bolivar, the liberator of the South Americans, died on this day in 1831.
It is a soldier's day.

On this day died:
Sir John de Mandeville, 1372,
Mary Tudor, 1558,
Robert Owen, 1858,
Auguste Rodin, the sculptor, 1917.

THESE ARE MILITARY EVENTS OF CONSEQUENCE ON THIS
DAY:
RELIEF OF LUCKNOW, 1857,
JOPPA OCCUPIED, 1917,
BRITISH PARACHUTE TROOPS LANDED IN TUNISIA, 1942.

MEN MARKED THESE EVENTS TOO—ON NOVEMBER THE
SEVENTEENTH:
EDWARD AWARDED THE SCOTS CROWN, 1292,
SUEZ CANAL FORMALLY OPENED, 1869,
FIRST WAR LOAN, £300,000,000, 1914,
SEDITION BILL PASSED, 1934,
CONSTITUENT ASSEMBLY OF INDIA MET FOR THE FIRST
TIME AS PARLIAMENT OF THE DOMINION, 1947.

[336]

November the Eighteenth

Is life a boon?
If so it must befall
That death when e'er he call,
Must call too soon.

These are William Schwenck Gilbert's lines from the 'Yeoman of the Guard'. He held life sweet. He sweetened it for millions. He was born on November the Eighteenth in 1836—the year before Queen Victoria ascended the throne.
With Sullivan as his partner, he gave to the world a new form of entertainment, the English light opera.
As a humorous poet he is among the first with his immortal Bab Ballads.

Pierre Bayle, celebrated critic and controversial writer, in 1647,
Sir David Wilkie in 1785, and
Cezare Lombroso in 1836, were born on November the Eighteenth.

These died on this day, each in their appointed year.
Cardinal Pole, 1558,
Charles Heath, the engraver, 1848,
Captain George William Manby, inventor of apparatus for saving life in shipwrecks, 1854, near Yarmouth,
Professor Edward Forbes, eminent naturalist, 1854, Edinburgh,
General Sir Frederick Stanley Maude, 1917, Baghdad,
T. P. O'Connor, famous Irish journalist, politician and wit, 1929,
Rt. Hon. Henry Rushcliffe, P.C., a former Minister of Labour, 1949.

EVENTS OF THIS DAY ARE 'SEVERAL AND PECURIOUS':
HERE ARE SOME—
NOAH SAID TO HAVE LEFT THE ARK ON THIS DAY, 2347 B.C.
PRESUMABLY IN SEARCH OF FISH AS IT WAS FRIDAY,
THE STATUTES AT MARLBOROUGH ON THIS DAY, BY PARLIAMENT, ARE STILL THE BASIS OF ENGLISH LAW, 1267,
THAMES UNITED TO SEVERN BY CANAL, 1789,
FUNERAL OF DUKE OF WELLINGTON, 1852,
LEAGUE 'APPLIED' SANCTIONS TO ITALY, 1935,
GERMAN MAGNETIC MINES SOWN FROM AIR, 1939,
THE BATTLE OF BERLIN BEGAN, 1943,
ALL ON NOVEMBER THE EIGHTEENTH.

November the Nineteenth

At first Time was my faithful friend
Now it is coming to an end:
For me he now is short of days
He sends me seeking other ways.

November the Nineteenth, in 1600, saw the birth of Charles I, King of
Great Britain and Ireland—he whom the Jacobites called the Martyr King
and whose statue stands looking down Whitehall where he met his death on
the scaffold.
The Stuarts brought great colour and some may even say calamity to the
throne of Britain but none more than Charles I. A good and kind father, a
religious man, with profound conviction that it was his divine right to rule
the people, his memory as the years pass grows no less green.

Born on this day were:
Albert Thorwaldsen, Danish sculptor, 1770,
Ferdinand de Lesseps, 1805, and
Baron Ritchie, 1838.

Died on this day—these famous men are remembered for their
works:
Nicolas Poussin, painter, 1665, Rome,
John Wilkins, Bishop of Chester, philosopher and writer, 1672,
Franz Schubert, 1828,
Abraham John Valpy, editor of classics, 1854, London,
Sir William S. Crawford (advertising), 1950.

Events of the day down the years include,
Pitt the Younger's first ministry, 1783,
First treaty with U.S., 1794,
War declared against Abyssinia, 1867,
Monastir captured by the Allies, 1916,
Surrender of German Fleet, 1918, in the Firth of Forth,
Russians evacuated Zhitomir, 1943,
Geilenkirchen captured, 1944,
Pilgrim Trust gave £15,000 towards restoration of Peterborough
Cathedral, 1947.

IT WAS ON NOVEMBER THE NINETEENTH IN 1703 THAT THE
MAN IN THE IRON MASK DIED IN THE BASTILLE LEAVING HIS
STORY TO BE TOLD BY ALEXANDRE DUMAS.

[338]

November the Twentieth

Hours and minutes are but numbers
Taken when man works or slumbers
Nothing can halt the daily drain
Man can not have his hours again.

November the Twentieth crowds the calendar—away back in 1214, at
Bury St. Edmunds, it was on this day that Magna Carta was prepared;
Edward the First ascended the throne on this day in 1272; and on November
the Twentieth Vasco da Gama rounded the Cape of Good Hope in 1497.
These were the days but there were other things hid in the womb of Time.
On this day, in 1661, the bishops resumed their seats in the House of Lords
—in 1806 the decree of 'a new order' came from Berlin, and on this day
in 1858 the suppression of the Indian Mutiny was announced.

Thomas Chatterton was born in 1752,
Louis Alexandre Berthier, Prince of Wagram, one of Napoleon's
marshals, was born on this day in 1753, and
Sir Wilfred Laurier in 1841.

Sir Christopher Hatton, statesman and courtier of Queen
Elizabeth, died on this day in 1591,
Caroline, Queen of George II of England, in 1737,
Tom Hood, the humorist, 1874,
Rubinstein, 1894,
Admiral of Fleet, Earl Jellicoe, 1935.

IN 1875 THIS DAY SAW THE BEGINNING OF THE NEW
AMERICAN PASTIME, 'THE SPELLING BEE',
IN 1917 THIS DAY WITNESSED THE BATTLE OF CAMBRAI
AND 'TANKS' IN ACTION,
IN 1918, THE WAR OVER, NAVAL CENSORSHIP WAS
ABOLISHED ON NOVEMBER THE TWENTIETH,
TURIN WAS HEAVILY RAIDED, 1942,
RUSSIAN VICTORY IN THE CENTRAL CAUCASUS 1942—A
WELCOME ANNOUNCEMENT,
TRIAL OF MAJOR WAR CRIMINALS OPENED AT NUREMBERG,
1945,
PRINCESS ELIZABETH MARRIED LIEUT. PHILIP MOUNT-
BATTEN, DUKE OF EDINBURGH, IN WESTMINSTER ABBEY,
1947.

November the Twenty-first

Time's a torture: Time's a trance,
Time has a back and forward glance,
Time is time-less—has no sound
Neither on or underground.

Sir Thomas Gresham died on this day in 1579. Bankers do not figure much in history. They are the power behind the throne and prefer anonymity or someone else's name. Sir Thomas Gresham was the banker to the Tudors— to Henry VIII and Queen Elizabeth. His name is linked with the great economic truth that good money disappears but bad money persists—the fact that in currency the bad drives out the good in a wicked world which hoards the best and circulates the doubtful.

James Hogg, who knew little of London and less of banking, too, died on this day in 1835. A shepherd by calling, he educated himself and was known as 'The Ettrick Shepherd'. He was a tenant-farmer of the Duke of Buccleuch and a friend of Sir Walter Scott.

The registers show that these were born on this day,
Voltaire born in 1694,
Edmund, Lord Lyons, the British admiral in 1790, at Christchurch,
Sir Leslie Ward ('Spy'), 1851,
A. Gide, 1869,
Lord Kindersley in 1872.

These died on November the Twenty-first:
Marcus Licinius Crassus, the Roman triumvir, who was slain in Mesopotamia, 53 B.C.,
Henry Purcell, the musician, 1695,
Dr. Hill, 1775,
Abraham Newland, 1807,
General Hertzog, the South African Premier, 1942,
Sir Charles Edward Mallet, historian of Oxford University, 1947.

BRITISH HOSPITAL SHIP 'BRITANNIC' WAS SUNK IN 1916,
PARLIAMENT MET AT CHURCH HOUSE, 1940,
LIBYAN BATTLE OPENED, 1941,
2,300 UNITED STATES AIRCRAFT STRUCK OIL PLANTS IN GERMANY, 1944.

November the Twenty-second

The idle singer of an empty day.

She was born in 1819, on November the Twenty-second, as Mary Ann Evans, but she finds her fame under the name of George Eliot. She wrote Adam Bede, The Mill on the Floss, Mr. Gilfil's Love Story and Romola. These novels show profound insight into human character and enjoy lasting popularity. George Eliot was a free thinker and a pioneer of women's rights. She contracted an alliance—without a marriage—with the critic and historian George Henry Lewes—was a friend of Herbert Spenser and died in 1881.

The Scots philosopher, Dugald Stewart, was born on this day in 1735; at the age of nineteen he deputized as Professor of Mathematics in the University of Edinburgh.
General Charles André Joseph Marie de Gaulle was born in 1899.

The House of Commons in 1773 passed a resolution at five in the morning asserting that Robert Clive, Lord Clive, did render great and meritorious service to his country.
He founded British India and died on November the Twenty-second in 1774 by his own hand, only fifty years of age.

These, too, died on this day:
Sir Martin Frobisher, 1594,
John Stackhouse, botanist, 1819, Bath,
Sir Henry Havelock, 1857,
Professor George Wilson, 1859,
Mrs. Dickens, 1879,
John Delaney of *The Times*, 1879,
Sir Arthur Charles Sullivan, 1900,
James John Davis, a former United States Secretary of Labour, in 1947.

Some events are recalled:
U.S.A. Congress met for the first time at Washington in 1799, on this day,
Lord Grey's Ministry in 1830, marks November the Twenty-second,
A proposal by Edinburgh Town Council to censure Lord Provost was made in 1842 on this day,
The first train ran through Mersey Tunnel in 1885 on this day.

November the Twenty-third

What one day gives us, another takes away from us.

Looking back over travelled roads men saw on this day, The Times,
Mr. Walter sentenced for libelling the Royal Dukes, 1789,
First pillar-box erected, St. Helier, Jersey, 1852,
Halifax fisheries awarded to Canada, 1877,
Luxembourg separated from Netherlands, 1890,
Van der Lubbe declared he wanted to be sentenced at his Reichstag trial; he
had had enough of justice, 1933,
Rawalpindi *sunk, 1939, an opening action in the ocean war,*
Germans in Rostov, 1941, U.S.S.R. in retreat,
2,300 tons on Berlin, 1943—a monster bombing raid.

St. Clement, pope and martyr, 100,
St. Amphilochius, Bishop of Iconium, confessor, 100,
St. Daniel, bishop and confessor, 545, and
St. Tron, confessor, 693, are the saints with which November the
Twenty-third is associated.

John Wallis, mathematician, 1616, Ashford, Kent, and
Dr. Thomas Birch, historical and biographical writer, 1705,
London, were born on this day, and
Sir John Scoular Buchanan, pioneer of high-speed flying, born
in 1883.

Richard Hakluyt was born on November the Twenty-third in
1553. He lived in the spacious days of Queen Bess and was the
chronicler of her sea rovers and land raiders. The very title of his
book sounds like a fanfare of trumpets. He named his book:
The Principal Navigations, the Voyages, the Traffics and the Discoveries
of the English Nation, made by sea, or over land, to the remote and far
distant Quarters of the Earth at any time within the compass of these
Fifteen Hundred Years.

THESE TOO DIED ON NOVEMBER THE TWENTY-THIRD:
LOUIS, DUKE OF ORLEANS, BROTHER OF CHARLES VI, WHO
WAS ASSASSINATED AT PARIS IN 1407,
WILLIAM BENTINCK, FIRST EARL OF PORTLAND, THE
FAVOURITE MINISTER OF WILLIAM III, IN 1709,
THOMAS TALLIS, THE COMPOSER OF CHURCH MUSIC, IN
1858,
SIR RODGER NEWDIGATE, ENGLISH ANTIQUARY, IN 1806.

November the Twenty-fourth

O Phosphor Morning Star bring back day!
Why do you delay our delight?
Caesar is coming to us;
O Phosphor, bring us back the day!

John Knox died on the Twenty-fourth of November 1572. Scotland knew Edward I of England as the hammer of the Scots! John Knox hammered the Scots too—and especially the women. His most remembered work leaves no doubt as to what is its subject-matter. It is entitled Blasts of the Trumpet against the Monstrous Regiment of Women. *He was born in 1505 and his mark on Scotland, for much that is good, still remains.*

November the Twenty-fourth is a day of great birthdays,
A philosopher—the gentle Spinoza in 1632, and
Laurence Sterne, the clergyman whose *Sentimental Journey* all the world enjoys, in 1713,
John Bacon, the sculptor, in 1740, at Southwark,
Grace Darling in 1815, the brave girl whose name still inspires the Life-boat Service.
Mrs. Hodgson Burnett in 1849, and
Lord Ailwyn in 1887.

These died on this day:
Dr. Robert Henry, historian, 1790, Edinburgh,
Viscount Melbourne, statesman, 1848,
General Sir Henry Havelock, 1857,
Rev. Dr. George Croly, poet and romance writer, 1860, London,
Sir Hiram Maxim, in 1916, the inventor of the Maxim machine-gun.

On this day:
In 1548 Parliament decided that clergy may marry,
In 1642 Tasmania was discovered,
In 1861 in Edinburgh a tenement collapsed, fifty people were buried. ('Heave awa', lads' was the slogan of the rescuers),
Oesel Island cleared of the enemy, 1944.

NOVEMBER THE TWENTY-FOURTH:
THE DAY OF THE PILGRIMS AND ROAST TURKEY—IS USUALLY
THANKSGIVING DAY IN UNITED STATES—FIXED AS THE
LAST THURSDAY IN NOVEMBER.

November the Twenty-fifth

My days I gave to work and getting,
You mock'd at me, I'm told,
I'm not complaining: I'm not fretting,
But must you grab my gold?

It was my way to get and gather
I got that I might give.
Exploiter! miser! these I'd rather
Than choose the way you live!

In 1835, in Dunfermline in Scotland, Andrew Carnegie was born on November the Twenty-fifth. He was a self-made man who, acquiring a fortune by his own genius, devoted the remainder of his life to its disbursement.
The same energy he gave to the first—he gave to the second. He endowed libraries—created scholarships and founded institutes. He is a supreme example of some of the disadvantages of capitalism and—more notably—of its advantages—to a growing society.

These were born on the same day as Andrew Carnegie,
Lopez de la Vega, who is the Shakespeare in Spain, in 1562,
Charles Kemble, the most famed of the famous Kembles, 1775.

On this day died:
Herod, A.D. 4,
Edward Alleyn, founder of Dulwich College, 1626,
Isaac Watts, 1748, the hymn writer,
Richard Glover, poet, 1785,
Sir Francis Chantry, the sculptor, 1841,
Sir Augustus Wall Calcott, landscape painter, 1844, Kensington,
John Gibson Lockhard, son-in-law and biographer of Sir Walter Scott and editor of the *Quarterly*, 1854.

The authority is no longer here but it has been asserted that 2348 B.C. was the year and November the Twenty-fifth was the day on which the Deluge began. Noah was the hero of the occasion.

THESE, TOO, ARE REPORTED FOR THIS DAY,
PROCLAMATION AGAINST HACKNEY CARRIAGES, 1687,
BRITISH PURCHASE OF KHEDIVE'S SUEZ CANAL SHARES
ANNOUNCED, 1875,
GERMANY AND JAPAN MADE THE ANTI-COMINTERN PACT,
1936.

November the Twenty-sixth

O come my friend we're just in time,
Let's drop this endless grind and grime.
O let's quit the gritty city,
Let's seek the hills and tramp the dales,
And find again our youth in Wales,
You with Bet and I with Kitty.

Marshal of France—under Napoleon—Nicolas Jean de Dien Soult died
in the style of the Duke of Dalmatia on this day in 1851.
Prince William, the son of Henry I of England, perished on this day in the
White Ship *on his way to England in 1120.*
John Loudoun Macadam died on this day in 1836. To him the world
owes what are called macadamized roads.

On this day were born:
Sir James Ware, antiquary, 1594, Dublin,
Dr. William Derham, natural philosopher, 1657, Stowton,
Lord Armstrong, English inventor, 1810,
Sir Henry Coward, the composer, 1849,
Sir Oliver Harvey, 1893.

They died on this day:
John Spottiswoode, Archbishop of St. Andrews, 1639,
John Elwes, the miser, 1789,
Dr. Joseph Black, eminent chemist, 1799, Edinburgh,
J. L. McAdam in 1836,
Lord Armstrong in 1900,
Sir L. S. Jameson, 1917, known as Dr. Jim.

On this day,
First Eddystone lighthouse was blown down in 1703,
Bomb exploded in casino at Monte Carlo, 1882,
Surrender of King Theebaw, 1885,
Lord Rothermere became President of Air Council, 1917,
Attack on Moscow reached climax, 1941.

ST. PETER, MARTYR, BISHOP OF ALEXANDRIA, 311,
ST. CONRAD, BISHOP OF CONSTANCE, CONFESSOR, 976, AND
ST. NICON, SURNAMED METANOITE, CONFESSOR, 998,
CROWN THE DAY. THEY ARE THE SALUTED AND CHOSEN
SAINTS.

November the Twenty-seventh

Hold it! Seize it! Snatch it!
Defend your ivory tower
Find your rainbow! Catch it!
Grasp now your fleeting hour.

November the Twenty-seventh is the anniversary of the day when, in 1666,
the Scots took up arms for the solemn league and covenant and declared war
on Charles Stuart the Second—it is the anniversary of the great storm of 1703,
and many now still living remember it as the day of the flood—'Frozen Foot
Day'—on Gallipoli in the First World War in 1915,
Cologne attacked by the R.A.F., 1940,
Gondar captured, 1941,
French fleet scuttled, 1942,
Mr. Churchill, President Roosevelt and Marshal Stalin met in Teheran
for a four-day conference, 1943.

There were born on this day:
Marquis de Maintenon, 1636,
Robert Lowth, Bishop of London, biblical critic, 1710,
John Murray, the publisher—his name continues, 1778,
Fanny Kemble, the gracious actress, 1809,
Sir W. Orpen, 1878.

These died on November the Twenty-seventh.
Horace, 8 B.C.,
Clovis, first King of France, 511, Paris,
Maurice, Roman emperor, beheaded at Chalcedon, 602,
Countess of Lovelace, only child of Lord and Lady Byron, 1852,
Alexandre Dumas the younger, 1895,
Maj.-Gen. Sir Borlase Childs, Assistant Police Commissioner,
1946.

It is reported that on this day in 1784, a man rode a cow in
defiance of Pitt.

THE SAINTS ARE:
ST. JAMES, SURNAMED INTERCISUS, A MARTYR, 421 AND
ALSO IN
241 ST. MAHARSAPORA, MARTYR AND AN IRISH SAINT,
ST. SECUNDIN OR SEACHNAL, BISHOP OF DUNSEACHLIN OR
DUNSAGHLIN IN MEATH, 447.

November the Twenty-eighth

Time is a sluggard—lies a-bed,
But now by forelock he is led.
I can make him go much faster,
Time's now my slave and I am master.

November the Twenty-eighth was a day when much happened.
In 1885 Mandalay was occupied by the British on this day and it is the
anniversary of the Battle of Colenso in 1899.
A political movement, drawing its inspiration from Hungary and called
Sinn Fein, came into being in Dublin under the initiative of Arthur
Griffith, on November the Twenty-eighth, 1905. It became the source of
the movement which through blood and fire reached the present-day Republic
of Ireland, the Government of Southern Ireland. Arthur Griffith, the
founder of Sinn Fein, was elected President of Dail Eireann in 1922.

Other occurrences on this day include,
Independence of Albania declared, 1912,
First aeroplane raid on London, 1916,
Hey-day of German onslaught in Russia, 1941,
Re-opening of the Port of Antwerp, 1944.

Born on this day were:
Captain George William Manby, the inventor of life-saving
apparatus for shipwrecks, in 1765,
William Blake, 1757,
Victor Cousin, the moral philosopher, in 1792.

ON NOVEMBER THE TWENTY-EIGHTH—
EDWARD PLANTAGENET, EARL OF WARWICK, WAS BE-
HEADED, 1499,
CHARLES BULLER, STATESMAN AND WRITER, 1848,
IN 1859 WASHINGTON IRVING DIED. POLITICIAN, WIT AND
MAN OF LETTERS, THIS AMERICAN HELD TO THE TRADITION
OF ENGLISH CULTURE—A FRIEND OF BRITAIN AND INTER-
PRETER OF U.S.A. AND U.K. TO EACH OF THESE PEOPLES.
BARON C. C. J. BUNSEN, PRUSSIAN STATESMAN, PHILO-
SOPHICAL WRITER, 1860,
JOHN AMERY SENTENCED TO DEATH FOR HIGH TREASON,
1945, AND
GENERAL LECLERC, OUTSTANDING FRENCH WAR COMMAN-
DER, WAS ACCIDENTALLY KILLED ON THIS DAY IN 1947.

November the Twenty-ninth

Our little systems have their day,
They have their day, and cease to be.

*His thirty-two years of life took him, at the end, to Zutphen in the Low
Countries, where his uncle, the Earl of Leicester, led Queen Elizabeth's
soldiers to war. Mortally wounded and dying he was being given a cup of
water but seeing another soldier in like condition exclaimed 'Give him the
water—his need is greater than mine'. Sir Philip Sidney was the name of
this gentle knight—a courtier, a traveller, a poet, a soldier—the idol of the
camp of Queen Elizabeth—he was born on November the Twenty-ninth in
1554 at Penshurst in Kent. He died in 1586.*

This was the day when
Steam was first applied to printing *The Times* (1,100 sheets an
hour) in 1814,
Florence Nightingale Fund for first Nursing Association started
in 1855,
Battle of Modder River was fought in 1899,
Beatty became Commander of Grand Fleet, 1916,
Newfoundland agreed to accept Commissioner Government in
1933,
The Eighth Army opened the offensive in 1943.

Pope Clement IV in 1268 died on this day,
Roger Mortimer executed in 1330,
Cardinal Wolsey, 1530,
Prince Rupert of the Rhine, 1682,
Maria Theresa, Queen of Hungary, in 1780,
Horace Greeley, American journalist, 1872,
Martin Tupper, poet and inventor, 1889,
Giacomo Puccini, Italian composer, 1924,
Sir Robert Blyth Greig, Agricultural Research Authority, 1947.

NOVEMBER THE TWENTY-NINTH WAS THE BIRTHDAY OF
MARGARET, DAUGHTER OF HENRY VII AND QUEEN OF
JAMES IV OF SCOTLAND, 1489,
DR. PETER HEYLIN, THEOLOGICAL AND HISTORICAL
WRITER, 1600,
JOHN RAY, EMINENT NATURALIST, 1628, BLACK NOTLEY,
ESSEX,
LOUISA MAY ALCOTT ('LITTLE WOMEN'), 1832.

November the Thirtieth

Restore thy light, O excellent chief, to the country;
For it is like spring where thy countenance has appeared;
To the people the day passes
More pleasantly and the sun more brightly.

'*I have seen this man under all circumstances and I have come to the conviction he is invincible.*' *These words are reported to be the words of one who knew Winston Leonard Spencer Churchill intimately in the Second World War. None will dispute them. The English people draw from and find fresh greatness in this most distinguished man of their long history. His life has not all been victories. He has lived through defeats which would have soured men of ordinary temper. He has known all the rigours of the game— political ostracism, personal antagonism, humiliating exclusion from public affairs, but he has triumphed over himself and all his enemies. He was born in 1874, on this, St. Andrew's Day.*

Winston Churchill has good companies to share his birth day,
Sir Henry Savile, an eminent scholar and mathematician, in 1549,
Jonathan Swift in 1667,
Mark Twain in 1835,
Lord Haldane, a great Secretary of War, in 1856.

They died on this day:
Edmund Ironside, colleague of King Canute, 1016,
John Selden in 1644,
Marshal Saxe in 1750,
James Sheridan Knowles, a dramatist, 1862,
Oscar Wilde in 1900.

THESE ARE EVENTS—GREAT AND SMALL—
BISHOPS REGAINED SEATS IN THE HOUSE OF LORDS, 1661,
PROVISIONAL ARTICLES OF PEACE SIGNED WITH AMERICA, 1782,
MEDICAL MISSIONARY SOCIETY ORGANIZED IN EDINBURGH, 1841,
REMAINS OF NAPOLEON ARRIVED IN FRANCE, 1840,
COMMANDER BYRD FLEW OVER THE SOUTH POLE, 1929,
DESTRUCTION OF CRYSTAL PALACE BY FIRE, 1936,
RUSSIA INVADED FINLAND, 1939.

SAINT ANDREW IS THE SAINT OF THE DAY, THE PATRON SAINT OF SCOTLAND.

[349]

DECEMBER

THIRTY-ONE DAYS

December the First

'And help us this and every day,
To live more nearly as we pray . . .'

Henry I of England, 1135,
Pope Leo X, 1521,
Sir James Ware, antiquary, 1666, Dublin,
Susanna Centlivre, dramatist, 1723,
Alexander I, Emperor of Russia, 1825,
Dr. George Birkbeck, promoter of scientific education, 1841,
Ebenezer Elliot, 1849,
Samuel Courtauld, industrialist, 1947, all died on this day.

These occurred on December the First . . .

In the seventeenth century,
The Grand Remonstrance in 1641, and
The passing of the Navigation Act in 1651 are recorded.

In the nineteenth century,
The Young Roscius, who died in 1874, well over the eighties, made
his first appearance in London on this day in 1801,
The Declaration of Frankfort was made on this day in 1813,
The Hull Watch Committee met in 1859,
The Albert Memorial Chapel, Windsor, was opened in 1875.

In the twentieth century:
Lady Astor took her seat in the House of Commons in 1919—the
first woman to do so, but not the first to be elected.
De Wet captured by the S. African forces, 1914,
The Treaty of Locarno was signed on this day in 1925,
Air raids on Helsinki, 1939,
The points rationing scheme came into being on this day in 1941,
and
Britain's greatest battleship was launched by Princess Elizabeth,
1944.

PRINCESS ANNA COMNENA, HISTORIAN, WAS BORN IN 1083,
JOHN KEILL, THE MATHEMATICIAN AND NATURAL PHILO-
SOPHER, WAS BORN ON THIS DAY AT EDINBURGH IN 1671,
QUEEN ALEXANDRA WAS BORN ON DECEMBER THE FIRST,
1844,
THE EARL OF SHREWSBURY WAS BORN, 1914.

December the Second

They lived, they died, creatures forlorn,
For some a thought, for few a sigh,
Why, Oh! why, then, were they born,
And for what purpose am I—I?

John Brown, of Harper's Ferry, Virginia, U.S.A., was hanged on this day in 1859 for endeavouring to free negro slaves from prison. Some Americans are not sure of the rights and wrongs of this occurrence but the American poets are sure. John Brown is the subject of many poems particularly Stephen Vincent Benet's, called John Brown's Body, *the finest narrative poem written in U.S.A. It is perhaps sufficient to repeat that John Brown's body lies a-mouldering in the grave, but unmistakably his soul—it goes marching on.*

Born on this day were:
Francis Xavier Quadrio, historical writer, 1695, Valtellina,
Henry Gally Knight, illustrator of architectural antiquities, 1786, and
Sir John Barbirolli, 1899.

On this day there died:
Herman Cortes, 1547,
Geraldus Mercator (Kaufmann), geographer, 1594, Doesburg,
Queen Adelaide, 1849,
Amelia Opie, novelist, 1853, Norwich,
Sir Thomas Callender, the man who was responsible for the lighting of London, 1938,
Sir Francis Noel Curtis Bennett, 1950.

THE EVENTS OF THE DAY INCLUDE:
THE SURRENDER OF JERUSALEM TO THE SALADIN, 1187,
ST. PAUL'S OPENED, 1697,
AUSTERLITZ, 'THE BATTLE OF THE EMPERORS', 1805,
ABDICATION OF THE EMPEROR OF AUSTRIA, IN FAVOUR OF HIS NEPHEW FRANZ JOSEPH, 1848,
LOUIS NAPOLEON ABOLISHED CONSTITUTION OF THE REPUBLIC, 1851,
NAPOLEON III BEGAN TO REIGN, 1852,
PRINCE OF WALES LEFT SOUTH AFRICA FOR HOME, 1928,
H.M.A.S. 'SYDNEY' LOST, 1941,
B.O.A.C. PLANE FLEW FROM NEW YORK TO SHANNON IN 8 HRS. 32 MINS., 1946.

December the Third

What of it friend,
It is the end—
Why, then, want more—
You have three score
And ten—enough
Of smooth and rough—
Accept the end,
And, good night, friend.

These five men were each born on December the Third:
Samuel Crompton, in 1753, who invented the spinning mule and was granted by Parliament £5,000 for his invention,
Robert Bloomfield, in 1706, who wrote The Farmer's Boy *and other poems,*
Sir Rowland Hill, in 1795, who was the author of the now lamentably lost penny-post system,
Robert Stephen Hawker, in 1803, who became vicar of Morwenstow and wrote And shall Trelawny die,
And fifthly, Frederick Leighton, in 1830, who became Baron Leighton of Stretton and a famous painter.

There died on this day:
John Flaxman, 1826,
Robert Montgomery, the poet, 1855,
Christian Rauch, sculptor, 1857, Dresden,
Archbishop Tait, 1882,
R. L. Stevenson, 1894,
Mary Baker Eddy, founder of Christian Science, 1910.

These are the events of the day:
Mauritius capitulated, 1810,
Gladstone's first ministry, 1868,
General Townsend reached Kut-el-Amara, 1915,
H.M. the King broadcast a message of thanks to the Home Guard, 1944.

THE SAINTS OF THE DAY ARE:
ST. LUCIUS, KING AND CONFESSOR, END OF SECOND CENTURY,
ST. BIRINUS, BISHOP AND CONFESSOR, 650,
ST. SOLA, HERMIT, 790,
ST. FRANCIS XAVIER, APOSTLE OF THE INDIES, CONFESSOR, 1552.

December the Fourth

The great, the important day, big with fate.

He gave his name to a word . . . and few have that fame. The word is galvanic—with its variations, galvanize, galvanism—and these come from the name of an Italian doctor, Luigi Galvani, who died on this day in 1737. He made a lasting contribution to the study of electricity.

Born on this day were:
Thomas Carlyle, 1795,
Dr. John Kitto, biblical illustrator, 1804, Plymouth,
Lilian Russel, 1861,
Edith Cavell, 1865.

On this day there died, too,
Pope John XXII, 1334,
Cardinal Richelieu, 1642,
William Drummond of Hawthornden, 1649,
Thomas Hobbes, 1679,
John Gay, 1732,
Lord Liverpool, 1828,
John Tyndall, 1893.

THESE ARE THE EVENTS RECORDED:
HADRIAN IV, AN ENGLISH POPE, ELECTED, 1154,
NAVY OFFICE FOUNDED, 1644,
HIGHLAND REBELS REACHED DERBY, 1745,
PITT INTRODUCED INCOME TAX, 1798,
SUTTEE ABOLISHED BY THE BRITISH, 1829,
ROYAL COURTS OF JUSTICE IN STRAND OPENED, 1882,
SUPREME ALLIED NAVAL COUNCIL FORMED, 1917,
FRANCE AND GERMANY SIGNED A 'GOOD NEIGHBOUR'
TREATY IN 1938,
MOSCOW ANNOUNCED THE TEHERAN CONFERENCE, 1943,
CAIRO CONFERENCE, 1943,
LEIPZIG BOMBED, 1943,
MILITARY TARGETS IN WESTERN GERMANY HEAVILY
BOMBED, 1944,
H.M. THE KING APPOINTED SEVEN KNIGHTS OF THE GARTER
—ADDISON, CRANBORNE, MOUNTBATTEN, ALANBROOKE,
PORTAL, ALEXANDER AND MONTGOMERY—1946.

December the Fifth

Time flies—who cares?
He lives who dares!

December the Fifth marked the end of a great attempt to make men better by passing laws. It was on this day by the repeal of the Twenty-first Amendment in 1933, that Prohibition was ended in U.S.A. It was the end of a long story. Prohibitionists first entered U.S.A. politics in 1869—they achieved their aim in 1918—and gangsterdom and racketeering came to full fruition—public opinion chose freedom as a lesser evil than prohibition.

Born on this day were:
Robert Harley, 1661,
Christina Rossetti, 1830,
Admiral Lord Jellicoe, 1859.

There died on this day:
Francis II of France, husband of Queen of Scots, 1560,
Sir Henry Wotton, poet and miscellaneous writer, 1639, Eton,
Wolfgang Mozart, 1791,
John Bewick, wood-engraver, 1795,
Carlo Giovanni Maria Denina, historical writer, 1813,
Leopold Frederick, Count Stolberg, poet and miscellaneous writer, 1819,
Captain S. A. Warner, inventor of projectiles, 1853, Pimlico,
Alexandre Dumas, the Elder, 1870,
G. J. Whyte-Melville (Katerfelto), 1878.

THESE ARE THE EVENTS OF THE DAY:
INDEPENDENCE OF SCOTLAND RESTORED BY RICHARD I, 1189,
AN INCIDENT OF PUBLIC PENANCE IN WALTON, 1838,
NEW POSTAGE LAW OF A GENERAL RATE OF 4D. CAME INTO OPERATION, 1839,
CAMPBELL-BANNERMAN'S MINISTRY, 1905,
MR. ASQUITH RESIGNED, 1916,
FINLAND STUBBORNLY DEFENDED HER TERRITORY, 1939,
91 ENEMY PLANES SHOT DOWN OVER BERLIN, 1944,
KING AND QUEEN GAVE LUNCHEON PARTY AT BUCKINGHAM PALACE FOR LORD WAVELL AND THE FOUR INDIAN LEADERS VISITING LONDON FOR DISCUSSIONS WITH THE GOVERNMENT, 1946.

December the Sixth

You have an hour—perhaps a minute:
Seize it: use it: forthwith begin it—
For neither time nor task will wait,
You cannot find a better date!

Burke and Sheridan baited him, impeached by Parliament for his conduct of the affairs of the East India Company, he was acquitted of all charges, as a memorial tablet in Westminster Hall witnesses. He was one of the builders of the Empire of India and native and British alike testify that no greater administrator appears in the long history of the British connection. Who was he? Warren Hastings, who was born in poverty on this December the Sixth, in 1732.

On this day were born:
Henry VI, 1421,
Sir David Baird, hero of Seringapatam, 1757, Newbyth, Scotland,
Richard Barham, 1788,
Lord Darling, 1849,
Von Mackensen, 1849,
Joseph Conrad, 1857,
Sir Osbert Sitwell, 1892.

On this day there died:
Pope Clement VI, 1352,
Dr. John Lightfoot, divine and commentator, 1675, Great Munden,
Anthony Trollope, the novelist, 1882,
Jefferson Davis, American statesman, 1889.

THE EVENTS OF THE DAY INCLUDE:
TRIAL OF JOHN HAMPDEN, 1637,
'PRIDE'S PURGE' OF THE LONG PARLIAMENT, 1648,
FIRST TIME A JEW WAS ELECTED ALDERMAN OF LONDON,
(SOLOMONS OF THE CORDWAINERS), 1847,
THIRD REFORM ACT, 1884,
TRANSVAAL AND ORANGE FREE STATE GRANTED SELF-
GOVERNMENT, 1906,
IRISH PEACE TREATY SIGNED, 1921,
BRITAIN INDICATED DECLARATION OF WAR ON FINLAND,
HUNGARY AND RUMANIA, 1941,
DR. JULIAN HUXLEY, FIRST DIRECTOR-GENERAL OF
UNESCO, 1946.

[357]

December the Seventh

How goes it, friend, I've done my fifty,
Fifty of the best—not out.
But of the future, I am thrifty,
Wond'ring what it's all about.

In 1542, on December the Seventh, Mary Stuart, Queen of Scots, was born.
The Scots, who were her unruly subjects in her lifetime, have adored her
memory. Her faults are forgotten, the memory of her beauty—her courage—
her spirit—her unhappy fate alone remain. Poets for generations have
found her fit subject for their art and common folk cherish her memory.

There were born on this day:
St. Columba, 521,
Giovanni Lorenzo Bernini, architect and sculptor, 1598,
Rev. Richard Valpy, D.D., compiler of classic grammars, 1754,
Allan Cunningham, 1784.

There died on this day:
Cicero, assassinated, 43 B.C.,
Robert Ket (Ket's rebellion), 1549,
Algernon Sydney, 1683,
Maréchal Ney, 1815,
de Lesseps, 1894,
Dr. Nicholas Murray Butler, 1947.

The events of the day include—
Stephen restored, 1141,
First Covent Garden Theatre opened, 1732,
Grand Lodge of Luxemburg constituted, 1849,
Australian Federal Council formed, 1883,
First D.S.O. investiture, 1886,
Battle of Falklands, 1914,
Lloyd George became Premier, 1916,
Japanese attacked Pearl Harbour, 1941,
Chinese Communists attacked and forced United Nations troops
to retire, 1950.

THESE ARE THE SAINTS OF THE DAY:
ST. AMBROSE, BISHOP AND CONFESSOR, DOCTOR OF THE
CHURCH, 397,
ST. FARA, VIRGIN AND ABBESS, 655.

December the Eighth

Some spend their hours in healing,
Some spend their time in talk,
Time, I have the feeling
Never cares to walk.
Whether at days beginning,
Or when day is done,
Time is always winning,
Time is on the run.

Herbert Spencer died on December the Eighth, 1903. He was born in 1820.
He lived into the twentieth century but he was of the nineteenth. His belief
in science—his hatred of the State—his passionate belief in individuals and
in individualism as a philosophy, make him an historic figure. His synthetic
philosophy, man and the State, and especially his autobiography, will always
command attention.

These, too, died on this day:
John Pym in 1643,
Richard Baxter in 1691,
Vitus Behring in 1741,
Edward Irving in 1834,
Thomas de Quincey, at Edinburgh, in 1859.

The events of the day are:
William the Lion, King of Scotland, signed away independence of
Scotland to Henry II, 1174,
Sir Robert Peel, Premier, 1834,
Four German cruisers sunk off Falkland Islands, 1914,
Cambridge refused women students, 1920,
American Aid for Greece pledged, 1940,
Singapore raided 1941 and Great Britain and United States
declared war on Germany and Japan,
London–Australia air mail inaugurated, 1934,
Last British troops left Italy in 1947.

THE BIRTHS OF THE DAY INCLUDE:
QUEEN CHRISTINA OF SWEDEN, 1626,
CHARLES WENTWORTH DILKE, EDITOR OF THE ATHENAEUM,
1789,
JAMES THURBER, 1894,
LORD WILLOUGHBY DE ERESBY, 1907.

December the Ninth

Last night I watched the fading sun
And marked its lustred ray.
I prayed, give me, now day is done,
Another perfect day.

John Milton was born on this day in 1608,
Vandyke—Sir Anthony Vandyke—died on this day in 1641,
These two must have known of each other—one the portrayer of Paradise
Lost *and the other the painter of kings.*
Which of these twain did most and left most for men today? The question
is an idle one.

These were born on this day:
Gustavus Adolphus the Great, of Sweden, 1594,
William Whitson, 1667,
Joel C. Harris (Uncle Remus), 1848,
Gen. Sir Frank Messervy, one of the most brilliant leaders of the
last war, was born 1893.

These died on this day:
Pope Pius IV, 1565,
Earl of Clarendon, 1674,
Thomas Brassey, the railway contractor, 1870,
Sir Arthur Pearson, 1921,
Sir George S. Barnes, a former member of the Viceroy's Council,
1946,
Dr. E. D. Logie Danson, 1946.
George Mozart, comedian, 1947.

THE EVENTS OF THE DAY ARE:
WILLIAM THE LION OF SCOTLAND BEGAN HIS REIGN, AND
THE WORD 'PARLIAMENT' WAS USED FOR THE FIRST TIME
ON THE SAME DAY, IN 1174,
FIRST EXECUTION IN NEWGATE, 1783,
SIERRA LEONE FOUNDED, 1786,
FIRST STEAM VOYAGE FROM GREAT BRITAIN TO INDIA,
1825,
JERUSALEM FELL TO THE BRITISH, 1917,
HOARE-LAVAL PROPOSALS, 1935,
FIRST BRITISH INFANTRY SOLDIER KILLED IN SECOND
GERMAN WAR, 1939,
FIRST BRITISH ATTACK IN WESTERN DESERT, 1940.

December the Tenth

Lord it is here: my prayer you grant,
I'm succoured from the pit,
But for the life in me I can't
Think what to do with it.

December the Tenth is the anniversary of the death of Llewelyn, Prince of Wales, in 1282.
December the Tenth is the anniversary of the birth day of General Sir Harold Alexander in 1891, who commanded the evacuation of the British Armies at Dunkirk and who is Governor-General of the Dominion of Canada.
December the Tenth is the anniversary of the untimely death of Damon Runyon in 1946—the humorous interpreter of Broadway who with O. Henry makes the American of today comprehensible to the English.

These were born on this day:
Thomas Holcroft, dramatist and translator, 1745, London,
General Sir William Fenwick Williams, hero of Kars, 1800, Nova Scotia,
Eugène Sue, 1804,
George Macdonald, 1827,
Viscount Alexander of Tunis, 1891.

There died on this day:
Duncan Forbes, 1747,
General Viscount Hill ('Daddy'), 1842,
Professor Empson, editor of *Edinburgh Review*, 1852,
General Beresford, 1853,
Alfred Nobel, 1896,
Duncan George Stewart, Governor of Sarawak, murdered, 1949.

THE EVENTS OF THE DAY ARE:
JAMES BROKE COVER FOR FRANCE, 1688,
JOHN LAW LEFT PARIS, 1720,
HANOVERIAN TROOPS VOTED, 1742,
DR. FRANKLIN ARRIVED IN LONDON, 1764,
QUEENSLAND SEPARATED FROM NEW SOUTH WALES, 1859,
SPANISH AMERICAN TREATY, 1898,
SIR ROSS SMITH COMPLETED FLIGHT TO AUSTRALIA, 1919,
'PRINCE OF WALES' LOST, 1941,
ZNAMENK CAPTURED, 1943,
HEAVY FIGHTING IN ATHENS, 1944.

December the Eleventh

It is mine—this minute,
This twinkling of an eye.
What can I put in it,
I who am doomed to die?

December the Eleventh reminds some of 'l'affaire Fashoda' in 1890. It might have been a war between France and Britain but wiser and more temperate counsels prevailed and the two countries, when the dust of disagreement had died away, went forward into l'entente cordiale. December the Eleventh in 1890 is little remembered, but some have speculated to what extent it led to German fears and the war in 1914.

December the Eleventh is a day for the affairs of kings:
On this day in 1688 King James II of England peacefully abdicated,
On this day the United States and Cuba signed a Treaty in 1902,
Germans attempted, unsuccessfully, to 'smash through' at Ypres in 1914,
George VI ascended the throne in 1936,
Edward VIII abdicated on the same day,
Italy left the League of Nations in 1939,
Sidi Barrani was captured by British forces in 1940.
Germany and Italy declared war on the United States in 1941.

These were born on this day:
Dr. William Cullen, illustrious professor of medicine, 1712,
Paul Joseph Barthez, physiologist, 1734, Montpelier,
Charles Wesley, musician, 1757, Bristol,
Hector Berlioz, 1803,
de Mousset, 1810.

THESE TOO, DIED ON THIS DAY:
MICHAEL VIII PALAEOLOGUS, GREEK EMPEROR, 1282,
LOUIS, PRINCE OF CONDÉ (THE GREAT CONDÉ), 1686,
SIR RODGER L'ESTRANGE, TRANSLATOR OF CLASSIC AUTHORS, 1704,
CHARLES XII OF SWEDEN KILLED AT FREDERICKSHALL, 1718,
THEODORE NEUHOFF, EX-KING OF CORSICA, DIED ON THIS DAY IN 1756, LONDON,
RICHARD DOYLE, OF 'PUNCH', 1883,
SIR DOUGLAS J. JARDINE, 1946.

December the Twelfth

Friends, today I have lost a day.

On December the Twelfth Robert Browning died in 1889. Just about the day he died, his last book of poems was published. It is called Asolando Fancies and Facts *and ends with a poem epilogue. In it is all the optimism of Robert Browning who, in his farewell, bid us in 'the bustle of man's worktime—greet the unseen with a cheer'.*

On this day these were born:
Nicholas Sanson, geographer, 1599,
Samuel, Viscount Hood, admiral, 1724,
Dr. Erasmus Darwin, poet, 1731,
Sir William Beechey, artist, 1753,
Archduchess Maria Louisa, second wife of Napoleon, 1791,
The Rev. Philip Thomas Clayton, c.h., m.c., Chaplain to the King, in 1885.

On this day these deaths are recorded:
John Craig, Scottish reformer, 1600,
Henry, Viscount Bolingbroke, 1751,
Sir Marc Isambard Brunel, 1849,
Douglas Fairbanks, 1940,
Lord Lothian, 1940,
Sir William J. Collins, 1946,
Sir Basil Clarke, war correspondent, 1947.

This day, in years gone by, marked these events:
German peace proposals, 1916,
Holland adopted woman suffrage, 1917,
All loyalty to British Crown rejected by I.F.S., 1936,
Sheffield bombed, 1940,
Burma raided, 1941,
Essen attacked, 1944,
M. Léon Blum, elected French Premier, 1946.

FOR THOSE WHOSE HOURS ARE HEAVY THERE ARE ALWAYS THE SAINTS'-DAYS:
THESE MEN FILLED THEIR DAYS TO PURPOSE . . .
SAINTS EPIMACHUS, ALEXANDER AND OTHERS, MARTYRS, 250,
ST. CORENTIN, BISHOP AND CONFESSOR, FIFTH CENTURY,
ST. COLUMBA, ABBOT IN IRELAND, 548.

December the Thirteenth

Earth breaks up, time drops away,
In flows heavenwards with its new day.

December the Thirteenth recalls four birthdays for four centuries.
On this day in 1585 was born William Drummond of Hawthornden, the poet,
On this day in 1797 was born Heinrich Heine, the ironical Jewish poet,
whose hopes of a Liberal Germany never fructified,
On this day in 1815, Dean Stanley—Arthur Penrhyn Stanley—was born—
to become the friend of Queen Victoria and the constant fighter for the poor,
On this day in 1906 was born Princess Marina, the younger daughter of
Prince Nicolas of Greece, who married the Duke of Kent.

Henry IV of France was born on this day in 1553,
Sir Frederick Rees, Principal of University College of South
Wales and Monmouthshire, 1883.

Conrad Gesner, eminent naturalist, 1565,
Anthony Collins, freethinking writer, 1729,
Rev. John Strype, historical writer, in 1737,
Dr. Johnson in 1784,
Earl of Aberdeen in 1860,
Calcraft, the executioner, in 1879,
Samuel Gompers in 1924, and
R. J. S. Rayleigh, Baron, scientist, in 1947, all died on December
the Thirteenth.

THE EVENTS WHICH MARK THE DAY ARE:
POPE CELESTINE FORCED TO ABDICATE, 1294,
COUNCIL OF TRENT, 1545,
NEW ZEALAND DISCOVERED, 1642,
ORDER IN COUNCIL AGAINST KIDNAPPING PEOPLE FOR
PLANTATIONS, 1682,
ELECTRIC LIGHT ON THE THAMES EMBANKMENT, 1878,
BRITISH SUBMARINE B.11 DIVED UNDER FIVE ROWS OF
MINES IN THE DARDANELLES AND TORPEDOED THE
TURKISH WARSHIP 'MESSUDIYEH', 1914,
'GRAF SPEE' BATTLE, 1939,
TWENTY-YEAR TREATY SIGNED BETWEEN THE SOVIET
UNION AND CZECHOSLOVAKIA, 1943,
UNITED NATIONS WITHDREW DIPLOMATIC REPRESENTA-
TIVES FROM SPAIN, 1946.

December the Fourteenth

O day, long to be remembered.

George Washington, the first President of the United States of America, died on this day in 1799. Americans hail him as the man who made them, giving him an even higher place than Lincoln or Roosevelt.
James V of Scotland died on December the Fourteenth, 1542.
The consort of Queen Victoria, Prince Albert, died on this day in 1861, as also did Britain's inter-war Prime Minister, Stanley Baldwin, in 1947, ennobled as Earl Baldwin of Bewdley.

These were born on this day:
Tycho Brahe, 1546,
Daniel Neal, divine and author, 1678, London,
James Bruce, 1730,
Charles Wolfe, author of *The Burial of Sir John Moore*, 1791, Dublin,
King George VI, 1895,
King Paul of Hellenes, 1901.

There died on this day:
Sir John Oldcastle, Lord Cobham, burned, 1417,
Thomas Rymer, 1713,
George Hudson, 'The Railway King', 1871,
Sir Henry Vaughan Markham, 1946,
Will Fyffe, Scottish character actor, 1947,
Edward John Higgins, C.B.E., third leader of Salvation Army, 1947.

THE EVENTS INCLUDE:
JAMES ARRESTED BY FISHERMAN, 1689,
BEGINNING OF LUDDITE RIOTS AGAINST MACHINERY, 1811,
THE BOTTLE PLOT, 1822,
FIRST SECTION OF THE LONDON AND GREENWICH RAILWAY
OPENED, 1836, THE FIRST RAILWAY IN LONDON,
ST. PAUL'S CATHEDRAL DECLARED OPEN TO THE PUBLIC,
FREE OF CHARGE, 1837,
FIRST WOMAN ELECTED TO PARLIAMENT—DID NOT TAKE
HER SEAT, 1918,
HAIG TOOK COMMAND OF BRITISH ARMIES, 1915,
LAST SESSION OF ITALIAN CHAMBER OF DEPUTIES, 1938,
RUSSIA EXPELLED FROM LEAGUE OF NATIONS, 1939,
CHERKASSY CAPTURED, 1943,
INFANTRY REINFORCEMENTS FLOWN TO ATHENS, 1944.

[365]

December the Fifteenth

The day is cold, and dark, and dreary;
It rains, and the wind is never weary.

Izaak Walton was a shopkeeper in the City of London who had many friends about whom he wrote, and in addition left the world The Compleat Angler. *He died on December the Fifteenth in 1683 and no writer leaves behind him a seemlier or more wholesome memory.*
Jan Vermeer, the Dutch painter, was a contemporary who died, too, on this day in 1675, leaving, as did Izaak Walton, much the world has learned to love.

These, too, died on this day:
Timoleon, 337 B.C.,
Benjamin Stillingfleet in 1771,
Jean Baptiste Carrier, revolutionary terrorist, guillotined, 1794,
David Don, 1841,
Léon Faucher, eminent French statesman and publicist, 1854,
Rasputin in 1916, and
Admiral Sir Herbert Richmond, naval historian, in 1946.

The births for December the Fifteenth include:
George Romney, portrait painter, 1734, Dalton, Lancashire,
Cowden Clarke in 1767,
Jerome Bonaparte, youngest brother of Napoleon, 1784, Ajaccio,
R. S. Hudson, 1886,
General Sir Miles Christopher Dempsey in 1896.

THESE EVENTS OCCURRED:
NAPOLEON'S REMAINS DEPOSITED IN THE TUILERIES, 1840,
'ALABAMA' CLAIMS COMMISSION BEGAN ITS SITTING, 1871,
BULLER'S FORCES DEFEATED AT COLENSO, 1899,
ALLIED WAR COUNCIL ESTABLISHED AT VERSAILLES, 1917,
RUSSO-GERMAN ARMISTICE SIGNED, 1917,
BOLSHEVIKS PROCLAIMED ESTHONIA A REPUBLIC, 1918,
INCORPORATION OF B.B.C., 1922,
LAVAL DISMISSED FROM VICHY GOVERNMENT, 1940,
ROMMEL IN RETREAT, MERSA BREGA, 1942,
U.S. FORCES LANDED IN ISLAND OF MINDORO, 1944,
BREAKDOWN OF FOUR-POWER CONFERENCE ON GERMANY, 1947,
GENERAL WU REJECTED CEASE-FIRE PROPOSALS, 1950.

December the Sixteenth

As soon as I was born I wept,
And every day shows why.

December the Sixteenth matters much for the Union of South Africa . . .
it is Dingaan's Day . . . the great national Boer festival in 1838—it was
the day of the proclamation of Boer independence in 1880—and December
the Sixteenth was, in 1904, the day of the Public Funeral of President Paul
Kruger—'Oom Paul' as he was affectionately called by his people.
Across the Atlantic the U.S.A. mark this December the Sixteenth as
the anniversary of the Boston Tea Party in 1773.

Born on this day were:
John Selden, 1584,
George Whitefield, 1714,
Marshal von Blücher, 1742,
Ludwig von Beethoven, 1770,
Jane Austen, 1775,
J. B. Hobbs, 1882,
Noel Coward, 1899.

These died on this day:
Sir William Petty, eminent political economist, 1687,
Abbé Desfontaines, translator of Virgil and Horace, 1745,
Thomas Pennant, naturalist, 1798, Downing, Flintshire,
Antoine François de Fourcroy, distinguished French chemist,
1809,
Rev. Samuel Lee, Orientalist, 1852, Barley, Herts, and
William Grimm, 1859.

The following events are recorded:
'The Instrument of Government' published, 1653,
Cromwell became Lord Protector, 1653,
Dryden received a hiding from three men at Wills Coffee House,
1680, 'soundly cudgelled',
Amundsen discovered South Pole, 1911,
Sollum and Fort Capuzzo captured, 1940,
Innsbruck and Berlin bombed, 1943.

THE SAINTS OF THE DAY ARE:
ST. ADO, ARCHBISHOP OF VIENNE, 875,
ST. ALICO OR ADELAIDE, EMPRESS OF GERMANY, 999.

December the Seventeenth

At the close of the day, when the hamlet is still,
And mortals the sweets of forgetfulness prove.

December the Seventeenth, in 1851, saw the culmination of the revolution of 1848 for Henry John Temple, Lord Palmerston. It was on this day that he was dismissed from office as Foreign Secretary by Lord John Russell, he became in due time, however, one of the great Prime Ministers of Britain, laying great stress on the place, purpose, and duty of Britain in the world. He died in office in 1865, and was buried in Westminster Abbey. It is to Palmerston Parliament owes the doctrine that a British subject, wherever he is, must be protected by his Government against peril, injustice and wrong doing.

Born on this day were:
Anthony A. Wood, 1632,
Gabriel Émile, Marquise du Chastelet, 1706,
Sir Humphrey Davy, 1778,
John Greenleaf Whittier, 1807,
William Lyon McKenzie King, 1874.

There died on this day:
Sir William Gascoigne, Lord Chief Justice, 1413,
Simon Bolivar, 1830,
Kasper Hauser, 1833,
Rear Admiral Sir A. Branfort, the hydrographer, 1857,
Bernard Quaritch, 1899,
Lord Kelvin, 1907,
Pierre A. Renoir, 1919,
Sir Bernard H. Spilsbury, pathologist, 1947.

THE EVENTS OF THE DAY INCLUDE:
CHELSEA HOSPITAL PROPOSED BY CHARLES II, 1684,
BILL FOR ADMISSION OF JEWS INTO PARLIAMENT CARRIED, 1847,
LORD DERBY RESIGNED, 1852,
MAN'S FIRST AIRPLANE FLIGHT, 1903,
BREST-LITOVSK, 1917,
GERMAN FORCES IN LIBYA IN FULL RETREAT, 1941,
BRITISH PARACHUTE TROOPS LANDED IN TUNISIA, 1942,
ROMMEL'S ARMY CUT IN TWO, 1942,
FAENZA CAPTURED BY NEW ZEALAND FORCES, 1944.

December the Eighteenth

Daylight will peep through a very small hole.

There were marvels among men in those days. If it is true of any it is true of Prince Rupert, Duke of Bavaria and Count Palatine of the Rhine, who was born on December the Eighteenth in 1619. The grandson of King James I, he must have shocked his philosophic mind by a passion for action. He was in the Thirty Years War before he joined his uncle, Charles I, as the leader of the cavalry in the Civil War. Cromwell's Fairfax brought him to surrender but his fortunes rose again. He was Admiral of the Fleet before he died in 1682 and in his leisure hours had found time to be inventor, scientist and artist.

Carl von Weber, German composer, 1786,
Sir Jos. Thomson, English physicist, author, 1856,
Edwin H. Armstrong, American engineer inventor, 1890,
Prince William of Gloucester was born on this day in 1941.

There died on this day:
Robert Nanteiul, celebrated engraver, 1678,
Heneage Finch, Earl of Nottingham, 1682,
Dr. Alexander Adam, the Scots educator, 1809,
Thomas Dunham Whitaker, writer, 1821,
Samuel Rogers, poet, 1855,
William Sheldon, organizer of the old London Omnibus Service, 1883,
Sir Richard Owen, 1892.

THESE ARE THE EVENTS OF THE DAY:
WILLIAM ARRIVED AT ST. JAMES'S, 1688,
ANTIQUARIAN SOCIETY INSTITUTED AT EDINBURGH, 1780,
ROBERTS AND KITCHENER COMMANDER-IN-CHIEF AND CHIEF-OF-STAFF, 1899,
'ELEMENTARY' SCHOOLS EDUCATION ACT ENGLAND AND WALES, 1902,
EGYPT PROCLAIMED A BRITISH PROTECTORATE, 1914,
PARIS GAVE U.S. PRESIDENT WILSON A GOLD MEDAL, 1918,
U.S. SUBMARINE S.4 SALVAGED IN 70 MINUTES, 1929,
'ADMIRAL GRAF SPEE', SCUTTLED AT MONTEVIDEO, 1939,
FIRST CANADIAN DIVISION REACHED BRITAIN, 1939,
KEDAH EVACUATED, 1941,
DUTCH TROOPS INVADED INDONESIA, 1948.

December the Nineteenth

Boast not thyself of tomorrow;
For thou knowest not what a day may bring forth.

It was on December the Nineteenth it all began again. Germany launched her first post-treaty battleship on this day in 1931.
Adolph Hitler became chancellor in 1933.
December the Nineteenth in 1848 saw the world made poorer by the death of Emily Brontë—the sister of Charlotte, Anne and Patrick. Few could write with less fear of challenge the opening lines of her poem—Last Verses:

> *No coward soul is mine*
> *No trembler in the world's*
> *storm-troubled sphere.*

These too, died on this day:
David Hartley, first mover in the House of Commons for abolition of slavery, 1813,
Benjamin Smith Barton, American naturalist, 1815,
J. M. William Turner, the artist, 1851,
Marquess of Dalhousie, 1860,
Sir Paul Vinogradoff, 1925,
The thirteenth Dalai Lama, 1933,
Harold McKenna, 1946,
Von Ludendorff, German war lord, 1937.

The births of the day include,
Charles William Scheele, distinguished chemist, 1742, Stralsund,
Captain William Edward Parry, Arctic navigator, 1790, Bath,
Lord Rowallan, Chief Scout, in 1895.

THE EVENTS OF THE DAY ARE:
ACCESSION OF HENRY II, 1154,
EARL OF ABERDEEN'S MINISTRY, 1852,
BRITISH FORCES WITHDREW FROM ANZAC AND SUVLA, 1915,
MONASTIR CAPTURED BY ALLIES, 1916,
GERMAN LINER 'COLUMBUS' SCUTTLED, 1939,
SHIP'S COMPANY OF 'GRAF SPEE' INTERNED AT BUENOS AYRES, 1939,
FOUR WAR CRIMINALS DIED BY HANGING AT KHARKOV, RUSSIA, 1943,
OMURA AIRCRAFT FACTORY BOMBED, 1944.

December the Twentieth

He never broke his hour that kept his day.

December the Twentieth was a fateful day for Charles Edward Stuart—Bonnie Prince Charlie—who on that day began his retreat from England back to Scotland in 1745.
Calamity, too, marked this day, in 1920, when Farrows Bank crashed into bankruptcy.
It was on the same day, in 1941, that the Japanese landed in Hong Kong, the prelude to its capture.
There were other and brighter events, fortunately, in history on this day.
In 1849, Queen's College was inaugurated at Belfast.
The independence of Belgium was proclaimed on this day in 1830.

Born on this day were:
J. W. Croker, 1780,
Harvey S. Firestone, senior, American manufacturer, 1868,
Rt.-Hon. Robert Gordon Menzies (Prime Minister of Australia), 1894,
Lieut.-General Sir Frederick A. M. Browning, 1896.

There died on this day:
Louis the Dauphin, father of Louis XVI, 1765,
Emeric de Vattel, the Swiss jurist, 1767,
Thomas Hill, patron of literary men, and prototype of Paul Pry, 1840, Adelphi, London,
Lord Francis Xavier Russel of Killowen, 1946,
George, Earl of Stradbroke, a former governor of Victoria, 1947.

OTHER EVENTS INCLUDE:
PILGRIM FATHERS LAND AT PLYMOUTH, 1620,
CORPORATION ACT, 1661,
STAGE PLAY SUPPRESSED BY COMMONWEALTH, 1649,
U.S. TOOK POSSESSION OF LOUISIANA PURCHASE, 1803,
TREATY SIGNED IN LONDON BY WHICH FRANCE, AUSTRIA AND RUSSIA ADOPTED BRITISH ANTI-SLAVE LAWS, 1841,
LOUIS NAPOLEON BONAPARTE DECLARED PRESIDENT OF FRENCH REPUBLIC, 1848,
HOUSE OF COMMONS DECIDED AGAINST A FIXED EASTER, 1934,
DUISBURG HEAVILY BOMBED, 1942,
AUSBURG, INNSBRUCK, BREMEN BOMBED, 1943.

December the Twenty-first

I'm sixty and it's time I went
To see the scented Orient.
To Time too long I've been a slave,
Soon I'll be lying in a grave.

The name is Giovanni Boccaccio and he died on this day in 1375. He made
the modern short story in his famous Decameron *but he was more than a*
teller of tales. He was one of the founders of the Renaissance, the friend of
Petrarch and of Dante, the source of the inspiration of the Elizabethan poets.
Catherine of Braganza, the Queen of Charles II, died on this day in 1705.
The Duke de Sully, the French statesman, died on this day in 1641.

Born on this day were,
Jean Racine, 1639,
Earl of Beaconsfield, 1804,
Stalin, 1879.

These died on this day,
James Harris, author of Hermes, 1780,
Arnauld de Berquin, author of *L'Ami des Enfants*, 1791,
Rev. Dr. Harris, author of *Mammon*, 1856,
Frank Billings Kellogg, 1937.

THESE EVENTS OCCURRED ON THIS DAY:
APPROPRIATIONS OF MARLBOROUGH REPORTED TO THE
HOUSE, 1711,
JONATHAN HALL'S STEAM-BOAT PATENTED, 1736,
PRINCE OF WALES MARRIED MRS. FITZHERBERT, 1781,
GENERAL SHERMAN CAPTURED SAVANNAH, 1864,
COLLIERY DISASTER AT PRETORIA PIT, BOLTON, 344 LIVES
LOST, 1910,
SOVIET CHEKA (SECRET POLICE), 1917, LATER OGPU,
CROWN JEWELS OF BAVARIA AUCTIONED AT CHRISTIE'S
FOR £39,000 IN 1931,
HITLER YOUTH FORMED OUT OF THE EVANGELICAL YOUTH
MOVEMENT, 1933,
HITLER PERSONALLY IN COMMAND OF GERMAN ARMIES,
1941,
GERMAN FORCES RETREATED BETWEEN THE DON AND
DONETZ, 1942,
GERMAN COUNTER-OFFENSIVE HELD ON THE FLANKS, 1944.

December the Twenty-second

I did not think of time at seven
When dew was on the grass.

Moody and Sankey were a partnership which millions knew in the nineties.
Ira D. Sankey and Dwight Lyman Moody were American evangelists who
stirred men and women into active religion by their combination of oratory
and singing. D. L. Moody died on December the Twenty-second in 1899.
They would have been among the saints in other days—preaching friars
maybe—but the saints in the calendar for this day are:
St. Ischyrion, the martyr, Saint Cyril and Saint Methodius, confessors.

Born on this day were,
John Crome, 1768,
Archbishop Tait, 1811, and
C. S. Calverley, 1831,
Sir Norman Angell, 1874,
The Earl of Sefton, 1898.

There died on this day,
Emperor Vitellius, beheaded at Rome, A.D. 69,
Richard Allein, nonconformist divine, 1681,
Mrs. Mapp, 1737,
Sir Philip Frances, 1818,
Rev. M. J. Routh, D.D., Magdalen College, Oxford, 1854,
George Eliot, the novelist, 1880,
Henry Watterson, American journalist, 1921,
Sir Montague John Eddy, C.B.E., 1949.

THESE EVENTS ARE RECORDED:
KING OF SCOTS DID PUBLIC HOMAGE TO JOHN AT LINCOLN,
1200,
PRETENDER LANDED AT PETERHEAD, 1715,
GUINEA ORDERED TO BE VALUED AT 21S., 1717,
DREYFUS CASE OPENED, 1894,
RIOTING IN BERLIN, 1918,
AIR RAID PRECAUTIONS ACT PASSED, 1937,
MANCHESTER SEVERELY RAIDED, 1940,
RANGOON RAIDED, 1941,
MANILA BOMBED, 1941,
SIR EUSTACE MISSENDEN RESIGNED CHAIRMANSHIP OF
RAILWAY EXECUTIVE, 1951.

[373]

December the Twenty-third

Tell me this day what means this life
Tell me why I am born:
Is it for peace—is it for strife,
Or am I all forlorn.

He was ninety-two when he died at Kensington in 1904 but he was born at
Haddington in Scotland on this December the Twenty-third in 1812.
He was one of a family of eleven—became a doctor and made himself the
exponent of the duty of hard work, achievement and success. He epitomized
the industrial revolution. His books were translated into many languages
and his 'self help' still is a model for those who would put their trust in
themselves. His influence is less than it was on previous generations: a fact
which may account for their decline in character. He was Samuel Smiles.

Born on this day were,
R. Barclay, 1648,
Sir Martin Archer Shee, portrait painter, 1770, Dublin,
Sir Hugh Allen, 1869,
J. Arthur Rank, film magnate, in 1888.

There died on this day,
Henri de Lorraine, Duke of Guise, 1588,
William Davison, Secretary of State to Queen Elizabeth, 1608,
Michael Drayton, the poet, 1631,
John Cotton, 'Patriarch of New England', 1652,
T. R. Malthus, 1834,
J. C. Pritchard, 1848,
Hugh Miller, 1856.

THESE EVENTS ARE RECORDED:
EARLIEST COMMISSION OF ARRAY, 1334,
DANISH WEST INDIES TAKEN, 1807,
FIRST APPEARANCE IN SCOTLAND (HADDINGTON) OF
CHOLERA, 1831,
RUMANIA FORMED FROM THE OLD PRINCIPALITIES OF
MOLDAVIA AND WALLACHIA, 1861,
FIRST PERFORMANCE OF HUMPERDINCK'S 'HANSEL AND
GRETEL', 1893,
SOVIET RUSSIA BEGAN NEGOTIATIONS FOR SEPARATE
PEACE, BREST-LITOVSK, 1917,
BENGHAZI CAPTURED BY BRITISH, 1941.

December the Twenty-fourth

Let me gather the hours
And make them—all of them—yours.
Do with them what you will,
Time we are doomed to kill.

His father was the headmaster of Rugby and he was born on December the Twenty-fourth, 1822, to become the foremost critic of his time. Matthew Arnold sought to see life steadily and see it whole and to find in culture a satisfaction amid the confusions of existence. Another poet born, also, on this day, in 1754, was George Crabbe. He saw life steadily, too, and put realism in the forefront of his approach to life.
On this day, too, was born Saint Ignatius Loyola who, beginning his career as a fighting man, founded the Society of Jesus.

Born on this day were,
King John, 1167,
William Warburton, Bishop of Gloucester, 1698, Newmark,
'Kit' Carson, American frontiersman, 1809,
Viscount Morley, 1838, and
Sir Harry Brittain, 1873.

There died on this day:
George of Cappadocia, noted Arian bishop, A.D. 361,
Thomas Beaufort, Duke of Exeter, 1426,
Vasco da Gama, 1524,
Davies Gilbert, antiquarian and man of science, 1839,
Archdeacon Henry John Todd, 1845,
Patrick Fraser Tytler, the Scots historian, 1849,
W. M. Thackeray, 1863,
Admiral Darlan, assassinated, 1942,
Sir Richard R. Cruise, 1946.

THESE EVENTS OCCURRED ON THIS DAY:
PEERS ASSUMED EXECUTIVE FUNCTIONS OF THE CROWN, 1689,
PEACE BETWEEN GREAT BRITAIN AND UNITED STATES, 1814,
ZOG TOOK OVER THE GOVERNMENT OF ALBANIA, 1924,
CODEX SINAITICUS BOUGHT FROM SOVIET FOR £100,000, 1933,
COMMANDER-IN-CHIEF OF ALLIED ARMIES ANNOUNCED, 1943.

December the Twenty-fifth

. . . I saw three ships come sailing in . . . on Christmas Day in the morning . . .

Twenty-fifth December, 1901, is the birthday of the Duchess of Gloucester. It was on this day that Dorothy Wordsworth was born in 1771. She was the life-time companion of William Wordsworth and doubtless no small inspirer and guide of that curiously reticent genius.
Sir Isaac Newton, the great scientist, was born on this day in 1642. He found significance in a falling apple nor was it the first time that an apple had its place in the human story.

These died on this day:
Persius, satiric poet, A.D. 62,
Sir Matthew Hale, eminent judge, 1676,
Rev. James Hervey, author of *Meditations*, 1758,
Mrs. Chapone, moral writer, 1801,
Col. John Gurwood, editor of *Wellington's Dispatches*, 1854,
W. C. Fields, actor, 1946.

Born on this day were:
Johann Jacob Reiske, oriental scholar, 1716, Zorbig, Saxony,
William Collins, poet, 1721,
Richard Porson, Greek scholar, 1759,
Clara Barton, the American Florence Nightingale, 1821, U.S.A.,
Rebecca West, 1892.

These events occurred on this day:
William the Conqueror crowned, 1066,
Stephen recrowned, 1141,
Mr. Pepys on Christmas Day 1662 took a walk in Whitehall, was too late for church and spent his time looking over pictures of ships in *Henry the Eighth's Voyage to Bullaen*,
Grand Lodge of Sweden inaugurated, 1759,
Seventeen degrees below freezing on Christmas Day in London in 1860, believed to be the severest till then experienced,
Hankow occupied by Japanese, 1938,
Hong Kong surrendered to Japanese, 1941,
The King broadcast his thirteenth Christmas Message, 1950.

THE SAINTS OF THE DAY ARE,
ST. EUGENIA, VIRGIN AND MARTYR, ABOUT 257,
ST. ANASTASIA, MARTYR, 304.

December the Twenty-sixth

I've had enough of hours,
Outside of Time there towers
Eternity. I can
Endure it. I am man.

On December the Twenty-sixth John Wilkes died in 1797. Few Members of Parliament have had a greater personal following. 'Wilkes and Liberty' was the cry of the London crowds and no action of Government caused John Wilkes to lose their esteem. He was seventy years of age when he died. The deviser of Holloway's Pills—the great Thomas Holloway—died, too, on this day in 1883 with the world still, despite his efforts, uncured of its ills.

On this day these were born,
Gulielmus Xylander, translator of the classics, 1532,
Thomas Gray, 1716,
George Romney, artist, 1734,
Charles Mathews, the actor, 1803,
Dion Boucicault, 1822.

These died on this day:
Antoine Houdart de la Motte, dramatist, 1731,
Joel Barlow, American author and diplomatist, 1812,
Stephen Girard, millionaire, 1831.

These events are recorded,
Dedication of the first Westminster Abbey, 1065,
Treaty of Pressburg, 1805,
Belgium gained her independence, 1830,
First contingent of Australian airmen trained under Empire Training Scheme arrived, 1940,
Lofoten Raid, 1941,
Scharnhorst sunk, 1943,
Budapest encircled, 1944,
Britain and Yugoslavia signed five-year trade pact, 1949.

THE SAINTS OF THE DAY ARE:
ST. STEPHEN, FIRST MARTYR,
ST. DIONYSIUS, POPE AND CONFESSOR, 269,
ST. IARLATH, CONFESSOR, FIRST BISHOP OF TUAM, IN IRELAND, SIXTH CENTURY.

December the Twenty-seventh

I've passed the span—I've run the race—
I have three score years and seven:
I feel that I can calmly face
More years—a hell or heaven.

In 1822 on December the Twenty-seventh, Louis Pasteur was born. His name
is associated with cures of hydrophobia and the heat treatment of milk. He
died in 1895.
In 1834, on December the Twenty-seventh, Charles Lamb died—'the
gentle Elia', as he is styled, brought to the English essay a grace and a
pathos which none has excelled. His life was, more than most, one of
difficulty and indeed tragedy, but Charles Lamb lived out his days all serene.

These were born on this day:
Johann Kepler, 1571,
Dr. Conyer Middleton, philosophical writer, 1683,
Pope Pius VI, 1717,
Arthur Murphy, dramatist and miscellaneous writer, 1727,
Earl Cairns, 1819.

On this day there died:
Pierre de Ronsard, French poet, 1585,
Thomas Cartwright, Puritan divine, 1603,
Thomas Guy, founder of Guy's Hospital, 1724,
Joanna Southcote, 1814,
Josiah Conder, editor, 1855,
Dean Ramsay, died at Edinburgh, 1872,
Victor Emmanuel III, ex-king of Italy, 1947.

These events occurred on this day:
Grand Lodge of the Netherlands constituted, 1756,
The *Bounty* left Spithead, 1787,
United Grand Lodge of England formed, 1813,
A naval expedition set out against the crofters of Lewis, 1884,
Attempted assassination of Prince Regent Hirohito, 1923,
Japanese bombed Manila, 1941,
End of German 'come-back', 1944.

ST. JOHN, APOSTLE AND EVANGELIST,
ST. THEODRUS GRAPT, CONFESSOR, EIGHTH CENTURY,
ARE THE SAINTS OF THE DAY.

December the Twenty-eighth

Just cast like nothing to the void
My years have been:
I've toiled—I've grieved and I have joyed
What does it mean?

Thomas Babington Macaulay died on December the Twenty-eighth in
1859. He is remembered for his history and his Lays of Ancient Rome,
but he had a great public career. He was Member of Parliament for the
city of Edinburgh and later Secretary of State for War as well as adviser to
the Government of India. He was a great Victorian.
Sir Eric Hambro, the London banker who died on this day in 1947.

Thomas Henderson, astronomer, 1798, Dundee,
Alexander Keith Johnstone, geographer, 1804,
Woodrow Wilson, 1856,
Sir A. S. Eddington, 1862, and
Lord Pethick-Lawrence, 1871, were born on this day.

These died on this day:
Mary, wife of William of Orange, 1694,
William Carstairs, 1715,
Rob Roy, 1734,
Dr. John Campbell, miscellaneous writer, 1775, London,
John Logan, poet, 1788, London,
Theodore Dreiser, 1945.

These events occurred on this day:
Oldest recorded minute of any Masonic lodge, 1598,
Term 'Roundhead' first used, 1642,
Endowed Schools Inquiry appointed, 1864,
Tay Bridge disaster, 1879,
National Indian Congress, formed, 1886,
Calabrian earthquake disaster, 156,000 lives lost, 1908,
Commando forces raided Vaagso, Norway, 1941,
Germans retreated before Americans; Russians advanced on
Vienna, 1944,
Egyptian Prime Minister Nokrashy Pasha assassinated, 1948.

ST. THEODRUS, ABBOT OF TABENNA, CONFESSOR, 367, IS
THE SAINT OF THE DAY.

December the Twenty-ninth

He is not born for fame who knows not the value of Time.

December the Twenty-ninth is a day of first occasions.
On this day in 1940 the first incendiary air raid took place over the City of London.
On this day in 1923 the Dominion of Canada concluded its first treaty with a foreign power—to wit—the U.S.A.
On this day in 1860 the first British ironclad, H.M.S. Warrior, was launched.
On this day in 1881 a London theatre, the Savoy, was lit for the first time with electricity.
On this day in 1895 Dr. Jameson, later Sir Leander Starr Jameson, led a raid on Johannesburg for which he was arrested and imprisoned.

Born on this day were:
Madame de Pompadour, 1721,
Sir Archibald Alison, the historian, 1792,
William Ewart Gladstone, 1809,
Louisa May Alcott, the novelist, 1832,
The Earl of Home, 1873.

These died on this day:
Thomas à Becket, murdered, 1170,
Viscount William Stafford, victim of 'Popish Plot' executed, 1680,
Dr. Thomas Sydenham, distinguished physician, 1689, London,
Brook Taylor, algebraist, 1731,
Jacques Louis David, painter, 1825,
William Crotch, musical composer, 1847,
W. H. Maxwell, novelist and historian, 1850, Musselburgh,
James, Marquis of Dalhousie, statesman, 1860.

THESE EVENTS ARE RECORDED:
GREAT BRITAIN SUBSIDIZED THE KING OF PRUSSIA, £670,000, IN 1761,
MONTENEGRO UNITED WITH SERBIA UNDER KING PETER, 1918,
SECOND FIRE OF LONDON, 1940,
BERLIN HEAVILY BOMBED, 1943,
TERRORISTS KIDNAPPED A BRITISH MAJOR FROM AN HOTEL AT NATANYA AND THREE N.C.O.S FROM OTHER PLACES AND FLOGGED THEM BEFORE RELEASING THEM, 1946.

December the Thirtieth

The dawn is here, what can I make
Of hours that are not mine to take,
Except to mar—except to use—
Help me, O Lord, my work to choose.

Rudyard Kipling was born on December the Thirtieth, 1865. He held a unique place in English literature, none, not even William Shakespeare or Sir Walter Scott, has expressed in writing so abounding, exuberant and admiring love for this country, and its glorious achievements. His fame for a time after his death appeared to diminish but recent years have witnessed a revival of the appreciation of his talent. The high-brows have, to their credit, been not the least backward in this recognition of his abiding genius.

These were born on this day,
Titus, Roman emperor, A.D. 41,
Sir John Holt, Lord Chief Justice, 1642, Oxfordshire,
John Philips, poet, 1676,
Stephen Leacock, 1869.

There died on this day:
Roger Ascham, scholar, 1568,
The Hon. Robert Boyle, the physicist, 1691,
The Old Pretender, James Francis Edward Stuart, 1765,
Rear-Admiral Maitland (the man to whom Napoleon surrendered), 1839,
Sir Samuel Baker, 1893,
Romain Rolland, French writer, 1944.

THESE EVENTS OCCURRED ON THIS DAY,
ROYAL SOCIETY INSTITUTED, 1660,
NO MEMBER OF PARLIAMENT ALLOWED TO ACCEPT AN APPOINTMENT WITHOUT PERMISSION OF THE HOUSE, 1680,
U.S. BOUGHT A BIT OF MEXICO FOR SOUTHERN PACIFIC RAILROAD, 1853,
'UNIVERSAL DAY', 'ASTRONOMICAL DAY' AND 'CIVIL DAY' MADE TO COINCIDE, 1884,
PROCLAMATION OF AUSTRALIAN COMMONWEALTH, 1900,
KERCH AND FEODOSIA RECAPTURED, 1941,
BRITISH MADE FORTY-SIX MILES ADVANCE IN BURMA, 1944,
KING MICHAEL OF RUMANIA ABDICATED, 1947.

[381]

December the Thirty-first

The books, they tell of what they did,
Of good displayed and evil hid,
Of notices alas! too rarely seen,
Of deeds undone that might have been.

These are sad recollections to the end of the year.
John Wycliffe died on the last day of the year 1384.
Guy Fawkes was executed on December the Thirty-first in 1606,
There was a great fire in a cinema at Paisley on this day in 1929.

It was on this day in 1600 that the East India Company got its first charter.
The Order of the Military Cross for gallantry in the British Army was
established on December the Thirty-first, 1914.

Born on this day were:
Prince Charles Edward Stuart, 1720,
Dr. Johann Gaspar Spurzheim, phrenologist, 1776,
Henri Matisse, 1869,
General George Marshall, 1880.

These died on this day,
Thomas Erastus, physician, 1583,
John Flamsteed, astronomer, 1719, Greenwich,
Jean François Marmontel, tale-writer, 1799,
William Gifford, reviewer and satirist, 1826, London,
Sir Frank Benson, 1940,
Sir John Eldon Bankes, 1946.

THESE ARE SOME OF THE EVENTS ON DECEMBER THE
THIRTY-FIRST:
WINDOW TAX IMPOSED, 1695,
NUMEROUS MEETINGS HELD DURING THIS MONTH, TO
COMPLAIN OF THE INVOLVED AND MEDDLESOME REQUIRE-
MENTS SCHEDULES OF THE NEW INCOME TAX, 1847,
GERMANS ATTACKED CAMBRAI, WITH LIQUID FIRE, 1917,
WASHINGTON NAVAL TREATY OF 1922 AND LONDON NAVAL
TREATY OF 1930 AND 1936,
KALUGA RECAPTURED, 1941,
MR. MOLOTOV, IN A STATEMENT IN MOSCOW, DECLARED
UNITED STATES DELEGATION HAD DISRUPTED ENTIRE
WORK OF LONDON CONFERENCE, 1947.

PRINTED AT
THE CURWEN PRESS
PLAISTOW
E.13